OUTLINES OF ECCLESIASTICAL HISTORY

A Text Book

By ELDER B. H. ROBERTS

AUTHOR OF: "The Life of John Taylor," "The Gospel," "New Witness for God," "Missouri Persecutions," "Rise and Fall of Nauvoo," "Defense of the Faith and the Saints," "The Mormon Doctrine of Deity," "The Prophet Teacher," "History of the Mormon Church," etc., etc.

CLASSICS IN MORMON LITERATURE

Deseret Book Company
Salt Lake City, Utah
1979

DEDICATION.

To the Seventies: That body of men upon whom—under the direction of the Twelve Apostles—devolves the responsibility of preaching the gospel, and defending the truth in all the world, this work is affectionately dedicated.

Library of Congress Cataloging in Publication Data

Roberts, Brigham Henry, 1857-1933.
    Outlines of ecclesiastical history.

    (Classics in Mormon literature)
    Includes bibliographical references and index.
    1. Church history.   2. Mormons and Mormonism.
I. Title.   II. Series.
BR148.R6   1979   289.3   79-9744
ISBN 0-87747-748-5

CONTENTS

A WORD WITH STUDENTS AND TEACHERS.

Before you take up the study of **Outlines of Ecclesiastical History,** I beg leave to call your attention to the structure of the work, and the purpose for which it was written. First, then, as to its structure.

The work is divided into four parts. Part I. deals with **The Establishment of the Church** through the ministry of Messiah and his apostles; Part II. with **The Apostasy,** brought about through the severe persecution to which the early saints were subjected, the rise of false teachers, changing the ordinances of the gospel, intermingling pagan philosophy with Christian doctrine, and a transgression of the laws of God; Part III. deals with **"The Reformation,"** treating it, however, as a revolution instead of a reformation since the so-called reformation by no means re-established primitive Christianity, either in its form or essence, but it did overthrow the power of the Catholic Church in the greater part of Western Europe, gave larger liberty to the people, and thus prepared the way for the great work which followed it—the introduction of the Dispensation of the Fullness of Times. Part IV. treats of **The Restoration of the Gospel,** in the aforesaid Dispensation, through the revelations which God gave to the Prophet Joseph Smith.

The parts above enumerated are separated into sections, these sub-divisions being determined by the several subjects into which the main idea of the respective parts naturally divides. The sections are again separated into topics, the titles of which are printed in bold-face type, and the paragraphs are numbered for reference. These divisions, it is believed, will better enable the student to discern the relation of the respective parts to the main subject, and at the same time afford a convenient division for the assignment of lessons to classes. Ordinarily it will be found that a section will be sufficient for a lesson for either a class or quorum; but in some instances two of the shorter sections may be taken for a lesson; but some of the longer sections should be divided into two or more.

At the end of each section will be found a collection of notes bearing upon the important points treated in the text of the work, at which place reference will be found to the note at the end of the section. The author cannot, in his opinion, too emphatically urge upon the student the importance of turning to the notes to which he is directed in the text and reading them. They will be found to throw additional light upon the subject treated in the text, either by giving the statement of a recognized authority, supplying pointed argument—with which it has been thought best not to burden the body of the work—or giving illustrations to the statement made in the text. Another purpose for placing these notes at the end of the sections has been to arouse an interest in the works of the authors quoted; that the students of this text book may be induced to delve deeper into the study of Ecclesiastical History than a perusal of these pages will enable them to do. And here let the author confess, while he believes he is presenting a very valuable collection of facts to those who will take up the study of his work—yet if the study of these pages shall result in merely awakening in the minds of the elders and the youth of Israel an interest in the subject, he will account the objects of his efforts successfully attained.

At the end of each section also will be found Review Questions, covering the main points treated in the text and in the notes. It is hoped that they will be found useful in conducting class exercises, and to the private student who wishes to ascertain if he has mastered the subject matter of each section. Let him put to himself the questions found in the review at the end of the section, when completing it, and if he can give a satisfactory answer to each one, the author feels assured that the student has mastered the salient points.

The purpose of the work is two-fold: first, it is to sustain the position taken by the church of Christ in the last days. What that position is may be readily discerned by the very first revelation the Lord gave to Joseph Smith. In answering the young prophet's question—which of all the sects of religion was acknowledged of him as his church and kingdom—the Lord said they were all wrong; that all their creeds were an abomination in his sight; that those professors were all corrupt; that they drew near to him with their lips, but their hearts were far from him; that they taught for doctrine the commandments of men—having a form of godliness, but denying the power thereof.*

It has been to bring together the historical evidences of the truth of this divine announcement that, in part, this work has been written; and therefore prominence has been given to those facts of history which support that announcement. But no fact has been suppressed that has a tendency to support the opposite view. No such fact either of history or prophecy exists. The whole stream of evi-

---

*Pearl of Great Price, p. 48. Writings of Joseph Smith.

dence proves that there has been a universal apostasy from the religion taught by Jesus Christ and his apostles; and the existing differences between the present teachings of "Christendom" and the doctrines of the scriptures is a proof so palpable that it admits of no contradiction. As this position of the church is one which the seventies and elders will have to maintain against all the world, it is of first importance that they become familiar with those facts of history and prophecy that will enable them to maintain that position intelligently and successfully.

The second purpose of the work is to teach the principles of the gospel. This, the author is convinced, can best be done in connection with their history. Relate the historical events which resulted in the introduction and establishment of the gospel and the church of Christ; then in all the centuries from the second to the tenth show how the doctrines of Messiah were departed from, how the ordinances were changed and the laws of God transgressed; relate the principal events of the sixteenth century revolution—miscalled the "Reformation"—and point out how that revolution, however salutary in bringing to pass an enlargement of popular liberty, failed to re-establish the gospel of the Lord Jesus Christ, or re-organize the church as at first founded by Messiah; then relate the events connected with the restoration of the gospel through the revelations given to the great prophet of the Dispensation of the Fullness of Times, Joseph Smith—and in so doing you are not only teaching the interesting facts of Ecclesiastical History to your students, but at the same time you are making them acquainted with the principles of the gospel. Under such a presentation the students, without being conscious of it, perhaps, will examine those principles under a variety of circumstances. They will see them stated in connection with the leading events of the Messiah's life; they will see them corrupted by an apostate church; they will hear them discussed by men during the attempt at Reformation; and after witnessing the unavailing efforts of the "Reformers" to re-establish the gospel and the church of Christ, they will see how the heavens were opened and every principle, doctrine, ordinance, law, officer and institution known to the church of Christ, restored. Such a presentation of the principles of the gospel, we repeat, must lead to a very comprehensive understanding of them, and such is one of the purposes of this work, and one which the author hopes will give it a claim upon the attention of all those desiring information on the subject of the gospel, as well as to the quorums of seventies and elders to whom we believe it will be of special service.

Before the work went to press the manuscript was submitted to a committee of brethren appointed by the First Presidency. Elders John Nicholson, George Reynolds and James E. Talmage constituted that committee. The author is very much indebted to them for their patient consideration of his manuscript, and for the very valuable suggestions and corrections made by them. They reported favorably to the First Presidency on the work, and it is now presented to the students of Ecclesiastical History— in which the church of Christ should abound—in the hope that it will be of service to them in their researches in this most interesting department of knowledge.

This, the fifth edition, is uniform with the previous edition, in every respect.

The Publishers

PREFACE TO
"CLASSICS IN MORMON LITERATURE" EDITION

B.H. Roberts, who immigrated to Utah from England in 1866 as a youth of nine, grew to manhood with an insatiable desire to digest every book he could find. He took particular interest in Hellenistic thought and Hebrew tradition. Following his call to the First Council of the Seventy in October 1888, his primary emphasis became that of the ministry. Despite his heavy ecclesiastical commitments, however, he sought every opportunity to continue his search of gospel-related source materials and make those findings available to the Church. In the process he became one of the most prolific and accepted writers among LDS authors, leaving an exceptional legacy of historical and doctrinal masterpieces.

Notable among his sterling contributions was **Outlines of Ecclesiastical History,** first published in 1893. His avowed purpose was to sustain the declaration of the Savior, through the Prophet Joseph Smith, that the existent creeds had become corrupt. He also wished to instruct his readers in the true principles of the gospel now available through a reestablishment of the ancient order. Documentation of his thesis followed a fourfold pattern of investigation. A vivid description of the ministry of the Messiah and the apostles was followed by an examination of the subsequent rise of false teachers and incumbent universal apostasy from the teachings of Jesus Christ; the reformation or "revolution" preparatory to a new dispensation of truth; and the final restoration of that lost truth and divine authority through revelation from God to the Prophet Joseph.

The 1951 edition of Elder Roberts's work, which is reprinted here, reflects revisions and refinements necessary to a detailed volume of this nature. The original text was prepared in a period when the knowledge of original sources was considerably restricted, and many items had not yet been translated from the Greek, Latin, and Hebrew. It is interesting that Elder Roberts considered his own work to be narrow and limited, and he evidenced a desire to do it over. He would have been the first to recognize the existence of some generalizations and limited documentary support for certain of his premises. Although his ultimate conclusions would not vary, it is probable that were he to undertake a revision of his work today, his use of source materials would have undergone extensive alterations in deference to a host of new documents that have surfaced in recent years.

Elder Roberts was a nonspecialist; that is, he was not formally trained in the disciplines of ancient studies. However, it must also be affirmed that he was no amateur. He studied available sources in great depth. In addition, he had access to a particular fund of knowledge not granted to a majority of the investigators of his era—the insights and gifts provided by the Holy Spirit interacting on a worthy and inquiring mind.

Now, decades later, this astute study supplies us with an invaluable resource for examining those events and circumstances leading to the restoration. Elder Roberts's arrangement of materials combined with the collection of salient notes at the end of each section provides a reservoir of valuable insights designed to induce the student "to delve deeper into the study of Ecclesiastical History."

PART I.

THE ESTABLISHMENT OF THE CHURCH.

SECTION I.

1. Birth of Messiah:—Jesus Christ, the Son of God and Savior of the world, was born, most probably, in the year of Rome 753; at a period of the year corresponding to our month of April (see note 1, 2, end of section). The place of His birth was Bethlehem [Beth-le-hem],* a small town about four miles south of Jerusalem. The birth-place of Messiah was foretold by Micah [Mi-kah], the prophet, more than seven hundred years before the event, in the following prophecy: "But thou, Bethlehem Ephratah [Ef-ra-tah], though thou be little among the thousands of Judah, yet out of thee shall he come forth unto me that is to be ruler in Israel; whose goings forth have been from of old, from everlasting."†

2. Parentage of Christ:—Messiah was born of the virgin Mary, a descendant of David, and the espoused wife of Joseph, a carpenter in the little village of Nazareth [Naz-a-reth], who, notwithstanding his humble station in life, was also a descendant of the royal house of David. An angel appeared unto Mary previous to her conception, and thus addressed her: "Hail thou that art highly favored, the Lord is with thee: blessed art thou among women. And when she saw him, she was troubled at his saying, and cast in her mind what manner of salutation this should be. And

---

*It is also called Ephrath [Ef-rath] and Ephratah [Ef-ra-tah.] It was the scene of Rachel's death and burial, the native place of Samuel's father, the residence of Boaz and Ruth, and the birthplace of David; it was also the last rallying point of the remnant of Judah after the invasion of Nebuchadnezzar.

†Micah v: 2.

the angel said unto her, Fear not, Mary: for thou hast found favor with God. And, behold, thou shalt conceive in thy womb, and bring forth a son, and shall call his name Jesus. He shall be great, and shalt be called the Son of the Highest: and the Lord God shall give unto him the throne of his father David: and he shall reign over the house of Jacob forever; and of his kingdom there shall be no end. Then said Mary unto the angel, How shall this be, seeing I know not a man? And the angel answered and said unto her, The Holy Ghost shall come upon thee, and the power of the Highest shall overshadow thee: therefore also that holy thing which shall be born of thee, shall be called the Son of God. * * * And Mary said: Behold the handmaid of the Lord; be it unto me according to thy word."*

3. These two, the mother of Jesus and her betrothed husband, had left their home in Nazareth to enroll their names as members of the house of David, in a census which had been ordered by the Emperor Augustus, and while at Bethlehem Mary was delivered of her son. The enrollment ordered by the emperor had called so many strangers into the little town of Bethlehem that on the arrival of Joseph and Mary there was no room at the inn for them, and they had to take up quarters in the stable adjacent. There, among the hay and straw spread for the food and rest of the cattle, Christ was born.   (Note 2, end of section.)

4. **The Angelic Announcement:**—The birth of Christ was announced to a few shepherds watching their flock by night—about a mile distant from the village of Bethlehem—by an angel, surrounded about by the glory of God, who said: "Fear not: for, behold, I bring you good tidings of great joy, which shall be to all people. For unto you is born

---

*Luke 1:28-38.

this day in the city of David a Savior, which is Christ the Lord. And this shall be a sign unto you; ye shall find the babe wrapped in swaddling clothes, lying in a manger. And suddenly there was with the angel a multitude of the heavenly host, praising God, and saying, Glory to God in the highest, and on earth peace, good will toward men."* A visit to the village confirmed the strange proclamation of the angel— they found the mother and child.

5. **The Inquiry of the Magi:**—Not alone by voice of angels was the birth of Messiah announced, but "wise men from the east" who had seen his star in the firmament came to Jerusalem about the time of his birth, inquiring— "Where is he that is born King of the Jews? for we have seen his star in the east, and are come to worship him."†

6. Nor were signs of Messiah's birth seen alone on the eastern hemisphere; to the people of the western hemisphere signs were also given; "a new star did appear," according to the words of the Nephite prophets, at Zarahemla; the Nephites saw it and to them, as well as to the wise men of the east, a star announced the birth of him who was to be King of the Jews‡ and the Savior of the world. Another sign was given to the Nephites, which had also been predicted by their prophets; the night before§ Jesus was born remained beautifully light on the western hemisphere. This event is thus recorded in the Book of Mormon: "And it came to

---

*Canon Farrar translates this passage: "Glory to God in the highest, and on earth peace among men of good will," maintaining that such is the reading of the best Mss. Dear to us as the reading in King James' translation of the Bible is, if looked upon as announcing the effect of Christianity in this world—"On earth peace among men of good will," comes more nearly to the truth than "on earth peace, good will toward men."

†Matt. ii: 2.

‡ III Nephi 1: 21.

§ III Nephi 1: 13.

pass that the words which came unto Nephi were fulfilled, according as they had been spoken; for behold at the going down of the sun, there was no darkness; and the people began to be astonished, because there was no darkness when the time of night came. * * * There was no darkness in all that night, but it was light as though it was midday. And it came to pass that the sun did rise in the morning again, according to its proper order; and they (the Nephites) knew that it was the day that the Lord should be born, because of the sign which had been given."*

7. **The Alarm of King Herod:**—The inquiry made by the "wise men" from the east concerning the one who was "born King of the Jews," alarmed the jealousy of Herod, and learning from the chief priests and scribes that Bethlehem was the place where the deliverer of Israel was to be born, he sent the wise men there, strictly charging them to search diligently, and when they had found the child to bring him word that he too might worship him. On the way to Bethlehem the star they had seen in the east went before them until it stood over where the child was. They found the babe with Mary his mother and they worshipped him, giving him presents of gold and frankincense and myrrh. They were commanded of God in a dream, however, not to return to Herod, so they departed into their own country another way.

8. Joseph, too, after the departure of the wise men, was warned in a dream to flee out of the land, for Herod would seek the young child to destroy him. He was commanded to go into Egypt and remain there until the Lord should call him to return. In obedience to these divine commandments,

---

*III Nephi 1: 15-19.

Joseph took the mother and child and fled in the night into Egypt.

9.   Herod's wrath knew no bounds when he found that the wise men had not obeyed him; and in order that he might not be baffled in his determination to destroy the one he feared would supplant himself or his posterity in the throne of Israel, he sent out an edict commanding that all the children in Bethlehem two years old and under should be slain.   Then was fulfilled the prophecy of Jeremiah: "In Rama [Ra-ma] was there a voice heard, lamentation, and weeping and great mourning, Rachel weeping for her children, and would not be comforted because they were not."* (See note 3, end of section.)

10.   **Death of Herod:**—(note 4 end of section) After Herod's death, Joseph was again visited, in a dream, by an angel, who commanded him to return with the child and his mother into the land of Israel; for they who had sought the young child's life were dead.   Then was fulfilled that which was spoken by the prophet of the Lord, (Hosea)—"Out of Egypt have I called my son."   Joseph obeyed the commandment, but as he approached Judea and learned that Archelaus [Ar-ke-la-us] the son of Herod reigned in his father's stead, he was fearful and instead of remaining in Judea, he went into Galilee [Gal-i-lee] and dwelt in the little town of Nazareth—his former home—"That it might be fulfilled which was spoken by the prophets, He shall be called a Nazarene"† [Naz-a-reen].

*Matt. ii: 18.
†Matt. ii: 23.

NOTES.

1. The Year of Messiah's Birth:—"The Birth of Christ was first made an era, from which to reckon dates," says the learned translator of Dr. Mosheim's *Institutes*,—Murdock—"by Dionysius Exiguus, [Di-o-nish-i-us Exs-ig-u-us] about A. D. 532. He supposed Christ to have been born on the 25th of December, in the year of Rome 753, and this computation has been followed in practice to this day; notwithstanding the learned are well agreed that it must be incorrect."
It will be seen, however, from what follows, from the same author, that all is uncertainty with the learned in respect to this subject:

"To ascertain the true time of Christ's birth, there are two principal data afforded by the Evangelists: I. It is clear, from Matt. ii: 1, etc., that Christ was born before the death of Herod the Great, who died about Easter, in the year of Rome 749 or 750. Now, if Christ was born in the December next before Herod's death, it must have been in the year of Rome 748 or 749; and, of course, four, if not five years anterior to the Dionysian or Vulgar era: II. It is probable, from Luke iii: 1, 2, 23, that Jesus was 'about' thirty years of age in the fifteenth year of the reign of Tiberius Caesar. Now, the reign of Tiberius may be considered as commencing at the time he became sole emperor, in August of the year of Rome 767; or (as there is some reason to suppose that Augustus made him partner in the government two years before he died), we may begin his reign in the year of Rome 765. The fifteenth year of Tiberius will therefore be either the year of Rome 781 or 779. From which deduct 30, and we have the year of Rome 751 or 749 for the year of Christ's birth; the former two and the latter four years earlier than the Dionysian computation. Comparing these results with those obtained from the death of Herod, it is generally supposed the true time of Christ's birth was the year of Rome 749, or four years before the Vulgar era. *But the conclusion is not certain, because there is uncertainty in the data.* (1.) It is not certain that we ought to reckon Tiberius' reign as beginning two years before the death of Augustus. (2.) Luke says '*about* thirty years of age.' This is indefinite and may be understood of twenty-nine, thirty, or thirty-one years. (3.) It is not certain in which of the two years mentioned Herod died; nor how long before that event the Savior was born. Respecting the month and day of Christ's birth, we are left almost wholly to conjecture."

It will be demanded on what authority I have gone counter to the conclusions of the learned on this subject by keeping to the Dionysian date—so far, at least, as the year is concerned. My answer is that in the revelation on Church government in the Doctrine and Covenants (Sec. XX.) the following in respect to the rise of the Church is given: "The rise of the Church of Christ in these last days, *being one thousand eight hundred and thirty years since the coming of our Lord and Savior Jesus Christ in the flesh*, it being regularly organized and established agreeable to the laws of our country, by the will and commandments of God, in the fourth month, and on the sixth day of the month, which is called April."

I believe that this—better than any other authority, fixes the time of the birth, or the "coming of our Lord and Savior Jesus Christ in the flesh;" and that, as to the year at least, agrees with the Dionysian computation. It must be remembered that this revelation in Section twenty of the Doctrine and Covenants was given before the Church was organized—at sundry times between the first and the sixth of April—and that the prophet was instructed to organize the Church on the sixth day of April, 1830, hence it was not mere chance that determined the day on which that organization took place, a fact that is significant in view of the above considerations and those which follow in note 2.—*Roberts.*

2. **The Day of Messiah's Birth:**—"Strictly speaking, if this Church was organized 'one thousand eight hundred and thirty years since the coming of our Lord and Savior in the flesh," then the sixth of April must have been the anniversary of the Savior's birthday. If the organization of the Church had been before or subsequent to that date, if only by one or any number of days, the great event would have been more or less than one thousand eight hundred and thirty years by just so many days. (This argument also holds good as to the year of Christ's birth.) Opinions formed by the study of chronological events may or may not be accurate. But we would scarcely think the Lord would make any mistake about dates. Least of all he who was born on that day, and on that day thirty-three years later was crucified."—*Joseph F. Smith.*

"Let us inquire if the day observed by the Christian world as the day of His (Christ's) birth—the 25th of December—is or is not the real Christmas day. A great many authors have found out from their researches, that it is not. I think that there is scarcely an author at the present day that believes that the 25th of December was the day that Christ was born on * * * It is generally believed and conceded by the learned who have investigated the matter, that Christ was born in April. * * * It is stated that according to the best of their (the learned) judgment from the researches they have made, Christ was crucified on the 6th of April. That is the day on which this Church was organized. But when these learned men go back from the day of his crucifixion to the day of his birth, they are at a loss, having no certain evidence or testimony by which they can determine it."—*Orson Pratt.*

In support of Elder Pratt's contention relative to the uncertainty of Christian scholars as to the day on which Jesus was born, I quote the statement of Rev. Charles F. Deem, Author of "The Light of the Nation." and President of the American Institute of Christian Philosophy "It is annoying to see learned men use the same apparatus of calculation and reach the most diverse results." In a foot note at page 32, in "Light of the Nation," he refers to fifteen different authors all of whom are writers of note, who give different years for the birth of Christ varying from B. C. 1 to B. C. 7.

3. **Humble Nativity of Messiah:**—"In the rude limestone grotto attached to the inn as a stable, among the hay and straw spread for the food and rest of the cattle, weary with their day's journey, far from

home, in the midst of strangers, in circumstances so devoid of all earthly comfort or splendor that it is impossible to imagine a humbler nativity, Christ was born. Distant but a few miles, on the plateau of the abrupt and singular hill now called *Jebel Fureidis* or 'Little Paradise Mountain,' towered the palace—fortress of the Great Herod. The magnificent houses of his friends and courtiers crowded around its base. The humble wayfarers, as they passed near it, might have heard the hired and voluptuous minstrelsy with which its feasts were celebrated, or the shouting of the rough mercenaries whose arms enforced obedience to its despotic lord. But the true King of the Jews—the rightful Lord of the universe—was not to be found in palace or fortress. They who wear soft clothing are in kings' houses. The cattle stables of the lowly caravan-serial were a more fitting birthplace for him who came to reveal that the soul of the greatest monarch was no dearer or greater in God's sight than the soul of his meanest slave; for him who had not where to lay his head; for him who, from his cross of shame, was to rule the world!"—*Canon Farrar.*

4. **Character of Herod:**—"Now some there are who stand amazed at the diversity of Herod's nature and purposes; for when we have respect to his magnificence, and the benefits which he bestowed on all mankind, there is no possibility for even those who had the least respect for him, to deny, or not openly confess, that he had a nature vastly beneficent; but when anyone looks upon the punishment he inflicted and the injuries he did, not only to his subjects, but to his nearest relatives, and takes notice of his severe and unrelenting disposition there, he will be forced to allow that he was brutish, and a stranger to all humanity. * * * If anyone was not very obsequious to him in his language, and would not confess himself to be his slave, or but seemed to think of any innovation in his government, he was not able to contain himself, but prosecuted his very kindred and friends and punished them as if they were enemies; and this wickedness he undertook out of a desire that he might be himself alone honored. * * * A man he was of great barbarity towards all men equally, and a slave to his passion; but above the consideration of what was right."—*Josephus.*

5. **Last Illness of Herod:**—"But now Herod's distemper greatly increased upon him after a severe manner, and this by God's judgment upon him for his sins; for a fire glowed in him slowly, which did not so much appear to the touch outwardly, as it augmented his pains inwardly; for it brought upon him a vehement appetite to eating, which he could not avoid to supply with one sort of food or other. His entrails were exulcerated, and the chief violence of his pain lay on his colon; an aqueous and transparent liquor also had settled itself upon his feet; * * * and when he sat upright, he had a difficulty of breathing which was very loathsome, on account of the stench of his breath, and the quickness of his returns. He had also convulsions in all parts of his body, which increased his strength to an unsufferable degree. It was said by those who pretended to divine, and who were endowed with wisdom to foretell such things, that God inflicted this punishment on the king on account of his great impurity; yet was he still in hopes of recovering, though his afflictions seemed greater than anyone could bear."—*Josephus.*

REVIEW.

1.   In what year of Rome was Messiah born?

2.   State the reasons for placing the date of Messiah's birth in the year of Rome 753.   (See notes 1 and 2.)

3.   Give the name of Messiah's birthplace.

4.   For what is Ephratah noted?   (Note.)

5.   Who was the mother of Jesus?

6.   Relate what you can of Mary, and the announcement that she should be the mother of the Son of God.

7.   Relate the circumstances under which Christ was born.

8.   Give an account of the visitation of the angels to the shepherds.

9.   What is Canon Farrar's translation of the title of the angelic song?

10.   Give an account of the Magi's visit to Jerusalem in search of the Christ.

11.   What signs were given of Messiah's birth to the people on the Western Hemisphere?

12.   By what divine providence was Messiah's life preserved in infancy?

13.   What was the character of Herod the Great?   (Note 4.)

14.   Describe Herod's last illness and death.   (Note 5.)

15.   Where did Joseph settle on his return from Egypt?

16.   What prophecies were fulfilled by Messiah being taken into Egypt and Nazareth?

SECTION II.*

1.   State of the Religious World at Messiah's Birth:—
At the time of the birth of the Son of God, the enfeebled
world was tottering on its foundations.   The national religions which had satisfied the parents, no longer proved
sufficient for the children.   The new generations could not
repose contented within the ancient forms.   The gods of
every nation, when transported to Rome—then the domi-
nant political power in the world—there lost their oracles,
as the nations themselves had there lost their liberty.   Brought
face to face in the capital, they had destroyed each other,
and their divinity had vanished.   A great void was thus
occasioned in the religion of the world.

2.   A kind of deism, destitute alike of spirit and of life,
floated for a time above the abyss in which the vigorous
superstitions of antiquity had been engulfed.   But like all
negative creeds it had no power to reconstruct.   All nations
were plunged in the grossest superstition.   Most of them,
indeed all, except the Jews, supposed that each country and
province was subjected to a set of very powerful beings whom
they called gods, and whom the people, in order to live
happily, must propitiate with various rites and ceremonies.
These deities were supposed to differ materially from each
other in sex, power, nature and offices.   Some nations

---

*I have condensed much of the matter in the first part of this section
from the learned works of D'Aubigne, Dr. Mosheim, Gibbon and Josephus, sometimes using even their phraseology without further acknowledgment than this note.—*The Author.*

went beyond others in impiety of worship, but all stood chargeable with absurdity, if not gross stupidity in matters of religion. (See note 1, end of section.)

3. Thus every nation had a class of deities peculiar to itself, among which one was supposed to be pre-eminent over the rest, and was their king, though subject himself to the laws of *fate*, or to an eternal destiny. The oriental nations had not the same gods as the Gauls, the Germans, and the other northern nations; and the Grecian deities were essentially different from those of the Egyptians, who worshipped brute animals, plants, and various productions of nature and art. Each nation, likewise, had its own method of worshiping its gods; differing widely from the rites of other nations. But, from their ignorance or from other causes the Greeks and Romans maintained that their gods were universally worshipped; and they therefore gave the names of their own gods to the foreign deities which has caused great confusion and errors in the history of ancient religions even in the works of the learned.

4. Heathen Toleration—Its Cause:—The variety of gods and religions in the Pagan nations produced no wars or feuds among them. Each nation without concern allowed its neighbors to enjoy their own views of religion, and to worship their own gods in their own way. Nor need this tolerance greatly surprise us. For they who regard the world as divided like a great country into numerous provinces each subject to a distinct order of deities, cannot despise the gods of other nations nor think of compelling all others to pay worship to their national gods. The Romans in particular, though they would not allow the public religions to be changed or multiplied, yet gave the citizens full liberty to observe foreign religions in private, and to hold meetings and feasts and to erect temples and groves to these foreign

deities, in whose worship there was nothing inconsistent with the public safety and existing laws.   (See note 2, end of section.)

5.   **Character of Heathen Gods:**—The greater part of the gods of all nations were ancient heroes, famous for their achievements and their worthy deeds; such as kings, generals and the founders of cities; and likewise females who were highly distinguished for their deeds and discoveries, whom a grateful posterity had deified.   To these some added the more splendid and useful objects in the natural world, among which the sun, moon, and stars being pre-eminent, received worship from nearly all, and some were not ashamed to pay divine honors to mountains, rivers, trees, the earth, the ocean, the winds, and even to diseases, to virtues and vices, and to almost every conceivable object, or, at least, to the deities supposed to preside over these objects.

6.   The worship of these deities consisted in numerous ceremonies with sacrifices, offerings, and prayers.   The ceremonies, for the most part, were absurd and ridiculous; and what was worse yet, debasing, obscene and cruel.   The whole pagan system had not the least efficacy to excite and cherish virtuous emotions in the soul.   For in the first place, the gods and goddesses to whom the public homage was paid, instead of being patterns of virtue, were patterns rather of enormous vices and crimes.   They were considered as superior to mortals in power and as exempt from death, but in all things else as on a level with man.   In the next place, the ministers of this religion, neither by precept nor by example, exhorted the people to lead honest and virtuous lives, but gave them to understand that all the homage required of them by the gods was comprised in the observance of the traditional rites and ceremonies.   And lastly, the doctrines inculcated respecting the rewards of the

righteous and the punishments of the wicked in the future world were some of them dubious and uncertain, and others more adapted to promote vice than virtue. Hence the wiser pagans themselves, about the time of the Savior's birth condemned and ridiculed the whole system.

7. **Mysteries of Paganism:**—It is contended by those who would dignify paganism, that back of its common worship, among the orientals and Greeks at least, certain recondite and concealed rites called mysteries—containing in them the essence of true religion—existed: and that back of its idolatry stood and was recognized the true God, of which the images worshipped were but the material representatives. To these mysteries, however, very few were admitted. Candidates for initiation had first to give satisfactory proof of their good faith and patience, by various most troublesome ceremonies. When initiated they could not divulge anything they had seen without exposing their lives to imminent danger. Hence the interior of these hidden rites is at this day but little known, and therefore but an imperfect judgment may be formed as to their virtue. But what glimpses are obtained of the rites of these mysteries do not prepossess one in their favor; for in many of them many things were done which are repugnant to modesty and decency, and in all of them that are known the discerning may see that the deities there worshipped were more distinguished for their vices than for their virtues. (See note 3, end of section.)

8. **Paul's Arraignment of the Pagan World:**— Paul, the great apostle of the Gentiles, brings a terrible indictment against the pagan world of his day, and also against the more ancient pagans, and avers that there was no excuse for their idolatry or wickedness: "For the wrath of God is revealed from heaven against all ungodliness and

unrighteousness of men, who hold the truth in unrighteousness; because that which may be known of God is manifest in them; for God hath showed it unto them. For the invisible things of him from the creation of the world are clearly seen, being understood by the things that are made, even his eternal power and Godhead; so that they are without excuse: because that, when they knew God, they glorified him not as God, neither were thankful; but became vain in their imaginations, and their foolish heart was darkened. Professing themselves to be wise, they became fools, and changed the glory of the incorruptible God into an image like to corruptible man, and to birds, and four-footed beasts and creeping things. Wherefore God also gave them up to uncleanness through the lusts of their own hearts, to dishonor their own bodies between themselves; who changed the truth of God into a lie and worshiped and served the creature more than the Creator. * * * For this cause God gave them up unto vile affections; * * * and even as they did not like to retain God in their knowledge, God gave them over to a reprobate mind, to do those things which are not convenient; being filled with all unrighteousness, fornication, wickedness, covetousness, maliciousness; full of envy, murder, debate, deceit, malignity; whisperers, backbiters, haters of God, despiteful, proud, boasters, inventors of evil things, disobedient to parents, without understanding, covenant-breakers, without natural affection, implacable, unmerciful: who knowing the judgment of God, that they which commit such things are worthy of death, not only do the same, but have pleasure in them that do them."*   (See note 4, end of section.)

---

*Epistle to Romans 1: 18-32.

9. Political State of the World at Messiah's Birth:—
At the birth of Jesus Christ the greater part of the civilized
world on the eastern hemisphere was subject to the Romans.
Their remoter provinces they either ruled by means of temporary governors and presidents sent from Rome, or suffered
them to live under their own kings and laws, subject to the
control of the Roman emperors.

10. The senate and people of Rome, though they had
not lost all the appearance of liberty, were really under the
authority of one man, Augustus; who was clothed with the
titles of emperor, sovereign pontiff, censor, tribune of the
people, pro-consul; in a word, he was given every office which
conferred general power and pre-eminence in the commonwealth.

11. The Roman government, if we regard only its
form and laws, was sufficiently mild and equitable. But
the injustice and avarice of the nobles and provincial governors, the Roman lust of conquest and dominion, and the
rapacity of the publicans who farmed the revenues of the
state, brought many and grievous evils upon the people.
The magistrates and publicans fleeced them of their property
on the one hand, while, on the other, the Roman lust of
dominion required armies to be raised in the provinces—
a thing which was very oppressive to them, and the occasion
of almost perpetual insurrection. This, however, is true
more especially of the days which preceded the reign of
Augustus [Au-gus-tus]. The principal conquests of the
Romans were achieved under the republic. It was left for
Augustus to adopt that policy which aimed merely to preserve those dominions which had been acquired by the policy
of the senate, the active emulation of the consuls and the
martial enthusiasm of the people. Under his reign the
Roman people themselves seem to have relinquished the

ambitious design of subduing the whole earth.   (See note 5, end of section.)

12.   This widely extended dominion of one people, or rather, of one man, was attended with several advantages: 1, it brought into union a multitude of nations differing in customs and languages; 2, it gave freer access to the remotest nations; 3, it gradually civilized the barbarous nations, by introducing among them the Roman laws and customs; 4, it spread literature, the arts and philosophy in countries where they were not before cultivated, and guaranteed the protection of its laws to the people even in the remotest provinces.   (See note 6, end of section.)

13.   Moreover, at the birth of Messiah, the Roman empire was freer from commotion that it had been for many years.   Though it cannot be said that the whole world was in profound peace, yet there can be no doubt that the period when the Savior was born, if compared with the preceding times, was peculiarly peaceful—a condition quite essential to the introduction of the gospel and the extensive preaching of it.   Nor is it too much to say that the Lord raised up the great Roman empire that under its beneficent yet powerful sway, the glad tidings of great joy, the gospel of Jesus Christ, might be widely preached among men.

14.   Of the state of those nations which lay beyond the boundaries of the Roman empire we may not learn so much as of Rome.   It is sufficient to know, however, that the Oriental nations were pressed down by a stern despotism, which their effeminacy of mind and body, and even their religion, led them to bear with patience; while the northern nations enjoyed much greater liberty, which was protected by the rigor of their climate and the consequent energy of their constitutions, aided by their mode of life.

15. Political and Religious State of the Jews:— The condition of the Jewish people among whom the Savior was born was scarcely any better than that of other nations. Herod, called the Great, then governed, or rather, oppressed the Jewish nation, though only a tributary king under the Romans. He drew upon himself universal hatred by his cruelties, jealousies and wars; and he exhausted the wealth of the unhappy nation by his mad luxury, his excessive magnificence, and his immoderate largesses. Under his administration Roman luxury and licentiousness spread over Palestine. In religion he was professedly a Jew, but he copied the manners of those who despise all religion.

16. The Romans did not wholly prohibit the Jews from retaining their national laws, and the religion established by Moses. "They had their high priests, council or senate (Sanhedrin)*, and inflicted lesser punishments. They could apprehend men and bring them before the council; and if a guard of soldiers was needful, could be assisted by them upon asking the governor for them; they could bind men and keep them in custody; the council could summon witnesses, take examinations, and when they had any capital offenders, carry them before the governor. This governor usually paid a regard to what they offered, and if they brought evidence of the fact, pronounced sentence according to their laws. He was the proper judge in all capital causes."†

17. The measure of liberty and comfort allowed to the Jews by the Romans was well nigh wholly dissipated, first by the cruelty and avarice of the governors, and by the frauds and repacity of the publicans; and second, by the profligacy and crimes of those who pretended to be patriots and guardians of the nation. Their principal men,

*See note (7), end of section.
†Dr. Lardner.

their high priests, were abandoned wretches, who had purchased their places by bribes or by deeds of iniquity, and who maintained their ill-acquired authority by every species of dishonest acts.   The other priests, and all who held any considerable office, were not much better.   The multitude, excited by such examples, ran headlong into every sort of iniquity, and by their unceasing robberies and seditions they excited against themselves both the justice of God and the vengeance of man.

18. **Religious Divisions:**—Two religions may be said to have flourished in Palestine at the times of which we write; *viz.*, the Jewish and the Samaritan; between the followers of which there was a deadly hatred.   The nature of the former is set forth in the Old Testament.   But in the age of the Savior it had been corrupted by the traditions of the people who were divided into sects filled with bitterness against each other.   Chief among these sects were the Pharisees [Fa-ri-sees,] and Sadducees [Sad-du-seezs.]

19. **Pharisees and Sadducees.**—While these two sects agreed as to a number of fundamental principles of the Jewish religion, they differed on questions of the highest importance, and such as related to the salvation of the soul. First, they disagreed respecting the law which God had given them.   The Pharisees superadded to the written law an oral or unwritten law, handed down by tradition, which the Sadducees rejected, adhering alone to the written law. They differed, too, as to the import of the law.   The Pharisees held to a double sense of the scripture, the one literal, the other figurative; while the Sadducees held only to the literal sense of the Bible.   To these contests concerning the laws were added others on subjects of the highest moment; particularly in respect to the rewards and punishments announced in the sacred writings.   The Pharisees supposed

them to affect both body and spirit—in whose pre-existence and eternal existence they believed—and that punishments and rewards extended beyond the present life. The Sadducees believed in no future retributions. They were sceptical of the miraculous; and denied the existence of spiritual beings, the immortality of the soul, the resurrection of the body. They were deists, in fact; viewing the Supreme Being as a quiescent Providence calmly surveying and ruling the regular working of natural laws. They gave themselves up to ease, luxury, self-indulgence, and were not indisposed to view with indifferent liberality the laxity of heathen morals and the profanity of idol worship. They included in their numbers the leading men of the nation, were the aristocracy in fact, while the Pharisees, on the other hand, were the common people; proud of their unblemished descent from Abraham, exclusive, formal, self-righteous, strict observers of external rites and ceremonies, even beyond the requirements of the law.

20. Such were the chief sects among the Jews. There were others but they were of minor importance. Both Sadducees and Pharisees looked for a deliverer; not, however, such an one as God had promised; but a powerful warrior and a vindicator of their national liberties, a king, a ruler. All placed the sum of religion in an observance of the Mosaic ritual, and in certain duties toward their countrymen. All excluded the rest of mankind from the hope of salvation, and, of course, whenever they dared, treated them with hatred and inhumanity. To these fruitful sources of vice, must be added the various absurd and superstitious opinions concerning the divine nature, genii, magic, etc., which they had imbibed from surrounding nations.

21. Samaritans:—The Samaritans [Sa-mar-i-tans] were colonists sent by the king of Assyria [As-syr-rya], Shalma-

neser [Shal-ma-ne-zer], to people the land after he had carried captive the Israelites, in the latter part of the eighth century, B. C. They were a mixed people from various eastern nations, conquered by this same king—and they brought with them their various forms of national idolatry. A plague breaking out among them, however, led them to petition for a priest of the god of the country, to teach them the old form of worship. He was stationed at Bethel [Beth-el], and the Samaritans endeavored to combine a formal reverence of God with the practice of their own idolatrous rites. After the captivity of Judah, they sought an alliance with the returned Jews (536 B. C.), with whom they intermarried. On Ezra enforcing the Mosaic law against mixed marriages—three-quarters of a century later— Manasses [Ma-nas-ses], a Jewish priest, who had married the daughter of Sanballat [San-bal-lat], chief of the Samaritans, headed a secession at Shechem [Shek-em]. The Samaritans taught the Mosaic ritual and erected a rival temple to that at Jerusalem, on Mount Gerizim [Ger-i-zim]. This mixed community before the time of the Savior began to claim descent from the patriarchs and a share in the promises. Their religion was less pure than that of the Jews, as they adulterated the doctrines of the Old Testament with the profane rites of the pagan religion.

22. Such was the state of the world—such the condition of the Jews at the time of Messiah's birth; and surely that condition justified the pity and also the stern reproofs— nay, the severe rebukes administered, as we shall see, by the Son of God in the course of his ministry.

NOTES.

1. State of the World at Messiah's Birth:—The world had grown old, and the dotage of its paganism was marked by hideous excesses. Atheism in belief was followed, as among all nations it has always been, by degradation of morals, iniquity seemed to have run its course to the very farthest goal. Philosophy had abrogated its boasted functions except for the favored few. Crime was universal, and there was no known remedy for the horror and ruin which it was causing in a thousand hearts. Remorse itself seemed to be exhausted, so that men were past feeling. There was a callosity of heart, a petrifying of the moral sense, which even those who suffered from it felt to be abnormal and portentous. Even the heathen world felt that "the fullness of the time" had come.—*Canon Farrar.*

2. Policy of Rome in Respect to Religion:—The policy of the emperors and the senate, so far as it concerned religion, was happily seconded by the reflections of the enlightened, and by the habits of the superstitious part of their subjects. The various modes of worship, which prevailed in the Roman world, were all considered by the people as equally true; by the philosopher as equally false; and by the magistrate as equally useful. And this toleration produced not only mutual indulgence, but even religious concord. * * * Avarice and taste very frequently despoiled the vanquished nations of the elegant statues of their gods and the rich ornaments of their temples; but in the exercise of the religion which they derived from their ancestors, they uniformly experienced the indulgence, and even protection of the Roman conquerors. The province of Gaul seems, and indeed only seems, an exception to this universal toleration. Under the specious pretext of abolishing human sacrifices, the emperors Tiberius and Claudius suppressed the dangerous power of the Druids; but the priests themselves, their gods and their altars, subsisted in peaceful obscurity till the final fall of paganism. * * * Rome gradually became the common temple of her subjects; and the freedom of the city was bestowed on all the gods of mankind.—*Gibbon.*

3. Mysteries of the Pagan Religion:—It has been maintained that the design of at least some of these mysteries was to inculcate the grand principles of natural religion, such as the unity of God, the immortality of the soul, the importance of virtue, etc., and to explain the vulgar polytheism as symbolical of these great truths. But this certainly needs better proof. It is more probable that the later pagan philosophers, who lived after the light of Christianity had exposed the abominations of polytheism, were the principal authors of this moral interpretation of the vulgar religion, which they falsely pretended was taught in the mysteries, while in reality, those mysteries were probably mere supplements to the vulgar mythology and worship, and of the same general character and spirit.—*Murdock*—Translator of Mosheim Ecclesiastical History.

4. State of Religion in Rome:—A modern writer describing the religious state of Rome at the time of Julius Caesar—it could not have been much changed at the birth of Messiah, sixty years later—says: "Religion, once the foundation of the laws and rule of personal conduct, had subsided into opinion. The educated in their hearts disbelieved it. Temples were still built with increasing splendor; the established forms were scrupulously observed. Public men spoke conventionally of Providence, that they might throw on their opponents the odium of impiety; but of genuine belief that life had any serious meaning, there was none remaining beyond the circle of the silent, patient, ignorant multitude. The whole spiritual atmosphere was saturated with cant—cant moral, cant political, cant religious; an affectation of high principle which had ceased to touch the conduct, and flowed on in an increasing volume of insincere and unreal speech. The truest thinkers were those who, like Lucretius, spoke frankly out their real convictions, declared Providence was a dream, and that man and the world he lived in were material phenomena, generated by natural forces out of cosmic atoms, and into atoms to be again resolved."—*Froude.*

5. **Policy of Augustus as to Conquests:**—Inclined to peace by his temper and situation, it was easy for him to discover that Rome, in her present exalted situation, had much less to hope than to fear from the chance of arms; and that, in the prosecution of remote wars, the undertaking every day became more difficult, the event more doubtful and the possession more precarious and less beneficial. The experience of Augustus added weight to these salutary reflections, and eventually convinced him that by prudent vigor of his counsels, it would be easy to secure every concession which the safety or the dignity of Rome might require from the most formidable barbarians * * * On the death of the emperor, his testament was publicly read in the senate. He bequeathed, as a valuable legacy to his successors, the advice of confining the empire within those limits which nature seemed to have placed as its permanent bulwarks and foundations; on the west the Atlantic ocean; the Rhine and Danube on the north; the Euphrates on the east; and towards the south the sandy deserts of Arabia and Africa.—*Gibbon, Decline and Fall, Vol. I, Chap. 1.*

6. **Mission and Character of the Roman Empire:**—As the soil must be prepared before the wheat can be sown, so before the kingdom of heaven could throw up its shoots there was needed a kingdom of this world, where the nations were neither torn to pieces by violence nor were rushing after false ideals [as to governments] and spurious ambitions. Such a kingdom was the empire of the Caesars—a kingdom where peaceful men could work, think and speak as they pleased, and travel freely among provinces ruled for the most part by Gallios who protected life and property, and forbade fanatics to tear each other to pieces for their religious opinions. "It is not lawful for us to put a man to death," was the complaint of the Jewish priests to the Roman governor. Had Europe and Asia been covered with independent nations, each with a local religion represented in its ruling powers, Christianity must have been stifled in its cradle. If St. Paul had escaped the Sanhedrin of Jerusalem, he would have been torn to pieces

by the silversmiths at Ephesus. The appeal to Caesar's judgment seat was the shield of his mission, and alone made possible his success. —*Froude.*

7. The Sanhedrin of the Jews:— "The Council" of the Jewish church and people was a theocratic oligarchy, which after the return from the captivity (536 B. C.), ruled the new settlement, being in all causes and over all persons, ecclesiastical and civil, supreme. It is supposed to be suggested by the old institution of seventy-two Elders (six from each tribe), appointed by Moses, at Jethro's [Jeth-ro's] suggestion, to relieve him in the administration of justice (Ex. xviii: 14; Num. xi: 16.) Having died out in the age succeeding Joshua, and being superceded under the monarchy, it was revived either by Ezra, or after the Macedonian ascendancy. It consisted of an equal number of priests, scribes and elders, all of whom must be married, above thirty years of age, well instructed in the law, and of good report among the people. This constituted the Supreme Court of judicature and administrative Council, taking cognizance of false doctrine and teaching, as well as breaches of the Mosaic Law, and regulating both civil and religious observances peculiar to the Jewish nation. The power of life and death had been taken from it by the Roman government, which otherwise covenanted to respect its decrees. The council usually met in the hall Gazith, within the Temple precincts, though special meetings were sometimes held in the house of the High Priest, who was generally (though not necessarily) the president. There were also two vice-presidents, and two scribes—clerks—or "heralds," one registering the votes of acquittal (or noes), and the other those of convictions (or ayes), and a body of lictors or attendants. The assembly set in the form of a semi-circle, the president occupying the center of the arc, the prisoner that of the center of the chord, while the two "heralds" sat a little in advance of the president, on his right and his left.—*Oxford Teacher's Bible—Addenda.*

REVIEW.

1.   State the religious condition of the world at Messiah's birth?
2.   What was the cause of heathen religious toleration?
3.   What was the policy of Rome in respect to religion? (Note 2.)
4.   What was the nature of the heathen gods?
5.   Describe the character of heathen worship.
6.   What can you say of pagan mysteries?   (Note 3.)
7.   Give the substance of Paul's arraignment of the pagan world.
8.   What was the political state of the world at Messiah's birth?
9.   Describe the general character of the Roman government.
10.   Enumerate the advantages the Roman government gave to the world.
11.   How did these advantages affect the work of the Christ?
12.   What was the state of the nations outside of the Roman empire?

13. Who was the king of the Jews at Messiah's birth?
14. What was the political state of the Jews at that time?
15. What can you say of religion among the Jews at this period?
16. What were the religious divisions in Palestine?
17. State the doctrines of the Pharisees.   The Sadducees.
18. What was the character of the Deliverer expected by both Pharisees and Sadducees?
19. Did Jesus Christ answer their expectations?
20. Tell what you can of the Samaritans.
21. Describe the Sanhedrin of the Jews.   (Note **7.**)

SECTION III.

1. Childhood and Youth of Messiah:—Returning from Egypt in obedience to the commandment of God, Joseph, the husband of Mary, with the infant Savior, went into Galilee, and lived at Nazareth—the most despised village of the most despised province in all Palestine. (Note 1, end of section.) Of his childhood but little information can be obtained from any authentic source. All that may be learned from the biographies in the Gospels is that after the settlement in Nazareth, the child grew and waxed strong in spirit, filled with wisdom; and the grace of God was upon him.

2. Luke tells us that when twelve years of age, Jesus accompanied his mother and Joseph to Jerusalem, to attend the feast of the Passover. (See note 2, end of section.) When they started on the return to Nazareth, Jesus remained behind at Jerusalem without their knowledge. They supposed him to be in the company, but when after a whole day's journey he did not appear, they made inquiry for him among their kindred, and not finding him, returned to Jerusalem in search of him. After three days' anxious inquiry they found him in the temple, sitting in the midst of the doctors, both hearing them and asking questions. Answering his mother's gentle reproof for remaining behind, he said: "How is it that ye sought me? Wist ye not that I must be about my Father's business?" Thus early in life, just emerging from childhood, it seems that the Son of God had the inspiration of his mission resting upon him. Yet in loving obedience he went with them down into Nazareth, "and was subject unto them." With the return to Nazareth the authentic history of the childhood and youth of the Son of God ends; further than we learn from the remark of Luke that "Jesus increased in wisdom and stature, and in favor with God and man." But what the details of his life and development were for the next eighteen years, we do not know. (See note 3, end of section.)

3. In the New Testament apocrypha there are wonderful and miraculous stories of his carrying spilt water in his robe; of his pulling a short board to its requisite length; of moulding sparrows out of clay and then clapping his hands at which they are made alive and fly away; how he vexes and shames and silences those who wish to teach him; how he rebukes Joseph or turns his playmates into kids; how he strikes dead with a curse the boys who offend or run against him, until at last there is a storm of popular indignation, and his mother fears to have him leave the house*—and a hundred other things equally absurd which mar rather than embellish the childhood and youth of Jesus, which the silence of his reliable biographers dignifies and exalts.

4. **John the Baptist:**—In the fifteenth year of the reign of Tiberius Caesar, there came preaching throughout the wilderness of Judea [Ju-de-a] a strange character, called John the Baptist. He was the son of Elizabeth, who was a descendant of Aaron, and a cousin to Mary, the mother of Jesus. His father was a priest of the temple, named Zacharias. Zacharias and Elizabeth were both well stricken in years, when there appeared unto the former, in the temple, as he was burning incense upon the altar, the angel Gabriel [Ga-bri-el], who announced to him that his wife should bear

---

*See The First Gospel of the Infancy, Apocryphal New Testament (Colley & Rich, publishers, Boston, 1891.)

him a son, and that he must call his name John. The angel
also said that John should be great in the eyes of the Lord;
that he should be filled with the Holy Ghost, even from his
mother's womb. He was to have power also to turn unto
their God many of the children of Israel, and to go before the
Lord in the spirit and power of Elias to turn the hearts of
the fathers to the children, and the disobedient to the wisdom of the just; to make ready a people prepared for the
Lord.*

5. In due time all that the angel promised came to pass.
The child was born, and when eight days old he was cir-
cumcised and named John. On that occasion his father who
had been dumb from the time of the visitation of the angel
prophesied that the child should be called the prophet of the
Highest; that he should go before the face of the Lord to
prepare his ways; give knowledge of salvation unto his people
by the remission of their sins, through the tender mercy of
God; and give light to them that sit in darkness, and in the
shadow of death.†

6. That the child grew and waxed strong in spirit, and
was in the deserts till the day of his showing unto Israel;‡
that he had his raiment of camel's hair; a leathern girdle
about his loins; that his food was locusts and wild honey† is
all we know of him until the word of the Lord came to him
in the wilderness‡ commanding him to cry repentance, and
proclaim the coming of the kingdom of heaven.

7. **The Voice from the Wilderness:**—The burden of
John's message consisted of three great declarations: Repent
for the kingdom of heaven is at hand; prepare ye the way of
the Lord, make his paths straight; there cometh one after me

---

*Luke i.
†Matt. iii.
‡Luke iii.

mightier than I am, whose shoe latchet I am unworthy to loose, he will baptize you with fire and with the Holy Ghost.

8.   When the multitude flocked to hear the teaching of John the Pharisees and Sadducees came also—with guile in their hearts and deceit on their lips, he rebuked them, called them a generation of vipers and told them to bring forth fruits mete for repentance, and not to pride themselves on being the children of Abraham, for God was able of the very stones about them to raise up children unto Abraham. He warned them that the ax was laid at the root of every tree, and that tree which brought not forth good fruit was to be destroyed.

9.   That was a strange voice to the people of that generation, accustomed as they were to hear only the accents of flattery or subserviency.   Without a tremor of hesitation he rebuked the tax gatherers for their extortion; the soldiers for their violence; the Sadducees and Pharisees for their pride and formalism; and warned the whole people that their cherished privileges were worse than valueless if without repentance they regarded them as a protection against the wrath to come.

10.   So unusual a teacher as John the Baptist could not fail to attract attention in Judea where all men were anticipating the coming of a deliverer.   Hence, as the Jews listened to his teachings so inspired with the power of God, they wondered if he were not the Messiah.   This he denied. They asked him then if he were not Elias.   This too he denied (see note 5, end of section); and claimed only to be the voice of one crying in the wilderness: "Make straight the way of the Lord." *

11.   **The Baptism of Jesus:**—When John came into the

---

*John 1: 19-23.

region about Bethabara [Beth-ab-a-rah], on the Jordan,* among others who came to be baptized was Jesus. When John saw him he hesitated, and knowing by the inspiration within him what he was soon to know by a more splendid manifestation of God's power, *viz.*, that this was the Son of God, he said: "I have need to be baptized of thee, and comest thou to me?" "Suffer it to be so now," replied Jesus, "for thus it becometh us to fulfill all righteousness."†

12.   Then John baptized him, and as Jesus came up out of the water the heavens were opened unto him (that is, unto John; see note 6, end of section), and he saw the Spirit of God descending like a dove and lighting upon him; and he heard a voice from heaven saying: "This is my beloved Son, in whom I am well pleased."‡   This splendid spiritual manifestation was a sign to John that this was the Son of God, the One who was to baptize with fire and the Holy Ghost, the Messiah, who was to take away the sins of the world.   For he who had sent him to baptize with water, had said to him: "Upon whom thou shalt see the Spirit descending, and remaining on him, the same is he which baptizeth with the Holy Ghost."§

13.   **The Martyrdom of John:**—Having borne witness that Jesus was the Son of God, John seems to have completed the mission given to him at that time, and soon after fell a victim to the malice of a wicked woman and a weak prince. Herod Antipas [Anti-pas], the son of Herod the Great, who was made Tetrarch of Galilee on the death of his father, married the daughter of Aretas [Ar'-e-ta], king of Arabia. But forming also an unholy attachment for Herodias [He-ro'-

---

*The location of Bethabara is uncertain.
†Matt. iii.
‡Matt. iii.
§John 1: 32, 33.

di-as], his brother Philip's wife, he soon became involved in a course of guilt with her. For this he was reproved by John, who told him it was not lawful for him to have her. Herod at the instance of Herodias cast John into prison for his temerity in reproving their wicked course, and would have put him to death, but he feared the multitude, who esteemed John a prophet.

14. The revengeful spirit of Herodias, however, was not satisfied with the bonds and imprisonment of John; she determined to have his life. On Herod's birthday, in the midst of the feast, she sent her daughter to dance for the amusement of the company, which greatly pleased Herod, and he promised her with an oath that he would give her whatsoever she should ask; and the damsel being instructed of her mother demanded the head of John the Baptist. It was with sorrow that Herod, bad as he was, heard this demand, yet for his oath's sake, and ashamed to manifest weakness in the presence of those who sat at meat with him, he sent and beheaded John in the prison, and had the head brought in and given to the damsel in a charger. Thus fell the first martyr in that dispensation. (See note 7, end of section.)

NOTES.

1. Nazareth:—Nazareth was in Galilee, a part of Palestine, which was held in disesteem for several reasons: It had a provincial dialect; lying remote from the capital, its inhabitants spoke a strange tongue, which was rough, harsh, and uncouth, having a peculiar combination of words, and words also peculiar to themselves. Its population was impure, being made up not only of provincial Jews but also of heathens of several sorts, Egyptians, Arabians, Phoenicians. As Galilee was a despised part of Palestine, so was Nazareth a despised part of Galilee, being a small, obscure, if not mean place. Accordingly its inhabitants were held in little consideration by other Galileans, and, of course, by those Jews who dwelt in Judea. Hence the name of Nazarene came to bear with it a bad odor and was nearly synonymous with a low, ignorant and uncultivated, if not un-Jewish person.—*Biblical Litera-ture, Kitto.*

2. The Passover:—The Passover, like the Sabbath and other in-stitutions had a two-fold reference—historical and typical. As a com-memorative institution it was designed to preserve among the Jews a grateful sense of their redemption from Egyptian bondage, and with the protection granted to their first born, on the night when all the first born of the Egyptians were destroyed (Exodus xii: 27), as a typical institute its object was to shadow forth the great facts and consequences of the Christian sacrifices (I. Cor. v: 7). That the ancient Jews un-derstood this institution to prefigure the sufferings of the Christ is evident, not only from the New Testament, but from the Mishna, where, among the five things said to be contained in the *Great Hallel* (a hymn composed of several songs and sung after the Paschal supper,) one is, the suffering of Messiah, for which they refer to Ps. cxvi. * * * * The Passover also denotes the whole solemnity, commencing on the 14th and ending on the 21st day of Nisan.— *Kitto.*

3. The Youth of Christ:—It is written that there was once a pious, godly bishop who had often earnestly prayed that God would manifest unto him what Jesus had done in his youth. Once the bishop had a dream to this effect. He seemed in his sleep to see a carpenter working at his trade, and beside him a little boy who was gathering up chips. Then came in a maiden clothed in green, who called them both to come to the meal, and set porridge before them. All this the bishop seemed to see in his dream, himself standing behind the door that he might not be perceived. Then the little boy began and said: Why does that man stand there? Shall he not also eat with us? And this so frightened the bishop that he awoke. Let this be what it may, a true history or a fable, I none the less believe that Christ in his childhood and youth looked and acted like other children, yet without sin, in fashion like a man.— *Martin Luther.*

4. Messiah's Life for Thirty Years:—What was his manner of life during those thirty years? It is a question which the Christians cannot help asking in deep reverence, and with yearning love; but the words in which the gospels answer it are very calm and very few. * * * * * His development was a strictly human development. He did not come to the world endowed with infinite knowledge, but, as St. Luke tells us, he gradually advanced in wisdom. He was not clothed with in-finite power, but experienced the weakness and imperfections of human infancy. He grew as other children grow, only in a childhood of stain-less and sinless beauty—as the "flower of roses in the spring of the year and as lilies by the waters." * * * * * It was in utter stillness, in prayerfulness, in the quiet round of daily duties—like Moses in the wilderness, like David among the sheep folds, like Elijah among the tents of the Bedouin, like Jeremiah in his quiet home at Anathoth, like Amos in the sycamore groves of Tekoa—that the boy Jesus prepared himself, amid a hallowed obscurity, for his mighty work on earth. His outward life was the life of all those of his age, and station and place of birth. He lived as lived the other children of peasant

parents in that quiet town, and in great measure as they live now.—
Canon Farrar.

5.   Was John the Elias?—"Art thou Elias?" said the messengers
from Jesus to John.   "And he saith, I am not;" (John i.)   Afterwards,
as Jesus, Peter, James and John were descending the mountain on
whose summit they had seen in vision Moses and Elias, the following
conversation occurred:

Jesus: "Tell the vision to no man, until the Son of man be risen again
from the dead.

Disciples: "Why then say the scribes that Elias must first come*?*

Jesus: "Elias truly shall first come, *and restore all things*; but I say
unto you that Elias is come already, and they knew him not, but have
done unto him whatsoever they listed.   *   *   *   Then the disciples
knew that he spake unto them of John the Baptist."   (Matt. xvii.)
From this it appears that John denied being Elias, while Jesus declared
that he was, and in consequence much controversy has arisen on this subject.   The matter may be easily understood, however, when it is known
that Elias is the name of a person, the name of a prophet who lived,
doubtless, in the days of Abraham (Doc. and Cov. Sec. cx: 12) and
who also appeared to Jesus on the occasion above named; Elias is also
the name of an office—the office of Restorer.   "The spirit of Elias,"
said the Prophet Joseph (March 10, 1844) "is to prepare the way for
a greater revelation of God, which is the priesthood of Elias.   *   *
And when God sends a man into the world to prepare for a greater
work holding the keys of the power of Elias, it was called the doctrine
of Elias, even from the early ages of the world."   Hence any man who
came to prepare the way for a greater revelation was "an Elias," and
in this sense John the Baptist was pre-eminently Elias; but it is equally
true that he was *not* Elias, the prophet who lived in the days of Abraham, who appeared unto Jesus in the mountain and who also appeared
to the Prophet Joseph and Oliver Cowdery in the Kirtland Temple.

In the revision of the New Testament, by the Prophet Joseph Smith,
often improperly called the "new translation," the difficulty in respect
to the denial of John that he was Elias is easily understood.   We
quote the passage: "This is the record of John, when the Jews sent
priests and Levites from Jerusalem, to ask him: Who art thou?
And he confessed and denied not that he was Elias; but confessed,
saying, I am not the Christ.   And they asked him, saying: How
art thou then Elias?   And he said, *I am not that Elias who was to restore
all things.*   And they asked him, saying, Art thou that Prophet?   And
he answered, No."   (St. John i: 20-22.)   From the above it may be
plainly seen that while John was not the particular Elias who is to restore *all* things, yet he is *"an* Elias," because he restored some things
in respect to the gospel.—*Roberts.*

6.   John the Only Witness of the Descent of the Holy Ghost:—
I suppose that John the Baptist was the only one who was a witness
of the Holy Ghost resting upon Jesus in the form of a dove.   In all
the accounts given of this event, except by Luke, the pronoun "he"
referring to John, is used.   While in Luke it is not said that anyone else
saw the Holy Ghost; it is merely stated that "the Holy Ghost descended

in bodily shape like a dove and rested upon him.   John's own testimony is as follows: "I saw the Spirit descending from heaven like a dove, and it abode upon him. And I knew him not; but he that sent me to baptize with water, the same said unto me, upon whom thou shalt see the Spirit descending and remaining on him, the same is he which baptizeth with the Holy Ghost."—*The Gospel* (note), *Roberts*.

7.   **The Fate of Herod Antipas:**—He was not allowed to enjoy his prosperity long. His nephew Agrippa having obtained the title of king, Herodias urged him to make a journey to Italy and demand the same honor. He weakly assented to his wife's ambitious representations; but the project proved fatal to them both. Agrippa anticipated their design; and when they appeared before Caligula, they were met by accusations of hostility to Rome, the truth of which they in vain attempted to disprove. Sentence of deposition was accordingly passed upon Herod, and both he and his wife [Herodias] were sent into banishment and died at Lyons in Gaul.— *Kitto*.

8.   **The Sign of the Dove:**—"The Holy Ghost descended in the form of a dove, or rather in the *sign* of a dove, in witness of that administration (Messiah's baptism.)   The sign of the dove was instituted before the creation of the world, a witness for the Holy Ghost, and the devil cannot come in the sign of a dove. The Holy Ghost is a personage, and is in the form of a personage. It (he) does not confine itself (himself) to the form of a dove, but in the sign of a dove. The Holy Ghost cannot be transformed into a dove; but the sign of a dove was given to John to signify the truth of the deed, as the dove is an emblem or token of truth and innocence."—*Joseph Smith*.

REVIEW.

1.   State what you can of the childhood of Christ.
2.   What can you say of Nazareth?
3.   What happened when Jesus was twelve years old?
4.   Describe the Passover. (Note 2.)
5.   What can you say of the fabulous stories related of the childhood and youth of Christ?   (Consult Apocryphal New Testament.)
6.   At what time did John the Baptist appear as a preacher?
7.   Who were the parents of John?   What their descent?
8.   Relate all you can concerning John's birth and childhood.
9.   What was the burden of John's message?
10.   How did he treat the deceitful Pharisees and Sadducees?
11.   As whom did some of the Jews regard John?
12.   What was the extent of his pretensions?
13.   What can you say of Elias?   (Note 5.)
14.   Relate the baptism of Jesus.
15.   Tell the story of John's martyrdom.
16.   What was the fate of Herod Antipas?   (Note 7.)

SECTION IV.

1. The Temptations of Jesus:—After his baptism Jesus was led by the Spirit into the wilderness, where he fasted forty days and forty nights. Then at the moment of his great physical weakness Lucifer came tempting him, but all the allurements of the wily foe were thwarted, from the challenge to turn the stones into bread to the offer of the kingdoms of this world and the glory of them. After his failure to seduce Jesus to sin, Lucifer left him—"for a season," and angels came and administered unto him. (See notes 1 and 2, end of section.)

2. Commencement of Christ's Ministry:—Having in all things resisted the temptations of Lucifer, Jesus returned from the wilderness into Galilee, the Spirit of God resting upon him in mighty power. It was then that he began his great ministry among the people, teaching in their synagogues, astonishing all with the graciousness of his doctrines and his power in healing the sick, until his fame extended throughout the land, and great multitudes of people from Galilee, and also from Decapolis [De-kap-o-lis], Jerusalem and other parts of Judea followed him.

3. The Doctrines Christ Taught:—The burden of Messiah's teaching at this period of his ministry seems to have been: "Repent for the kingdom of heaven is at hand."* In addition to this, he also taught beautiful truths and moral precepts in brief, emphatic sentences (see note 3, end of sec-

---

*Matt. iv.

tion), that were especially comforting to the poor; such as, "Blessed are the poor in spirit; for theirs is the kingdom of heaven: Blessed are they that mourn; for they shall be comforted: Blessed are the meek; for they shall inherit the earth: Blessed are they which do hunger and thirst after righteousness; for they shall be filled: Blessed are the pure in heart; for they shall see God."

4. In some things His teachings seemed to come in conflict with the traditions of the people; and, indeed, with the law of Moses itself, as witness the following: "Ye have heard that it was said by them of old time, thou shalt not kill; and whosoever shall kill shall be in danger of the judgment: but I say unto you, whosoever is angry with his brother without cause shall be in danger of the judgment: and whosoever shall say unto his brother, Raca,* shall be in danger of the council; but whosoever shall say, thou fool, shall be in danger of hell fire." Again: "Ye have heard that it hath been said by them of old time, thou shalt not forswear thyself, but shall perform unto the Lord thine oaths: But I say unto you, swear not at all, * * * but let your communications be yea, yea; nay, nay. Ye have heard that it hath been said, an eye for an eye, and a tooth for a tooth; but I say unto you, that ye resist not evil. * * * Ye have heard that it hath been said, thou shalt love thy neighbor, and hate thine enemy: But I say unto you, love your enemies, bless them that curse you, do good to them that hate you, and pray for them which despitefully use you, and persecute you."

5. Yet Jesus claimed that He came not to destroy the law nor the prophets, but to fulfill them, and declared that though heaven and earth should pass away, not one jot nor

---

*That is, vain fellow.

tittle of the law should pass away but all should be fulfilled. Still it cannot be denied that some of His teachings set aside many parts of the law of Moses, and seemed to be in conflict with its spirit.

6. **The Gospel Supplants the Law:**—The seeming conflict, referred to in the last paragraph, between the law of Moses and the teachings of Messiah disappears when it is understood that the gospel of Jesus Christ was about to supplant the law. The gospel, under Moses was offered to ancient Israel before they received the law of carnal commandments; but they would not live in accordance with its divine precepts, but hardened their hearts against it until the gospel, as also the higher priesthood, was taken from among them. The lesser priesthood, which holds the keys of the ministering of angels and the preparatory gospel, repentance and baptism, and the law of carnal commandments (the spirit of which is an eye for an eye, a tooth for a tooth) remained with them,* to educate and instruct them, that they might be prepared eventually for the fullness of the gospel. When Jesus began his ministry by proclaiming his gospel, the law of Moses was about fulfilled, and many of the carnal commandments and precepts were being pushed aside by the more excellent precepts of the gospel, even as many of the sacrifices and burnt offerings were to be discontinued after Messiah should be offered up as a sacrifice, of which the sacrifices before mentioned were but types and symbols. (See note 4, end of section.) It should not be overlooked, however, that between the law of Moses and the gospel there must always remain much in common. The Ten Commandments, for instance, are still in force, in the main, being modified only by the more spiritual inter-

---

*Doc. and Cov. lxxxiv: 17-27.

pretations given to the law by the Christ, or by those specific
or clearly implied changes authorized by him.

7. **Twelve Apostles Called:**—From among the disciples which followed him Jesus selected twelve men whom
he called apostles. Their names were: Simon, commonly
called Peter; Andrew, brother to Peter; James, the son of
Zebedee, sometimes called James the elder; John, brother
to James above named; Philip, Bartholomew; Thomas;
Matthew, the publican, author of the book of Matthew in
the New Testament; James, the son of Alphaeus, also called
James the less, perhaps to distinguish him from James
the elder, or because of his small stature;* Lebbaeus, usually
called by his surname Thaddaeus; Simon, the Canaanite;
Judas Iscariot, who betrayed him.

8. These twelve men Jesus sent out on a mission to the
cities of Israel, forbidding them to go into the way of the
Gentiles, or into the cities of the Samaritans. Their mission
was to "the lost sheep of the house of Israel."† They were
sent without purse and without scrip, nor were they to pro-
vide themselves with two coats, nor take thought as to what
they should eat, or wherewithal they would be clothed; but
they were to trust in the Lord for these things, being assured that the laborer is worthy of his hire."

9. The burden of their message was to be: "The kingdom of heaven is at hand." They also received power from
their Master to heal the sick, cleanse the lepers, raise the
dead, cast out devils; and were admonished, since they
had received freely, to give as freely to others. Jesus told
them they were going as sheep among wolves; that they would
be brought before governors and kings for his sake; that they

---

*Biblical Literature.— *Kitto.*
†Matt. x.

would be delivered up to councils, and scourged in the synagogues; that they would be hated of all men for his sake; but they were also given the comforting assurance that they who would endure to the end should be saved.* These apostles went forth through the towns of Judea preaching the gospel and healing the sick.

10. Seventies Called:—The harvest being great and the laborers few, Jesus called "seventies" into the ministry to aid the twelve apostles. He sent them two and two before him into every city and place where he himself expected to go. The commission, powers and instructions which the "seventies" received were nearly the same as those given to the twelve apostles.† These seventies went forth as the apostles had done and returning from their labor bore record that the power of God was with them in their ministry and that the very devils were subject to them in the name of Jesus.‡

11. The Order of Events.—It would be difficult, if not impossible, to relate even the chief events in the life of Messiah in the order in which they occurred, since no little confusion exists in respect to the succession of events in the narratives of the New Testament. (See note 5, end of section.) Nor is it necessary to our purpose to dwell in detail or in sequence upon those matters. It is sufficient for us to know that after the events we have already noted Messiah's mission was more boldly declared. He proclaimed himself to be the Son of God; the Messiah of which the scriptures had borne record.§ He taught men that God so loved the world that he gave his only begotten Son to redeem it; that who-

---

*Matt. x.
†Compare Luke x with Matt. x.
‡Luke x.
§John v.

soever would believe in him might have everlasting life.*
In addition to this great doctrine he taught repentance; he
likewise taught that men must be born (baptized) of the
water and of the Spirit before they could enter into the
kingdom of heaven;† he made and baptized more disciples
than John;‡ he also taught the doctrine of the resurrection
of the dead, and announced himself as possessing the keys
and powers thereof.§

12.   **The Divinity of Messiah's Mission:**—Jesus sustained the divinity of his mission by pointing to the con-
formity of the facts connected with his career with the pre-
dictions of the scriptures;|| by the testimony which John the
Baptist bore;¶ by the works which he did—his wonderful
miracles wherein the power of God was made manifest;**
and lastly, and best of all, the testimony of the Father himself which was promised unto all those who would do his
(the Father's) will.††

NOTES.

1.   **Order of the Temptations:**—The order of the temptations is
given differently by St. Matthew and St. Luke. St. Matthew places
second the scene on the pinnacle of the temple, and St. Luke the vision
of the kingdoms of the world   Both orders cannot be right, and possibly
St. Luke may have been influenced in his arrangement by the thought
that a temptation to spiritual pride and the arbitrary exercise of miraculous power was a subtler and less transparent, and therefore more
powerful one than the temptation to fall down and recognize the power
of evil.   *   *   *   The consideration that St. Matthew, as one of the
Apostles, is more likely to have heard the narrative immediately from
the lips of Christ—gives greater weight to the order which he adopts.—
Canon Farrar.

---

*John iii.
†John iii.
‡John iv.
§John v:24-30.
||John v:39-47.
¶John v:32-35.
**John v:36 ; x:25.
††John v:37, 39; vii:14-18.

2. More than Three Temptations:—The positive temptations of Jesus were not confined to that particular point of time when they assailed him with concentrated force. [In the wilderness.] * * * But still more frequently in after life was he called to endure temptation of another kind—the temptation of suffering, and this culminated on two occasions, viz., in the conflict of Gethsemane, and in that moment of agony on the cross when He cried, "*My God, my God! why hast thou forsaken me?*— *Ullman.*

3. Manner of Christ's Teaching:—Next to what our Savior taught, may be considered the manner of his teaching, which was extremely peculiar; yet, I think, precisely adapted to the peculiarity of his character and situation. His lessons did not consist of disquisitions; of anything like moral essays, or like sermons, or like set treatises upon several points which he mentioned. When he delivered a precept, it was seldom that he added any proof or argument, still more seldom that he accompanied it with, what all precepts require, limitations and distinctions. His instructions were conceived in short, emphatic, sententious rules, in occasional reflections or in sound maxims. I do not think this was a natural, or would it have been a proper method for a philosopher or a moralist or that it is a method which can be successfully imitated by us. But I contend that it was suitable to the character which Christ assumed, and to the situation in which, as a teacher, he was placed. He produced himself as a messenger from God. He put the truth of what he taught upon authority. [*I* say unto you, swear not at all; *I* say unto you, resist not evil; *I* say unto you, love your enemies.] In the choice, therefore, of his mode of teaching, the purpose by him to be consulted was *impression*; because conviction, which forms the principal end of our discourse, was to arise in the minds of his followers from a different source, from their respect to his person and authority. Now, for the purpose of impression singly and exclusively, I know nothing which would have so great force, as strong, ponderous maxims, frequently urged and frequently brought back to the thoughts of the hearers. I know nothing that could in this view be said better than, Do unto others as ye would that others should do unto you; The first and great commandment is Thou shalt love the Lord thy God; and the second is like unto it, Thou shalt love thy neighbor as thyself.— *Christian Evidences—Paley.*

4. The Law Added to the Gospel:—The Mosaic Law never was considered, by those who understood it, "an everlasting covenant." It was given for a special purpose, and when it had accomplished that purpose, it was laid aside. We read in Galatians iii:8, that "the scriptures foreseeing that God would justify the heathen through faith, preached before the gospel unto Abraham, saying, In thee shall all the nations of the earth be blessed." From this it appears that the gospel was preached unto Abraham. In Hebrews (iv:2), Paul in speaking of ancient Israel says: "For unto us was the gospel preached, as well as unto them [ancient Israel]; but the word preached did not profit them, not being mixed with faith in them that heard it." Not only then was the gospel preached unto Abraham but also unto the children of Israel.

Now let us go back to the third chapter of Galatians; for Pau having stated that the gospel was preached unto Abraham, asks this question (verse 19): "Wherefore then serveth the law" [i. e. if the gospel was preached unto Abraham]? "It was added because of transgression, till the seed" (Christ) "should come to whom the promise was made." Added? Added to what? Added to the gospel, which before that time had been preached unto Abraham, and also to ancient Israel. But the Israelites under Moses were unable to live the perfect law of the gospel. They were not strong enough to overcome evil with good, as the gospel requires; so a law of carnal commandments was "added" to the gospel —a law which breathed of the spirit of an eye for an eye, a tooth for a tooth—a law which was suited to their capacity. Paul, speaking of this subject in the same chapter of Galatians (23-25 verses), says: "Before faith came we were kept under the law, shut up unto the faith which should afterwards be revealed. Wherefore the law (the law of Moses) was our school-master to bring us unto Christ, that we might be justi-fied by faith. But after that faith has come we are no longer under a school-master." From these passages of scripture we learn this: The gospel was preached unto Abraham, and also to ancient Israel. The Israelites were unable to live the law of the gospel, hence a law of carnal commandments, known as the law of Moses was given as a school master to bring them up to a higher law; Christ came and introduced that higher law—the gospel; explained its principles and pointed out the difference between it and the law of Moses. The gospel took the place of the law of Moses, which was laid aside, having fulfilled the object for which it was "added" to the gospel.—*Lecture on Mission of Joseph Smith, Roberts.*

   5. **Neglect of Chronological Order in New Testament Narra-tives:**—The four gospels narrate the principal events connected with our Lord's abode on earth, from his birth to his ascension. There must, therefore, be a general resemblance between them, though that of John contains little in common with the others, being apparently supple-mentary to them. Yet there are considerable diversities both in the order in which facts are narrated, and in the facts themselves. Hence the difficulty of weaving the accounts of the four into a continuous and chronological history. It is our decided conviction that all the evangel-ists have not adhered to chronological arrangement. The question then arises, have all neglected the order of time? Newcome and many others espouse this view. "Chronological order," says the writer, "is not precisely observed by any of the Evangelists; St. John and St. Mark observe it most; and St. Matthew neglects it most."—*Davidson, Bibli-cal Literature.*

REVIEW.

1. What followed the baptism of Jesus?
2. What can you say of the order of the temptations? (Note 1).
3. What was the commencement of Christ's ministry?
4. What was the character of Christ's doctrines at this period?

5. State how the gospel supplanted the law of Moses. (Note 4.)

6. Name the Apostles whom Jesus called.

7. What was the first mission of the Twelve?

8. What was the nature of the commission given to the Apostles?

9. State the calling and commission of the Seventies.

10. What can you say of the order of chronological events in the New Testament?   (Note 5.)

11. To what several circumstances did Messiah point as giving evidence of the divinity of His mission?

12. Quote the several passages of scripture cited in the text.

SECTION V.

1. The Common People Hear Jesus Gladly:—The mission of Jesus was full of comfort to the poor. As one of the signs that he was the promised Messiah, he said to a delegation of John's disciples—"The poor have the gospel preached to them."* He claimed to be anointed of the Lord to that work; and in doing it was fulfilling that which had been predicted by the prophets.† He often reproved the rich, not because they were rich, however, but because of their pride and hypocrisy which led them to oppress the poor. In like manner he reproved the chief elders and scribes and Pharisees who loved fine clothing, and loved to receive salutations in the market places, who coveted the chief seats in the synagogues and the uppermost rooms at the feasts; who devoured widows houses, and for a pretense made long prayers.‡ This with a free reproof of their other vices and crimes brought upon him the enmity of the wealthy, and of the rulers of the people; but "the common people heard him gladly."‡ (See note 1, end of section.)

2. Religious Jealousy—Political Fear:—Another thing which embittered the minds of the chief priests and elders against Jesus was religious jealousy. The numerous evidences of his divine authority, to be seen in his character and works, led many of the Jews to revere him as the Son of

---

*Matt. xi:26.
†Matt. iv:16-24.
‡Mark xii.

God. This awakened the jealousy of the priests and the chief rulers. Especially was this the case after he raised Lazarus from the dead.* They said: "If we let this man alone all men will believe in him; and the Romans will come and take away both our place and nation." It was religious jealousy that dictated the first half of the sentence; and political fear the rest. The Jews had but a precarious hold upon their political privileges; already it had been intimated that Jesus was king of the Jews;† and if the people should under a sudden impulse accept him as king, the result in the judgment of the ruling class, must be a loss of those political privileges which the Romans permitted them to exercise. To allow Jesus, therefore, to continue preaching was dangerous to their supposed honors and privileges; and this consideration was sufficient to induce the leading men among all parties to plot against his life.

3. **The Charges Against Jesus:**—The principal charges which the Jews brought against Jesus were: (1) violation of the Sabbath; he had healed a man on the Sabbath day, and had commanded him to take up his bed and walk:‡ (2) blasphemy; he had said God was his Father, "making himself equal with God" (see note 2, end of section):§ (3) It was said that he was king of the Jews; and, on one occasion, the people hearing of his coming to Jerusalem took palm branches and went out to meet him shouting Hosannah, blessed is the king of Israel that cometh in the name of the Lord.‖ For this he was said to be an enemy to. Caesar's government and a seditious person.

---

*John xi.
†Matt. ii.
‡John v:1-18.
§John v:17, 18.
‖John xii.

4. Treason of Judas:—For some time the efforts of the chief priests to arrest Jesus were baffled. They feared to proceed openly against him lest the people should stand in his favor and overthrow them. At last, however, Judas Iscariot, one of the twelve, met with some of the chief rulers and promised to betray him to them in the absence of the multitude. This offer they gladly accepted and agreed to pay him thirty pieces of silver for his treachery.

5. Institution of the Sacrament:—The time chosen by Judas for the betrayal of his Master was the night of the passover feast. Jesus with the twelve ate the feast in an upper room in Jerusalem. It was on this occasion that he instituted the Sacrament of the Lord's supper. He took bread and gave thanks, broke it and gave it to his disciples, saying: This is my body which is given for you; this do in remembrance of me. He also took wine, gave thanks, saying as He gave it to them: This cup is the New Testament in my blood, which is shed for many for the remission of sins.*

6. After the supper was over, having sung a hymn, Jesus with the twelve, excepting Judas Iscariot, went out to the garden of Gethsemane [Geth-sem-e-na] where Jesus prayed in great agony of spirit "so that he sweat great drops of blood." He prayed that the bitter cup of suffering now about to be held to his lips might be removed from him. Thrice he so prayed, but closed each petition to his Father with—"yet, not my will, but thy will be done."

7. The Betrayal:—Meantime, Judas Iscariot having stolen out in the midst of the feast, went to the chief priests and directed a multitude with a company of Roman soldiers to the garden, and running to Jesus cried, "Hail, Master!"

---

*Luke xxii. Matt. xxvi.

and kissed him. That was the sign agreed upon by the traitor and those who came to make the arrest, that they might know which one to take. And when they had secured him, they took him first to the house of Annas [An-nas], who, after questioning him, sent him bound to Caiaphas [Kai-ya-fas], the high priest, where he was arraigned before the Sanhedrin [San-he-drin].

8. **The Trial:**—The court before which Jesus was arraigned was not one before which his case was to be investigated, they had come together with the fixed determination to adjudge him guilty; hence they sought for witnesses who would testify something against him that would furnish a pretext for putting him to death. Many false witnesses testified against him; but their testimony was unsatisfactory and failed of its purpose. At last the high priest, evidently losing patience at the silence of the prisoner—for he made no defense against the charges of the false witnesses—adjured him by the living God to say if he were the Christ, the Son of God. Jesus acknowledged that he was, and told them that hereafter they should see him at the right hand of Power, coming in the clouds of heaven. At this the high priest rent his clothes, saying, "he hath spoken blasphemy," and claimed that they had no need of further witnesses, since they themselves had heard his "blasphemy" (see note 3, end of section). The council at once decided him worthy of death.

9. **Christ Before Pilate and Herod:**—The Romans had taken from the Sanhedrin of the Jews the power of executing those whom it adjudged guilty of death, unless the sentence was confirmed by the Roman governor; hence after sentence of death was passed upon Jesus by the Sanhedrin they took him to Pilate's judgment hall to have that sentence confirmed.

10. Learning incidentally that Jesus was a Galilean, and belonged to Herod's jurisdiction, Pilate sent him to Herod who, at the time, was in Jerusalem. Before Herod Jesus was silent; neither the contempt of the murderer of his forerunner, nor the mockery of the common soldiers could provoke him into breaking his dignified silence. So in ridicule of his claims to kingship—although, as Jesus himself said, his kingdom was not of this world*—Herod clothed him in gorgeous apparel and sent him back to Pilate.

11. Satisfied that there was nothing in Messiah's conduct worthy of death, Pilate sought to let him go; but the Jews insisted upon his execution. It was the custom among the Jews to have released to them a prisoner at the feast of the Passover, and on that ground Pilate sought to release Jesus; but the Jews would not listen to it, and preferred that the robber, Barabbas, a murderer, should be released. They told Pilate that whosoever made himself a king was an enemy to Caesar; and if he let Jesus go he was not Caesar's friend. By such arguments on the part of the chief priests, and the persistent cry of the people to crucify him, Pilate was over-awed, and at last confirmed the sentence of death. (See note 4, end of section.)

12. The Crucifixion:—From the hall of judgment Jesus was led into the common hall, where the soldiers stripped him of his own raiment, and put upon him a scarlet robe in mockery of his claims to kingship. They also platted a crown of thorns and placed it on his brow, and for a scepter gave him a reed in his right hand. They bowed the knee before him, and mockingly cried: "Hail, king of the Jews!" They spit upon him, beat him with their hands and with the reed they had given him for a scepter.

---

*John xviii:36.

13. From the common hall he was led away under a guard of soldiers to a place called Golgotha [Gol-go-tha], which, as well as its Latin equivalent—*Calvaria—Calvary**—means, the place of a skull. Here Jesus was stripped, and nailed to the cross, which was erected between two other crosses, on each of which was a thief. Above the Christ's head in Latin, Greek and Hebrew was fixed the superscription written by Pilate—*"This is the King of the Jews."* As he hung there between the two thieves, the soldiers mocked him as did also the chief scribes and the Pharisees, saying: He saved others, let him save himself; if he is Christ, the chosen of God, let him come down from the cross and we will believe him; he trusted in God, let him deliver him now, if he will have him; for he said, "I am the Son of God." In the midst of his great suffering, in which his mental agony was greater than his physical pain, the Son of God cried, "Father, forgive them, they know not what they do."

14. At the sixth hour—mid-day—there was a darkness that spread over the whole land, and continued until the ninth hour (see note 5, end of section). About the ninth hour Jesus said: "Father, into thy hands I commend my spirit," then he bowed his head and expired. At the same moment the veil of the Temple was rent from top to bottom, an earthquake shook the solid earth and rent the rocks, all the elements of nature seemed agitated as if anxious to bear witness that a God had died!

15. **The Convulsions of Nature on the Western Hemisphere:**—On the western hemisphere during the crucifixion of our Lord, the elements of nature were more

---

*Luke alone calls it *Calvary*; Matthew, Mark and John call it Golgotha. They each have reference to the same place, which was known by the two different names.

disturbed than on the eastern hemisphere. During the time that Jesus was upon the cross, great and terrible tempests accompanied with terrific lightning raged throughout the land. Earthquakes shattered cities into confused piles of ruins; level plains were broken up and left in confused mountainous heaps; solid rocks were rent in twain; many cities were swept out of existence by fierce whirlwinds; others were sunk into the depths of the sea; others covered with mountain chains thrown up by the convulsions of the trembling earth; and others still were burned with fire. For the space of about three hours this awful disturbance of the elements continued, during which the whole face of the land both in North and South America was greatly changed, and most of the inhabitants destroyed. After the storm and tempest and the quakings of the earth had ceased, there followed intense darkness which lasted for three days, the time that Jesus was lying in the tomb.*

16. **The Burial:**—Towards evening of the day of the crucifixion, Joseph of Arimathaea [Ar-ra-ma-thee-ya], a rich man and a disciple of Jesus, went to Pilate, and begged that the body of the Lord be given him that he might bury it. Pilate granted the request; and Joseph took the body, wrapt in clean linen and put it in his own new tomb. The Pharisees also went to Pilate and reminded him how Jesus had said when living that after three days in the tomb he would rise again, and asked that the sepulchre wherein he was buried should be placed under guard until the third day should pass, lest his disciples should come and steal his body by night, and then spread abroad the rumor that he had arisen from the dead. Pilate granted them permission to seal up the sepulchre and set a watch to guard it. (See note 6, end of section.)

---

*III Nephi viii.

NOTES.

1. Reforms Begin Among the Common People:—The case of the common people hearing Jesus gladly is not singular; it may be said to be true in nearly all great movements. It is a truth so generally accepted that a modern writer (Lew Wallace) has said: "To begin a reform, go not into the palaces of the great and rich; go rather to those whose cups of happiness are empty—to the poor and humble."

2. Jesus' Defense Against the Charge of Blasphemy:—The following scene occurred in Solomon's porch, at the temple, where Jesus was walking. A number of Jews gathered about him and said: How long dost thou make us to doubt? If thou be the Christ tell us so plainly.

Jesus:—I told you and ye believed not; the works that I do in my Father's name, they bear witness of me * * * I and my Father are one. [Then the Jews took up stones to stone him.]

Jesus:—Many good works have I showed you from my Father; for which of those works do you stone me?

Jews:—For a good work we stone thee not; but for blasphemy; and because that thou, being a man, makest thyself God.

Jesus:—Is it not written in your law; I said ye are Gods? If he called them Gods unto whom the word of God came, and the scripture cannot be broken, say ye of him whom the Father hath sanctified, and sent unto the world, thou blasphemest; because I said, I am the Son of God? If I do not the works of my Father, believe me not.

Then they sought again to take him, but he escaped out of their hands. (John x.)

3. The Law Against Blasphemy:—The law against blasphemy is to be found in Leviticus (xxiv:15, 16) and is as follows: "Whosoever curseth his God shall bear his sin; and he that blasphemeth the name of the Lord, he shall surely be put to death, and all the congregation shall certainly stone him; as well the stranger as he that is born in the land, when he blasphemeth the name of the Lord, shall be put to death." The Jews claimed that Jesus was guilty of blasphemy, because he claimed to be the Son of God, thus making himself equal with God; when to their eyes he was merely a man. Therein consisted his alleged blasphemy. Christ's own defense against the charge (see note above) is the best answer to the sophistry of the Jews by which they tried to make it appear that he had broken this law.—*Roberts.*

4. Character of Pilate:—If we now wish to form a judgment of Pilate's character, we easily see that he was one of that large class of men who aspire to public offices, not from a pure and lofty desire of benefitting the public and advancing the good of the world, but from selfish and personal considerations, from a love of distinction, from a love of power, from a love of self indulgence; being destitute of any fixed principles, and having no aim but office and influence, they act right only by chance and when convenient, and are wholly incapable of pursuing a consistent course, or of acting with firmness or self-denial in cases in which the preservation of integrity requires the exercise of these qualities. Pilate was obviously a man of weak, and therefore, with his temptations, of corrupt character.—*J. R. Beard, D. D., Member of the Historical Theological Society, Leipzig.*

5.   The Three Hours' Darkness:—In the gospel of Matthew and Luke, we read that while Jesus hung upon the cross, "from the sixth hour there was darkness over all the land to the ninth hour." Most of the ancient commentators believed that this darkness extended to the whole world. But their arguments are now seldom regarded as satisfactory, and their proofs even less so. Of the latter the strongest is the mention of an eclipse of the sun, which is referred to this time by Phlegon Trallianus, and, after him by Thallus. But even an eclipse of the sun could not be visible to the whole world; and neither of these writers names the place of the eclipse. Some think it was Rome; but it is impossible that an eclipse could have happened from the sixth to the ninth hour both at Rome and Jerusalem. * * * That the darkness could not have proceeded from an eclipse of the sun is further placed beyond all doubt by the fact that, it being then the time of the Passover, the moon was at the full. This darkness may, therefore, be ascribed to an extraordinary and preternatural obscuration of the solar light, which might precede and accompany the earthquake which took place on the same occasion. For it has been noticed that often before an earthquake such a mist arises from sulphurous vapors as to occasion a darkness almost nocturnal.—*Biblical Literature— Kitto.*

6.   Fate of the Chief Actors in Christ's Crucifixion:—Before the dread sacrifice was consummated, Judas died in the horrors of a loathsome suicide. Caiaphas (the High Priest and President of the Sanhedrin) was deposed the year following. Herod died in infamy and exile. Stripped of his procuratorship very shortly afterwards, on the very charges he had tried by a wicked concession to avoid. Pilate, wearied out with misfortunes, died in suicide and banishment, leaving behind him an execrated name. The house of Annas was destroyed a generation later by an infuriated mob, and his son was dragged through the streets and scourged and beaten to his place of murder. Some of those who shared in and witnessed the scenes of that day—and thousands of their children—also shared in and witnessed the long horrors of that siege of Jerusalem, which stands unparalleled in history for its unutterable fearfulness.—*Canon Farrar.*

REVIEW.

1.   What class of people heard Jesus gladly?
2.   What classes of people did Jesus reprove? Why?
3.   What was it that embittered the minds of the chief priests and rulers against Jesus?
4.   Enumerate the charges against Jesus.
5.   In what manner did Jesus defend himself against the charge of blasphemy?   (Note 2.)
6.   Who betrayed Jesus?
7.   What time was chosen by Judas to betray Jesus?

8. Give an account of the institution of the sacrament.

9. Tell the story of the betrayal.

10. State the circumstances of the trial of Jesus before the Sanhedrin.

11. Why did the Jews take Jesus before Pilate?

12. Why did Pilate send him to Herod?

13. What was Messiah's treatment at the hands of Herod?

14. What the deportment of Jesus?

15. How did Pilate look upon Jesus?

16. In what manner did the Roman governor try to save Jesus?

17. What was the character of Pilate?   (Note 4.)

18. Tell the story of the crucifixion.

19. What occurred on the Western hemisphere at the crucifixion, and during the time Jesus was in the tomb?

20. Tell about the burial of Jesus.

21. What was the fate of those who judged and condemned Jesus? (Note 6.)

SECTION VI.

1. The Resurrection:—Notwithstanding the sealed sepulchre, the armed watch, on the third day after his burial, the Son of God arose from the dead, as he himself predicted he would.* A number of women coming to the sepulchre early in the morning, for the purpose of finishing the work of embalming his body, found the grave untenanted and the angel present who announced the resurrection of the Lord; and commanded them to go and inform his disciples that he was risen from the dead and would go before them into Galilee, where he would appear unto them.

2. According to Matthew's account of the resurrection an angel from heaven came to the sepulchre wherein Jesus was laid, and rolled back the stone from its mouth; at his presence the soldiers who had been stationed as a guard to prevent the disciples from coming and stealing the body, became as dead men. Recovering from their stupor, some of the watch made their way to the chief priests and related what had happened. The chief priests and elders immediately assembled in council, and bribed the soldiers to say that they had fallen asleep, and during that time the followers of Christ had come and stolen his body. They agreed also that if the rumor of their falling asleep while on watch—a capital offense for a Roman soldier—should come to the ears of the governor, they would pursuade him and

---

*Those predictions are found in the following passages: John ii: 18-22; x: 17, 18; xiii:31-33. Matt. xii:38-42; xvi:21-23; xvii:1-9. Mark ix:30-32; x:32-34.

secure them from punishment. It was in this way that the disappearance of the body of Jesus was commonly explained by the Jews who crucified him.[*]

3. The Appearances of Jesus After His Resurrection:—There are some slight discrepancies in the writings of Matthew, Mark, Luke and John in respect to the order of the appearances of Messiah after his resurrection, as indeed there is in respect to the order of the events connected with his trial, condemnation and death; but the following may be regarded as being as nearly correct as may be ascertained. (See notes 1, 2, and 3, end of section):

4. First, he appeared to Mary Magdalene, in the garden where the tomb in which he was laid was located;[†] second, to the women returning from the sepulchre on their way to deliver the angel's message to the disciples;[‡] third, to two disciples going to Emmaus;[§] fourth, to Peter;[||] fifth, to ten apostles in an upper room;[¶] sixth, to the eleven apostles, also in the upper room;[**] seventh, to seven apostles at the sea of Tiberias;[††] eighth, to eleven apostles in a mountain in Galilee;[‡‡] ninth, to above five hundred brethren at once;[§§] tenth, to James;[|| ||] and finally to Paul while on his way to Damascus.[¶¶]

5. In all Jesus was with his disciples on the eastern

---

[*]Matt. xxviii.
[†]John xx:14-17
[‡]Matt. xxviii:9.
[§]Luke xxiv:13-31.
[||]Luke xxiv:34 and I Cor. xv:5.
[¶]John xx:19.
[**]John xx:26; Mark xvi:14.
[††]John xxi:1-24.
[‡‡]Matt. xxviii:16.
[§§]I Cor. xv:6.
[|| ||]I Cor. xv:7.
[¶¶]I Cor. xv:8.

hemisphere for forty days after his resurrection,* appearing eleven times in all; during which time and occasions he taught them all things pertaining to the kingdom of heaven, and authorized them to go into all the world and preach the gospel to every creature, baptizing them in the name of the Father and of the Son and of the Holy Ghost, teaching them to observe all things whatsoever he had commanded them; and promised that he would be with them even unto the end of the world.†

6. Moreover, he told them that these signs should follow them that believed: In his name they should cast out devils: they should speak with new tongues, take up serpents, and even if they drank any deadly thing he promised that it should not harm them; they should lay hands on the sick, and they should recover.‡

7. **The Ascension:**—Having thus taught the gospel to the people of the eastern hemisphere, organized his church and commissioned his apostles to teach the gospel to all nations, he prepared to depart from them. It was most probably at Bethany [Beth--any] that this solemn parting occurred. His forerunner, John the Baptist, had promised that he who should come after him, Jesus Christ, would baptize them with the Holy Ghost, and just previous to leaving the apostles he told them that the promise was about to be fulfilled. He therefore commanded them to tarry in Jerusalem until they were endowed with that power from on high. Then he lifted up his hands and blessed them, after which he was parted from them, and a cloud received him out of their sight.§

---

*Acts 1.
†Matt. xxviii.
‡Mark xvi:16.
§Luke xxiv:49, 53; Acts 1.

8. As they were still looking steadfastly toward heaven, two men—angels—in white apparel stood by them, and declared that this same Jesus whom they had seen go into heaven, should come in like manner, that is, in the clouds of heaven and in great glory.*

9. The Appearing of Messiah to the Nephites:— Jesus, before his crucifixion, told his disciples at Jerusalem that he was the good shepherd that would lay down his life for the sheep. He told them plainly, also, that he had other sheep which were not of that fold; "Them also I must bring," said he, "and they must hear my voice; and there shall be one fold and one shepherd."†

10. This saying, like many others which he delivered to them, the apostles did not understand, because of their unbelief. And because of their unbelief and their stiff-neckedness Jesus was commanded by his Father to say no more to them about it.‡ But it was the Nephites on the continent of America whom Jesus had in mind when he uttered the saying recorded in John's gospel,§ "Other sheep I have which are not of this fold," etc. (See note 4, end of section.)

11. What length of time intervened between Messiah's departure from his disciples at Jerusalem and his appearance among the Nephites is not known. It was not, however, until after he had ascended into heaven.‖ His appearing to them was in this manner:

12. The few people upon the western hemisphere—and they were the more righteous part both of the Nephites

---

*Acts 1; Matt. **xvi.**
†John x:16.
‡III Nephi xv:18.
§III Nephi xv:21.
‖III Nephi xi:12.

and the Lamanites—who survived that terrible period of destruction which lasted during the time that Jesus hung upon the cross,* and the three succeeding days of darkness, were gathered together about the temple in the land Bountiful.† And as they were pointing out to each other the changes that had occurred because of the earthquakes and other convulsions of the elements while the Messiah suffered upon the cross, they heard a voice speaking unto them as if from heaven. They at first did not understand the voice they heard; but the third time it spoke they understood it, and it made their hearts burn within them and their whole frame to quake, and these are the words which the voice spake: "Behold my beloved Son in whom I am well pleased, in whom I have glorified my name; hear ye him." And looking up into heaven from whence the voice came, they saw a man descending clothed in a white robe. The multitude were breathlessly silent, for they supposed an angel had appeared unto them; but as soon as Jesus was in their midst he stretched out his arm and said: "Behold I am Jesus Christ, whom the prophets testified should come into the world. * * * I am the light and life of the world; and I have drunk out of that bitter cup which the Father hath given me, and have glorified the Father in taking upon me the sins of the world."

13. At this announcement the people fell prostrate and worshiped him. But he commanded them to arise and come unto him that they might thrust their hands into his side, and feel the prints of the nails in his hands and in his feet, that they might know that he was the God of

---

*Section v, paragraph 14.
†The Land of Bountiful is supposed to have been in the northern part of South America.

Israel, and the God of the whole earth who had been slain for the sins of the world.* (See notes 5, 6, and 7, end of section.) This the people did, and then again they worshiped him, and shouted aloud: "Hosanna! blessed be the name of the Most High God!"

14. **The Church Established in America:**—After these things, Jesus proceeded to teach them his gospel and establish his church among them. It will be sufficient to say here that the Messiah taught the people on the western continent the same great moral truths that he taught the Jews; that he established the same ordinances for the salvation of the people; that he chose Twelve Apostles to whom he committed power to preach his gospel and administer in its ordinances; that a church was organized which was called "the Church of Christ;" that Jesus bore record of the great truth of the resurrection of the dead; that the Saints enjoyed the same spiritual graces and powers that the church in Palestine did, only more abundantly because of their greater faith; that two years after the appearance of Messiah all the people on the continent accepted the gospel and were baptized; that they had all things common and were a blessed and prosperous people among whom were no strifes or jealousies or contentions, "and every man did deal justly one with another."

15. They increased rapidly in numbers and went forth and built up the waste places, and rebuilded many of the cities which had been ruined by the earthquakes and by fires. They walked no more after the ordinances of the law of Moses, but they practiced the principles of the doctrines of the gospel of Christ, and thus the first century of the Christian era passed away.

---

*III Nephi xi:14.

16. All the members of the first quorum of the twelve whom Jesus called on the western hemisphere died within the first century of the Christian era, except the three to whom he had granted the privilege, as he did unto John the beloved disciple,* of remaining on the earth until he should come in his glory. The places of those who died were filled by ordaining others, and thus the quorum of apostles was perpetuated.†

NOTES.

1. The Gospels but Fragmentary Histories:—Although skeptics have dwelt with disproportioned persistency upon a multitude of discrepancies in the four-fold narrative of Christ's trial, condemnation, death, and resurrection, yet these are not of a nature to cause the slightest anxiety to a Christian scholar; nor need they awaken the most momentary distrust in anyone who—even if he have no deeper feelings in the matter—approaches the gospels with no preconceived theory, whether of infallibility or of dishonesty, to support and merely accept them for that which, at the lowest, they claim to be—histories, honest and faithful, up to the full knowledge of the writers, *but each, if taken alone, confessedly fragmentary and obviously incomplete.* After repeated study, I declare, quite fearlessly, that though the slight variations are numerous—though the lesser particulars cannot in every instance be rigidly and minutely accurate—though no one of the narratives taken singly would give us an adequate impression—yet, so far from there being, in this part of the gospel story, any irreconcilable contradiction, it is perfectly possible to discover how one Evangelist supplements the details furnished by another, and perfectly possible to understand the true sequence of the incidents by combining into one whole the separate indications which they furnish.—*Canon Farrar.*

2. The Bible Corrupted by the Gentiles:—And it came to pass that I, Nephi, beheld that they (the Gentiles) did prosper in the land (America); and I beheld a book (the Bible), and it was carried forth among them. And the angel said unto me, Knowest thou the meaning of the book? And I said unto him, I know not. * * * And he said unto me, The book which thou beholdest, is a record of the Jews, which contains the covenants of the Lord which he hath made unto the house of Israel. * * * Thou hast beheld that the book proceeded forth from the mouth of a Jew; and when it proceeded forth from the

---

*See John xxi:21-25; III Nephi xxviii.

†Let those who would be more minutely informed upon the ministry of Messiah on the western hemisphere, study carefully the book of III Nephi, where the history of that important event is recorded, and which book has been called—not inaptly—a "Fifth Gospel."

mouth of the Jew, it contained the plainness of the gospel of the Lord, of whom the twelve apostles bear record; and they bear record according to the truth which is in the Lamb of God; wherefore these things go forth from the Jews in purity, unto the Gentiles, according to the truth which is in God. And after they go forth by the hand of the twelve apostles of the Lamb, from the Jews unto the Gentiles, thou seest the foundation of a great and abominable church, which is most abominable above all other churches; for behold, they have taken away from the gospel of the Lamb, many parts which are plain and most precious; and also many covenants of the Lord have they taken away; and all this have they done, that they might pervert the right ways of the Lord; that they might blind the eyes and harden the hearts of the children of men. * * * Because of these things which are taken away out of the gospel of the Lamb, an exceeding great many do stumble, yea, insomuch that Satan hath great power over them.—*Vision of Nephi, I Nephi xiii.*

3. **Missing Parts of the Scripture:**—No better evidence can be given that the Jewish scriptures are fragmentary and corrupted than the fact that reference is made in them to books and scriptures which are not now extant—that have been destroyed. The following are a few such references taken from the New Testament:

Scriptures of Abraham's Time:—And the scriptures foreseeing that God would justify the heathen through faith, preached before the gospel unto Abraham" (Gal. iii:18). The Christian world says, "Moses was God's first pen;" but it appears from the above quotation that some one wrote scripture even before Abraham's days, and he read them, learned the gospel from them, and also learned that God would justify the heathen through faith.

Prophecy of Enoch:—Speaking of characters who were like "raging waves of the sea foaming out their own shame," Jude says: "And Enoch the seventh from Adam prophesied of these, saying, Behold the Lord cometh with ten thousand of his saints, to execute judgment upon all, etc. (Jude 15, 16). From this it appears that Enoch had a revelation concerning the glorious coming of the Son of God to judgment. May not the prophecy of Enoch have been among the scripture with which Abraham was acquainted?

Another Epistle of Jude:—"When I gave all diligence to write unto you of the common salvation, it was needful for me to write unto you, and exhort you that ye should contend earnestly for the faith once delivered unto the Saints." (Jude 3). We have but one epistle of Jude. Would not the epistle on the "common salvation" be as important as the one and the only one we have from Jude's pen?

Another Epistle to the Ephesians:—In Ephesians iii and 3rd, Paul alludes to another epistle which he had written to that people, but of which the world has no knowledge except this reference which is made by its author. This epistle contained a revelation from God.

An Epistle to the Laodiceans:—"When this epistle (Colossians) is read among you, cause that it be read also in the church of the Laodiceans, and that ye likewise read the epistle from Laodicea." (Col. iv:16.) The epistle to the Laodiceans is among the scripture that is lost.

Another Epistle to the Corinthians:—In the first letter to the Corinthians is this statement: "I wrote unto you in the epistle not to keep company with fornicators" (I Cor. v:9). From this it would appear that our so-called first epistle to the Corinthians, is really not the first, since Paul in it speaks of a former letter he had written, and which was doubtless as good scripture as the two which have been preserved.

The books mentioned in the Old Testament, but which are missing, are more numerous than those in the New Testament. In the following passages some few of the many lost books are referred to: I Chron. xxix:29; II Chron. ix:29; II Chron. xii:15; I Sam. x:25; I Kings iv:32, 33. —*Roberts.*

4. If it should be said that the Christ here had reference to his gospel going to the Gentiles, and that they were the "other sheep not of this fold," the answer would be that the language evidently refers to a personal visit of the Messiah to some lost sheep—"them also I must bring, and they shall hear my voice." On one occasion when one not of Israel asked a certain blessing of him, the Master answered her not a word; and when the disciples intervened in the case, he said to them: "I am not sent but to the lost sheep of the house of Israel." (Matt. 15:24.) Therefore, when he said: "Other sheep I have which are not of this fold, them also I must bring, and they shall hear my voice," he undoubtedly meant some branch of the house of Israel and not the Gentiles; he had reference to the branch of the house of Israel in America.

5. **Traditions of Aborigines Respecting Messiah:**—It is beyond all question that the descendants of the Nephites and Lamanites—the American Indians—have kept in their traditions a recollection—though perhaps a distorted one—of the memorable visit of Messiah to their forefathers. "The chief divinity of the Nahua nations," says Bancroft in his Native Races, "was Quetzalcoatl, the gentle God, ruler of the air, controller of the sun and rain, and source of all prosperity. * * * From toward the rising sun Quetzalcoatl had come; and he was white, with large eyes and long, black hair and copious beard. He finally set out for some other country*and as he departed from them his last words were that "one day bearded white men, brethren of his, perhaps he himself, would come by way of the sea in which the sun rises, and would enter in and rule the land;" and from that day, with a fidelity befitting Hebrews waiting for the coming of Messiah, the Mexican people watched for the fulfillment of this prophecy, which promised them a gentle rule, free from bloody sacrifices and oppression."— *Roberts.*

6. **The Incarnation Believed by the Mexicans:**—How truly surprising is it to find that the Mexicans who seemed to have been unacquainted with the doctrine of the migration of the soul, should have

*It must be remembered, that Jesus told the Nephites that he was going to visit the lost tribes whom the Father had led away. They, too, were to have a personal visit from him, and also to have the gospel preached to them (III Nephi xv and xvi.)

believed in the incarnation of the only Son of the supreme God !— *Humboldt.*

7. Crucifixion and Atonement Believed in by Mexicans:— Quetzalcoatl is there (in a certain plate where that God is represented) painted in the attitude of a person crucified, with the impression of nails in his hands and feet, but not actually upon the cross.   *   *   * The seventy-third plate of the Borgian MS. is the most remarkable of all, for there Quetzalcoatl is not only represented as crucified upon a cross of Greek form, but his burial and descent into hell are also depicted in a very curious manner.   *   *   * The Mexicans believe that Quetzalcoatl took human nature upon him, partaking of all the infirmities of man, and was not exempt from sorrow, pain or death, which he suffered voluntarily to atone for the sins of man."—*Antiquities of Mexico—Kingsborough*

8. Christ and Quetzalcoatl:—The story of the life of the Mexican divinity, Quetzalcoatl, closely resembles that of the Savior; so closely indeed that we can come to no other conclusion than that Quetzalcoatl and Christ are the same being. But the history of the former has been handed down to us through an impure Lamanitish source, which has sadly disfigured and perverted the original incidents and teachings of the Savior's life and ministry.—*Mediation and Atonement—President John Taylor.*

9. The Date of Christ's Crucifixion:—The day of the month in which Jesus was crucified has for decades been a vexed problem in New Testament research, especially in view of the fact that the Synoptic Gospels and the Gospel of John seem not to agree on this point. An entirely new effort to solve the matter has been made by Prof. Hans Acholis, of the University of Konigsberg, and the result is published in the Nachrichten (No. 5) of the Gottingen Academy of Science. The novelty of the effort lies in this, that Professor Achelis tries to figure out the date astronomically and reaches the conclusion that it was Friday, April 6, A. D. 30. His process is as follows:

Jesus was crucified on a Friday, according to Matt. xxvii:62; xxviii:1; Mark xv:42; Luke xxiii:54; John xix:31. According to John, he was crucified on the 14th of Nisan; according to the other evangelists, on the 15th of Nisan. The year is not mentioned.

Pilate was governor between 26 and 36, and at Easter of the latter year had been deposed. In the year 26, the 14th of Nisan fell on Saturday; in the year 27, on Wednesday; in 28, on Monday; in 29, on Sunday; in 30, on Friday, April 6; in 31, on Tuesday; in 32, on Monday; in 33, on Friday, April 3; in 34, on Tuesday; in 35, on Monday. During all of these years the 15th never fell on Friday. From these facts two conclusions can be drawn: one, that John and not the synoptics have the correct date, and Jesus could not have been crucified on the 15th of Nisan; second, that we must choose between April 6, A. D. 30, and April 3, A. D. 33.

To decide between these two, we must appeal to other data taken from Luke and John. Christ began his public ministry, according to Luke, in immediate connection with the activity of John the Baptist, and the latter began (1) in the fifteenth year of Tiberius; (2) at the time when Pontius Pilate was ruler in Judea; (3) when Herod was tetrarch in Galilee; (4) when Herod's brother Philip was tetrarch in Itureah, etc.; (5) when Lysanias was tetrarch in Abelene; and (6) when Annas and Caiaphas were high priests. These data fix the time between August 19, A. D. 28, and August 18, A. D. 29.

According to John ii:20, the Jews said to Christ, when he entered upon his ministry, that the Temple had been in process of erection forty-six years. This brings us to the year 27-28. Since Christ, according to Luke, was engaged in his ministry for one year—according to John, two or three years—both writers have taken the year 30, as the year of his death. Accordingly we can with good reason regard Friday, April 6, A. D. 30, as the date of the crucifixion.

This computation has, however, not been satisfactory to all, and a critic in the Christliche Welt (No. 14) tries to show that it is unreliable in method, although correct in result. He says:

The Jewish month is not a fixed date like the Roman month. It went from new moon to new moon; or, better, from the time when the new moon became visible to the next time this occurred. It is accordingly only 27 or 28 days long, and twelve months is accordingly not a solar year, but only 354 days. Accordingly, at least once every three years the Jews had to add an intercalary month. The Jewish year began in spring, with the month of Nisan. If the month begins with the new moon, then the full moon falls upon the 14th-15th. The month of Nisan, as the first spring month, was so arranged that its full moon fell after the vernal equinox. In this way the beginning of Nisan and the beginning of the year were determined with reasonable certainty. But there are two ways of determining the 1st of Nisan, and we no longer know which of these two ways the Jewish almanac-makers observed. Did they adopt the most reliable way, namely, of counting backward from the full moon to the first? This is probably the case; but, if so, then they were at times compelled, as is seen by a glance at our own calendar, to begin the 1st of Nisan before the new moon had really become visible. But if they followed the more certain way, namely, not to declare the 1st of Nisan until they really had seen the new moon, then the latter dates of the month could also have been changed. Much of this calculation, therefore, is uncertain, since in case of cloudy weather, the new moon would be seen later than in clear. Nevertheless, a careful comparison of these calculations with the two chronological data concerning the beginning of Christ's ministry leads to the conclusion that Christ's death occurred on Friday, April 6, A. D. 30.—(*Literary Digest*, May 16, 1903, pp. 723-4).

REVIEW.

1. What occurred on the third day of Christ's burial?
2. State the several prophecies made by Jesus which were fulfilled in his resurrection? (Footnote.)
3. Relate the account of the resurrection as given by Matthew.

4.   In respect to what are there slight discrepancies in the writings of Matthew, Mark, Luke and John?

5.   What can you say of the fragmentary character of the New Testament "gospels?" (Notes 1 and 2,)

6.   State the most probable order in which Jesus made his several appearances after the resurrection.

7.   How long was Jesus with his disciples on the eastern hemisphere after his resurrection?

8.   What notable commission did Jesus give to the apostles before leaving them?

9.   What signs did Messiah say should follow believers?

10.   Describe the last parting of Jesus from his disciples.

11.   What prophecy did Jesus make to his disciples at Jerusalem that they did not understand?

12.   Give an account of Messiah's visit to the Nephites.

13.   What did Jesus do among the Nephites?

14.   What was the effect that followed the preaching of the gospel and the organization of the church?

15.   What course was pursued as to the quorum of the apostles?

16.   Relate the several traditions of the Mexicans respecting the visit of Messiah to this land.

SECTION VII.

1. Vacancy in the Quorum of the Twelve Filled:— The first official business which occupied the attention of the authorities of the church after the ascension of the Lord—according to our Christian annals—was filling up the quorum of the twelve. Judas by his treason had forfeited his apostleship and was dead, and hence it became necessary to ordain another to fill his place. Peter when presenting this matter before the church, appeared to lay some stress upon the necessity of choosing some one of the brethren who had been with them from the beginning— "from the baptism of John unto that same day that he (Christ) was taken up," that he might be a witness with the rest of the apostles of the things which Jesus did and also a witness of his resurrection.

2. "And they appointed (nominated) two, Joseph called Barsabas, who was surnamed Justus, and Matthias. And they prayed. * * * Thou, Lord, which knowest the hearts of all men, show whether of these two thou hast chosen. * * * And they gave forth their lots [or, gave their votes];* and the lot fell upon Matthias." From that

---

*In his *Comment de Rebus Christ*, p. 78-80, the learned Dr. Mosheim has a note on this passage in which his aim is to prove that the correct translation from the Greek of the phrase usually rendered *they gave forth their lots*, should be *they gave their votes*. While it is but proper to say that the Doctor's translation is very generally rejected by the learned, still there will be no question with those who understand the order - of the priesthood and the manner of filling vacancies in its quorums, that Dr. Mosheim is correct in his interpretation as to the meaning of the passage.

time he was numbered with the apostles.* (See note 1, end of section.)

3. The filling of this vacancy in the quorum of the twelve—the only instance of the kind mentioned in the New Testament—may be taken as a proof that it was clearly the understanding of the apostles that the quorum of the twelve was to be perpetuated. It was so understood in the church on the western hemisphere, for the fourth Nephi informs us that as the apostles whom Jesus had chosen passed away, others were ordained in their stead;† and thus the quorum was kept full, but for how long cannot be ascertained.

4. **The Holy Ghost Given:**—The first time the gospel was preached publicly, after the ascension of Messiah, was on the day of Pentecost, most probably seven days after the ascension.‡ The church had assembled and suddenly the promised baptism of the Holy Ghost—promised both by John the Baptist and Messiah§—took place, for the Spirit came like the rushing of a mighty wind and filled the house where the saints were assembled; and they were all filled with the Holy Ghost. It rested upon them visibly like cloven tongues of fire; and they began speaking in other tongues, that is, in languages before unknown to them, as the spirit gave them utterance.

5. The occurrence was soon noised about the city and the multitude came together, to witness this strange event.

---

*Acts i:15-26.
†IV Nephi 1:14.
‡Pentecost came fifty days after the Passover, on which day the Lord Jesus was crucified. Allowing that he lay three days in the tomb, and was with his disciples forty days after his resurrection (Acts 1:3), forty-three days of the fifty between Passover and Pentecost are accounted for, leaving but seven days between ascension and the day of Pentecost, when the promise of the baptism of the spirit was fulfilled.—*The Gospel—Roberts*, note p. 189.
§Luke iii:16. Matt. iii:2. Acts i:4, 5.

In that great concourse of people thus hastily assembled were devout men out of every nation under heaven (see note 2, end of section), and they were confounded with astonishment since every man heard the gospel in his own language.* "Are not all these which speak Galileans," said they, "and how hear we every man in his own tongue, wherein we were born?" All were amazed, and some inquired one of another, "What meaneth this?" Others mockingly said, "These men are full of new wine."

6. To this latter remark the apostle Peter replied that the brethren were not drunken as had been supposed, and reminded the accusers that it was but the third hour of the day. Men were not likely to be drunk so early. The apostle further informed them that his power which they witnessed was the same as that of which Joel† spoke when he said that in the last days the Spirit of God should be poured out upon all flesh, and make the sons and daughters of men to prophesy, young men to see visions and old men to dream dreams, etc. (See notes 3 and 4, end of section.)

7. Having corrected the slander uttered by those inclined to mock at the power of God, Peter continued his discourse, and proved from the scriptures and from the marvelous works of the Lord Jesus while among them, that he was both Lord and Christ. Then a great multitude was converted, and cried as with one voice, "Men and brethren, what shall we do?" To which Peter answered, "Repent and be baptized every one of you in the name of Jesus Christ for the remission of sins, and ye shall receive

---

*The languages spoken are enumerated by the writer of *The Acts* ii: 9-11.
†Joel ii:28.

the gift of the Holy Ghost."* He informed them that this promise of the Holy Ghost—and, of course, of salvation— was both to them and to their children, in fact to all whom God should call.† There were added to the church that day, three thousand souls.

8. **The Rise of Opposition:**—Being now endowed with power from on high, the apostles continued to preach in and about Jerusalem with great success, the Lord working with them and confirming their ministry by signs and wonders following the believers.

9. The chief priests and rulers among the Jews became alarmed at the boldness of the disciples of Jesus and the rapidity with which faith in the gospel spread among the people. They were in imminent danger of being adjudged by the people, guilty of executing an innocent man; nay, more, of putting to death Messiah!

10. They therefore had some of the apostles brought before them and sought to intimidate them with threats, warning them not to preach any more in the name of Jesus. To these threats the apostles made answer: "Whether it is right in the sight of God to hearken unto you more than unto God, judge ye."‡ Leaving the presence of the council the apostles preached even more boldly in the name of Jesus.

---

*I think it proper here to call the attention of the student to the fact that the principles of the gospel in this discourse of Peter's are stated in the same order that they were unfolded in the ministry of John the Baptist and Messiah. First, John came bearing witness of one who should come after him—Christ, the Lord. Hence, he taught faith in God (John 1:15, 16, also verses 19-36). After that, the burden of his message was, "Repent for the kingdom of heaven is at hand;" then followed his baptism in water with a promise that they should receive the Holy Ghost. So Peter first taught the people faith in the Lord, proving from the scripture that Jesus was both Lord and Christ; and when they believed that, then he taught them repentance and baptism for the remission of sins, and promised them the Holy Ghost.

†Acts ii:38, 39.
‡Acts iv:19.

A second time they were brought before the chief rulers, to answer for a disregard of the orders of the council which charged them with threats not to teach in the name of Jesus; "and behold," said they, "ye have filled Jerusalem with your doctrine and mean to bring this man's blood upon us."

11. The answer of Peter, who spoke also for the rest of the apostles, was even bolder than before. "We ought to obey God rather than man," said he. "The God of our fathers raised up Jesus, whom ye slew and hanged on a tree. Him hath God exalted with his right hand to be a Prince and a Savior, for to give repentance to Israel and forgiveness of sins. And we are witnesses of these things; and so is also the Holy Ghost, whom God hath given to them that obey him."*

12. The boldness of his answer gave deep offense and led the chief rulers to take counsel how they might slay them. But Gamaliel [Ga-ma-li-el], a learned doctor of the law, advised them against such proceedings. His advice was to let the men alone, for if the work they had in hand was of men it would come to naught. If it was of God, nothing which they could do would overthrow it; and they might be found fighting against God.†

13. The counsel of Gamaliel prevailed in part at least. The apostles were not killed at that time; but they were once more forbidden to speak in the name of Jesus, beaten and then set free. The apostles rejoiced at being found worthy to suffer shame for the name of Jesus, and not heeding the orders of the council continued preaching in the temple and in private houses.

14. **Temporal Concerns:**—So completely did the apos-

*Acts v:26-32.
†Acts v:34-42.

tles and the other disciples give themselves to the work of the ministry, that complaint was made by the Grecians because the widows and poor were neglected. Whereupon the twelve called the church together and proposed that seven men of good report be chosen and set apart to see to these affairs, that they themselves might give their attention wholly to the ministry, as it was not profitable for them to neglect that in order to "wait on tables." The plan pleased the church and the seven men were appointed.*

15. **All Things in Common:**—The effect of the gospel upon the saints of Jerusalem was very marked. They were of one heart and of one mind; they had all things in common, and those who possessed houses or lands sold

---

*It is generally supposed by Biblical scholars, Mosheim, Neander, Kitto, Murdock and many others, that these men were deacons only. There is nothing, however, in the Acts of the Apostles or other parts of the New Testament which would lead one to believe that such was the case. We have evidence on the other hand that one of them at least held a higher priesthood than the office of deacon. In modern revelation we have it stated that neither teachers nor deacons have authority to baptize, administer the sacrament or lay on hands for the Holy Ghost (Doc. and Cov., Sec. xx:58); yet we have Philip, one of the seven, going down into Samaria, teaching the gospel *and baptizing the people* (Acts viii), hence we may know that he held a higher priesthood than that of deacon. Yet when it became necessary to confer the Holy Ghost upon these same converts by the laying on of hands, Philip, it would seem, had not the authority to do it; but the Apostles hearing that Samaria had received the word, sent Peter and John down and they conferred upon the Samaritans the Holy Ghost. And though Philip was present he appears to have taken no part in it. It is therefore reasonable to conclude that since Philip had authority to baptize, he therefore must have held an office higher than that of deacon, or even of teacher; but since he evidently had *not* authority to lay on hands for the gift of the Holy Ghost, his office was something less than that of an Elder. Hence it is most likely that he was a priest—priests have the right to baptize but not to lay on hands for the reception of the Holy Ghost (Doc. and Cov. Sec. xx)—as perhaps also were his six associates, appointed to preside over the temporal affairs of the Church, especially to see after the poor.

them and brought the price of the things and laid it at the apostles' feet.   Distribution was made unto every man as he had need; and there was none among them that lacked for that which was necessary.*

16.   Persecution:—A great persecution arose against the church at Jerusalem, within the first year after Messiah's ascension, so that most of the brethren, except the apostles, were scattered abroad throughout Judea and Samaria.   Everywhere they went they preached the gospel, so that great good came out of what was intended to be an evil, as the gospel was more widely preached.   Philip, one of the seven who had been appointed to look after the temporal affairs of the church, was among the number driven from Jerusalem by the persecution.   He went to the city of Samaria, where the people listened to his teachings, accepted his testimony and were baptized both men and women.   The apostles hearing of his success, sent to Samaria Peter and John; and when they came they laid their hands upon those who had been baptized and they received the Holy Ghost;† and thus the work was established there.

17.   Paul:—It was during this persecution that Saul, of Tarsus, afterwards better known as Paul, the apostle of the Gentiles, manifested his bitterness toward the saints. He witnessed the stoning to death of Stephen, one of the seven men appointed to look after the temporal affairs of the church at Jerusalem.   He held the clothes of those who killed him; and being exceedingly vexed at what he regarded as a superstition, he followed the saints into distant cities,

---

*Acts iv:32-37.

†Acts viii: The student will observe that the same order of presenting and accepting the gospel is observed in the account given of its introduction into Samaria as was observed in the teaching of John the Baptist and Jesus, and also of Peter, on the day of Pentecost.

breathing out threatenings and slaughter against them. He went to the high priest and obtained letters of authority from him to the rulers of the synagogue at Damascus, that if he found any of the saints there he might bring them bound to Jerusalem.   On his way to Damascus, however, the Lord Jesus appeared to him, and Paul, blinded by the glory of the vision, and humbled because he found he had been fighting against God, was led by his companions into the city where a disciple of the name of Ananias was sent by the Lord to restore to Paul his sight and baptize him.   He was afterwards made an apostle and became zealous for the truth.*   (See note 4, end of section.)

18.   **The Gospel Taken to the Gentiles:**—The apostles, being Jews themselves, appear to have shared the common prejudices of their race against the Gentiles; and treated them as if they had no lot nor part in the gospel of Christ. It was not the design of the Lord, however, to thus restrict the application of the gospel.   Jesus, himself, while he had said that he was sent but to the lost sheep of the house of Israel,† had also said: "And I, if I be lifted up from the earth, *will draw all men unto me.*"‡   Hence when Cornelius, of Caesarea, a devout man, one that feared God, though a Gentile, sought the Lord by prayer and good works, he found him; for an angel was sent to him who told him his prayers and alms were accepted of God, and that he had come to direct him to send men to Joppa for Simon Peter, who would be able to tell him what he ought to do.   The devout Gentile immediately started the messengers to find the apostle

---

*Acts ix.
†Matt. xv:24.
‡John xii:32.

19. Meantime Peter himself was prepared by a vision to go with the gospel unto one whom both he and all his race regarded as unclean. In vision he thought he beheld a great net let down from heaven, filled with all manner of four-footed beasts, fowls of the air and creeping things. And a voice said to him, "Rise, Peter, kill and eat." "Not so, Lord," was his reply, "for I have never eaten anything that is common or unclean." "What God hath cleansed," said the voice that spoke to him, "that call not thou common or unclean." This was done thrice, and as he was yet pondering what the vision could mean, the messengers of Cornelius were at the gates enquiring for him; and he was commanded by the spirit to go with them, doubting nothing, for God had sent them.

20. Peter was obedient to the inspired commandment, and went to the house of Cornelius, where he found many of the devout Gentile's friends and kinsmen gathered together in anticipation of his coming. Cornelius having informed the apostle how he came to send for him, Peter exclaimed: "Of a truth I perceive that God is no respecter of persons; but in every nation he that feareth him and worketh righteousness, is accepted with him."* He then proceeded to preach the gospel to Cornelius and all present. As he did so the Holy Ghost fell upon them to the astonishment of all the Jews who had accompanied Peter; for they heard them speak in new tongues and magnify God. Cornelius and his friends were baptized and thus the door of the gospel was opened to the Gentiles.†

21. Rapid Growth of the Work:—The knowledge once established in the minds of the apostles that God

---

*Acts 10.

†This case of Cornelius marks an exception—the only one recorded in the New Testament—to that order in the gospel to which attention

granted to the Gentiles repentance unto life, seemed to unshackle those who were to preach the gospel, and gave a broader meaning in their minds to their commission to "Go unto all the world and preach the gospel unto every creature." Evidently before this they did not comprehend it in its fullest sense.

22. The apostles appear to have remained in Jerusalem a number of years—twelve years, tradition says—presiding over the church and directing the labors of those preaching the gospel. Churches, or, more correctly speaking, branches of the church, were built up in Antioch [An-ti-ok], Damascus [Da-mas-kus] and other cities of Syria [Sir-ia]. The work also spread into Asia Minor, Greece and Rome; and everywhere great success attended the preaching of the elders, until the gospel was firmly established in various parts of the Gentile world. So extensive was the preaching of the ambassadors of Christ in those early days of the church, that we have Paul saying (about thirty years after the ascension of Messiah) that it had been preached to every creature under heaven.* (See note 5, end of section.)

---

has been drawn several times in this section; that is, these Gentiles received the Holy Ghost before baptism in water. The object of the deviation from the rule is obvious. It was that the Jews might have a witness from God that the gospel was for the Gentiles as well as for the house of Israel. But according to the Scriptures, and I may say according to the nature and relationship of these several principles and ordinances of the gospel to each other, the reception of the Holy Ghost comes after repentance and baptism, the one leading up logically to the other, which follows in beautiful and harmonious sequence.

*Col. :23.

NOTES.

1. Was Matthias Called of God?—In consequence of Matthias having been chosen by "lot," it may be a question in the minds of some as to his being called of God. A careful consideration of all that was done in connection with that circumstance will dispel all doubt in relation to it. It must be observed that after Joseph Barsabas and Matthias were nominated for the place in the quorum of the Twelve, the Apostles prayed, saying: "Thou Lord, which knowest the hearts of all men, show whether of these two *Thou* hast chosen." Before his ascension Jesus had said to these men, "If ye abide in me, and my words abide in you, ye shall ask what ye will, and it shall be done unto you. * * * Ye have not chosen me, but I have chosen you, and ordained you; * * * that whatsoever ye shall ask of the Father in my name, he may give it you." Therefore when these Apostles asked which of the two men nominated God had chosen, and they gave their votes and Matthias was the one selected, God in that way answered their prayer, and Matthias was thus called of God. Again, to be called by a divinely appointed authority is to be called of God. No one can deny that the Apostles were a divinely appointed authority, hence to be called by them was to be called of God.—*Roberts.*

2. Pentecost:—Pentecost is the name given in the New Testament to the Feast of Weeks, or of Ingathering, celebrated on the fiftieth day from the Passover. It was a festival of thanks for the harvest. It was also one of the three great yearly festivals, in which all the males were required to appear before the Lord at the place of his Sanctuary. Josephus in three places in his writings, *viz.* in the fourteenth book of *Antiquities*, ch. xiii:4; *Ibid* xvii, ch. x:2; and in his second book of the *Wars of the Jews*, ch. iii :2,—speaks of this festival as bringing together great numbers of the Jews from all parts of the world, and sustains the statement in Acts ii, that there were in Jerusalem at Pentecost "Jews; devout men, out of every nation under heaven," who came running together on hearing that the disciples of Jesus were speaking in unknown tongues. We cannot refrain from remarking that it was a most opportune time for such a demonstration, since these men would carry the rumor of these things and the substance of the remarkable sermon they heard to the distant lands from which they had come, and thus the news of the gospel would be spread abroad.—*Roberts.*

3. Joel's Prophecy:—It is very generally supposed among Christians, that this outpouring of the Holy Ghost on the day of Pentecost was the fulfillment of Joel's prophecy, that is, its complete fulfillment. A careful examination of the prophecy, however, will clearly demonstrate that this is not the case. The prophecy will be found in Joel ii:28-32, and the particulars enumerated in it are as follows: The spirit of the Lord is to be poured out upon *all flesh*: At Pentecost it was poured out upon a few of the disciples of Jesus only; the sons and daughters of the people were to prophesy; we have no account of their doing so at Pentecost: old men were to dream dreams and young men see visions; there is no account of this taking place on the occasion in question; wonders were to be shown in the heavens and in the earth, blood and fire and pillars of smoke; the sun is to be turned into darkness, the moon into blood, before the great and terrible day of the Lord come, yet on Mount Zion and in Jerusalem deliverance was to be found. These things unquestionably point to the glorious coming of the Son of God to judgment (see Matt. xxiv); and certainly they were not fulfilled on the day of Pentecost by the outpouring of the Holy Ghost on a few of the disciples of Jesus. Still Peter said, referring to the spirit poured out upon the disciples: "This is that which was spoken by the prophet Joel," and then quoted the passage. He doubtless meant: This spirit which you now see poured out upon these few men, is that spirit which Joel spoke of, and which will eventually be poured out upon *all flesh*, not only upon men and women, but upon the brute creation as well, so that the lion and lamb shall lie down together and a little child shall lead them, and they shall not hurt nor destroy in all God's holy mountain. I have deemed it necessary to make this note, first, because of the very general belief among Christians that the prophecy of Joel was fulfilled on the day of Pentecost; and second, because the prophecy is one that was quoted by the angel Moroni on the occasion of his first visit to Joseph Smith, concerning which he said, it was not yet fulfilled but soon would be (Pearl of Great Price, page 51), hence, since this heavenly messenger puts its fulfillment in the future, it could not have been fulfilled on the day of Pentecost two thousand years ago.— *Roberts*.

4. **Description of Paul:**—He is about five feet high; very dark hair; dark complexion; dark skin; large Roman nose; sharp face; small black eyes, penetrating as eternity; round shoulders; a whining voice, except when elevated, and then it almost resembled the roaring of a lion. He was a good orator, active and diligent, always employing himself in doing good to his fellow-man.—*Joseph Smith, at the organization of a school for instruction, Jan. 5th*, 1841.

Paul was small in size, and his personal appearance did not correspond with the greatness of his soul. He was ugly, stout, short, and stooping, and his broad shoulders awkwardly sustained a little bald head. His sallow countenance was half hidden in a thick beard; his nose was aquiline, his eyes piercing, and his eyebrows heavy and joined across his forehead. Nor was there anything imposing in his speech, for his timid and embarrassed air gave but a poor idea of his eloquence. He shrewdly, however, admitted his exterior defects, and even drew advantage therefrom. The Jewish race possesses the peculiarity of at the same time presenting types of the greatest beauty, and the most thorough ugliness; but this Jewish ugliness is something quite apart by itself. Some of the strange visages which at first excite a smile, assume, when lighted up by emotion, a sort of deep brilliancy and grandeur.—*Renan—Life of the Apostles, p.* 165.

5. **Travels of the Apostles Uncertain:**—The ambassadors of Christ on leaving Jerusalem traveled over a great part of the world, and in a short time collected numerous religious societies in various countries. Of the churches they founded, not a small number is mentioned in the sacred books, especially in the Acts of the Apostles. Be-

sides these, there can be no doubt they collected many others, both by their own efforts and by the efforts of their followers. But how far they traveled, what nations they visited, or when and where they died, is exceedingly dubious and uncertain.—*Mosheim.*

6. **Divine Aid in Propagation of the Gospel:**—The causes must have been divine which could enable men destitute of all human aid, poor and friendless, neither eloquent nor learned, fishermen and publicans, and they too *Jews*, that is persons odious to all other nations, in so short a time to persuade a great part of mankind to abandon the religion of their fathers, and to embrace a new religion which is opposed to the natural dispositions of men. In the words they uttered there must have been an amazing and a divine power controlling the minds of men. To which may be added miracles, prophecies, the detection of men's secret designs, magnanimity in the midst of perils, contempt for all the objects of ordinary ambition, a patient and cheerful endurance of sufferings worse than death, as well as of death itself, and finally, lives of the purest and most unblemished character. That the ambassadors of Jesus Christ were in fact thus furnished for their work, is a truth perfectly clear and obvious. And if we suppose them not to have been so furnished, no probable reason can be assigned for so rapid a propagation of Christianity by this small and feeble band.—*Mosheim.*

7. **The Rapid Spread of the Gospel:**—Thus, then, under a celestial influence and co-operation, the doctrine of the Savior, like the rays of the sun, quickly irradiated the whole world. Presently, in accordance with divine prophecy, the sound of his inspired evangelists and apostles had gone throughout all the earth, and their words to the ends of the world. Throughout every city and village, like a replenished barn floor, churches were rapidly abounding and filled with members from every people. Those who, in consequence of the delusions that had descended to them from their ancestors, had been fettered by the ancient disease of idolatrous superstition, were now liberated by the power of Christ, through the teachings and miracles of his messengers.—*Eusebius, writing of the period between 37-41 A. D.*

REVIEW.

1. What was the first official business of the authorities of the church after the resurrection of the Christ?

2. State the manner of filling the vacancy in the quorum of the twelve.

3. What of Mosheim's translation of the phrase: "They gave forth their lots?" (Note.)

4. Was Matthias called of God? (Note 1.)

5. What evidence can you refer to in proof that the quorum of Twelve Apostles was to be perpetuated?

6. When was the gospel first publicly preached after the resurrection of the Christ?

7. How long between the ascension and Pentecost? (Note 2.)

8. Describe the events in the church on the day of Pentecost.

9. What circumstance is an evidence that the statement of scripture is true that there were devout men from many nations in Jerusalem at that time?   (Note 2.)

10. Was the outpouring of the Holy Ghost on the day of Pentecost a complete fulfillment of Joel's prophecy quoted by Peter?   (Note 3.)

11. How does the order of principles taught by Peter on the day of Pentecost compare with the order of principles taught by John the Baptist and Messiah?   (Note.)

12. Describe the rise of opposition to the church.

13. What answer did Peter make to the mandates of the rulers not to teach in the name of Jesus?

14. What was the counsel of Gamaliel to the Jews?

15. To what extent did his counsel prevail?

16. What arrangements were made in the church in respect to looking after the poor?

17. What priesthood did the seven most likely hold?   (Note.)

18. Give an account of the introduction of the gospel among the Samaritans.

19. What was Paul's course at the first towards the church?

20. Relate the circumstances of his conversion.

21. Give a description of Paul.   (Note 4.)

22. What were the views entertained by the Jews toward the Gentiles?

23. Relate how the gospel was introduced to the Gentiles.

24. State the exception to the order of the gospel in the case of Cornelius.

25. What was the object of the exception made?

26. What effect on the church did carrying the gospel to the Gentiles have?

27. How long is it supposed that the Twelve remained at Jerusalem?

28. What can you say of the spread of the work during the first century?   (Notes 5, 6, 7.)

SECTION VIII.

1. Review:—We have now related the chief events connected with the introduction of the gospel and the establishment of the Church by the personal labors of Messiah and those immediately connected with him. We may now review the doctrines that he taught, which, taken in the aggregate, constitute the gospel; and examine the character of the organization he founded—the Church.

2. The Mission of Messiah:—Jesus Christ came into the earth to accomplish three great purposes; first, to redeem mankind from the consequences of Adam's transgression; second, to save them from the consequences of their own sins; third, to be the complete, and perfect revelation of God to men—"God manifested in the flesh."

3. The Purpose of God in the Earth-Life of Man:— In order to a right understanding of the first and second items in the mission of the Christ, an outline, at least, as to the purpose of God in the earth-life of man must be given. This may not be learned directly from either the Old Testament or the New; but happily is made clear in the revelations given in the New Dispensation of the Gospel, the dispensation of the Gospel given to the world through Joseph Smith, the prophet* of that New Dispensation.

---

*I make no apology for thus bluntly stating what examination of the Old Testament and the New will clearly prove—there is no passage in those sacred books which clearly or definitely states what the purpose of God was in the earth-life of man. It was reserved for the New Dispensation of the Gospel to disclose that purpose.

"Behold this is my work and my glory," saith the Lord, "to bring to pass the immortality and eternal life of man."*

"The elements are eternal, and spirit and element inseparably connected receive a fullness of joy; and when separated man cannot receive a fullness of joy.†

"Behold all things have been done in the wisdom of him who knoweth all things. Adam fell that men might be; and men are that they might have joy.‡

God's purpose in the earth-life of man, is here disclosed to be the bringing to pass the eternal life of man, that he might have a fullness of joy. This high purpose of God, however, may not be achieved except through an eternal union of spirit and of element; and this, in turn, can only be achieved through an earth-life by which is secured a union of spirit and element.

4.   **Needed Experience**:—One other thing is also needed before a fullness of joy can be attained in that eternal life of man—viz.,—Experience in the midst of broken harmonies; by man coming in contact with evil, that good might be appreciated; with sorrow, that joy might stand revealed; with sin, that righteousness might the more be loved; with sickness, that the boon of health might more be prized; with pain, that ease might be more blessed; with death itself, that eternal life—God's greatest gift to man—and the consummation to be attained in the work and the glory of God, might be understood and rightly valued.

5.   **The Ground of Free Redemption from Death**:— To attain this end one thing is a necessity—it is inevitable. It is a thing forced by reason of the conditions that must

---

*Book of Moses—a fragment revealed to Joseph Smith—Ch. 1:39 —found in Pearl of Great Price.

†Revelations in Doc. & Cov. Sect. 93: 33, 34.

‡Book of Mormon II Nephi ii: 24, 25.

exist in order to make the whole of God's purpose possible. That one thing is *death*, and its results, a world of broken harmonies; a world where temptations and sin shall abound; where good and evil shall strive for mastery; where man shall have full opportunity to exercise his choice for good or for evil; make use of his agency—his power to choose his life and what it shall be. And since this death is *necessary* to the plan, and man is not, and can be in nowise responsible for that *necessity* in the plan, justice demands that there shall be, in some way, a free deliverance from the consequences of this element of *necessity* in the plan. Not because man's agency is not involved in acceptance of the plan, for it was involved in it. "At the first organization in heaven," says our Prophet of the New Dispensation of the Gospel—Joseph Smith—speaking of what happened in the spirit life of man before his earth-life began—"At the first organization in heaven we were all present, and saw the Savior chosen and appointed, and the plan of salvation made, *and we sanctioned it.*" Man's agency, then, was involved in the acceptance of God's scheme, and the plea that man—meaning the race—all men—had no lot or part in the fall of Adam and its consequences, death, temporal and spiritual, may not be urged as a reason why free deliverance from death and its consequences should be provided. But that which may reasonably be pleaded as a ground for free and universal deliverance from death and its consequences is this: Where necessity enters as a constituent part of a scheme pertaining to man, and is not a product of man's action, but is something inherent in the conditions on which the plan rests, then man should not be held responsible for those conditions and the consequences that grow out of them. From those consequences man should have free deliverance.

6. General Salvation Provided from the Consequences of Adam's Transgression:—And that is what takes place in the Gospel, the scheme of man's progress toward eternal life and fullness of joy. He is unconditionally redeemed from death, physical and spiritual death, so far as these are produced by necessity of conditions in the plan itself, and that is not a product of man's agency or action. That the benefits of this free redemption are to be universal, is evident from the following facts:

First, That the resurrection from the dead is universal, as the scriptures witness:—"And many of them that sleep in the dust of the earth shall awake, some to everlasting life, and some to shame and everlasting contempt."* "For as the Father hath life in himself, so hath he given to the Son to have life in himself. * * * Marvel not at this; for the hour is coming, in which all that are in their graves shall hear his voice, and shall come forth; they that have done good unto the resurrection of life, and they that have done evil unto the resurrection of damnation."† Or, as the last two clauses were given to the Prophet Joseph Smith by inspiration—"They who have done good in the resurrection of the just; and they who have done evil in the resurrection of the unjust."‡ After giving a full account of the resurrection of the righteous and their reign upon the earth for a thousand years, the writer of the Apocalypse [A-poc-a-lypse] says: "And I saw the dead, small and great, stand before God. * * * And the sea gave up the dead which were in it; and death and hell delivered up the dead which

---

*Dan. xii: 2.
†John v: 26, 28, 29.
‡Doc. and Cov. lxxvi: 16, 17.

were in them, and they were judged every man according to his works."*

Second, The scriptures plainly declare that the redemption of men from the consequences of Adam's transgression shall be universal: "For as by the offense of one [Adam] judgment came upon *all men* to condemnation; even so by the righteousness of one the free gift came *upon all men* to the justification of life."† "Since by man came death, by man came also the resurrection of the dead. For as in Adam *all die,* even so in Christ shall *all be made alive.* But every man in his own order; Christ the first fruits; afterwards they that are Christ's at his coming. Then cometh the end, when he shall have delivered the kingdom to God, even the Father; when he shall have put down all rule and all authority and power. For he must reign till he hath put all enemies under his feet. The last enemy that shall be destroyed is death."‡ "Behold, he (Christ) created Adam, and by Adam, came the fall of man. And because of the fall of man, came Jesus Christ, even the Father and the Son; and because of Jesus Christ, came the redemption of man. And because of the redemption of man, which came by Jesus Christ, they are brought back into the presence of the Lord; yea, this is wherein all men are redeemed, because the death of Christ bringeth to pass the resurrection, which bringeth to pass a redemption from an endless sleep, from which sleep all men shall be awakened by the power of God, when the trump shall sound; and they shall come forth, both small and great, and all shall stand before his bar,

---

*Rev. xx: 12, 13.
†Rom. v: 18. See whole chapter.
‡I Cor. xv: 21-26.

being redeemed and loosed from this eternal band of death, which death is a temporal death."*

7. Through the atonement made by Messiah, therefore, a full and complete redemption from the consequences of Adam's transgression is brought about; that is, a victory over the grave is secured, and that, too, through the merits of Jesus Christ. And while the law transgressed by Adam has been vindicated, the posterity of Adam who became subject to death through his disobedience, are redeemed from the grave without anything being required of them. For as their agency was not concerned in bringing about the mischief, nothing is required of them in order to obtain redemption from it. So far salvation is free and universal. (See notes 1, 2 and 3, end of section.)

8. **The Atonement a Fact Proven by Evidence:**— It is often asked: "How is it that through the sacrifice of one who is innocent, salvation may be purchased for those under the dominion of death?" We observe, in passing, that what should most concern man is, not so much *how* it is that such is the case; but is it a *fact*. Is it true that God has established such a scheme of redemption, is what should concern him. To that question the blood sprinkled upon a thousand Jewish altars, and the smoke that darkened the heavens for ages from burnt offerings, answer yes. For those sacrifices, and that sprinkled blood were but typical of the great sacrifice to be made by the Messiah.

Even the mythology of heathen nations retains the idea of an atonement that either has been, or is to be made for mankind. Fantastic, distorted, confused, buried under the rubbish of savage superstition it may be, but it never-

*Mormon ix: 12, 13. Other evidences from the Nephite scriptures will be found in Alma xi: 40-44.   III Nephi xxvii: 13-15.   II Nephi ii.   Mosiah xv: 18-27.   Alma xxxiv: 7-17.   Alma xiii. 1-26.

theless exists. So easily traced, so distinct is this feature of heathen mythology, that some writers* have endeavored to prove that the gospel plan of redemption was derived from heathen mythology. Whereas the fact is that the gospel was understood and extensively preached in the earliest ages; men retained in their tradition a knowledge of those principles, or parts of them, and however much they may have been distorted, traces of them may still be found in nearly all the mythologies of the world.

The prophets of the Jewish scriptures answer the question in the affirmative. The writers of the New Testament make Christ's atonement the principal theme of their discourses and epistles. The Book of Mormon, speaking as the voice of entire nations of people whose prophets and righteous men sought and found God, testify to the same great fact. The revelations of God as given through the Prophet Joseph Smith are replete with passages confirming this doctrine. The evidence is more than sufficient, to establish the *fact* of the atonement beyond the possibility of a doubt; and if there are some things in it not within the scope of our comprehension, still there is sufficient foundation for the glorious hope of eternal life through its power.

9. **Claims of Mercy and Justice Balance:**—In the atonement there is a nice balancing of the relative claims of justice and mercy. The law given to man having been transgressed, justice demanded the payment of the penalty, which was death. And as Adam had no power to liberate himself from the captivity thereof, his sleep in the grave must have been eternal; so also with all his posterity to whom his mortality was bequeathed as an evil legacy, had not Mercy put in her claims and prevented Justice from

---

*See The World's Sixteen Crucified Saviors (by Kersey Graves).

being cruel. The Son of God having it given to him to have life in himself,* and being capable of making an infinite atonement, he stood forth as the great friend of man and offered himself as a sacrifice to satisfy the claims of Justice. That offering was accepted by the great Law Giver, and upon the demands of Justice being satisfied,—the law having no further claim upon him,—the captive is set free from the dominion of death. Mercy is not permitted to rob Justice, but she claims her own. Justice is not permitted to be cruel, but he retains his dignity—his demands are satisfied. As the late President Taylor very beautifully says: "Is justice dishonored? No; it is satisfied; the debt is paid. Is righteousness departed from? No; there is a righteous act. All requirements are met. Is judgment violated? No; its demands are fulfilled. Is Mercy triumphant? No; she simply claims her own. Justice, judgment, mercy and truth all harmonize as the attributes of Deity. Justice and truth have met together, righteousness and peace have kissed each other, justice and judgment triumph as well as mercy and peace; all the attributes of Deity harmonize in this great, grand, momentous, just, equitable, merciful and meritorious act."†

10. **The Sacrifice of Messiah Voluntary:**—Unbelievers delight to represent God, the great Law Giver, as unspeakably cruel in demanding such an atonement as Christ made for the salvation of the children of men. But let it be borne in mind that he who made the atonement did so voluntarily. Testifying to his disciples respecting the matter, he says: "Therefore doth my Father love me, because I lay down my life that I may take it up again. No man

---

*John v: 26.
†Mediation and Atonement, **xxiv.**

taketh it from me, but I lay it down of myself. I have power to lay it down, and I have power to take it again. This commandment have I received of my Father."* When his enemies gathered about him—a former friend betraying him with a kiss—and Peter prepared to defend him with the sword, he chided him for his rashness, commanding him to put up his sword, and added: "Thinkest thou that I cannot now pray to my Father, and he shall presently give me more than twelve legions of angels? But how then shall the scriptures be fulfilled, that thus it must be?"† Thus down to the very last moment, it appears that Jesus could have been delivered from the sacrifice had he so willed it. But the principle which was the guiding star of his life—"Father, not my will, but thy will be done"—influenced him in this instance, and he drank of the cup given him of his Father, and wrung out the dregs in agony; but he did it voluntarily, and that, too, out of his great love for mankind.

11. **The Love of God Made Manifest in the Atonement:**—By this atonement of Messiah's there is especially one fact thrown out in bold relief, that is, the great love of God and Christ for mankind. When one thinks of the unspeakable agony, of the anguish of heart, of the pains that racked the body and distressed the mind of the Savior in Gethsemane the scene of his blood-sweat, at the time of his betrayal, and during his trial and crucifixion, he may see how great the love of the Father for mankind must be, when he would consent for his only begotten Son to pass through this great humiliation and affliction, in order to redeem mankind from the bonds of death. On such contemplation, increased emphasis will be given to the passage—"In this

---

*John x:17, 18.
†Matt. xxvi: 53, 54.

was manifested the love of God towards us, because that God sent his only begotten Son into the world that we might live through him."* And also to this—"For God so loved the world, that he gave his only begotten Son, that whosoever believeth in him should not perish, but have everlasting life. For God sent not his Son into the world to condemn the world, but that the world through him might be saved."† Equally great appears the love of the Son of God, who of his own free will volunteered to take upon himself the task of man's redemption. Vicarious suffering may appear to have some element of injustice in it, but in no other way can love be so perfectly manifested.

12. **Individual Salvation:**—As before stated, Messiah came not only to redeem man from the consequences of the fall, but to save him also from the consequences of his own personal sins. The redemption from the fall is universal and unconditional, because the penalties following it were entailed upon the race through no action of theirs, but through the transgressions of Adam. The redemption from the consequences of man's personal sins, however, is bottomed upon conditions, because his agency is more completely a factor in the violations of the law. He sins knowingly, willfully, and sometimes wantonly. He transgresses the laws of God and of nature in spite of the protests of his conscience, the convictions of his reason, and the promptings of his judgment. He becomes desperately wicked and so depraved that in some cases he actually seeks evil and loves it. He hugs it to his bosom and cries: Evil, be thou my good; sin, be thou my refuge!

13. In cases of such violation of the laws of God, Justice

---

*I John iv: 9.
†John iii: 16, 17.

demands that the outraged laws should be vindicated by the punishment of the transgressor. But here again the principle of Mercy is active. By the sacrifice which he made, Messiah purchased mankind as an inheritance for himself, and they came of right under his dominion; for he not only ransomed them from an endless sleep in the grave, but "He hath borne our griefs and carried our sorrows. * * * He was wounded for our transgressions, he was bruised for our iniquities, the chastisement of our peace was upon him; and by his stripes we are healed. The Lord hath laid on him the iniquity of us all."* (See note 4, end of section.) It was these considerations, doubtless, which led the Apostle to say to the saints—"Ye are not your own; for ye are bought with a price."†

Still more plain in relation to the effect that Messiah's Atonement has upon the personal sins of men, is the word of the Lord through the Prophet Joseph Smith to Martin Harris, warning him to repent lest his sufferings be sore—how sore, how exquisite, how hard to bear, he knew not: "For behold, I God, have suffered these things for all, that they might not suffer if they would repent; but if they would not repent, they must suffer even as I, which suffering caused myself, even God, the greatest of all, to tremble because of pain, and to bleed at every pore, and to suffer both body and spirit; and would that I might not drink the bitter cup, and shrink—nevertheless, glory be to the Father, I partook and finished my preparations unto the children of men."‡

14. **Conditions of Salvation:**—Messiah having thus ransomed mankind by his own suffering and death, he

---

*Isaiah liii: 5, 6.

†I Cor. vi: 19, 20.

‡Doc. and Cov., Sec. xix, 16-18. See also Mosiah iii: 20, 21. *The Gospel*, Roberts, page 25.

becomes the law-giver to our race and of right prescribes the conditions upon which the full benefits of his great atonement shall be applied to individuals. Those conditions he has prescribed, and they constitute the Gospel. It was these conditions which he authorized his Apostles to proclaim to the world, saying: "All power is given unto me in heaven and in earth. Go ye therefore, and teach all nations, baptizing them in the name of the Father, and of the Son, and of the Holy Ghost; teaching them to observe *all things* whatsoever I have commanded you."*

15. Following the Apostles in their fulfillment of this commission, we have them persuading people to believe on the Lord Jesus Christ as the Savior of the world, as the only one to whom they may look for salvation†—the resurrection and the life. Men in whose minds this faith was created they commanded to repent and be baptized in the name of Jesus Christ for the remission of sins; and promised them on the condition of their obedience the gift of the Holy Ghost.‡ By repentance they meant a deep and heart-felt sorrow for sin, accompanied by a reformation of life;§ by baptism they meant immersion in water in the likeness of Christ's burial and resurrection;‖ and the Holy Ghost was imparted by the laying on of hands and prayer.¶

16. These things connected with a Godly walk and conversation—after obeying them**—constitute the laws of

---

*Matt. xxviii: 18-20.
†Acts iv: 12.
‡Acts ii: 22-47. Acts viii: 5-25.
§II Cor. vii: 8-10.
‖Rom. vi: 3-5.
¶Acts viii: 14-18.
**The injunction placed upon those who accept the faith of the gospel is that they add to their faith virtue; and to virtue, knowledge; and to knowledge, temperance; and to temperance, patience; and to patience godliness; and to godliness, brotherly kindness; and to brotherly kind

adoption into the Church of Christ. These are the conditions on which man receives the full benefit of the atonement of Jesus Christ—a forgiveness of sins and power through the Holy Ghost to overcome all evil propensities within himself, until he becomes pure in heart and every way made ready and worthy for the kingdom of heaven. This is the gospel of Jesus Christ, as taught by Jesus and his apostles.   (See note 6, end of section.)

17. **The Church:**—In order to propagate the gospel, and teach, encourage, instruct, preserve and finally perfect those who accepted it, Messiah organized his Church. He bestowed upon its members certain great and precious spiritual gifts and graces, such as the power to speak in new tongues and interpret them; to receive revelation, to prophesy, to see visions, receive the visitation of angels, to possess the gift of wisdom, knowledge, faith, discernment of spirits, and healing the sick.*

18. The description of the Church organization in the New Testament is extremely imperfect, owing, no doubt, to the fragmentary character of the Christian annals.

The distinctions between the respective offices in the Priesthood, and the definition of the duties of each officer are even less satisfactory; still there is enough written to enable us to get an outline of the organization.

19. Messiah, during his personal ministry, organized a quorum of Twelve Apostles, to whom he gave very great powers and authority; they were to be special witnesses of him among the people; to build up his Church by the proclamation of the gospel, to heal the sick, open the eyes of the

---

ness, charity. For if these things be in you, and abound, they make you that ye shall neither be barren nor unfruitful in the knowledge of our Lord Jesus Christ.   (II Peter 1: 5-8.)—*The Gospel,* Roberts, page 37.

*Mark xvi. I Cor. xii.

blind, raise the dead, and cast out devils.* He likewise
organized quorums of seventy, unto whom he gave similar
powers to those bestowed upon the apostles.†

20. After his resurrection Messiah was with his apostles
and disciples forty days, during which time he was teaching
them all things concerning the kingdom of God.‡ Hence
we have these men, after Messiah's ascension, organizing
branches of the church wherever they found people who
received their testimony. In some instances they ordained
elders to preside over these branches;§ and in other instances
bishops were appointed.||

21. Paul in giving a description of the organization of
the church says: "And God hath set some in the church,
first apostles, secondarily prophets, thirdly teachers, after
that miracles, then gifts of healing, helps, governments,
diversities of tongues. Are all apostles? Are all prophets?
Are all teachers? Are all workers of miracles? Have all the
gifts of healing? Do all speak with tongues? Do all interpret?"¶ The implied answer is that all are not apostles, nor prophets, nor teachers, etc., in the church of Christ,
but that the whole body, is fitly joined together and com-
pacted by that which every part and every joint supplieth.**

22. Paul also, compares the church of Christ to the body
of a man, which, though it be composed of many members,
yet it is but one body, and all the members thereof are
needful to it. "The eye cannot say unto the hand, I have no
need of thee; nor again the head to the feet, I have no need

---

*Matt. x ; Acts i: 4-8.
†Compare Luke x with Matt. x.
‡Acts i: 3.
§Acts xiv: 23. Acts xx: 17, 28.
||Phil. i: 1 ; Titus i: 5-7.
¶I Cor. xii: 28-30.
**Eph. iv: 16.

of thee. Nay, much more, those members of the body which seem to be more feeble are necessary." This is equivalent to saying that the apostle cannot say to the elder, I have no need of thee; nor the deacon to the bishop, I have no need of thee; nor the seventy to the priest, I have no need of thee. The argument is that all the offices, even those which seem the least necessary, are all needful to the existence of the church of Christ, and everyone is forbidden to hold as unnecessary his brother officer.

23.   Moreover, Paul insists that there should be the same bond of sympathy between the members of the church of Christ that there is in the members of the human body; that there should be no schism in it, and that the members should have a care one for another; that when one member suffers all the members suffer with it; or if one member be honored all rejoice with it.*

24.   In another description of the church the same writer, after saying again that God had given to men "some apostles, and some prophets, and some evangelists, and some pastors and teachers"—also enumerates the objects for which this peculiar organization was given:—1. For the perfecting of the Saints. 2. The work of the ministry. 3. Edifying the body of Christ. 4. To prevent the Saints being carried about by every wind of doctrine, by the sleight of men, and cunning craftiness whereby they lie in wait to deceive.

25.   He very plainly intimates, too, that this organization was designed to be perpetuated until the saints all come to the "unity of the faith and the knowledge of the Son of God—unto a perfect man, unto the measure of the stature of the fullness of Christ."† We suggest that it must be ob-

---

*I Cor. xii.
†Eph. iv.

vious, since the church organization was given to perfect the saints, to work the ministry, to edify the body of Christ, to prevent the saints being carried about by every wind of doctrine, or deceived by cunning men—that so long as there are saints who need perfecting, so long as there is a necessity for work in the ministry, so long as the church of Christ needs edifying, or the saints need to be guarded from heresy, or the deceitfulness of false teachers—just so long will this organization of the Church with apostles and prophets, seventies, and elders, bishops and teachers and deacons be needed; and since the kinds of work enumerated in the foregoing will always be necessary, we reach the conclusion that the Church organization as established by the Apostles was designed to be perpetual.   (See note 5, end of section.)

26.   Officers of the Church to be Divinely Appointed: —Moreover it is apparent that these officers of the church were called of God.   Concerning the apostles Jesus said: "Ye have not chosen me, but I have chosen you, and ordained you, that ye may bring forth fruit."* When seven men were chosen to look after the poor and minister to them they set them before the apostles, who, when they had prayed, laid their hands upon them and ordained them to their calling.†

27. So in the case of Paul.   It was not enough that he saw and spoke with Messiah, for afterwards when the Lord would have him engage in the work of preaching the gospel and administering in the ordinances thereof, the Holy Ghost said unto certain prophets at Antioch: "Separate me Barnabas and Saul for the work whereunto I have called them.   And when they had fasted and prayed, and laid their hands on them, they sent them away."‡

---

*John xv: 16.
†Acts vi: 1-6.
‡Acts xiii: 1-3.

28. Furthermore, as Paul went about confirming the souls of saints, he *ordained* elders in every church.* He did not suffer men to take the authority on themselves to minister in the things of God; but warned the saints against such characters. "Take heed unto yourselves," said he to the elders of Ephesus, "and to all the flock over which the Holy Ghost hath made you overseers, to feed the flock of God * * * For I know this, that after my departing, shall grievous wolves enter in, not sparing the flock. And of your own selves shall men arise, speaking perverse things, to draw away disciples after them."†

29. The general law of the church is expressed in the following:—"Every high priest taken from among men is ordained for men in things pertaining to God that he may offer both gifts and sacrifices for sins. * * * And no man taketh this honor unto himself, but he that is called of God as was Aaron."‡ The manner in which Aaron was called to the priest's office is recorded in the writings of Moses as follows: The word of the Lord came to that prophet saying: "Take thou unto thee Aaron thy brother, and his sons with him, from among the children of Israel, that he may minister unto me in the priest's office, even Aaron, Nadab and Abihu, Eleazer and Ithamar, Aaron's sons."§

30. It may be objected that this was the law relating to the calling of high priests alone, but if high priests were to be called in this manner, is it not reasonable to conclude that all who administer in things "pertaining to God" must be called in the same manner—that is, of God? So

---

*Acts xiv: 2, 3.
†Acts xx: 28, 29.
‡Heb. v: 1, 5.
§Ex. xxviii: 1.

far as the scriptures are concerned, and on subjects of this character their authority is conclusive, wherever we have an account of men administering in the things pertaining to God, and their administrations are accepted of him, they have either been called directly by revelation from him, or through inspiration in those who already had authority from God to act in his name; and to be called by a legitimate, divinely established authority is to be called of God. (See note 6, end of section.)

31. The Church on the Western Hemisphere:—The Book of Mormon is no more explicit in its description of the church organization than the New Testament. This is owing to the fact that the Book of Mormon is but an abridgement of the Nephite annals, and we are informed by Mormon, who made the abridgement, that not an hundredth part of the things which Jesus taught to the Nephites could be recorded in his abridged record—hence the meagre description of the church organization.* From Mormon's abridged account of Messiah's visit and labors among the Nephites, however, it appears that Jesus chose from among the faithful men who believed on him, twelve "disciples",† unto whom he gave power to preach repentance, baptize for remission of sins,‡ lay on hands for the Holy Ghost,§ and organize the Church.‖ But the details of this work are not given. It is evident, however, that the twelve disciples ordained subordinate officers, since Moroni informs us of the manner in which they ordained priests and teachers;¶ and he also refers to the office of elders.**

---

*III Nephi xxvi. 6, 7.
†III Nephi xii.
‡III Nephi xi.
§III Nephi xviii: 37; also Moroni ii.
‖III Nephi xxvii and IV Nephi i: 1.
¶Moroni iii.
**Moroni vi.

32. Thus in the Book of Mormon, as in the New Testament, may be seen only the faint outlines of the organization of the church of Christ. A full description of it, together with the callings and authority of the respective officers and members of which it is composed, will be reserved for Part IV of this work.

33. The acceptance of the gospel by the Nephites was followed by the same results as when accepted by the Jews and Gentiles of the eastern hemisphere. The sick were healed, the dead were raised, the lame walked, the deaf heard, and the blind received their sight. Peace, love, sobriety, justice and an absence of greed and pride characterized the conduct of the saints of the western hemisphere; and here, too, they had "all things common among them, therefore they were not rich and poor, bond and free, but they were all made free, and partakers of the heavenly gifts."*

NOTES.

1. **The Redemption Unconditional:**—We believe that through the sufferings, death and atonement of Jesus Christ, all mankind without one exception, are to be completely and fully redeemed, both body and spirit, from the endless banishment and curse to which they were consigned by Adam's transgression; and that this universal salvation and redemption of the whole human family from the endless penalty of the original sin, is effected without any conditions whatsoever on their part; that is, that they are not required to believe or repent, or be baptized, or do anything else, in order to be redeemed from that penalty; for whether they believe or disbelieve, whether they repent or remain impenitent, whether they are baptized or unbaptized, whether they keep the commandments or break them, whether they are righteous or unrighteous, it will make no difference in relation to their redemption, both soul and body, from the penalty of Adam's transgression. * * * —*Remarkable Visions—Orson Pratt.*

2. **The Atonement Universal in its Application:**—Transgression of the law brought death upon all the posterity of Adam, the restoration through the atonement restored all the human family to

---

*IV Nephi 1: 1-7.

life. "For since by man came death, by man came also the resurrection of the dead. For as in Adam all die, even so in Christ shall all be made alive." So that whatever was lost by Adam was restored by Jesus Christ. The penalty of the transgression of the law was the death of the body. The atonement made by Jesus Christ resulted in the resurrection of the human body. Its scope embraced all peoples, nations and tongues.

> "For all my Lord was crucified,
> For all, for all my Savior died."
> *Mediation and Atonement—John Taylor.*

3. The Atonement a Mystery:—As stated elsewhere, in some mysterious, incomprehensible way, Jesus assumed the responsibility which naturally would have devolved upon Adam; but which could only be accomplished through the mediation of himself, and by taking upon himself their sorrows, assuming their responsibilities and bearing their transgressions or sins. In a manner incomprehensible and inexplicable, he bore the weight of the sins of the whole world; not only of Adam, but of his posterity; and in doing that, opened the kingdom of heaven, not only to all believers and all who obeyed the law of God, but to more than one-half of the human family who died before they came to years of maturity, as well as to the heathen, who having died without law, will through his mediation be resurrected without law, and be judged without law, and thus participate according to their capacity, works and worth, in the blessings of his atonement.—*Mediation and Atonement—John Taylor.*

4. The Means of Escape from Penalties of Personal Sins:— After this full, complete and universal redemption, restoration, and salvation of the whole of Adam's race through the atonement of Jesus Christ, * * * all and every one of them will enjoy eternal life and happiness, never more to be banished from the presence of God *if they themselves have committed no sin.* * * * We believe that all mankind, in consequence of the fall, after they grow up from their infant state and come to the years of understanding, know good and evil and are capable of obeying or disobeying law, and that a law is given against doing evil, and that the penalty affixed is a second banishment from the presence of God, both body and spirit, *after* they have been redeemed from the first banishment and restored into his presence. * * * We believe that all who have done evil, having a knowledge of the law, or afterwards in this life coming to the knowledge thereof, are under its penalty, which is not inflicted in this world but in the world to come. * * * "But," inquires the sinner, "is there no way of escape? Is my case hopeless?" * * * The answer is, if thou canst hide thyself from the all-searching eye of an omnipresent God, that he shall not find thee, or if thou canst prevail with him to deny justice its claim, or if thou canst clothe thyself with power, and contend with the Almighty and prevent him from executing the sentence of the law, then thou canst escape. * * * But be assured, O sinner, that thou canst not devise any way of thine own to escape, nor do anything which will *atone* for thy sins.   Therefore thy case is hopeless, unless God hath devised some way for thy deliverance; but do not let despair seize upon thee;   *   *   *   for he who gave the law has devised a way for thy deliverance.   That same Jesus, who hath atoned for the original sin (Adam's transgression), and will redeem all mankind from the penalty thereof, hath also atoned for thy sins, and offereth salvation and deliverance to thee, on certain conditions to be complied with on thy part.   *   *   *   The first condition to be complied with on the part of sinners is to believe in God, and in the sufferings and death of his Son Jesus Christ   *   *   *   and in the Holy Ghost.   *   *   *   That the second condition is to repent.   *   *   *   That the third condition is to be baptized for the remission of sins.   *   *   *   And that the fourth condition is to receive the laying on of hands for the gift of the Holy Ghost.   *   *   *   They are then required to be humble, to be meek and lowly in heart, to watch and pray and deal justly.   *   *   * And, in short, to continue faithful to the end in all the duties enjoined upon them by the word and Spirit of Christ.—*Remarkable Visions— Orson Pratt.*

5.   Four Opinions on Church Government:—How far even wise men and Christian scholars have gone astray in relation to church government may be judged from the following opinions on the subject:

Those who imagine that Christ himself or the apostles by his direction or authority appointed a certain fixed form of church government are not agreed what that form was.   The principal opinions that have been adopted upon this head may be reduced to the following four:

First, The Roman Catholics maintain that Christ's intention and appointment was that his followers should be collected into one sacred empire subject to the government of St. Peter and his successors, and divided like the kingdoms of this world into several provinces; that in consequence thereof Peter fixed the seat of ecclesiastical dominion at Rome, but afterwards to alleviate the burden of his office divided the church into three greater provinces according to the division of the world at that time, and appointed a person to preside in each who was dignified with the title of Patriarch; that the European Patriarch resided at Rome, the Asiastic at Antioch, and the African at Alexandria; that the bishops of each province among whom there were various ranks, were to reverence the authority of their respective patriarchs, and that both bishops and patriarchs were to be passively subject to the supreme dominion of the Roman Pontiff.   This romantic account scarcely deserves a serious refutation.

The *second* opinion concerning the government of the church makes no mention of a supreme head or of patriarchs constituted by a divine authority; but it supposes that the apostles divided the Roman empire into as many ecclesiastical provinces as there were secular or civil ones; that the metropolitan bishops, that is, the prelate who resides in the capital city of each province, presides over the clergy of that province, and that the other bishops were subject to his authority.   This opinion has been adopted by some of the most learned of the Romish church, and has also been favored by some of the most eminent British divines.

Some Protestant writers of note have endeavored to prove that it is not supported by sufficient evidence.

The *third* opinion is that of those who acknowledge that when the Christians began to multiply exceedingly, metropolitans, patriarchs and archbishops were indeed created but only by human appointment and authority; though they confess at the same time that it is consonant to the orders and intentions of Christ and his apostles that there should be in every Christian church one person invested with the highest authority and clothed with certain rights and privileges above the other doctors of that assembly. This opinion has been embraced by many English divines of the first rank in the learned world; and also by many in other countries and communions.

The *fourth*, and last opinion is that of the Presbyterians who affirm that Christ's intention was that the Christian doctors and ministers should all enjoy the same rank and authority without any sort of pre-eminence or subordination or distinction of rights and privileges.—Mosheim vol. I, pages 67, 68. Note—Murdock.

"The truth of the matter is," remarks **Dr.** Maclaine, "that Christ by leaving this matter undetermined, has of consequence, left Christian societies a discretionary power of modeling the government of the church in such a manner as the circumstantial reasons of times, places, etc., may require; and therefore the *wisest* government of the church is the *best* and the *most divine*; and every Christian society has a *right* to make laws for itself; provided that these laws are consistent with charity and peace and with the fundamental doctrines and principles of Christianity."

Of this it is only necessary to say that Christ did not leave this matter undetermined but established his church government as explained in the text of this work. The *wisest* form of church government is that which God gave; it is at the same time, the *best* and not only the *most divine* but the *only* one that can lay any claim to being so; and for the church or any branch thereof to establish any other government for itself is an unjustifiable departure from the order of God.—*Roberts*.

6. Authority from God Needful:—We are informed in the scriptures, that the Lord wrought special miracles by the hands of Paul, whom he had called to be his servant. The sick were healed, and evil spirits were cast out of those who were possessed. "Then certain of the vagabond Jews, exorcists, took upon them to call over them which had evil spirits, the name of the Lord Jesus, saying: We adjure you, by Jesus whom Paul preacheth. And there were seven sons, of one Sceva, a Jew, and chief of the priests, which did so. And the evil spirit answered and said, Jesus I know, and Paul I know, but who are ye? And the man in whom the evil spirit was, leaped on them, and overcame them, and prevailed against them, so that they fled out of the house, naked and wounded." (Acts xix; 13-16.) These men presumptuously took it upon themselves to act as those who had authority, and the result was that not even the devils would respect their administrations, much less the Lord. There is a principle of great moment associated with this incident. The question is, if these men, when acting without authority from God could not drive out an evil spirit, would their administration be of force, or have any virtue in it, had they administered in some other ordinance of the gospel, say baptism for the remission of sins, or the laying on of hands for the reception of the Holy Ghost? Manifestly it would not. Hence we come to the conclusion, so well expressed in one of our (L. D. S. 5) articles of faith—"A man must be called of God by prophecy and by the laying on of hands by those who are in authority to preach the gospel and administer in the ordinances thereof."—*The Gospel—Roberts.*

REVIEW.

1. What two great purposes were contemplated in Messiah's mission?

2. Relate the fall of man and its consequences.

3. What is general salvation?

4. How do you prove that there will be a general salvation?

5. Why is redemption from Adam's transgression unconditional? (Notes 1 to 4.)

6. How are the claims of justice and mercy balanced in the atonement?

7. Was Messiah's atonement voluntary?

8. What can you say of the love of God as it appears in the atonement?

9. What is meant by individual salvation?

10. In what does it differ from general salvation?

11. By what consideration does mercy mitigate the claims of justice in the plan of redemption?

12. What are the conditions of salvation?   (Note 6.)

13. For what several purposes did Messiah institute his church?

14. Why is it that the description of the Church of Christ is so imperfect in the New Testament?

15. Enumerate the powers granted to the Twelve.

16. What other officers did Jesus call to the ministry upon whom he bestowed similar powers?

17. What other officers were appointed in the church?

18. Give Paul's description of the church.

19. State the particular objects to be accomplished by the church organization.

20. What reasons can you give for believing that the church as organized by Messiah is to be perpetuated?

21. What are the four leading opinions in respect to church government?   (Note 5.)

22. What is the truth in respect of church government?   (Note 5.)

23. Is the Book of Mormon description of church organization more complete than that of the New Testament?   Why?

24. Give an account of the organization of the church on the western hemisphere.

25. What followed the preaching of the gospel and the organization of the church on the western hemisphere?

PART II.

THE APOSTASY.

SECTION I.

In Part I our narrative was confined mainly to those propitious circumstances which made for the successful introduction of the gospel and the founding of the church of Christ. In Part II we are to deal with those adverse events which led finally to the subversion of the Christian religion. We commence with the

1. Persecution of the Christians by the Jews:— The Messiah forewarned his disciples that they would be persecuted by the world, pointed out the reasons for it, and comforted them by reminding them that the world had hated him before it hated them; that the servant was not greater than his lord; and for that matter all the prophets which were before them had been persecuted by the generations in which they lived, and that, for the reason that they were not of the world, therefore the world hated and destroyed them.*

2. Two special reasons may be assigned for the persecution of the saints by the Jews. 1. They looked upon Christianity as a rival religion to Judaism, a thing of itself sufficient to engender bitterness, jealousy, persecution. 2. If Christianity should live and obtain a respectable standing, the Jews of that generation must ever be looked upon as not only putting an innocent man to death, but as rejecting and slaying the Son of God. To crush this rival religion and escape the odium which the successful establishment of it would inevitably fix upon them, were the incentives which

---

*These statements are sustained in the following scriptures. Matt. x:16-40. Luke vi:22-26. John xv:18-22.

prompted that first general persecution which arose against the church in Jerusalem, and that commenced in the very first year after Messiah's ascension.

3.   The extent of the persecution or the time of its continuance may not be determined; but that it was murderous may be learned from the fact that Stephen was slain,* as was also James, the son of Zebedee,† and James, the Just, brother of the Lord.‡   The Apostle Peter was imprisoned and would doubtless have shared in the fate of martyrdom but that he was delivered by an angel.§

4.   Nor was this persecution confined alone to Jerusalem; on the contrary, the hate-blinded high priests and elders of the Jews in Palestine conferred with the Jews throughout the Roman provinces, and everywhere incited them to hatred of the Christians, exhorting them to have no connection with, and to do all in their power to destroy the "superstition," as the Christian religion was then called.   Nor were they content with what they themselves could do, but they exhausted their ingenuity in efforts to incite the Romans against the Christians.   To accomplish this they charged that the Christians had treasonable designs against the Roman government, as "appeared by their acknowledging as their king one Jesus, a malefactor whom Pilate had most justly put to death."‖

5.   The Jews themselves, however, were in no great favor with the Romans since their impatience of Roman restraint led them to be constantly on the eve of rebellion and sedition, and frequently to break out into deeds of

---

*Acts vii: 55-60.
†Acts xii: 1, 2.
‡Eusebius Bk. II, ch. xxiii.
§Acts xii.
‖Mosheim Part I, ch. v.

violence against the Roman authority. This lack of favor rendered the power of the Jews unequal to their malice against the church of Christ.

6. The imperious nation, too, whose forefathers had rejected the prophets and at the last had crucified the Son of God, with every circumstance of cruelty, crying out in the streets of their holy city, "crucify him, and let his blood be upon us and on our children,"* were about to meet the calamities which their wickedness called down upon them. The Roman emperor Vespasian [Ves-pa-zhe-an], tired of their repeated seditions, at last sent an army under Titus to subjugate them. The Jews made a stubborn resistance and a terrible war followed. Jerusalem, crowded with people who had come into the city from the surrounding country to attend the Passover, was besieged for six months, during which time more than a million of her wretched inhabitants perished of famine. The city was finally taken, the walls thereof thrown down and the temple so completely destroyed "that not one stone was left upon another." Thousands of Jews were cut to pieces and nearly a hundred thousand of those taken captive were sent into slavery.† All the calamities predicted by the Messiah befell the city and people.‡ Jerusalem from that time until now has been trodden down of the Gentiles; and will be until the times of the Gentiles are fulfilled.

7. According to Eusebius, the Christians escaped these calamities which befell the Jews; for the whole body of the church at Jerusalem, having been commanded by divine revelation, given to men of approved piety, removed from Jerusalem before the war and dwelt at Pella, beyond Jordan,

---

*Matt. xxvii: 22-25.
†Josephus' Wars of the Jews, Bk. vi, ch. ix.
‡Luke xxi: 5-9, 20-24.

where they were secure from the calamities of those times.*

8. Persecution by the Romans:—It is more difficult to understand why the Romans should persecute the Christians than it is to see why the Jews did it. The Romans were polytheists, and affected the fullest religious liberty. The author of the *Decline and Fall of the Roman Empire* claims that this period of Roman history was the golden age of religious liberty. And such was the multitude of deities collected in Rome from various nations, and such the variety of worship to be seen in the great capital of the empire, that Gibbon has said: "Rome gradually became the common temple of her subjects; and the freedom of the city was bestowed on all the gods of mankind."† Furthermore, the same high authority says: "The various modes of worship which prevailed in the Roman world, were all considered by the people as being equally true; by the philosophers as all equally false; and by the magistrates as equally useful. And thus toleration produced not only mutual indulgences, but even religious concord."‡

9. The student who would learn why the mild and beautiful Christian religion was alone selected to bear the wrath and feel the vengeful power of Rome, must look deeper than the reasons usually assigned for the strange circumstance. It is superficial to say that the persecution was caused by the charges of immorality. The Roman authorities had the best of evidence that the charges were false. (See note 1, end of section.) Equally absurd is it to assign as a cause the supposed atheism of the Chris-

---

*Eusebius Bk. III, ch. v. The Saints were also warned to flee from Jerusalem by Messiah himself when they should see armies begin to encompass it.—See Luke xxi: 20-24.

†Decline and Fall Vol. I, ch. 1.

‡Ibid.

tians, for that was the condition of nearly all Rome; while the charge that they were traitors to the emperor, and expected to see the empire supplanted by the kingdom of Christ—which some assign as the chief cause of Roman persecution—was treated with contempt by the emperors. (See note 2, end of section.)

10. The true cause of the persecution was this: Satan knew there was no power of salvation in the idolatrous worship of the heathen, and hence let them live on in peace, but when Jesus of Nazareth and his followers came, in the authority of God, preaching the gospel, he recognized in that the principles and power against which he had rebelled in heaven, and stirred up the hearts of men to rebellion against the truth to overthrow it. This was the real cause of persecution, though it lurked under a variety of pretexts, the most of which are named in the above supposed causes.

11. The First Roman Persecution:—The first emperor to enact laws for the extermination of Christians was Nero. (See note 3, end of section.) His decrees against them originated rather in an effort to shield himself from popular fury than any desire that he had to protect the religion of the state against the advancement of Christianity. Nero, wishing to witness a great conflagration, had set fire to the city of Rome. The flames utterly consumed three of the fourteen wards into which the city was divided, and spread ruin in seven others. It was in vain that the emperor tried to soothe the indignant and miserable citizens whose all had been consumed by the flames, and neither the magnificence of the prince, nor his attempted expiation of the gods could remove from him the infamy of having ordered the conflagration.

12. "Therefore," writes Tacitus, one of the most trustworthy of all historians, "to stop the clamor, Nero falsely

accused and subjugated to the most exquisite punishments a people hated for their crimes, called Christians. The founder of the sect, Christ, was executed in the reign of Tiberius, by the Procurator Pontius Pilate. The pernicious superstition, repressed for a time, burst forth again; not only through Judea, the birth-place of the evil, but at Rome also, where everything atrocious and base centers and is in repute. Those first seized, confessed; then a vast multitude, detected by their means, were convicted, not so much of the crime of burning the city as of hatred of mankind. And insult was added to their torments; for being clad in skins of wild beasts they were torn to pieces by dogs; or affixed to crosses to be burned, were used as lights to dispel the darkness of night, when the day was gone. Nero devoted his garden to the show, and held circensian [sir-sen-shan] games, mixing with the rabble, or mounting a chariot, clad like a coachman. Hence, though the guilty and those meriting the severest punishment, suffered, yet compassion was excited, because they were destroyed, not for the public good, but to satisfy the cruelty of an individual."*

13. **Time of the Persecution:**—The time of this persecution is fixed by the date of the great conflagration, which Tacitus set down as commencing on the 18th of July, A. D. 65. It lasted six days; and soon after that the persecution broke out.

14. **Continuance and Extent of the Persecution:**— How long this persecution lasted, and whether it was confined to the city of Rome or extended throughout the empire is difficult to determine. From some remarks made by Tertullian [Ter-tul-li-an], writing in the next century,

---

*Annals lib. xv, ch. 44.

it would seem that the decrees of Nero against the Christians of Rome were general laws, such as those afterwards passed by Domitian. But the inferences of his language are generally discredited or accounted the result of Tertullian's fervid rhetoric; and Gibbon's conclusion that the persecution was confined within the walls of Rome generally accepted.* It was in this persecution, according to the tradition of the early Christian fathers, that Peter and Paul suffered martyrdom.

15. **The Second Persecution:**—The second persecution against the Christian church broke out in the year A. D. 93 or 94, under the reign of Domitian. It was during this persecution that the Apostle John was banished to Patmos. Eusebius states that at the same time, for professing Christ, Flavi Domitilla, the niece of Flavius Clemens, one of the consuls of Rome at the time, "was transported with many others, by way of punishment, to the island of Pontia." The pretext for this persecution is ascribed to the fears of Domitian that he would lose his empire. A rumor reached him that a person would arise from the relatives of Messiah who would attempt a revolution; whereupon the jealous nature of the emperor prompted him to begin this persecution. In it both Jews and Christians suffered, the emperor ordering that the descendants of David, especially, should be put to death. An investigation of the prospects of a revolution arising from such a quarter caused Domitian to dismiss the matter with contempt and order the persecution to cease.† (See note 2, end of section.)

---

*Decline and Fall I, ch. xvi. See also Guizot's note on same page.

†This is according to the testimony of Eusebius, quoting Hagesippus and Tertullian. (Eusebius Book III, ch. xx.) But other authorities claim that Domitian's edicts against the Christians were not revoked until after his death.

NOTES.

1. Pliny's Testimony to the Morality of the Christians:—
The character which this writer gives of the Christians of that age
(his celebrated letter was written to Trajan early in the second century), and which was drawn from a pretty accurate inquiry, because
he considered their moral principles as the point in which the magistrate was interested, is as follows:—He tells the emperor that some of
those who had relinquished the society, or who, to save themselves
pretended that they had relinquished it, affirmed "that they were wont
to meet together on a stated day, before it was light, and sang among
themselves alternately a hymn to Christ as a God; and to bind themselves by an oath, not to the commission of any wickedness, but that
they would not be guilty of theft, or robbery, or adultery; that they
would never falsify their word, or deny a pledge committed to them
when called upon to return it." This proves that a morality more
pure and strict than was ordinary, prevailed at that time in Christian
societies.—*Paley's Evidences.*

2. Interview of Domitian and the Relatives of the Lord:—
There were yet living of the family of our Lord the grandchildren of
Judas, called the brother of our Lord according to the flesh. These
were reported as being of the family of David, and were brought to
Domitian by the Evocaties. For this emperor was as much alarmed
at the appearance of Christ as Herod. He put the question whether
they were of David's race and they confessed that they were. He
then asked them what property they had, or how much money they
owned. And both of them answered that they had between them
only nine thousand denarii, and this they had not in silver, but in the
value of a piece of land, containing only thirty-nine acres; from which
they raised their taxes and supported themselves by their own labor.
Then they also began to show their hands, exhibiting the hardness of
their bodies, and the callosity formed by incessant labor on their lands,
as evidence of their own labor. When asked also, respecting Christ
and his kingdom, what was its nature, and when and where it was to
appear, they replied that it was not a temporal nor an earthly kingdom,
but celestial and angelic; that it would appear at the end of the world,
when coming in glory he would judge the quick and the dead, and give
to every one according to his works. Upon which Domitian despising
them, made no reply; but treating them with contempt, as simpletons,
commanded them to be dismissed, and by a decree ordered the persecution to cease.— *Hegesippus, quoted by Eusebius.*

3. Character of Nero:—Nero was the incarnation of depravity—
the very name by which men are accustomed to express the fury of
unrestrained malignity. Bad as he was, he was not worse than Rome.
She had but her due. Nay, when he died the rabble and the slaves
crowned his statue with garlands and scattered flowers over his grave.
And why not? Nero never injured the rabble, never oppressed the
slave. He murdered his mother, his brother, his wife, and was the
tyrant of the wealthy, the terror of the successful. He rendered poverty
sweet, for poverty alone was secure; he rendered slavery tolerable, for

slaves alone or slavish men were promoted to power. The reign of
Nero was the golden reign of the populace, and the holiday of the
bondman.—*Bancroft.*

REVIEW.

1. Of what did Messiah warn his followers?
2. What reason may be assigned for the hatred of the world towards the people of God?
3. What special reason can you assign for the persecution of the Christians by the Jews?
4. What can you say of the bitterness and extent of the first great persecution?
5. What circumstance rendered the Jewish power to injure the Christians unequal to their malice?
6. Describe the great conflict between the Jews and the Romans.
7. By what means did the Christians living at Jerusalem escape the calamities of those times?
8. What makes it difficult to understand why the Romans persecuted the Christians?
9. What can you say of the charges of immorality as justifying Roman persecution?   (Note 1.)
10. What of the charge of treason?   (Note 2.)
11. What was the true cause of the persecution?
12. Who was the first emperor to enact laws against the Christians?
13. What was the character of Nero?   (Note 3.)
14. What was the incentive which prompted Nero to persecute the Christians?
15. What was the duration and extent of the first Roman persecution?
16. Under whose reign did the second Roman persecution begin?
17. On what was the persecution based?

SECTION II.

1. Condition of the Church in the Second Century:—During the second century the church had many seasons of immunity from persecution. The Roman emperors for the most part were of a mild and equitable character, and at the beginning of the century there were no laws against the Christians, as those enacted both by Nero and Domitian had been repealed. The first by the senate, the second by his successor, Nerva.* Still it must not be supposed that the saints were free from persecution. Their troubles arose, however, rather from the tumults of the rabble at the instigation of the pagan priests than from any desire of the emperors to oppress them.

2. As the Christians had no temples, no altars, no clouds of incense, no smoking victims—in short, as they had none of the pomp and circumstance in their simple religion which attended pagan worship, they were open to the charge of atheism by the great body of the people of the Roman empire; and, in their judgment, deserved the severest tortures and death. "If the empire had been afflicted by any recent calamity," remarks Gibbon, "by a plague, a famine, or an unsuccessful war; if the Tiber had, or if the Nile had not, risen above its banks; if the earth had shaken, or if the temperate order of the seasons had been interrupted, the superstitious pagans were convinced that the crimes and impurities of the Christians, who were

---

*Mosheim's Eccl. Hist. I.   Second Cent., ch. 11.

spared by the excessive lenity of the government, had at
length, provoked the divine justice."* And however virtuous the emperors were, however mild or equitable in
character the governors of the provinces, it is certain they
did not hesitate to appease the rage of the people by sacrificing a few obnoxious victims.

3. **The Persecution Under Marcus Aurelius:**—The
strangest fact of all connected with the persecutions of
this century is that the saints suffered most under the most
virtuous of the emperors—Marcus Aurelius [Mar-cus Au-
re-li-us], who allowed the judges to put many of the saints
accused of crime to torture. Among those of note who
fell in this persecution were Polycarp, the bishop of Smyrna
(see note 1, end of section), and Justin Martyr, the philosopher. The persecution was most severe in Gaul (France),
the churches of Lyons and Vienne being well nigh utterly
destroyed. The unparalleled cruelties practiced upon the
saints in those cities are related at length by Eusebius† in
letters written by those who survived the persecution.
(See note 2, end of section.)

4. **Edicts of Severus:**—Early in the third century
a law was enacted by the Emperor, Severus [Se-ver-us,]
making it criminal for any reason to abandon the religion
of his fathers for that of the Christians or the Jews. The
object of the law was to stay the propagation of Christianity
which was spreading abroad on every hand; and while it
was not intended to increase the hardships of those already
Christians, it nevertheless encouraged the governors and
judges of some of the provinces—especially those of Egypt
and other parts of Africa and Asia—to sorely afflict the

---

*Decline and Fall, vol. I, ch. xvi.
†Eusebius Eccl. Hist. bk. v, ch. 1 and 11.

saints. Many of the poor were put to death—thousands
of them if we may credit Eusebius—and many of the rich
intimidated into paying large sums of money to the judges
to secure them from torture and death. Still this persecution was not long continued, nor was it general throughout
the empire, and after it subsided there was a long period of
peace—pity it is that we have to say that it was more hurtful
to the church than the periods of the cruelest persecution.

5. **Persecution Under Decius Trajan:**—In the middle
of this century, under the reign of Decius Trajan [De-ci-us
Tra-jan], the severest and most disastrous persecution of all
befell the Christians. The emperor must have been impelled both by his fear of the Christians and his attachment
to the ancient religion of the Romans to publish his terrible
edicts by which he hoped to destroy the Christian church.
The governors of the provinces were ordered, on pain of
forfeiting their own lives, either to exterminate all Christians utterly, or bring them back by pains and tortures to
the religion of their fathers. Even Gibbon, whose constant
effort is to belittle the sufferings of the early Christians, says
of this persecution: "The bishops of the most considerable
cities were removed by exile or death; the vigilance of the
magistrates prevented the clergy of Rome during sixteen
months from proceeding to a new election and it was the
opinion of the Christians that the emperor would more
patiently endure a competitor for the purple than a bishop
in the capital."*

6. For more than two years the persecution raged with
unmitigated fury; and great multitudes of Christians, in all
the Roman provinces, were butchered in the most inhuman
manner. "This persecution," writes Dr. Mosheim, "was

---

*Decline and Fall, vol. I; ch. xvi.

more cruel and terrific than any which preceded it; and immense numbers, dismayed, not so much by the fear of death as by the dread of the long continued tortures by which the magistrates endeavored to overcome the constancy of the Christians, professed to renounce Christ, and procured for themselves safety, either by sacrificing—i. e., offering incense before the idols—or by certificates purchased with money."* (See note 3, end of section.)

7. The immediate successors of Decius continued this persecution, which with a pestilential disease which prevailed in many of the Roman provinces greatly increased the hardships of the saints; but the latter part of the century passed away in peace.

8. **The Diocletian Persecution:**—In the commencement of the fourth century a peculiar state of affairs existed in the Roman empire. In 284 A. D., Diocletian [Di-o-kle-shan], a native of Dalmatia [Dal-ma-shi-a], whose parents were slaves, was proclaimed emperor. The year following, feeling that the extent of the empire was too vast to be managed by a single mind, he chose a colleague, one Maximian [Max-im-i-an], an unlettered soldier, with whom he shared the authority of emperor and the title of "Augustus." Soon afterwards they each chose a colleague with whom they shared their authority. These were Constantinus [Con-stan-ti-nus], Chlorus [Klo-rus] and Galerius, [Ga-le-ri-us]. On their ascension to this honor they each took the title of "Caesar," and so matters stood at the opening of the fourth century.

9. The church had peace at the opening of this century, and at first there were no indications that it would be broken. But early within that period Diocletian was persuaded to

*Mosheim's Eccl. Hist. vol. I, cent. iii, ch. ii.

undertake the suppression of the Christian religion. This he attempted by demanding that the Christians give up their sacred books; if they refused they were put to death. The constancy of all the Christians, no, not even that of all their bishops and clergy, was equal to this trial, and many voluntarily surrendered the sacred writings in their possession to save themselves from punishment and death.

10.   The royal palace at Nicomedia being twice set on fire, soon after the first edict of Diocletian was published, the crime was charged to the Christians, and led to the issuance of a second edict which caused many Christians to suffer the penalties inflicted on incendiaries—torture and death. Following this came rebellion against Roman authority in Nicomedia and Syria. This too was charged to the intrigue of Christians (see notes 4 and 5, end of section), and was made a pretext for throwing all bishops and ministers into prison. A third edict authorized the employment of torture to compel them to offer sacrifices to the gods of the heathen. It was hoped by Diocletian that if these leaders of the church could be forced into acts of apostasy the people would follow. A great multitude, therefore, of excellent men in all parts of Christendom—excepting Gaul— were put to death, and others condemned to labor in the mines.

11.   But Diocletian was disappointed in the effects of these assaults on the leaders of the church. The members thereof remained obdurate in their adherence to the Christian faith; whereupon he issued a fourth edict, directing the magistrates to compel all Christians to offer sacrifice to the gods and to use tortures for that purpose. As the governors yielded strict obedience to these orders, the Christian church was reduced to the last extremity."*

---

*Mosheim's Eccl. Hist. vol. I, cent. iv, ch. 1.

12. "With the exception of Gaul," says Schlegel, "streams of Christian blood flowed in the provinces of the Roman empire. Everywhere the Christian temples lay in ruins, and assemblies for worship were all suspended. The major part had forsaken the provinces and taken refuge among the barbarians. Such as were unable or unwilling to do this, kept themselves concealed, and were afraid for their lives if they appeared in public. The ministers of Christ were either slain, or mutilated and sent to the mines, or banished from the country. The avaricious magistrates had seized upon nearly all their church property and their private possessions. Many through dread of undergoing torture, had made away with their own lives and many apostatized from the faith; and what remained of the Christian community consisted of weak, poor, and timorous persons."* Truly it would appear from this that the beast unto whom was given power "to make war with the saints and overcome them"† had at last triumphed.

13. **End of Pagan Persecution:**—This, however, was to be the last great persecution of the Christians by the heathens. In 305 Diocletian, to the surprise of his own and all succeeding ages, resigned the empire and compelled his associate, Maximian, to do the same. This left the empire in the hands of the two Caesars, who became the emperors. Like their predecessors they chose colleagues; but Constantius Chlorus, dying at York, in Britain, his son, Constantine [Kon-stan-tin], afterwards called the Great, was proclaimed emperor by the army. The associate of his father, Galerius, and the two Caesars refused to ratify the election, and civil war ensued which lasted for eighteen

---

*Quoted by Murdock in Mosheim. See note—Mosheim Eccl. Hist. vol. I, p. 210.
†Revelation ch. xiii: 1-7.

years. Finally, however, Constantine prevailed over all his rivals and became sole emperor, A. D., 323. Being, like his father, favorably disposed towards Christianity, his accession to the throne brought universal peace to the church.

14. The Luminous Cross Seen by Constantine:— It was during the above-mentioned civil war, while marching against the forces of Maxentius [Max-en-ti-us], one of the rebellious Caesars, that Constantine and his army are said to have seen near midday, in the heavens, a luminous cross bearing this inscription in Greek: *"By This Conquer."* The same night Christ appeared to him in a dream accompanied with the same sign and instructed him to make a standard bearing the cross as a protection against his enemies. The circumstance is related at great length in the life of Constantine by Eusebius, on whose sole authority the story rests. It is regarded as suspicious that he makes no reference to the matter in Ecclesiastical History, written only twelve years after the event. (See note 7, end of section.) The story is altogether rejected by some writers as the cunning invention of interested priests seeking to make the cross an object of veneration; and even Christian writers of high standing—among them Mosheim—consider the story to be doubtful.

15. Constantine and his Friendliness to Christianity:—With the accession of Constantine to the imperial throne, as before remarked, the peace of the church was assured. His father had favored the Christians, and in the cruel persecution under Diocletian, he kept the provinces of Gaul free from the effusion of Christian blood; and his son seems to have fallen heir to his father's friendliness for the Christian faith.

16. It is difficult to determine the motives of Con-

stantine for favoring the Christian cause and resolving
upon the destruction of the pagan religion. Whether it
was the appearance of the miraculous cross in the heavens,
as some aver, the influence of Helena, his mother,* as Theo-
doret claims, or through the arguments of an Egyptian priest
who promised him absolution for the crime of murder if
he would accept Christianity.† But let the motive be what
it may, benevolence, policy, conviction or remorse, coupled
with a hope of forgiveness, Constantine from the time of his
accession to the throne became the avowed protector of the
Christian church; and at length by his powerful influence
made Christianity the reigning religion of the Roman empire.‡ The exiles were recalled; those condemned to labor
in the mines were released; those who had been robbed of
their property were reinstated in their possessions, and the
demolished Christian temples were ordered to be rebuilt and
enlarged. The church militant, after the emperor's edicts
of toleration, became the church tranquil, so far as external
opposition was concerned. Her ministers were welcomed
to the court of the emperor, admitted to the imperial table,
and even accompanied the monarch in his expeditions.
Wealth, honor and imperial patronage were bestowed almost without measure on the Christian church. From the
position of a despised, persecuted religion, Christianity was
suddenly exalted to the very throne of the Roman world.
Yet these things which are usually accounted among the
good fortunes of the church, were, as we shall yet see, disastrous to the purity of the Christian religion.

---

*According to Eusebius, however, Helena was converted to Christi-
anity by her son.—*de Veta Constantine* I, iii, ch. 47.

†Constantine had caused to be put to death, through jealousy and
on what, to say the least, was very slight and very suspicious testimony,
his son Crispus, his wife Fausta, and his brother-in-law Licinius.

‡Decline and Fall vol. 1, ch. xvi.

17. Progress of the Church Under the Patronage of Constantine:—The court of Constantine was converted of course; but it is to be feared that it was the hope of wealth and honor, the example of the emperor, his exhortations, his irresistible smile, rather than the truths of Christianity which wrought a change in the hearts of the obsequious crowd that filled the palace. A number of cities manifested a forward zeal in a voluntary destruction of their temples and idols, but it is more than likely that the municipal distinctions and popular donations which were held out as a reward for such conduct, rather than belief in the Christian faith are what inspired the iconoclasts. Twelve thousand men and a proportionate number of women and children were baptized in a single year in Rome; but how far did the twenty pieces of gold and a white garment promised to each convert by the emperor influence the conversion of this great number. Nor was the influence of Constantine in respect to the Christian religion confined within the provinces of the empire. It extended to the barbarous peoples outside; who, while they had held in disdain a despised and proscribed sect, soon learned to esteem a religion which had been so lately embraced by the greatest monarch and the most civilized nation of the globe.*

18. The Character of Constantine:—It is as difficult to come to a right conclusion as to the real character of Constantine as it is to decide the motives which led him to accept the Christian religion; for in the former as in the latter case the authorities are conflicting. The Christians who were favored by his actions extol him for his virtues; while the pagans who were despoiled by him, execrate him for his crimes. It is certain, however, that

---

*Decline and Fall, vol. I, ch. xvi.

he put to death his own son Crispus, and his wife Fausta, on a suspicion that was at least precarious. He cut off his brother-in-law Licinius, and his offending son, contrary to his plighted word; and, according to Schlegel and Gibbon, he was much addicted to pride and voluptuousness. The latter said of him: "He pursued the great objects of his ambition through the dark and bloody paths of war and policy, and after the victory, abandoned himself without moderation to the abuse of his good fortune. As he advanced in years he seems to have declined in the practice of virtue, blighting in his old age, when a convert to the Christian faith, and famed as the protector of the Christian church, the fair promises he gave in his youth, and while a pagan, of being a truly virtuous prince. It is not likely that the patronage of such an emperor would contribute to the real progress of religion or assist in the establishment of the church of Christ."

NOTES.

1. **The Martyrdom of Polycarp:**—Presently the instruments prepared for the funeral pile were applied to him. As they were on the point of securing him with spikes, he said: "Let me be thus, for he that gives me strength to bear the fire, will also give me power without being secured by you with these spikes, to remain unmoved on the pile." They therefore did not nail him, but merely bound him to the stake. But he, closing his hands behind him, and bound to the stake as a noble victim selected from the great flock an acceptable sacrifice to Almighty God, said: "Father of thy well-beloved and blessed Son, Jesus Christ, through whom we have received the knowledge of thee, the God of angels and power and all creation, and of all the family of the righteous, that live before thee, I bless thee that thou hast thought me worthy of the present day and hour to have a share in the number of the martyrs and in the cup of Christ, unto the resurrection of eternal life, both of the soul and body, in the incorruptible felicity of the Holy Spirit. Among whom may I be received in thy sight this day as a rich and acceptable sacrifice, as thou the faithful and true God hast prepared, hast revealed and fulfilled. Wherefore on this account, and for all things I praise thee, I bless thee, I glorify thee through the eternal

High Priest, Jesus Christ, thy well beloved Son. Through whom be glory to thee with Him in the Holy Ghost, both now and forever. Amen." After he had repeated Amen, and had finished his prayer, the executioners kindled the fire.—*Eusebius.*

2. A Second Century Persecution:—Would the reader know what a persecution in those days was, I would refer him to a circular letter written by the church at Smyrna soon after the death of Polycarp, who it will be remembered had lived with St. John; and which letter is entitled a relation of that bishop's martyrdom. "The sufferings," say they, "of all the other martyrs were blessed and generous which they underwent according to the will of God. For so it becomes us, who are more religious than others, to ascribe the power and ordering of all things unto him. And indeed who can choose but admire the greatness of their minds, and that admirable patience and love of their Master, which then appeared in them? Who when they were so flayed with whipping, that the frame and structure of their bodies were laid open to their very inward veins and arteries, nevertheless endured it. In like manner, those who were condemned to the beasts and kept a long time in prison, underwent many cruel torments, being forced to lie upon sharp spikes laid under their bodies, and tormented with divers other sorts of punishments; that so, if it were possible, the tyrants by the length of their sufferings might have brought them to deny Christ."—*Paley.*

3. The Persecution Under Decius Trajan:—This persecution was more terrible than any preceding one, because it extended over the whole empire, and because its object was to worry the Christians into apostasy by extreme and persevering torture.—The *certificated* or *libellatici*, are supposed to be such as purchased certificates from the corrupt magistrates, in which it was declared that they were pagans and had complied with the demands of the law, when neither of these was fact. To purchase such a certificate was not only to be partaker in the fraudulent transaction, but it was to prevaricate before the public in regard to Christianity, and was inconsistent with that open confession of Christ before men, which He Himself requires.—*Murdock.* (Note in *Mosheim*, vol. I., cent. iii, p. 1, ch. ii.)

4. The Insurrection of Syria and Nicomedia:—Some degree of probability could be attached to the charge against the Christians of causing the insurrection from the fact that their inconsiderate zeal sometimes led them to deeds which had an aspect of rebellion. At the commencement of this persecution, for example, a very respectable Christian tore down the imperial edict against the Christians which was set up in a public place.—*Schlegel.*

5. Unwise Zeal of the Christians:—Several examples have been preserved of a zeal impatient of those restraints which the emperors had provided for the security of the church. The Christians sometimes supplied by their voluntary declaration the want of an accuser, rudely disturbed the public service of paganism, and rushing in crowds round the tribunal of the magistrates, called upon them to pronounce and to inflict the sentence of the law. The behavior of the Christians was too remarkable to escape the notice of the ancient philosophers; but they seemed to have considered it with much less admiration than astonishment. Incapable of conceiving the motives which sometimes transported the fortitude of believers beyond the bounds of prudence or reason, they treated such an eagerness to die as the strange result of obstinate despair, of stupid insensibility or of suspicious frenzy.— *Gibbon.*

6. **Spirit of the Christian Martyrs:**—The spirit of the Christian martyrs, at least of the first three centuries, may be learned from the epistle of Ignatius of Antioch, who, early in the second century was taken from Syria to Rome where he suffered martyrdom by being thrown to the wild beasts. On his journey to Rome, under sentence of death, he wrote an epistle to the Roman saints from which the following passage is taken: "I write to the churches and I declare to all, that willingly I die for God, if it be that you hinder me not. I beg of you, do not become to me an unseasonable love. Let me be of the beasts, by whose means I am enabled to obtain God. I am God's wheat, and by the teeth of the beasts am I ground, that I may be found God's pure bread. Rather entreat kindly the beasts that they may be a grave for me and may leave nothing of my body; that not even when I am fallen asleep, I may be a burden upon any man. Then I shall be in truth a disciple of Jesus Christ, when the world seeth not even my body. Supplicate our Lord for me, that by these instruments I may be found a sacrifice to God. I am not commanding you like Peter and Paul; they were apostles, I am a condemned convict; they were free, I am hitherto a slave. But if I suffer, I am a free man of Jesus Christ, and I shall rise from the dead, in him a free man. And now since I am in bonds, I learn to desire nothing. From Syria to Rome I am cast among beasts by sea and by land, by night and by day; since I am bound between ten leopards, who get worse when I do good to them. But by their ill-treatment I am furthered in my apprenticeship; still by that I am not justified. May I have to rejoice of the beasts prepared for me! and I pray that they may be found ready for me, and I will kindly entreat them quickly to devour me, and not as they have done to some, being afraid of them, to keep from touching me. And should they not be willing, I will force them."—*Ignatius' Epistle to the Romans.*

7. **Constantine's Luminous Cross:**—Now if this narrative (by Eusebius) is all true, and if two connected miracles were actually wrought as here stated, how happens it that no writer of that age, except Eusebius, says one word about the luminous cross in the heavens? How came it that Eusebius himself said nothing about it in his Ecclesiastical History, which was written twelve years after the event, and about the same length of time before his life of Constantine? Why does he rely solely on the testimony of the emperor and not even intimate that he even heard of it from others; whereas, if true, many thousands must have been eye-witnesses of the fact. What mean his suggestions, that some may question the truth of the story; and his caution not to state anything as a matter of public notoriety, but to

confine himself simply to the emperor's private representation to himself. * * * But how came the whole story of the luminous cross to be unknown to the Christian world, for more than twenty-five years, and then to transpire only through a private conversation between Eusebius and Constantine?—*Murdock.*

REVIEW.

1. From what source did the persecution of the church come during the 2nd century?

2. What charge did pagan priests bring against the Christians?

3. What in the estimation of the ignorant pagans gave the color of truth to their charge?

4. To what circumstance were the calamities which befell the empire usually attributed?

5. What strange fact meets us in connection with the persecution of the 2nd century?

6. What two noted martyrs were put to death in the reign of Marcus Aurelius?

7. Describe the martyrdom of Polycarp.

8. What was the nature of some of the tortures inflicted on the Christians? (Note 2.)

9. What was the nature and purpose of the edicts of Severus?

10. What was the effect of this persecution and the period of peace which followed it?

11. What can you say of the persecution under Trajan?

12. What does Gibbon say of it?

13. How long did it continue?

14. What means of avoiding the severe tortures were offered the Christians?

15. What was the effect of this persecution?

16. What other circumstance added to the afflictions of the Christians?

17. What changes in respect to the Roman government took place early in the 4th century?

18. What method did Diocletian adopt for the suppression of the Christian religion?

19. What special crimes were charged to the Christians in the reign of Diocletian?

20. What can you say of the zeal of the Christians? (Notes 4 and 5.)

21. What effect did these persecutions have on the church?

22. What event put a stop to the pagan persecutions?

23. Relate the circumstances which led to Constantine becoming emperor of Rome.

24. What effect did his accession to the throne have upon the Christian church?

25. By what circumstance is Constantine said to have been converted to the Christian religion?

26.   What evidences exist against the probability of this story?
27.   What good service did the father of Constantine do the Christians in the Diocletian persecution?
28.   What are the several motives assigned for Constantine's friendliness to the Christian church?
29.   What can you say of the emperor's treatment of the Christians?
30.   What considerations very likely influenced converts when Constantine extended his patronage to the church?
31.   What was the character of Constantine?

SECTION III.

1. The Accusations of the Pagans:—The simplicity of the Christian religion was made a reproach to the church of Christ by the pagan priests. The saints were accused of atheism, an accusation which found support in the fact that the primitive church had no temples, no incense, no sacrifice, no incantations, pomp or ceremony in its worship. "The Christians have no temples, therefore they have no gods," was an argument sufficiently convincing to the heathen. It was but natural, perhaps, that the Christians should seek to cast off this reproach; but the desire to do so led to the introduction of many ceremonies quite at variance with the religion of Jesus Christ, and eventually subverted it altogether.

2. Outward Ordinances of the Christian Religion:—The outward ordinances of the gospel consisted of baptism, the laying on of hands for the imparting of the Holy Ghost, and the Lord's Supper. The laying on of hands was also employed in ordaining men to the Priesthood and in administering to the sick. In the latter case it was accompanied by anointing with oil.

3. While it does not appear that there was any specific law commanding or regulating fasts, the ancient saints occasionally joined abstinence from their food with their prayers, and especially when engaged in great undertakings. But the frequency of his fasts and the time of their continuance were left to each man's judgment.

4. They met on the first day of the week—Sunday—

for worship (see note 1, end of section) the meetings, during the first century, being held in most instances in private houses. The ceremonies were of the simplest character. They consisted of reading the scriptures, the exhortation of the president of the assembly—"neither eloquent nor long, but full of warmth and love;" the testimony of such as felt moved upon by the Holy Ghost to bear testimony, exhort or prophesy; the singing of hymns; the administration of the Sacrament and prayers.* (See note 2, end of section.)

5. **Baptism:**—Baptism was administered by immersing the candidate in water. The only pre-requisites were faith in Jesus Christ and repentance. As soon as the candidate professed these he was admitted into the church by baptism.† In a short time, however, the simplicity of this ordinance was corrupted and burdened with useless ceremonies. In the second century the newly baptized converts, since by baptism they had been born again, were taught to exhibit in their conduct the innocence of little infants. Milk and honey, the common food of infants, were administered to them, after their baptism to remind them of their infancy in the church. Moreover, since by baptism they were released from being servants of the devil, and became God's free men, certain forms borrowed from the Roman ceremony of manumission of slaves were employed in baptism. As by baptism also they were supposed to be made God's soldiers, like newly enlisted soldiers in the Roman army, they were sworn to obey their commander, etc.

6. **Further Additions of Ceremonies to Baptism:**— A century later (the third) further ceremonies were added. It was supposed that some evil spirit was resident in all

---

*Mosheim vol. I, Book 1, part ii, ch. iv.
†Acts ii: 41. Acts viii: 12, 35-40.

vicious persons and impelled them to sin. Therefore, before entering the sacred fount for baptism, an exorcist by a solemn, menacing formula declared them free from the bondage of Satan, and hailed them servants of Christ.* After baptism the new converts returned home, "decorated with a crown and a white robe; the first being indicative of their victory over the world and their lusts, the latter of their acquired innocence."†

7. We have already noted the fact that baptism was administered in the days of the apostles as soon as profession of faith and repentance were declared, but in the second and third century baptism was only administered twice a year, and then only to such candidates as had gone through a long preparation and trial.‡ The times chosen for the administration of the ordinance were on the vigils of Easter and Whitsuntide,§ and in the fourth century it had become the custom to accompany the ceremony with lighted wax candles, to put salt—an emblem of purity and wisdom— in the mouth of the baptized, and everywhere a double anointing was administered to the candidates, the one before, the other after baptism.‖

------

*That exorcism was not annexed to baptism till some time in the third century, and after the admission of the Platonic philosophy into the church, may almost be demonstrated. The ceremonies used at baptism in the second century are described by Justin Martyr in his second apology, and by Turtullian in his book *de Corono Militas*. But neither makes mention of exorcism. This is a cogent argument to prove that it was admitted by Christians after the times of these fathers, and of course in the third century. Egypt perhaps first received it. *Murdock's Mosheim vol.* 1, *p.* 190.—(Note.)

†Mosheim vol. I, book i, part ii, ch. iv.

‡According to Schlegel, the so-called apostolic constitution (b. viii, ch. 32) enjoined a three years' course of preparation; yet with allowance of some exceptions.

§That is, the evening preceding the day on which Messiah is supposed to have arisen from the dead, and the evening preceding the seventh Sunday after Easter, the anniversary of Pentecost when the Holy Ghost was poured out upon the Apostles in a remarkable manner (Acts ii.)

‖Mosheim vol. I, book ii, part ii, ch. iv.

8. The Form of Baptism Changed:—It must have been early in the third century that the form of baptism began to be changed. Up to this time it had been performed only by immersion of the whole body. But in the first half of the third century, Cyprian, Bishop of Carthage, during a controversy respecting the re-baptism of those who in times of persecution had denied the faith, decided that those whose weak state of health did not permit them to be immersed, were sufficiently baptized by being sprinkled.* The first case of this kind of baptism is related by Eusebius. The person to whom it was so administered was Novatus [No-va-tus], a desperate heretic, who created a schism in the church and became the founder of a sect. He was among the number of so-called Christians who put off baptism as long as he dared, in order to enjoy a life of sin and then through baptism, just before death, obtain forgiveness for them—a custom very prevalent in those times. Novatus being attacked with an obstinate disease, and supposed to be at the point of death, was baptized by having water sprinkled upon him as he lay in bed; "if indeed," says Eusebius, "it be proper to say one like him did receive baptism."†

9. This innovation continued to spread until now the general rule among so-called Christian sects is to baptize by sprinkling or pouring. For this change there is no warrant of revelation. It destroys the symbol there is in baptism as taught by Messiah and his apostles—that of a burial and a resurrection—of a death and a birth—a death unto sin, a birth unto righteousness. (See notes 3 and 4,

---

*Cyprian's Epistles, letter 76.
†Eusebius Eccl. Hist. b. vi, ch. 43.

end of section.)   It is one of those innovations which changed an ordinance of the everlasting covenant.

10.   **Baptism Misapplied:**—About the time that the form of administering baptism was changed it began to be misapplied, that is, it was administered to infants.   Just when this custom came into vogue may not be determined, but clearly it has no warrant for its existence either in the doctrines or practice of the apostles or any New Testament writer.   (See note 5, end of section.)   No truth is more plainly taught by the apostles than that baptism is for the remission of sins, and must be preceded by faith and repentance; and as infants are incapable of sin, or of exercising faith, or of repenting, evidently they are not fit subjects for baptism.

11.   Still it became the custom in the latter part of the second century or early in the third to baptize infants. In the year 253 A. D., a council of sixty bishops, in Africa— at which Cyprian, bishop of Carthage, presided, took under consideration the question whether infants should be baptized within two or three days after birth, or whether it should be deferred until the eighth day, as was the custom of the Jews in respect to circumcision.   The council decided that they should be baptized at once, that is within a day or two after birth.*   It will be observed that the question was not as to whether infants should be baptized at all, or not, but *when* they should be baptized, within a day or two after birth or not until they were eight days old.   The matter was treated in the council as if infant baptism was a custom of long standing.   This proves, not that infant baptism is a correct doctrine, or that it was derived from the teachings and examples of the apostles—as some aver†—but that in a cen-

---

*Milner's Church Hslt. vol. I, pp. 429, 430.
†Such is the opinion of Milner—*Church Hist. vol. I, p.* 430.

tury or so after the introduction of the gospel, men began to pervert the gospel by changing and misapplying its ordinances. The false doctrine of infant baptism is now practiced by nearly all so-called Christian churches, Catholic and Protestant.

12. **The Sacrament:**—Much as the simple rite of baptism was burdened with useless ceremonies, changed in its form and misapplied, it was not more distorted than was the sacrament of the Lord's supper. The nature of the sacrament—usually called the eucharist—and the purposes for which it was instituted are so plain that he who runs may read.

13. From Paul's description of the ordinance, it is clear that the broken bread was an emblem of Messiah's broken body; the wine an emblem of his blood, shed for sinful man; and his disciples were to eat the one and drink the other *in remembrance of him* until he should return; and by this ceremony show forth the Lord's death. *

14. It was designed as a memorial of Messiah's great Atonement for mankind, a token and witness unto the Father that the Son was always remembered. It was to be a sign that those partaking of it were willing to take upon them the name of Christ, to always remember him, and keep his commandments. In consideration of these things being observed, the saints were always to have the

---

*The Lord Jesus the same night in which he was betrayed took bread; and when he had given thanks, he broke it and said, "Take, eat; this is my body which is broken for you; this do in remembrance of me." After the same manner also he took the cup, when he had supped, saying: "This cup is the new testament in my blood; this do ye, as oft as ye drink it, *in remembrance of me*. For as often as ye eat this bread and drink this cup, ye do show the Lord's death till he come." —*Paul to the Corinthians.* (I Cor. xi: 23-26.)

Spirit of the Lord to be with them.* In this spirit and without great ceremony (see note 7, end of section) the sacrament was administered for some time.

15. Administration of the Sacrament Corrupted:— In the third century there were longer prayers and more ceremony connected with the administration of the sacrament than in the century preceding. Disputations arose as to the proper time to administer it. Some considered the morning, others the afternoon, and some the evening the most suitable time. All were not agreed either as to how often the ordinance should be celebrated. Gold and silver vessels were used, and neither those doing penance, nor those unbaptized, though believers, were permitted to be present at the celebration of the ordinance; "which practice it is well known, was derived from the pagan mysteries."† Very much of mystery began to be associated with it even at an early date. The bread and the wine through the prayer of consecration were considered to undergo a mystic change by which they were converted

---

*These facts are clearly taught by Messiah when he established the sacrament among the Nephites; and of course it was established among the Jews for the same purpose that it was among the Nephites. After having broken the bread and blessed it, and passed it to the multitude, Messiah said: "This shall ye do in remembrance of my body, which I have shown unto you. And it shall be a testimony unto the Father that ye do always remember me. And if you do always remember me, ye shall have my Spirit to be with you," So when he had administered the wine: "Blessed are ye for this thing which ye have done; * * * this doth witness unto the Father that ye are willing to do that which I have commanded you; And this shall ye always do to those who repent and are baptized in my name; and ye shall do it in remembrance of my blood which I have shed for you, that ye may witness unto the Father that ye do always remember me. And if ye do always remember me, ye shall have my Spirit to be with you." III Nephi xviii. See also Moroni, iv and v, where the prayer of consecration is given.

†Mosheim's Ecclesiastical History vol. I, book 1, cent. iii, part 2, chapter iv. The banishment of unbaptized people from sacrament meetings was forbidden among the Nephites by Messiah. III Nephi xviii: 22-23.

into and became the very body and the very blood of Jesus Christ; so that they were no longer regarded as emblems of Messiah's body and blood, but the body and blood itself.* This is the doctrine of transubstantiation.

16. This dogma established, it was but a short step to the "elevation of the host"; that is, the elevation of the bread and wine before they were distributed, so that they might be viewed with reverence by the people. Thus came the adoration of the symbols.

17. **Institution of the Mass:**—Hence came also the mass, or the idea of a sacrifice being connected with the celebration of the eucharist. It was held that as Jesus was truly present in the bread and wine he could be offered up, and was truly offered up as an oblation to his Eternal Father. The death of the victim was not supposed to occur in reality but mystically, in such a way, however, as to constitute a true sacrifice, commemorative of that of the cross, and not

---

*Protestants combating the Catholic idea of the real presence of the flesh and blood in the eucharist—transubstantiation—have endeavored to prove that this doctrine was not of earlier origin than the eighth century. In this, however, the evidence is against them. Ignatius, bishop of Antioch, writing early in the second century says of certain supposed heretics: "They do not admit of eucharists and oblations, because they do not believe the eucharist to be the flesh of our Savior Jesus Christ, who suffered for our sins." (Epistles of Ignatius to the Smyrneans.) So Justin Martyr, also writing in the first half of the second century:—"We do not receive them (the bread and the wine) as ordinary food or ordinary drink; but as by the word of God Jesus Christ, our Savior, was made flesh and took upon him both flesh and blood for our salvation, so also the food which was blessed by the prayer of the word which proceeded from him, and from which our flesh and blood, by transmutation, receive nourishment, is, we are taught, both the flesh and blood of that Jesus who was made flesh." (Justin's Apology to Emperor Antonius.) After Justin's time the testimony of the fathers is abundant. There can be no doubt as to the antiquity of the idea of the real presence of the body and blood of Jesus in the eucharist; but that proves—as we said of infant baptism—not that the doctrine is true, but that soon after the apostles had passed away, the simplicity of the gospel was corrupted or else entirely departed from.

different from it in essence. The same victim was present and offered up by Christ through his minister, the priest. The sacrifice at the cross was offered with real suffering, true shedding of blood, and real death of the victim; in the mass it was taught there was a mystical suffering, a mystical shedding of blood and a mystical death of the same victim.

18. Into such absurdities was the simple sacrament of the Lord's supper distorted! When attended with all the pomp and ceremony of splendid altars, lighted tapers, processions, elevations and chantings; offered up by priests and bishops clad in splendid vestments and in the midst of clouds of incense, accompanied by mystic movements and genuflections of bishops and priests, the church could congratulate itself on having removed the reproach at the first fastened upon the Christians for not having altars and a sacrifice. The mass took away the reproach; and the new converts to Christianity were accustomed to see the same rites and ceremonies employed in this mystical sacrifice of the Son of God as they had seen employed in offering up of sacrifice to their pagan deities. (See notes 8 and 9, end of section.)

19. **Suppression of Half the Sacrament:**—In time the idea became prevalent that as the body and blood of Messiah were equally and entirely present under each "species"—that is, equally and entirely present in the bread and in the wine—it was equally and entirely given to the faithful whichever they received. This idea, of course, rendered it unnecessary to partake of both bread and wine—hence the practice of communion in one kind. That is, the sacrament was administered by giving bread alone to the communicant. To remark that this was changing the ordinance of the sacrament as instituted by Messiah—suppressing half of it in fact—can scarcely be

necessary since it is so well known that Jesus administered both bread and wine when instituting the sacred ordinance.*

NOTES.

1. Reasons Why the Ancient Saints Worshiped on Sunday:— But Sunday is the day on which we all hold our common assembly, because it is the first day on which God, when he changed the darkness and matter, made the world; and Jesus Christ our Savior on the same day rose from the dead; for the day before that of Saturn he was crucified and on the day after it, which is Sunday, he appeared to his apostles and disciples and taught them these things which we have given to you also for your consideration.—*Justin Martyr.*

2. Description of Christian Public Worship in the Second Century:— On the day which is called Sunday there is an assembly in the same of all who live in cities or in country districts; and the records of the apostles, or the writings of the prophets, are read as long as we have time. Then the reader concludes, and the president verbally instructs and exhorts us to the imitation of these excellent things. Then we all rise together and offer up our prayers. And, as I said before, when we have concluded our prayer, bread is brought, and wine and water, and the president in like manner offers up prayers and thanksgivings with all his strength, and the people give their assent by saying Amen; and there is a distribution and a partaking by every one of the eucharistic elements (the sacrament), and to those who are not present they are sent by the hands of the deacons. And such as are in prosperous circumstances, and wish to do so, give what they will, each according to his choice; and what is collected is placed in the hands of the president, who assists the orphans and widows, and such as through sickness or any other cause are in want; and to those who are in bonds, and to strangers from afar, and, in a word, to all who are in need, he is a protector.—*Justin Martyr.*

3. Baptism a Symbol of Burial and Resurrection:— In writing to the saints of Rome, Paul says: "Know ye not, that so many of us as were baptized into Jesus Christ were baptized into his death? Therefore we are *buried* with him by baptism into death; that like as Christ was raised up from the dead by the glory of the Father, even so we also should walk in newness of life. For if we have been *planted* together in the likeness of his death, we shall be also in the likeness of his resurrection." (Rom. vi. 3-5.) In writing to the saints of Colosse, the same apostle reminds them that they had been "*buried* with him (Christ) in baptism, wherein also ye are risen with him through the faith of the operation of God who hath raised him from the dead." (Col. ii: 12.)

In these passages the terms "buried" and "planted" are in plain

---

*Luke xxii. Matt. xxvi. III Nephi xviii.

allusion to the manner in which the saints had received the ordinance of baptism, which could not have been by sprinkling or pouring, as there is no burial or planting in the likeness of Christ's death, or being raised in likeness of his resurrection in that but in immersion there is. —*The Gospel—Roberts*—page 185.

4.   The Manner of Baptism Instituted Among the Nephites:— "Verily, I say unto you, that whoso repenteth of his sins through your words, and desireth to be baptized in my name, on this wise shall ye baptize them: Behold, ye shall go down and stand in the water, and in my name shall ye baptize them.   And now behold, these are the words which ye shall say, calling them by name, saying, Having authority given me of Jesus Christ, I baptize you in the name of the Father, and of the Son, and of the Holy Ghost.   Amen.   And then shall ye immerse them in the water and come forth again out of the water. And after this manner shall ye baptize in my name."—*Jesus to the Nephites.*

5.   Infant Baptism not Ordained of Christ or the Apostles:— As faith and baptism are constantly so closely connected together in the New Testament, an opinion was likely to arise that where there could be no faith there could be no baptism.   It is certain that Christ did not ordain infant baptism.   *   *   *   We cannot prove that the apostles ordained infant baptism; from those places where the baptism of a whole family is mentioned (Acts xvi: 33; I Cor. i: 16), we can draw no such conclusions, because the inquiry is still to be made whether there were any children in those families of such an age that they were not capable of any intelligent reception of Christianity; for this is the only point on which the case turns.— *Neander* (Church History, vol. I, page 360.)

6.   Infant Baptism Forbidden Among the Nephites:—The word of the Lord came to me by the power of the Holy Ghost, saying: *   *   *   Behold, I came into the world to not to call the righteous, but sinners unto repentance; the whole need no physician, but they that are sick; wherefore little children are whole for they are incapable of committing sin; wherefore the curse of Adam is taken from them in me, that it hath no power over them; and the law of circumcision is done away in me.   *   *   *   Wherefore my beloved son, I know that it is solemn mockery before God that ye should baptize little children. *   *   *   Awful is the wickedness to suppose that God saveth one child because of baptism, and the other must perish because he hath no baptism.   Woe be unto him that shall pervert the ways of the Lord after this manner, for they shall perish, except they repent.—*Epistle of Mormon to Moroni* (Book of Moroni, chapter viii.)

7.   Manner of Administering the Sacrament—Second Century:—When the Christians celebrated the Lord's supper, which they were accustomed to do chiefly on Sundays, they consecrated a part of the bread and wine of the oblations, by certain prayers pronounced by the president, the bishop of the congregation.   The wine was mixed with water, and the bread was divided into small pieces.   Portions of the consecrated bread and wine were commonly sent to the absent and the sick, in testimony of fraternal affection towards them.   There is much evidence that this most holy rite was regarded as very necessary to the attainment of salvation.—*Mosheim.*

8. **Pagan Rites Introduced into the Christian Worship—Fourth Century:**—The Christian bishops introduced, with but slight alterations, into the Christian worship, those rites and institutions by which formerly the Greeks and Romans, and other nations had manifested their piety and reverence towards their imaginary deities; supposing that the people would more readily embrace Christianity, if they saw that the rites handed down to them from their fathers still existed unchanged among the Christians, and perceived that Christ and the martyrs were worshiped in the same manner as formerly their gods were. There was, of course, little difference in these times, between the public worship of the Christians and that of the Greeks and Romans. In both alike there were splendid robes, mitres, tiaras, wax tapers, crosiers, processions, illustrations, images, golden and silver vases, and numberless other things.—*Mosheim.*

9. **Superstitious Observances Connected with the Eucharist—Eighth Century:**—As evidence of the superstition which was associated with the eucharist, note the following: "If any one through negligence, shall destroy the eucharist, *i. e.,* the sacrifice; let him do penance one year. * * * If he lets it fall on the ground, carelessly, he must sing fifty Psalms. Whoever neglects to take care of the sacrifice, so that worms get into it, or it lose its color, or taste, must do penance thirty or twenty days; and the sacrifice must be burned in the fire. Whoever turns up the cup at the close of the solemnity of the mass must do penance forty days. If a drop from the cup should fall on the altar, the minister must suck up the drop and do penance three days; and the linen cloth which the drop touched, must be washed three times, over the cup, and the water in which it was washed be cast into the fire."—*Decisions of Pope Gregory III.* (*Harduin's Concilia.*)

REVIEW.

1. What reproach did the simplicity of the Christian religion lead to?

2. What effect did the endeavor to get rid of that reproach have on the Christian religion?

3. Enumerate the outward ordinances of the gospel.

4. What can you say of Christian fasts?

5. On what day did the Christians meet for worship?

6. What reasons do the early church fathers give for holding public worship on that day? (Note 1.)

7. Describe the meetings of the early Christians. (Note 2.)

8. How was baptism administered in the early church?

9. What does baptism represent? (Note 3.)

10. Tell how the simplicity of this ordinance was changed.

11. What additions were made to the ceremony of baptism in the third century?

12.   About when was the form of baptism changed?
13.   Relate the first known case of baptism by sprinkling.
15.   In what way was the orcinance of baptism misapplied?
15.   Was infant baptism ordained of the apostles? ˙(Note 5.)
16.   About when was infant baptism introduced into the church?
17.   Does the antiquity of infant baptism prove it to be a correct doctrine?
18.   What does it prove?
19.   What was said to the Nephites about infant baptism? (Note 6.)
20.   For what was the sacrament of the Lord's supper instituted?
21.   Give Paul's description of the introduction of the sacrament. (Footnote.)
22.   About what time was the manner of administering the sacrament changed?
23.   What was the nature of those changes?
24.   What custom crept into the practice of the Christian church that was forbidden by Jesus among the Nephites?   (Note.)
25.   What can you say of the antiquity of the doctrine of transubstantiation?
26.   What is the mass?
27.   What reproach did the institution of the mass remove from the Christians?
28.   At what cost was the reproach removed?
29.   Who introduced pagan rites into Christian worship?   (Note 8.)
30.   Why was it done?   (Note 8.)
31.   What reason is given for suppressing half the sacrament?

SECTION IV.

1. Early Church Organization Not Perpetuated:—
We have already stated in Part I of this work that the
church organization established by Messiah—consisting of
apostles, prophets, seventies, bishops, etc.—was designed
to be perpetual. It is a singular fact, however, that aside
from filling up the vacancy in the quorum of the twelve—
occasioned by the fall of Judas Iscariot—there is no account
in any of the writings of the apostles or fathers of the first
centuries—on the eastern hemisphere*—of any attempt
to perpetuate the quorum of the twelve by filling up the
vacancies occasioned by the death of the original apostles.
The same may also be said of the quorum of the seventies.

2. The reason for this will doubtless be found in the
fact that in the very days of the apostles the great "falling
away" which was to end eventually in the subversion of the
Christian religion, had begun.   (See note 2, end of section.)
And since "the mystery of iniquity" had already begun its
work in the days of the apostles, and men were rapidly
proving themselves unworthy of the church of Christ, the
Lord did not permit his servants to perpetuate these quorums of the higher Priesthood.

3. Establishment of the Church by the Apostles:—
Whenever in their travels the apostles converted any considerable number of persons, in a city or district, they or-

---

*It will be remembered that the quorum o_ the twelve was per-
petuated on the western hemisphere by filling up vacancies as fast as
they occurred (IV Nephii: 14), but for how long a period is uncertain.

ganized them into a church, or, speaking more precisely, into a branch of the great universal church of Christ, and appointed either a bishop or an elder to preside over them. As long as the apostles lived they were regarded as the presiding authority of the universal church, and were looked to for counsel and instruction in all difficult matters that arose concerning doctrine or discipline.   Their decisions were accepted as final, and well might it be so, since these men were guided in their counsels by revelation* as well as by the wisdom which their large experience in company with Jesus Christ had given them.

4.   But when the apostles died, and no one succeeded to their authority, the branches of the church were left separate and independent organizations, united, it is true, in faith and charity, but the visible, general presidency recognized in the apostles and cheerfully submitted to by all sections of the church, ceased when the apostles passed away, and each branch was left an independent organization of itself.† There is no evidence that there was such a thing as subordination among the churches when so left, or rank among the bishops.   Each church was a sort of independent commonwealth, of which the bishop was president and a vassal to no other bishop.‡

5.   **Manner of Electing Bishops:**—The manner in

---

*Acts xv: 1-30.   Rev. i-iv.

†During a greater part of this century (the second) all the churches continued to be, as at the first, independent of each other.   *   *   * Each church was a kind of small republic, governing itself by its own laws, enacted or at least sanctioned by the people.—*Ecclesiastical History*, Mosheim *Vol. I, book ii, Cent. ii, part ii, ch. ii.*

‡As might be expected, however, there was a peculiar respect paid to the churches founded by the apostles—the church at Jerusalem, Antioch, Ephesus, Corinth, Rome.   Those churches were appealed to in controversies on points of doctrine, "as most likely to know what the apostles taught," but the appeal had no other significance than that.

which bishops were first elected was for the apostles to nominate them, and then for the whole church over which they were to preside to sustain them by their vote. After the apostles had passed away then "other men of repute" made the nominations and the people sustained them as at first.* The duties and powers of the bishops in the first and in the greater part of the second century were limited to conducting the public worship, administering the ordinances of the gospel, settling difficulties which arose between brethren, attending in person the sick and the poor. They also were made the custodians and managers of the public fund. In all these duties they were assisted by the elders [presbyters] of the church and the deacons. Yet neither the bishops nor the elders, nor both of them together, seem to have had power to ordain or determine anything without the approbation and consent of the members of the church. The principle of common consent was closely adhered to in the primitive church. (See note 3, end of section.)

6. **Equality Among Bishops Changed:**—This equality of rank among the bishops, together with the simple form of church government, described above, was soon changed. The bishops who lived in cities, either by their own labors or those of the elders associated with them, raised up new

---

*Clement, the third bishop of Rome, is the authority for the above statement. It appears that the Corinthians had deposed some of their bishops, and Clement in an epistle which he wrote to them said: "Our apostles knew through our Lord Jesus Christ that there would be strife over the name of the bishop's office. For this cause therefore, having received complete foreknowledge, they appointed the aforesaid persons [the bishops], and afterward they provided a continuance [i. e., gave instructions] that if these should fall asleep, other approved men should succeed to their ministration. Those therefore who were appointed by other men of repute *with the consent of the whole church,* and have ministered unblamably * * * these men we consider to be unjustly thrust out of their ministration."—See also *Gibbon's Decline and Fall,* Vol. I, ch. xv.

churches in the adjacent villages and hamlets. The bishops of. these rural districts being nominated and ordained by the bishops presiding in the city, very naturally, perhaps, felt themselves under the protection and dependent upon the city bishops. This idea continued to grow until these bishops presiding in the city, very naturally, perhaps, felt themselves under the protection and dependent upon the city bishops. This idea continued to grow until these "bishops of the suburbs and the fields," were looked upon as a distinct order of officers, possessing a dignity and authority above the elders, and yet subordinate to the bishops of the cities, who soon came to be designated as archbishops.

7. **The Origin of Metropolitans:**—Gradually and almost imperceptibly the church in its government began to follow the civil divisions of the Roman empire. The bishops of the metropolis of a civil province, in time, came to be regarded as having a general supervision of all the churches in that province, over the archbishops and indirectly over the suburban bishops or suffragans, as they began to be called, and finally, bishops merely. The bishops of these provinces were soon designated as metropolitans.

8. **The Rise and Influence of Councils:**—Concurrent with these changes arose the custom, first derived from the Greeks, of holding provincial councils. The bishops living in a single province met in council to confer upon matters of common interest to the churches of the province. These provincial councils met at stated times of the year, usually in the spring and autumn. At the first the attending bishops looked upon themselves as merely the representatives of their respective churches, without jurisdiction further than to discuss and come to agreement on matters of common concern. But gradually they usurped the power to order by decree where at first they

were accustomed to advise or entreat—so easy is it to change the language of exhortation to that of command! Nor was it long ere the decrees of these provincial councils were forced upon the respective churches as laws to be implicitly obeyed. There was some resistance to this at first from the lower orders of the clergy; but that resistance was quickly overcome by the activity and ambition of the bishops, who were only too glad to escape from the restraints which the doctrine of "common consent"—a doctrine which made it necessary for the bishops to submit any matter of importance to their respective churches for the approbation of the people—imposed upon them. (See note 4, end of section.)

9. **Conduct of Lower Clergy:**—As many changes occurred among the lower orders of the clergy as among the bishops. The elders and deacons became too proud to attend to the humble duties of their offices and hence a number of other officers were added to the church, while the elders and deacons spent much of their time in indolence and pleasure.

10. **Corruption of Church Officials:**—To the evils of contention for power and place, which had its origin in arrogance and ambition—unbecoming those who profess to be followers and servants of Jesus Christ—must be added those of dissipation and voluptuousness. Many bishops, in the third century, affected the state of princes, especially those who had charge of the more populous and wealthy congregations; for they sat on thrones, surrounded by their ministers and other signs of their power, and dazzled the eyes and the minds of the populace with their splendid attire.*

11. **Church Government Modeled on the Plan of**

---

*Eccl. Hist. (Mosheim) Vol. I, bk. 1, cent. iii, part ii, ch. ii.

the Civil Government:—It was reserved for the fourth century to see the church government more completely modeled on the plan of the civil government of the Roman empire, to witness more pride and arrogance in its rulers, and an increase of vices both in clergy and people. Early in this century, it will be remembered, Constantine, the Emperor of Rome, avowed his conversion to Christianity, and as might have been expected that fact produced great changes in the fortunes of the church. It not only put an end to its persecutions but loaded its bishops with new honors and enlarged powers.

12. In saying that the church government was modeled upon the plan of the civil government we would not be understood as saying that the first was a *fac simile* of the second; there were some differences between them, but the civil divisions of the empire suggested the ecclesiastical divisions.

13. Under Constantine the Roman empire was divided into four prefectures, containing thirteen dioceses, embracing one hundred and sixteen provinces. Officers called praetorian prefects presided over the four prefectures—exarchs over the dioceses and governors over the provinces. The Bishops of Rome, Constantinople, Antioch and Alexandria, having gained a pre-eminence over all other metropolitans were made to correspond with the four prefectures by Constantine, and assumed, before the close of the century, the title of patriarchs. Next to the patriarchs stood the bishops, whose jurisdiction extended over several provinces, corresponding to the civil exarchs,* though the

---

*Dr. Mosheim in his *Institutes of Ecclesiastical History* states that next to the patriarchs were bishops called exarchs; but this his translator (Murdock) denies. Certain it is, however, that there were bishops who presided over several provinces, just as the civil exarchs did. These

bishops of this dignity did not equal in number the civil exarchs. Next came the metropolitan bishops, whose jurisdiction was limited to a single province. They corresponded to the civil governors of the provinces, whose authority was limited in like manner. After the metropolitans came the archbishops,* and then the bishops. Some of the latter were exempt from the jurisdiction of both metropolitans and archbishops, and hence were called independent bishops.

14. **Pre-Eminence of the Bishops of Rome:**—The distinctions of rank among the bishops of the Christian church first arose largely through the opulence and civil importance of the respective cities and provinces over which they presided—the membership of the church and its wealth usually bearing a just proportion to the size and civil importance of the city in which it was located. It is not surprising, therefore, that the metropolitans and patriarchs also struggled for pre-eminence upon the same basis. That basis gave the bishop of Rome great advantage; for, as stated by Gibbon, "the Roman church was the greatest, the most numerous, and, in regard to the west, the most ancient of all the Christian establishments, many of which had received their religion from the pious labors of her missionaries." The fact, too, that for so many ages Rome had been the capital of the great empire led men

---

Mosheim may have considered as corresponding to the civil exarchs; while his translator insists that they were merely the "first metropolitans of the civil dioceses." The difference seems to be one of terms rather than of facts; but there is this to say in favor of the translator, that the bishops exercising jurisdiction over several provinces did not exactly correspond to the number of civil exarchs. There was not an exarch bishop over each civil diocese, and perhaps this is the reason the learned translator objects to the term of ecclesiastical exarch.

*In course of time the terms arch-bishop and metropolitan came to be used interchangeably.

naturally to give pre-eminence to the church established there.

15.   Another thing which went far to establish the supremacy of the bishop of Rome was the tradition that Peter, the chief or "prince" of the apostles, had founded that church; that he became its first bishop; that the bishops succeeding him succeeded to his apostleship and to whatever of pre-eminence he held over his fellow apostles; and, that pre-eminence, it is claimed, amounted to the right of presidency over the universal church.

16.   **Objections to the Claims of the Bishop of Rome:**—That Peter, aided by Paul, did found the church at Rome there is little cause to doubt.   It is also true that Peter was the chief or president of the apostles; that to him had been given the keys of the kingdom of heaven.*   But that he became the bishop of Rome, or that the bishops of Rome succeeded to his apostleship and to that power which made him the president of the universal church of Christ, we cannot allow.

17.   Our first reason for saying that Peter was not bishop of Rome is that the office of apostle and bishop are not identical.   If Peter presided at all over the church at Rome he did so by virtue of his apostleship, not by becoming its bishop; but as his apostleship would give him the right to act in minor offices of the church—on the principle that the greater authority includes the lesser—he may have presided for a time over the church at Rome.

18.   Our second reason is that according to the very best authority on the subject, one Linus and not Peter was the first bishop of Rome.   Irenaeus writing in the second century, says: "The blessed apostles [Peter and Paul] then,

---

*Matt. xvi:19.

upon founding and erecting the church [at Rome], committed the office of administering the church to Linus. Of this Linus, Paul speaks in the epistle to Timothy. To him succeeded Anacletus [An-a-cle-tus], and after him, in the third place from the apostles, Clement received the bishopric."*

From this it plainly appears that Peter and Paul organized a church at Rome, and as in other cities they appointed a bishop to preside over it. Peter no more became the bishop of Rome than he did of the church at Jerusalem, or Paul of Antioch, Ephesus, or Corinth.

19. The bishop of Rome did not succeed to the apostleship of Peter, much less to the pre-eminence which he held among the apostles; and that for the very good reason that the office of bishop and that of apostle, as remarked above, are not identical. It would require an apostle to succeed an apostle, and as there is no account of an apostle being ordained to succeed to Peter's office, we conclude he had no successor. Here we might let the matter rest, but it will be proper to notice the arguments which are made by those who contend that the bishops of Rome are the true successors to the office and mission of the Apostle Peter.

20. **Scripture Basis of the Claims of the Bishop of Rome to Pre-Eminence:**—On one occasion Jesus said to his disciples: "Whom say ye that I am? And Simon Peter answered, * * * Thou art the Christ, the Son of the living God." To this Jesus said: "Blessed art thou, Simon Barjona; for flesh and blood hath not revealed it unto thee, but my Father which is in heaven. And I say unto thee, that thou art Peter, and upon this rock I will build my church; and the gates of hell shall not prevail against it."† He then gave to Peter the keys of the king-

---

*Irenaeus against Heresy, bk. III, ch. iii: 2, 3.
†Matt. xvi:15-18.

dom of heaven, power to bind and loose on earth and in heaven.   The argument is that since Peter, some time before this, had been given the name Cephas, which means a stone,* therefore when Jesus said, "Thou art Peter, and upon this rock I will build my church," it is claimed that he meant than on Peter, he would build his church.†

21.   That this is a clear misconception of the scripture is apparent. If Messiah had meant to found the church on Peter, how unfortunate that he did not say, Thou art Cephas, a stone, and upon *thee* will I build my church, etc. But he did not. He first assured Peter that the knowledge he had received that Jesus was the Christ, the Son of the living God, was received by revelation from God—"And I say unto thee, that thou art Peter, and upon this rock [principle] will I build my church," etc.; i. e., upon the principle of God revealing to men that Jesus was the Christ‡—on the principle of revelation.

22.   Another passage quoted in support of the theory that the apostles had successors in the bishops of Rome is found in the following: Jesus after his resurrection said to his apostles: "All power is given unto me in heaven and in earth.   Go ye therefore and teach all nations; * * * and lo I am with you always, even unto the end of the world."§   This is the argument—"The apostles themselves were only to live the ordinary term of man's life: therefore

---

*St. John 1:42.

†The words of Christ to Peter, spoken in the vulgar language of the Jews, which our Lord made use of, were the same as if he had said in English: Thou art a rock, and upon this rock I will build my church. So that by the plain course of the words, Peter is here declared to be the rock upon which the church was to be built.—*Footnote in Douay Bible on these passages.*

‡As if it read: "Flesh and blood hath not revealed it unto thee, but my Father which is in heaven; and I say unto thee, Peter, upon this principle I will build my church."

§Matt. xxviii:18-20.

the commission of preaching and ministering, together with
the promise of divine assistance, regards the successors of
the apostles, no less than the apostles themselves. This
proves that there must have been an uninterrupted series
of successors of the apostles, in every age since their time;
that is to say, successors to their doctrine, to their jurisdiction, to their orders, and to their mission."* Against
this argument we put that of the late Apostle Orson Pratt:
"We do not admit that the promise—'Lo, I am with you
always, even unto the end of the world,' had any reference
to any persons whatever only the eleven disciples mentioned. * * * They were the only persons whom he
[Jesus] addressed and to whom he made this great promise.
'But,' says Dr. Milner, 'they were only to live the ordinary
term of man's life,' and consequently he draws the conclusion
that the promise could not be fulfilled to them without
successors. According to this curious inference of the
learned bishop, the Lord must have forsaken the eleven
disciples as soon as they died; for if he admit that Jesus
continued with them after the period of the death of their
mortal bodies, and that he will continue with them even
unto the end of the world, then what need would there be
for successors in order that the promise might be fulfilled?
Prove that Jesus has not been with the eleven apostles from
the time of their death until the present time, and that he
will not be with them even unto the end of the world, and
after you have proved this, you will prove that Jesus has
falsified his word; for to be with the successors of the apostles
is not to be with them.   But whether the apostles have successors or not, Jesus will always be with them, and will bring
them with him when he shall appear in his glory, and they

---

*Milner's End of Religious Controversy—Letter xxviii.

shall sit upon thrones and judge the house of Israel during the great Millennium, while Jesus will not only be with them, but will reign with them even unto the end of the world."*

23. Those who believe that the church was founded on Peter; that he became the bishop of Rome; that those who succeeded to that bishopric became the heir to his apostleship and right of presidency over the universal church, are as weak in their arguments as they are wrong in their conceptions of the foundation of the church and the right of succession in the priesthood.

24. **Primacy of the Bishops of Rome Allowed by the Fathers:**—It cannot be denied that the early fathers of the Christian church conceded to the bishops of Rome a certain "primacy of order and association," but they did not concede to them any such authority as the popes wielded from the fifth and sixth centuries onward.   The assumption of autocratic powers was resisted in the third century by Cyprian, bishop of Carthage, who contended for the equality and independence of all bishops.   (See note 5, end of section.)

25. **Opposition of the Bishops of Constantinople:**— After Cyprian the Roman pontiffs found their chief opponents in the bishops of Constantinople. That city was made the capital of the empire early in the fourth century; and became a "New Rome." The importance given to the city by this act, and the lavish embellishments and increase of population which followed it, conferred great dignity on the patriarch appointed to preside there; and the council of Constantinople, held A. D. 381, conferred upon him the second place among the great bishops of the world— the bishop of Rome being first. The council of Chalcedon,

*Orson Pratt's Works, Divine Authenticity, No. 3.

held in the next century [A. D. 451], decreed that the bishop of "New Rome" ought to be equal in power and authority with the bishop of Rome, assigning as a reason that the cities where they resided were equal in rank and dignity.

26. It would appear that second place ill-suited the ambitious prelates of "New Rome," and in this century began that struggle for supremacy between the bishops of the ancient and the new capital of the empire which ended finally in the division of the church. The strife raged with varying fortunes; but in the main the Roman pontiffs were most successful. Still in the last half of the sixth century the bishop of Constantinople, John, called the Faster—on account of the austerity of his life—assumed the title of universal bishop and continued to hold it in spite of all the efforts and threats of the Roman prelates. Early in the seventh century the emperor, Phocas, being displeased with Cyriacus, the bishop of Constantinople, he divested him of the title of universal bishop and conferred it upon the Roman pontiff, Boniface III. "After Phocas' death the prelate of the east re-assumed the title. The two bishops each preserved it, and with equal ambition strove for the pre-eminence."* Instead of dwelling together as brethren and working for the spread of truth, they spent their time in vain disputes about the extent of their respective jurisdictions and wasted their revenues and strength in conquests and reprisals of each other's ecclesiastical provinces.

27. The Ascendency of the Roman Pontiffs.—Gradually, however, the Roman pontiffs surpassed their eastern competitors in the struggle for power. The first reason for this will be found in the superior activity and that restless energy of the western people. While the east was at a

---

*Milner's Church Hist. Vol. III, pp. 53, 69—note.

standstill in its missionary enterprises, at this period, the west was using its best endeavors to extend the faith among the barbarous peoples of Germany and Briton; and everywhere they went they taught submission to the decrees of the Roman pontiff. Not only did Rome send missionaries to the barbarians, but the barbarians came to Rome. They came with arms in their hands, and as conquerors, it is true, and in the closing years of the fifth century obtained an easy victory over the western division of imperial Rome. But if imperial Rome was vanquished, there rose above its ruins and above the kingdoms founded upon them by the all-conquering barbarians, papal Rome, in majesty no less splendid than imperial Rome in her palmiest days; and in the course of time, the victorious barbarians bowed in as humble submission to the wand of the popes as their ancestors had to the eagle-mounted standards of the emperors.

28. Another reason why the Roman pontiff outstripped his eastern rival in the struggle for supremacy will be found in the superstitious reverence in which the barbarous nations that fell under the influence of Roman missionaries were accustomed to hold their priests. In the days of paganism in Gaul (France) and Germany the priests reigned over both people and magistrates, controlling absolutely the jurisdiction of the latter. The proselytes to the Christian faith among them, readily transferred that devout obedience which they had given to pagan priests, to the Christian bishops. The latter were not slow in appropriating to themselves all the honors the rude barbarians had before paid to their pagan priests. While the extraordinary reverence—which amounted to worship, according to some authorities—they bestowed upon their chief priest, was readily transferred to the pope. (See note 6, end of section.)

29. **The Great Division of the Church in the Ninth Century:**—The jealousy of the bishops of Rome and Constantinople finally ended in a division of the church, which remains to this day. It occurred in this manner: About the middle of the ninth century the emperor of the east— Michael—removed Ignatius [Ig-na-shi-us], bishop of Constantinople—whom he accused of treason—and set up one Photius [Fo-shi-us] in his place. Ignatius appealed to the bishop of Rome, Nicolaus I. Nicolaus [Nik-o-laus] called a council, which decided that the election of Photius was irregular and unlawful, and pronounced that he, with all his adherents, was unworthy of Christian communion. Instead of being humbled by this decree, and much less frightened at it, Photius convened a council, and in turn excommunicated the bishop of Rome.

30. To follow the controversies in respect to religion which followed this action, and the contests which arose about the jurisdiction over certain ecclesiastical provinces, to note the criminations and recriminations, the excommunications and counter excommunications would be not only a dreary task but one which the limits of this work preclude. Let it be sufficient to say that the breach made in the church in the middle of the ninth century, and which had its origin in the mutual jealousies of the bishops of Rome and Constantinople, rather than in the wrong done to the deposed Ignatius, or doctrinal difference which afterwards arose—continued to widen and has proven to be a chasm which up to the present it has been impossible to bridge.

31. **Means by Which Roman Pontiffs Gained Ascendency:**—The popes of Rome, however, easily outstripped the prelates of Constantinople in wealth, in pride, in power, in the magnificence of their courts, in the veneration paid

them by their subjects, in the extent of territory they brought
under their jurisdiction, in the influence wielded in the affairs
of the world. For by encouraging appeals to themselves;
by assuming the care of all the churches, as if it were a part
of their official duty; by appointing vicars in churches, over
which they had no claims to jurisdiction; by assuming to be
judges where they should have only been mediators; by
requiring accounts to be sent to them of the affairs of foreign
churches; by imposing the rites and usages of their own
church upon all others, as being of apostolic origin; by in-
sisting that their elevation was due to the pre-eminence of
the Apostle Peter—whose successor they claimed to be; by
maintaining that their fancied prerogatives belonged to
them by divine right; by threatening with excommunication all who would not submit to their decrees;* by accepting the homage which the barbarians anciently bestowed
upon their pagan priests;† by assuming the temporal power
of princes, and obtaining large grants of lands from kings
and emperors‡ (see note 7, end of section)—by these means
was that splendid though corrupt power established, before
which monarchs trembled, and which for ages ruled the des-
tinies of Europe.

32. **Rise of the Temporal Power of the Pope:—**
The Roman pontiffs, not satisfied with claiming to hold
the keys of heaven, determined through the prestige which
this claim gave them to rule the earth.

33. The popes were at first dependent for their election upon the suffrages of the clergy and people of Rome.
The election after the days of Constantine had also to

---

*See Bossuet's Universal History Vol. I, p. 558. J. Andrew Cramer,
German translation.
†See Eccl. Hist. (Mosheim) bk. III, part ii, ch. ii:6.
‡Eccl. Hist. (Mosheim) bk. III, part ii, ch. ii:11.

receive the approval of the emperor. But in course of
time all this was changed. The popes succeeded at last
in conferring the privilege of electing a successor to the
chair of St. Peter upon the clergy alone; and finally lodged
that power in the college of cardinals.* The next step was
to render the election independent of the sanction of the
emperors. This, too, was finally accomplished. But no
sooner was the church thus made independent of kings and
emperors than the former began to dominate the latter,
whose power was weakness in comparison with that of the
popes.

34. They assumed the right not only to excommunicate and anathematize kings, but to free their subjects from
their allegiance, and thus encourage rebellions and regicides.
They assumed the power to inflict temporal punishments for
violations of God's laws; and then claimed the power to remit those punishments for a consideration paid into the
sacred treasury.† Claiming to be the true successors of

---

*The Cardinals are senators of the church and counselors of the suc-
cessors of St. Peter. There are now three orders of cardinals, viz.,
bishops, priests and deacons; six of these are bishops, fifty are priests
and fourteen deacons. Sixtus V. [between A. D. 1585 and 1590] fixed
the number of cardinals at seventy in order to imitate the ancient
Sanhedrin of the Jews which was composed of seventy elders, and it is
this assembly which is now called the Sacred College.—History of All
Religions (*Burder*) p. 336.

†Apologists for the popes may say what they will about purchased
indulgences not being intended to remit sins, or a grant of permission
to commit sin; and claim that they are only a remission of the whole
or part of the temporal punishment due to sin. But if indulgences remit
the temporal penalties of sins, what is that but the remission of sin or
at least of its effects, which, for all practical purposes, would be the
same as remission of sin? And if penalties attached to sins are set aside
in advance of the commission of the sins, what is that but a license
to commit sin? "Come," said Tetzel, in selling indulgences in Germany
early in the 16th century, "come and I will give you letters all properly
sealed, by which even the sins that you intend to commit may be par-
doned. * * * There is no sin so great but that an indulgence cannot
remit."— *Hist. Reformation, D'Aubigne's bk. III, ch. i.* Tetzel de-
fends this doctrine in his *Antithesis* 99, 100, 101. [See Note 8, end of
section.]

the humble fisherman of Galilee—St. Peter—and the vicars of the still more humble Nazarene, their crowns, and thrones and courts as far outshone in splendid worldly grandeur those of kings and emperors, as their pride and arrogance surpassed the pomp and vain glory of the princes of this world; until, at last, the pope exalted himself "above all that is called God, or that is worshiped; "so that he as God sitteth in the temple of God, showing himself that he is God."* (See notes 9 and 10, end of section.)

NOTES.

1. **Apostasy in the Days of the Apostles:**—The great apostasy [or "falling away"] of the Christian church commenced in the first century, while there were yet inspired apostles and prophets in their midst; hence Paul, just previous to his martyrdom, enumerates a great number who had "made shipwreck of their faith," and "turned aside unto vain jangling;" teaching "that the resurrection was already past;" giving "heed to fables and endless genealogies," "doubting about questions and strifes of words whereof came envyings, railings, evil surmisings, perverse disputings of men of corrupt minds, and destitute of the truth, supposing the gain is godliness." This apostasy had become so general that Paul declares to Timothy, "that all they which are in Asia be turned away from me;" and again he says "at my first answer no man stood with me, but all men forsook me;" he further says that "there are many unruly, and vain talkers, deceivers, teaching things which they ought not, for filthy lucre's sake." These apostates, no doubt, pretended to be very righteous; "for," says the apostle, "they profess that they know God; but in works they deny him, being abominable and disobedient and unto every good work reprobate."—*Orson Pratt.*

2. **Early Decline of the Church:**—About the year of our Lord sixty, he [James] wrote his Catholic epistle. * * * By the practical turn of his doctrine, by his descanting on the vices of the tongue, of partiality to the rich, and of contemptuous treatment of the poor in Christian assemblies, and by his direction against vain swearing, it is but too evident that the church had considerably declined from its original purity and simplicity; and that the craft of Satan, aided ever by human depravity, was wearing out apace the precious fruits of that effusion of the Spirit, which has been described (alluding to the effusion on the day of Pentecost.)—*Milner, Vol. I, page* 34.

---

*II Thess. II:4.

3. Powers and Duties of Bishops—First and Second Century:—We may define in a few words the narrow limits of their (the bishops) original jurisdiction, which was chiefly of a spiritual, though in some instances of a temporal nature. It consisted in the administration of the sacraments and discipline of the church, the superintendency of religious ceremonies which imperceptibly increase in number and variety, the consecration of ecclesiastical ministers to whom the bishops assigned their respective functions, the management of the public fund, and the determination of all such differences as the faithful were unwilling to expose before the tribunal of an idolatrous judge. These powers, during a short period, were exercised according to the advice of the presbyteral college (the Elders of the church), and with the consent and approbation of the assembly of Christians. The primitive bishops were considered only as the first of their equals, and the honorable servants of a free people. Whenever the Episcopal chair became vacant by death, a new president was chosen among the presbyters (Elders), by the suffrage of the whole congregation, every member of which supposed himself invested with a sacred and sacerdotal character.—*Gibbon (Decline and Fall, ch. xv.)*

4. Usurpation of Provincial Councils:—As the legislative authority of the particular churches was insensibly superseded by the use of councils, the bishops obtained by their alliance a much larger share of executive and arbitrary power; and as soon as they were connected by a sense of their common interest, they were enabled to attack, with united vigor, the original rights of their clergy (the Elders and deacons) and people. The prelates of the third century imperceptibly changed the language of exhortation into that of command, scattered the seeds of future usurpations, and supplied, by scripture allegories and declamatory rhetoric, their deficiency of force and reason. They exalted the unity and power of the church as it was represented in the Episcopal office, of which every bishop enjoyed an equal and undivided portion.—*Gibbon (Decline and Fall, ch. xv.)*

5. Cyprian's Opposition to the Bishop of Rome:—Rome experienced from the nations of Asia and Africa a more vigorous resistance to her spiritual than she had formerly done to her temporal dominion. The patriotic Cyprian, who ruled with the most absolute sway the church of Carthage and the provincial synods, opposed with resolution and success the ambition of the Roman pontiff, artfully connected his own cause with that of the eastern bishops, and, like Hannibal, sought out new allies in the heart of Asia. If this punic war was carried on without any effusion of blood, it was owing much less to the moderation than to the weakness of the contending prelates. Invectives and excommunication were then the only weapons; and these, during the progress of the whole controversy, they hurled against each other with equal fury and devotion.—*Gibbon (Decline and Fall, Vol. I, Ch. xv.)*

6. Reverence of the Barbarians for the Popes:—That these pagan nations had been accustomed to treat their idolatrous priests with extraordinary reverence is a fact well known. When they became Christians they supposed they must show the same reverence to the

Christian priests. Of course they honored their bishops and clergy as they had before honored their Druids; and this reverence disposed them to bear patiently their vices. Every Druid was accounted a very great character, and was feared by every one; but the chief Druid was actually worshiped. When these people became Christians, they supposed that the bishop of Rome was such a chief Druid; and that he must be honored accordingly. And this was one cause why the Roman pontiff obtained in process of time such an ascendency in the western countries. The patriarch of Constantinople rose indeed to a great elevation; but he never attained the high rank and authority of the Roman patriarch. The reason was that the people of the east had not the same ideas of the dignity of a chief priest as the people of the west had.—*Schlegel.*

7. **Grant of the Roman Dukedom to the Popes:**—Charles [Charlemagne,] being made emperor and sovereign of Rome and its territory, reserved indeed to himself, the supreme power, and the prerogatives of sovereignty; but the beneficial dominion, as it is called, and subordinate authority over the city and its territory, he seems to have conferred on the Romish church. This plan was undoubtedly suggested to him by the Roman pontiff; who persuaded the emperor, perhaps by showing him some ancient though forged papers and documents, that Constantine the Great (to whose place and authority Charles now succeeded) when he removed the seat of empire to Constantinople, committed the old seat of empire, Rome; and the adjacent territories or Roman dukedom, to the possession and government of the church, reserving, however, his imperial prerogatives over it; and that, from this arrangement and ordinance of Constantine, Charles could not depart, without incurring the wrath of God and St. Peter.—*Mosheim.*

8. **Copy of an Indulgence:**—May our Lord Jesus Christ have mercy on thee, N. N., and absolve thee by the merits of his passion! And I in virtue of the apostolic power that has been confided in me, absolve thee from all ecclesiastical censures, judgments, and penalties which thou mayst have incurred; moreover, from all excesses, sins and crimes that thou mayst have committed, however great and enormous they may be, and from whatsoever cause, were they even reserved for our most holy father the pope and for the apostolic see. I blot out all the stains of inability and all marks of infamy that thou mayst have drawn upon thyself on this occasion. I remit the penalties that thou shouldst have endured in purgatory. I restore thee anew to participation in the sacraments of the church. I incorporate thee afresh in the communion of saints, and re-establish thee in the purity and innocence which thou hadst at thy baptism. So that in the hour of death, the gate by which sinners enter the place of torments and punishments will be closed against thee, and, on the contrary, the gate leading to the paradise of joy shall be open. And if thou shouldst not die for long years, this grace shall remain unalterable until thy last hour shall arrive. In the name of the Father, Son, and Holy Ghost. Amen. (Friar John Tetzel, Commissary, has signed this with his own hand.)— *D'Aubugne's Hist. Ref., Book III, ch. i.*

9. The Absolute Power of the Popes (13th century:)—All who had any share in the government of the church, were alike sovereign lords; at least in their feelings and dispositions they stiffly maintained with violence and threats, with both wiles and weapons, those fundamental principles of the popish canon law, that the Roman pontiff is the sovereign lord of the whole world, and that all other rulers in church and state have so much power and authority as he sees fit to allow them to have. Resting on this eternal principle as they conceive it to be, the pontiffs arrogate to themselves the absolute power, not only of conferring sacred offices or benefices as they are called, but also of giving away empires, and of divesting kings and princes of their crowns and authority. The more intelligent indeed, for the most part, considered [general] councils as superior to the pontiffs; and such of the kings as were not blinded by superstition, restrained the pontiffs from intermeddling with worldly or civil affairs, bid them be contented with the regulation of things sacred, maintained their power to the utmost of their ability and even claimed for themselves supremacy over the church in their respective territories. But they had to do these things cautiously, if they would not learn by experience that the pontiffs had very long arms.—*Mosheim.*

10. Character of Language Employed by the Popes Against Kings (8th century:)—[As a sample of the arrogant language employed by the popes toward kings and emperors, we present the following taken from an epistle of Pope Gregory III, addressed to the eastern emperor Leo III. Leo at the time was opposing with commendable zeal the use of images in divine worship:] "Because you are unlearned and ignorant, we are obliged to write to you rude discourses, but full of sense and the word of God. We conjure you to quit your pride, and hear us with humility. You say that we adore stones, walls and boards. It is not so, my lord; but those symbols make us recollect the persons whose names they bear, and exalt our grovelling minds. We do not look upon them as gods; but if it be the image of Jesus, we say, 'Lord help us.' If it be his mother, we say, 'pray to your Son to save us.' If it be a martyr, we say, 'St. Stephen, pray for us.' We might, as having the power of St. Peter, pronounce punishments against you; but as you have pronounced the curse upon yourself, let it stick to you. You write to us to assemble a general council; of which there is no need. Do you cease to persecute images, and all will be quiet. We fear not your threats; for if we go a league from Rome toward Campania, we are secure."—Certainly this is the language of anti-Christ supporting idolatry by pretenses to infallibility, and despising both civil magistrates and ecclesiastical councils.—*Milner (Church History, Vol. III, Page 159.)*

REVIEW.

1. Was the early church organization perpetuated?
2. What reasons can you assign for the failure to do so?

3. What can you say of the early apostasy in the church?   (Note 1, 2.)

4. What course was pursued by the apostles in respect to organizing churches?

5. In what light were the apostles regarded by the saints?

6. In what condition were the churches left at the death of the apostles?

7. Was there such a thing as subordination among the churches, or rank among the bishops?

8. What was the manner of electing bishops?

9. What was the nature of the bishop's duties in the early churches? (Note 3.)

10. Describe the growth of iniquity among the bishops.

11. Give an account of the origin of metropolitan bishops.

12. Describe the rise and influence of councils.   (Note 4.)

13. What was the conduct of the lower officials in the church?

14. What was the moral status of the church officials in the 2nd and 3rd centuries?

15. Tell what important change was made in the form of church government in the 4th century?

16. Describe the outlines of Roman government under Constantine.

17. Tell how the church government was made somewhat to correspond with it.

18. What circumstances led to the pre-eminence of the bishop of Rome?

19. What reasons can be urged against the idea that the bishop of Rome succeeded to the apostleship of Peter, and the presidency of the universal church?

20. What is the scriptural basis of the claims of the bishops of Rome to preeminence?

21. Refute the idea that Jesus built his church upon Peter.

22. Refute the argument that the bishops of Rome must have succeeded to the apostleship of Peter, because Jesus promised to be with the apostles unto the end of the world.   (Par. 22.)

23. To what extent did the early Christian fathers admit a primacy to the bishops of Rome?

24. State the controversy which arose between the bishop of Rome and the bishop of Constantinople.

25. Through what cause did the Roman pontiffs finally force an acknowledgment of their independency?   (Note 6.)

26. What led to the great division of the church in the 9th century?

27. By what means did the Roman pontiffs outstrip their eastern rivals?   (Note 7.)

28. What of the sale of indulgences?   (Note.)

29. What was the climax of papal power?   (Par. 34.)

SECTION V.

1. Simplicity of Public Worship Changed:—The public worship of the primitive Christians, as we have seen,* was very simple, but its simplicity was soon corrupted. The bishops and other public teachers in the third century, framed their discourses and exhortations according to the rules of Grecian eloquence; "and were better adapted," says a learned writer,† "to call forth the admiration of the rude multitude who love display, than to amend the heart. And that no folly and no senseless custom might be omitted in their public assemblies, the people were allowed to applaud their orators, as had been practiced in the forums and theaters; nay, they *were instructed to applaud the preachers."

2. This was a wide departure from that spirit of meekness and humility enjoined by Messiah upon his ministers. And when to these customs was added the splendid vestments of the clergy, the magnificence of the temples, with all the pageantry of altars, surrounded with burning tapers, clouds of incense, beautiful images, the chanting of choirs, processions and other mummeries without number—one sees but little left of that simple worship instituted by the Messiah and his apostles. (See note 1, end of section.)

3. It was about the third century that incense began to be used. The Christians of the first and second centuries

---

*Section III.
†*Mosheim.*

abhorred the use of incense in public worship, as being a part of the worship of idols.*   It first became a custom to use it at funerals against offensive smells; then in public worship to disguise the bad air of crowded assemblies; then at the consecration of bishops and magistrates, and by these steps at last degenerated into a superstitious rite.

4.   In the fourth century matters became still worse. "The public supplications by which the pagans were accustomed to appease their gods, were borrowed from them, and were celebrated in many places with great pomp.   To the temples, to water consecrated in due form, and the images of holy men, the same efficacy was ascribed and the same privileges assigned as had been attributed to the pagan temples, statues and lustrations before the advent of Christ."†

5.   **The Worship of Martyrs:**—In the third century also arose the worship of martyrs.   It is true that worship or adoration was relative, and a distinction was made between the worship of martyrs and the worship paid to God; but by degrees the worship of the martyrs was made to conform with that which the pagans had in former times paid to their gods.‡   This was done out of indiscreet eagerness to allure the pagans to embrace Christianity.§   (See note 2, end of section.)

6.   **Decline of Spiritual Gifts:**—While pagan ceremonies and rites were increasing in the church, the gifts and graces characteristic of apostolic times, seemed to have gradually departed from it.   Protestant writers insist that the age of miracles closed with the fourth or fifth

---

*Tertullian's Apology, ch. xlii.

†Mosheim's Eccl. Hist. vol. I, bk, ii; part ii; ch. 4.

‡Historie de Manicheism, tom ii, p. 642.

§Eccl. Hist. (Mosheim) vol. I, bk. ii, part ii.

century, and that after that the extraordinary gifts of the Holy Ghost must not be looked for. Catholic writers, on the other hand, insist that the power to perform miracles has always continued in the church; yet those spiritual manifestations which they describe after the fourth and fifth centuries savor of invention on the part of the priests and childish credulity on the part of the people; or else what is claimed to be miraculous falls far short of the power and dignity of those spiritual manifestations which the primitive church was wont to witness.

7. The virtues and prodigies ascribed to the bones and other relics of the martyrs and saints are puerile in comparison with the healings, by the anointing with oil and the laying on of hands, speaking in tongues, interpretations, prophecies, revelations, casting out devils in the name of Jesus Christ; to say nothing of the gifts of faith, wisdom, knowledge, discernment of spirits, etc.—common in the church in the days of the apostles.*

8. Nor is there anything in the scriptures or in reason that would leave one to believe that they were to be discontinued. Still this plea is made by modern Christians —explaining the absence of these spiritual powers among them—that the extraordinary gifts of the Holy Ghost were only intended to accompany the proclamation of the gospel during the first few centuries until the church was able to make its way without them, and then they were to be done away. It is sufficient to remark upon this, that it is assumption pure and simple, and stands without warrant either of scripture or right reason; and proves that men had so far changed the religion of Jesus Christ that it became a form of godliness without the power thereof. (See notes 3 and 4, end of section)

---

*I Cor. xii: 8-10.

9. Causes and Manner of Excommunications:— It appears to have been the custom of the apostles in the case of members of the church grievously transgressing the moral law of the gospel to require repentance and confession before the church; and in the event of a stubborn adherence to sin the offender was excommunicated, that is, he was excluded from the communion of the church and the fellowship of the saints. For the crimes of murder, idolatry and adultery some of the churches excommunicated those guilty of them forever; in other churches they were received back, but only after long and painful probation.

10. The manner in which excommunication was performed in apostolic times is not clear, but there is every reason to believe the process was very simple. In the course of time, however, this simple order of excommunication was changed, by being burdened with many rites and ceremonies borrowed from pagan sources.* It was not enough that the fellowship of the saints be withdrawn from the offender and he left to the mercy of God, or the buffetings of Satan, according as he was worthy of the one or the other; but the church must load him down with anathemas too terrible to contemplate. The power of excommunication, too, eventually, passed from the body of the church into the hands of the bishops, and finally into those of the pope. At first excommunication meant the loss of the fellowship of the saints, and such other punishments as God himself might see fit to inflict; the church leaving the Lord to be the minister of his own vengeance. But gradually it came to

---

*That it was proper for the Christian bishops to increase the restraints upon the licentiousness of transgression, will be readily granted by all who consider the circumstances of those times. But whether it was for the advantage of Christianity, to borrow rules for this salutary ordinance from the enemies of truth, and thus to consecrate, as it were, a part of the pagan superstition, many persons very justly call in question.—*Eccl. Hist.* (*Mosheim*) Book I, Cent. 2, Part ii, ch. iii.

mean in some instances banishment from home and country, the confiscation of property, the loss not only of religious fellowship with the saints, but the loss of civil rights, and the rights of Christian burial. In the case of a monarch excommunication absolved his subjects from their allegiance;andin the case of a subject, it robbed him of the protection of his sovereign. No anathema was so terrible but it was pronounced against the excommunicated, until the sweet mercies of God were overshadowed by the black pall of man's inhumanity. Satan exalted himself "above all that is called God, or that is worshiped, so that he as God sitteth in the Temple of God, showing himself that he is God."*

11. **Admixture of Pagan Philosophy with the Christian Religion**:—The thing which contributed most to the subversion of the Christian religion was the employment of pagan philosophy to explain Christian doctrine. This brought about an admixture of these two discordant elements that, while it failed to purge pagan philosophy of its errors, corrupted the doctrines of Christ and laid the foundations for those false notions in respect of God which obtain in the so-called Christian world unto this day.

12. **Christian Doctrine Respecting God**:—The scriptural doctrine in regard to God—and of course, that is the true Christian doctrine—is this: There is a being of infinite goodness and power, in form like man—for man was created in his image†—who, with his Son, Jesus Christ, and the Holy Ghost, constitute the great creative, and governing power or grand Presidency of the heavens and

---

*II Thess. 2:4.

†Gen. 1: 26, 27. Jesus Christ was in the form of man, yet he is said to be the *express image of God's* person, as also the brightness of his glory. *Heb. i*: 1-3.

of the earth.   As persons, the Father, Son and Holy Ghost
are separate and distinct, yet one in attributes, one in purpose; the mind of one being the mind of the others—a
harmonized trinity of distinct intelligences.

13.   That they are distinct and separate as persons was
plainly manifested at the baptism of Jesus.   On that occasion, as Jesus came up out of the water, John saw the Holy
Ghost descend upon him, and at the same time the voice
of the Father was heard speaking from heaven, saying:
"This is my beloved Son, in whom I am well pleased."*
Here we have the persons of the Godhead present but distinct from each other.   Stephen, the martyr, in the presence
of the angry crowd which took his life, saw the heavens open
and "Jesus standing on the right hand of God."†   Here, too,
the Father and Son are seen; and, according to the testimony of the holy man, they are distinct personalities.

14.   Yet Jesus said to the Jews: "I and my Father are
one. * * * Believe that the Father is in me and I in
him."‡   But this oneness cannot have reference to the
persons of the Father and the Son, which we have seen are
distinct.   Their oneness, therefore, must consist in a unity
of attributes, purposes, glory, power.   Jesus in his great
prayer just previous to his betrayal, said, in praying for his
disciples: "Holy Father, keep through thine own name
those whom thou hast given me, that they may be *one*. * * *
That they all may be one; *as* thou, Father, art in me,
and I in thee, that they also may be *one* in us."§   Clearly
it is not the uniting of the persons of his disciples into one
person or body, that Jesus prayed for; but he would have

---

*Matt. iii: 16, 17.
†Acts vii: 55, 56.
‡John x: 30, and John xiv: 8-11.
§John xvii: 11, 21.

them of one mind and one spirit, one in nature, as he and the Father are one. So also he had no wish that the person of one of his disciples should be crowded into that of another, and so on until they all became one person or body—but "*as thou, Father, art in me, and I in thee.*" That is, while remaining distinct as persons, Messiah would have the mind or Spirit of God in his disciples as it was in him, and as his was in the Father, that God might be all in all:—the Father to be honored as the head and worshiped in the name of the Son; and the Holy Ghost to be revered as the witness and messenger of both the Father and the Son*—the bond of union between God and men and between men and men, as it is between the Father and the Son; in one word to be God in man.

15. Each of these persons in scripture is called God; and taken together they are God, or constitute the grand Presidency of heaven and earth, and as such are one, as well as one—or alike—in attributes. (See note 5, end of section.)

16. The spirit of the Son had an existence with the Father before he was born in the flesh;† and indeed it was by him, and through him—under the direction of the Father—that the worlds were made;‡ "and without him was not anything made that was made."§

17. Such is the simple doctrine of the Godhead taught to the primitive Saints by the apostles. It was implicitly believed as God's revelation to them upon the subject, and they were content to allow the revelation to excite their reverence without arousing their curiosity to the point where

---

*John xiv: 26. John xv: 26. John xvi: 13-15.
†John xvii: 4, 5.
‡Heb. iv: 2.
§John i: 3. (See note 1, end of section VI.)

men of finite minds attempt to grasp the infinite, or cir-
cumscribe God in their understandings. In a short time,
however, a change came, and men sought to explain the
revelation that God had given of himself by the vain bab-
blings of pagan science; and that led not only to much contention within the church, but to the adoption in the Christian creed of erroneous ideas in respect of Deity.

NOTES.

1. Christian Worship in the Fifth Century:—Public worship
everywhere assumed a form more calculated for show and for the grati-
fication of the eye. Various ornaments were added to the sacerdotal
garments in order to increase the veneration of the people for the
clerical order. The new forms of hymns, prayers and public fasts, are
not easily enumerated. * * * In some places it was appointed,
that the praises of God should be sung perpetually, day and night, the
singers succeeding each other without interruption; as if the Supreme
Being took pleasure in clamor and noise, and in the flatteries of men.
The magnificence of the temples had no bounds. Splendid images were
placed in them; and among these * * * the image of the Virgin
Mary, holding her infant in her arms, occupied the most conspicuous
place. Altars and repositories for relics, made of solid silver if possible,
were procured in various places; from which may easily be conjectured,
what must have been the splendor and the expense of the other sacred
utensils.—*Mosheim.*

2. Martyr Worship (3rd century:)—When Gregory [surnamed
Thaumaturgus on account of the numerous miracles he is said to have
wrought—born in Pontus, in the second decade of the third century]
perceived that the ignorant and simple multitude persisted in their
idolatry, on account of the sensitive pleasures and delights it afforded—
he allowed them in celebrating the memory of the holy martyrs, to
indulge themselves, and give a loose to pleasure, (i. e., as the thing
itself, and both what precedes and what follows, place beyond all
controversy, he allowed them at the sepulchres of the martyrs on their
fast days, to dance, to use sports, to indulge in conviviality, and do
all things that the worshipers of idols were accustomed to do in their
temples, on their festival days,) hoping that in process of time, they
would spontaneously come over to a more becoming and more correct
manner of life.— *Nyssen's Life of Gregory Thaumaturgus.*

3. On the Continuance of Spiritual Gifts:—The affliction of
devils, the confusion of tongues, deadly poisons and sickness (all of
which were to be overcome by the extraordinary gifts of the Spirit) are all
curses which have been introduced into the world by the wickedness of
man. The blessings of the gospel are bestowed to counteract these
curses. Therefore, as long as these curses exist, the promised signs

[Mark xvi: 17, 18] are needed to counteract their evil consequences. If Jesus had not intended that the blessings should be as extensive and unlimited in point of time as the curses, he would have intimated something to that effect in his word. But when he makes a universal promise of certain powers, to enable every believer in the gospel throughout the world to overcome certain curses, entailed upon man, because of wickedness, it would be the rankest kind of infidelity not to believe the promised blessing necessary, as long as the curses abound among men. —*Orson Pratt.*

4. **When and Why the Spiritual Gifts Ceased in the Church:**— It does not appear that these extraordinary gifts of the Holy Spirit [speaking of I Cor. xii] were common in the church for more than two or three centuries. We seldom hear of them after that fatal period when the Emperor Constantine called himself a Christian; and from a vain imagination of promoting the Christian cause thereby heaped riches, and power, and honor upon Christians in general, but in particular upon the Christian clergy. From this time they [the spiritual gifts] almost totally ceased; very few instances of the kind were found. The cause of this was not (as has been supposed) because there was no more occasion for them, because all the world was become Christians. This is a miserable mistake; not a twentieth part of it was then nominally Christian. The real cause of it was the love of many, almost all Christians, so-called, was waxed cold. The Christians had no more of the Spirit of Christ than the other heathens. The Son of Man when he came to examine his church, could hardly find faith upon the earth. This was the real cause why the extraordinary gifts of the Holy Ghost were no longer to be found in the Christian Church—because the Christians were turned heathens again and only had a dead form left.— *John Wesley (Wesley's Works, Vol. vii, Sermon 89, pages 26, 27.)*

5. **Illustration of the Oneness of the Godhead:**—The Godhead may be further illustrated by a council, composed of three men—all possessing equal wisdom, knowledge and truth, together with equal qualifications in every respect. Each person would be a separate, distinct person or substance from the other two, and yet the three would form but *one* council. Each alone possesses, by supposition, the same wisdom and truth that the three united or the *one* council possesses. The union of the three men in one council would not increase the knowledge or wisdom of either. Each man would be *one part* of the council when reference is made to his person; but the wisdom and truth of each man would be the whole wisdom and truth of the council, and not a part. If it were possible to divide truth, and other qualities of a similar nature into fractions, so that the Father should have the third part of truth, the third part of wisdom, the third part of knowledge, the third part of love, while the Son and the Holy Spirit possessed the other two-thirds of these qualities or affections, then neither of these persons could make "one God," "but only a part of a God." But because the divisibility of wisdom, truth or love is impossible, the whole of these qualities dwell in the Father—the whole dwells in the Son— the whole is possessed by the Holy Spirit. The Holy Spirit is *one part* of the Godhead in essence; but the whole of God in wisdom, truth,

and other similar qualities.   If a truth could become three truths, dis-tinct from each other, by dwelling in three substances, then there would be three Gods instead of one.   But as it is, the trinity is three in es-sence, but one in truth and other similar principles.   The oneness of the Godhead, as described in the scriptures, never was intended to apply to the essence, but only to the perfections and other attributes.— *Orson Pratt.*

REVIEW.

1.   Describe the simplicity of public worship in early Christian times.   (Note 2, end of section III.)

2.   What changes in the public worship were gradually introduced? (Note 1.)

3.   What was the object in introducing these changes?

4.   In what manner was incense introduced into public worship?

5.   What especially obnoxious practice became prevalent in the 4th century?

6.   What can you say of the worship of martyrs?   (Note 2.)

7.   Give an account of the decline of spiritual gifts in the church?

8.   On this point what difference exists between Catholics and Protestants?

9.   What can you say of Protestant excuses for the absence of the spiritual gifts of the gospel?   (Notes 3 and 4.)

10.   What does the absence of spiritual gifts prove?

11.   In what way were grievous offenses punished by the church?

12.   What ceremonies finally became associated with excommuni-cation?

13.   What temporal punishments were sometimes associated with excommunication?

14.   What can you say of the mingling of pagan philosophy with the Christian religion?

15.   Give the scriptural doctrine respecting God.

16.   Give an instance from scripture where the personages of the Godhead are seen to be distinct.

17.   In what does the oneness of the Father, Son and Holy Ghost consist?   (Note 5.)

18.   How did the early Christians regard the scriptural doctrine of the Godhead?

19.   By what means did men at last try to explain the revelation?

SECTION VI.

1. Gnostic and "New Platonic" Philosophy:— In order to give a clear explanation of the adoption of erroneous ideas in the Christian Creed respecting God, it will be necessary to invite the attention of the student to Gnosticism and to the Eclectic or "New Platonic" philosophy which arose in the early Christian centuries.

First, then, as to Gnosticism. The Gnostics taught that there existed from eternity a Being that embodied within himself all the virtues; a Being who is the purest light and is diffused throughout boundless space which they called Pleroma. This Being, after dwelling alone and in absolute repose for an infinite period, by an operation purely mental, or by acting upon himself, produced two spirits* of different sexes. By the marriage of these two spirits others of similar nature were produced, who, in their turn, produced others. Thus a celestial family was formed in the pleroma. These emanations from Deity, whether directly or from those spirits first begotten, by Deity acting upon himself, were called Aeons, a term which was doubtless employed to signify their eternal duration, and perhaps the mode of their production.

2. Beyond this pleroma where God and his family dwelt, existed a rude and unformed mass of matter, heaving itself continually in wild commotions.† This mass one of

---

*Some authorities say seven pairs were introduced in this manner.

†The statement is condensed from Mosheim; Dr. Benton, for years Professor of Divinity at Oxford, in his Brampton lectures states that the matter was "inert and powerless though co-eternal with the supreme God, and, like Him, without beginning."

the Aeons, wandering beyond the pleroma, discovered, and reduced to order and beauty and then peopled it with human beings and with animals of different species. This builder of the world the Gnostics called the Demiurge [Dem-i-urge.]* Though possessed of many shining qualities, the Demiurge was by nature arrogant and domineering, hence he claims absolute authority over the new world to the exclusion altogether of the authority of the supreme God, and requires mankind to pay divine honors exclusively to him.

3. Man, according to the Gnostic philosophy, is composed of a terrestrial, and therefore, a vicious body; and of a celestial spirit, which in some sense is a particle of the Deity himself. The, spirit is oppressed by the body, which is supposed to be the seat of all the lusts and other evils that flesh is heir to, and by it the spirit of man is drawn away from the. knowledge and worship of the true God, and led to pay reverence to the Demiurge and his associates. From this wretched bondage of evil, God labors to rescue his offspring. But the Demiurge and his associates, eager to retain their power, resist the divine purpose and labor to efface all knowledge of the supreme Deity. This philosophy maintained, however, that God would ultimately prevail; and having restored to liberty most of the spirits now imprisoned in bodies, he will dissolve the fabric of the world. Then the primitive tranquility will return, and God will

---

*The Gnostics desired to avoid making God the author of evil, hence it is a leading principle in their philosophy that all evil has its origin in matter, and as matter was created by one of the Aeons, not by God, the Lord in the Gnostic system is relieved from the responsibility of being the author of evil.

reign with the redeemed spirits in perfect happiness to all eternity.*

4. When the followers of this philosophy became converted to Christianity, they looked upon Jesus Christ and the Holy Ghost as the latest Aeons or emanations from the Deity, sent forth to emancipate men from the tyranny of matter by revealing to them the true God, to fit them—through perfect knowledge—to enter the sacred pleroma. In connection with this, however, some of these Christian Gnostics held that Jesus had no body at all, but was an unsubstantial phantom that constantly deceived the senses of those who thought they associated with him. Others of them said there doubtless was a man called Jesus, born of human parents, upon whom one of the Aeons, called Christ, descended at his baptism, having quitted the pleroma for that purpose; but who, previous to the crucifixion of the man Jesus, withdrew from him and returned to the Deity. (See note 2, end of section.)

5. **The Two Modes of Life to which Gnosticism Led:**—The Gnostic philosophy led to two widely different methods of life; one extremely ascetic and the other as extremely profligate. Gnostics believed matter to be utterly malignant, the source of all evil, therefore it was recommended by one party that the body should be weakened by fastings and the practice of other austerities, that the spirit might enjoy the greater liberty and be better able to contemplate heavenly things. The other party, on the contrary, maintained that men could safely indulge all their appetites and lustful desires, and that there was no moral difference in human actions. One leader of this

---

*The statement of the Gnostic philosophy I have condensed from Mosheim and Dr. Benton, than whom there can be no higher authority on this subject.

persuasion—Carpocrates, of Alexandria, who flourished in the second century—not only gave his disciples license to sin, but imposed on them the necessity of sinning, by teaching them the way to eternal salvation was open to those souls only which committed all kinds of enormity and wickedness. Such were the errors that grew out of Gnosticism, and which contributed to the corruption of the gospel soon after it was founded by the preaching of the apostles.

6. The New Platonic Philosophy: — The Eclectic or "New Platonic" philosophy which came into existence in the early Christian centuries, was compounded from all the systems which had preceded it, though following Plato more closely than any other teacher, for which reason they often assumed the name of "New Platonics." The founders of this philosophy professed simply to follow truth, gathering up whatever was accordant with it, regardless of its source, or in what school it was taught—hence the name eclectic. Still the teachings of Plato formed the basis of their doctrines, and they embraced most of his dogmas concerning God, the human soul and the universe. We shall therefore learn the fundamental principles of the Eclectics by considering what the Athenian sage taught on these subjects.

7. Plato held that God and matter existed from all eternity—that they were co-eternal. Before the creation of the world, matter had in itself a principle of motion, but without end or laws. This principle of motion Plato called the immortal soul of the universe. God wished to give form to this mass of eternal matter, regulate its motion, subject it to some end and to certain laws. Everything which exists in heaven or in earth, except Deity and unorganized matter, according to Plato's philosophy, had a beginning—there was a time when it did not exist; but there never was a time when the idea, that is, the form or plan of the thing, did not exist in the mind of Deity. This idea or intelligence existing with God from all eternity, is what Plato called the Logos—the word or intelligence of Deity. Many in the age of which we write saw in these doctrines a three-fold expression of the divine nature—viz., the First Cause, the Reason or Logos, and the Spirit of the Universe; while others saw in these three principles three Gods, united with each other by a mysterious and ineffable generation; in which the Logos is regarded in the character of the Son of an Eternal Father, and the creator and governor of the world.*

8. **Plato's "Logos" and John's "Word" Considered Identical:**—In the introduction of St. John's gospel, commencing—"In the beginning was the Word, and the Word was with God, and the Word was God"—in this Word, which the apostle in another verse of his opening chapter declares was "made flesh," and dwelt among men,—plainly alluding to the pre-existence and birth of Messiah—the New Platonics saw the incarnation of the Logos of Plato, and according to the fashion of the times attempted to harmonize the revelations of God with the philosophy of men. (See note 3, end of section.)

9. **The Rank of the Logos in the Trinity:**—It was trying to harmonize the revelations of God with these systems of philosophy which created the agitation in respect to the rank of the Logos, or Son of God, in the divine Trinity; and the nature of the Trinity itself—that is, whether the three persons, the Father, Son and Holy Ghost are distinct and separate, though of the same substance; or merely the same substance under different aspects.

Gibbon's Decline and Fall, Vol. ii, ch. xxii.

10. The Orthodox View:—The view held to be orthodox was that in God there are three persons, Father, Son and Holy Spirit; each really distinct yet so united as to constitute but one personal God—of the same substance, and equal as to their eternity, power, and glory and all other perfections.

11. Sabellian Theory:—On one side of this orthodox theory stood the doctrine of Sabellius [Sa-bel-i-us], who held that there was but one Divine person in the Godhead, and that the Father, Son and Holy Spirit were but different aspects of the same God, and that the Trinity was one of names, merely, not of distinct persons.* The Logos, in his theory, is an attribute of Deity rather than a person; and its incarnation is reduced to an energy or inspiration of the Divine wisdom, which filled the soul and directed all the actions of the man Jesus.

12. The Arian Theory:—On the other side of the orthodox line stood the theory of Arius [A-ri-us], who, while he maintained a real distinction in the persons of the Divine Trinity, taught that the Son was created out of nothing by the will of the Father; and though the longest astronomical periods would not measure the time of his duration, yet

---

*The subject is difficult of illustration; but the following will perhaps aid the student to grasp the Sabellian doctrine. We see the ocean is a liquid; let us next imagine it frozen into solid ice; next as entirely dissolved into vapor. Here we have the same substance in three different aspects—liquid, solid, vapor; but whether we speak of it as the liquid ocean, the frozen ocean or the ocean dissolved into vapor, it is always the same ocean, the same substance, but under different aspects. Whether he appeared as the Father, the Son, or the Holy Ghost, He was always the same God. Such was the Sabellian theory in respect to Deity. Mosheim represents Sabellius as teaching that the divine nature was divided into portions, that one portion became separate, was called the Son, and was joined to the man Jesus. The Holy Ghost was a similar portion or part of the Eternal Father. The weight of authority is against the learned Doctor in this matter, however, and in favor of the statement of Sabellius' views in the text of this work.

there *had* been a time when he was not. Upon the Son thus created the Father bestowed great glory, yet he shone only by a reflected light, and governed the universe only in obedience to the will of the Father; in other words, the Son was subordinate to the Father, unequal as to eternity, power, and glory.

13. The Nicene Council and Creed:—It was to still the rising commotion which arose in the church through the violent discussion of these several theories that the Emperor Constantine assembled the Council of Nice [Nes], A. D. 325.   In that council the theories of Arius were condemned and the orthodox creed stated thus: "We believe in one God, the Father, Almighty, the maker of all things visible and invisible; and in one Lord, Jesus Christ, the Son of God, begotten of the Father, only begotten, (that is) of the substance of the Father; God of God, Light of Light, Very God of Very God; begotten not made; of the same substance with the Father, by whom all things were made, that are in heaven and that are in earth; who for us men, and for our salvation, descended and was incarnate, and became man; suffered and rose again the third day, ascended into the heavens and will come to judge the living and the dead; and in the Holy Spirit.   But those who say there was a time when he [the Son] was not, and that he was not before he was begotten, and that he was made out of nothing, or affirm that he is of any other substance or essence, or that the Son of God was created, and mutable, or changeable, the Catholic Church doth pronounce accursed."*

14. The Creed of Athanasius:—Athanasius [Ath-a-

---

*This is the Nicene Creed as it was formulated by that celebrated council.   The so-called Nicene Creed, used in the Catholic, Lutheran and English Churches, is this creed as modified by the Council of Constantinople, A. D. 381.   There is no material difference in them.

na-shi-us], who was the most active opponent of Arius, thus explains the Nicene doctrine, in what is commonly known as the creed of Athanasius:* "We worship one God in Trinity, and Trinity in Unity, neither confounding the persons; nor dividing the substance. For there is one person of the Father, another of the Son, and another of the Holy Ghost. But the Godhead of the Father, Son and Holy Ghost is all one: The glory equal, the majesty co-eternal. Such as the Father is, such is the Son; and such is the Holy Ghost. The Father uncreate, the Son uncreate, and the Holy Ghost uncreate. The Father incomprehensible, the Son incomprehensible, and the Holy Ghost incomprehensible. The Father eternal, the Son eternal, and the Holy Ghost eternal. And yet these are not three eternals; but one eternal. As also there are not three incomprehensibles, nor three uncreated; but one uncreated and one incomprehensible. So likewise the Father is Almighty, the Son Almighty, and the Holy Ghost Almighty; and yet they are not three Almighties, but one Almighty. So the Father is God, the Son is God, and the Holy Ghost is God, and yet they are not three Gods, but one God.†

---

*Mosheim, Gibbon, Montfaucon and others insist that Athanasius is not the author of this creed, and this may be true, but I have not yet heard of its being rejected as an explanation of the Nicene Creed. Indeed, notwithstanding its authenticity has long been suspected, it still stands in the English prayer book and is recited in the church of England service upon the most notable feasts, Christmas, Epiphany etc.

†*Church of England Book of Common Prayer*, *p.* 49, Athanasius is credited with having confessed that whenever he forced his understanding to meditate on the divinity of the Logos, his toilsome and unavailing efforts recoiled on themselves; that the more he thought, the less he comprehended; and the more he wrote, the less capable was he of expressing his thoughts. (*Decline and Fall, Vol. II, ch. xxi.*) We would naturally think that whoever the author of the Athanasian Creed may be, that such would be his mental condition. Nor are we very much surprised when we hear Gennadius, patriarch of Constantinople, frankly pronouncing it the work of a drunken man.

15. Immateriality of God:—The evil which grew out of these contentions in respect to Deity is found in the conclusion arrived at that God is an incorporeal, that is to say, an immaterial being; without body, without parts, without passions. The following is the Roman Catholic belief in respect of God: "There is but one God, the creator of heaven and earth, the supreme, *incorporeal* uncreated being, who exists of himself, and is infinite in all his attributes, etc."* The Church of England teaches in her articles of faith—"There is but one living and true God, everlasting, without body, parts or passions; of infinite power, wisdom and goodness,"† etc. This plainly teaches the great error of the immateriality of God; and, indeed, that is the orthodox notion in respect of Deity, notwithstanding it finds so many express contradictions in the scriptures.

16. In the work of creation, God proposed to make man in his own image and likeness, and the proposition was executed.‡ Moreover, Jesus is said to be the brightness of God's glory, "and the express image of his person."§ Again it is said, that Jesus "being in the form of God, thought it not robbery to be equal with God."‖ All this teaches that God has a form similar to that of man's; that he has organs, dimensions, proportions; that he occupies space and has relation to other objects in space; that as a person, he moves from place to place; and that so far as his actual person is concerned he cannot be in two places at one and the same instant. The question here arises as to those passages of

---

*Catholic *Belief* (Bruno) p. 1. This work is endorsed by His Eminence Cardinal Manning.

†Church of England Book of Common Prayer, p. 311.

‡Gen. 1: 26, 27.

§Heb. 1: 3.

‖Phil. ii: 5, 6.

scripture which declare the omnipresence of God, a thing which is impossible—speaking of his person—if what is here contended for be true. But God may be and is omnipresent by his influence, by his power, if not in his person. While his person is confined to one place at a time, as other substances are, his influence extends throughout the universe, as does also his power, and through this means he is omnipotent and omnipresent.

17. To assert the immateriality of God as substance, is not only to deny his personality, but his very existence; for an immaterial substance cannot exist. It can have no relation to time or·space, no form, no extension, no parts. An immaterial substance is simply no substance at all; it is a contradiction of terms to say a substance is immaterial— it is the description of an infinite vacuum; and the difference between the atheist and the orthodox Christian is one of terms, not of fact; the former says, "There is no God;" the latter in his creed says, "God is nothing."* (See note 5, end of section.)

18. Such were the absurdities into which the vain

---

*It is remarkable how clearly men will reason upon the absurdity of immaterialism in everything except in respect to God. As an example take the reasoning of Rev. John Wesley in regard to the supposed immateriality of the fire in hell: "But it has been questioned by some whether there be any fire in hell; that is, any material fire. Nay, if there be any fire it is unquestionably material. For what is immaterial fire? The same as immaterial water or earth? Both the one and the other is absolute nonsense, a contradiction in terms. Either, therefore, we must affirm it to be material, or we deny its existence." Now apply that correct reasoning to the immaterial God of the orthodox Christian and what is the result? Let us try the experiment by substituting the word God, for the word fire in the quotation:—"But it is questioned by some whether there be any God; that is, any material God. Nay, if there be any God, he is unquestionably material. For what is an immaterial God? The same as immaterial water or earth! both the one and the other (that is, both immaterial God and immaterial earth,) is absolute nonsense, a contradiction in terms. Either, therefore, we must affirm him to be material, or we deny his existence."

philosophies of the pagans led the Christians even in the early centuries of the Christian era; so that through these errors they even denied the Lord who bought them.*

NOTES.

1. Messiah the Author of the Gospel and Creator of the World:—Christ is the author of this gospel, of this earth, of men and women, of all the posterity of Adam and Eve, and of every living creature that lives upon the face of the earth, that flies in the heavens, that swims in the waters, or dwells in the field. Christ is the author of salvation to all this creation, to all things pertaining to this terrestrial globe we occupy.—*Brigham Young (Discourse, August 8th, 1852.)*

2. The Phantom Theory of the Gnostics:—While the blood of Christ yet smoked on Mount Calvary, the Docetes (the name given to the Gnostic Christians) invented the impious and extravagant hypothesis, that, instead of issuing from the womb of the virgin, he had descended on the banks of the Jordan in the form of perfect manhood; that he had imposed on the senses of his enemies, and of his disciples; and that the ministers of Pilate had wasted their impotent rage on an airy phantom, who *seemed* to expire on the cross, and, after three days, to rise from the dead.—*Gibbon.*

3. The Fashion of Uniting Discordant Elements in Philosophy and Religion:—When we come to consider the state of philosophy at that time (the early Christian centuries,) and the fashion which prevailed of catching at anything new, and of uniting discordant elements into fanciful systems, we shall not be surprised to find the doctrines of the gospel disguised and altered, and that, according to the language of that age, many new heresies were formed.—*Burton's Brampton Lectures.*

4. The Mysteries of Religion Deepened Through Attempted Explanations:—That devout and reverential simplicity of the first ages of the church, which taught men to believe when God speaks, and obey when God commands, appeared to most of the doctors of this age (the fifth century) to be unphilosophical and becoming only in the vulgar. Many of those, however, who attempted to explain and illustrate these doctrines, opened the way rather to disputation than for a rational faith and a holy life; for they did not so much explain, as involve in greater obscurity, and darken with ambiguous terms and incomprehensible distinctions the deep mysteries of revealed religion. And hence arose abundant matter for difficulties, contentions and animosities which flowed down to succeeding ages, and which can scarcely be removed by the efforts of human power. It hardly need be remarked, that some, while pressing their adversaries, incautiously fell into errors of an opposite character which were no less dangerous.—*Mosheim.*

---

*II Peter ii: 1.

5. Immaterialists are Atheists:—There are two classes of atheists in the world.   One class denies the existence of God in the most positive language; the other denies his existence in duration or space.   One says, "There is no God."   The other says, "God is not *here* or *there*, any more than he exists *now* and *then*."   The infidel says, "There is no such a substance as God."   The immaterialist says, "There is such a substance as God, but it is 'without parts.' "   The atheist says, "There is no such substance as spirit."   The immaterialist says, "A spirit, though he lives and acts, occupies no room and fills no space, in the same way and after the same manner as matter, not even so much as does the minutest grain of sand."   The atheist does not seek to hide his infidelity; but the immaterialist, whose declared belief amounts to the same thing as the atheist's endeavors to hide his infidelity under the shallow covering of a few words.—*Orson Pratt* (*Absurdities of Immaterialism*, page 11.)

REVIEW.

1.   Give the Gnostic idea respecting God.
2.   How did the Gnostics account for the creation of the world?
3.   In what way did the Gnostics avoid making God the author of evil?
4.   What is the nature of man according to the Gnostic philosophy?
5.   What did the Gnostic philosophy look to as the culmination between the struggle of man with evil?
6.   In what light did the Gnostics look upon Jesus Christ?
7.   What fanciful theory did some of them hold respecting him? (Note 7.)
8.   To what two modes of life did the Gnostic philosophy lead?
9.   What was the New Platonic philosophy?
10.   What was Plato's idea of God?
11.   In what way was there an attempt to harmonize the philosophy of Plato with the writings of St. John?
12.   State the "orthodox" doctrine respecting Deity in those times.
13.   State the Sabellian theory.
14.   Give an illustration of it.
15.   State the Arian theory.
16.   In what way did the Nicene Council decide the Trinity controversy?
17.   What confession did Athanasius make as to his inability to comprehend the Nicene creed?
18.   What great error resulted from the controversy on the nature of Deity?
19.   What passages of scripture refute the "orthodox" Christian notion that God is immaterial?
20.   How from reason would you refute the notion that God is an immaterial Being?

SECTION VII.

1. Departure from Moral Precepts of the Gospel:—
There was as wide a departure from the moral precepts
of the gospel among the Christians as there was from the
doctrines, ordinances and government of the church.   From
the nature of the reproofs, the admonitions and warnings
to be found in the epistles of the apostles to the churches,
one may see that while they yet lived, the saints were
prone to wickedness, and great errors in regard to moral
conduct crept into the churches.   The writings of the early
fathers of the church who succeeded the apostles also bear
witness of the continuance and increase of these errors.

2. Double Rule of Life:—As early as the second
century the idea became prevalent that Messiah had prescribed a two-fold rule of moral conduct; the one ordinary,
the other extraordinary; one for those engaged in ordinary
affairs of life, the other for persons of leisure and such as
desired a higher glory in the future life.   This led the early
Christian doctors to divide whatsoever had been taught
by the apostles in respect to Christian life and morals, into
"precepts" and "counsels."   The precepts were those laws
which were equally binding on all men, the counsels were
binding only on those who aspired to a closer union with
God.

3. Of course there soon appeared a class of persons who
sought to attain to this closer union; and they adopted
the method of life practiced among the pagan philosophers
who wished to excel in virtue.   They considered many things
forbidden to them which were proper for ordinary Chris

tians to indulge in; such as wine, flesh, matrimony, and secular business. They thought the holiness of life they aspired to could sooner be attained by emaciating the body by fastings, watchings, excessive toil, hunger, insufficient and coarse raiment. In short, they "thought to merit heaven by making earth a hell." Those who engaged in this kind of life soon came to distinguish themselves by their dress as well as by the austerity of their lives. They soon began to withdraw themselves from association with their fellow Christians and the world and retire to the deserts and the wilderness, where by severe meditation, they sought to abstract their minds from external objects and those things which minister to sensual delights. They sometimes lived alone but oftener in association with those devoted to the same manner of life.

4. When peace was assured to the Christian church, early in the fourth century, the number of those who became ambitious for this austere righteousness greatly increased, until vast multitudes of monks and sacred virgins spread with remarkable rapidity throughout Christendom. About the year 305 A. D., the practice of collecting these people into associated communities and regulating their mode of living by fixed rules was introduced. St. Anthony of Egypt was the prime mover in this work. Thus monasteries and nunneries were established; and in a short time the east, especially, swarmed with persons who abandoned the conveniences, associations and business of ordinary life, to pine away in these institutions, amid hardships and sufferings, in order to attain a closer communion with God and a more excellent salvation.

5. **Origin of the False Idea of Moral Life:**—"The Christian church would have remained free from these numerous tortures of the mind and body," remarks Dr.

Mosheim, "had not that great and fascinating doctrine of the ancient philosophy gained credence among Christians that to attain to happiness and communion with God, the soul must be freed from the influence of the body, and for this purpose the body must be subdued."*

6. As a further evidence that these false notions of life and virtue came from the pagan philosophy rather than from the Christian religion, we quote again from Mosheim: "The causes of this institution [austere method of life] are at hand. First, the Christians did not like to appear inferior to the Greeks, the Romans, and the other people; among whom were many philosophers and sages, who were distinguished from the vulgar by their dress and their whole mode of life, and who were held in high honor. Now among these philosophers (as is well known), none better pleased the Christians than the Platonists and Pythagoreans [Pyth-a-go-re-ans]; who are known to have recommended two modes of living, the one for philosophers who wished to excel in virtue, and the other for the people engaged in the common affairs of life."† The Platonists prescribed the following rules for philosophers: "The mind of a wise man must be withdrawn, as far as possible, from the contagious influence of the body, and as the oppressive load of the body and social intercourse are most adverse to this design, therefore all sensual gratifications are to be avoided; the body is to be sustained or rather mortified, with coarse and slender fare; solitude is to be sought for; and the mind is to be self-collected, and absorbed in contemplation, so as to be detached as much as

---

*Mosheim, Book II, Cent. iv, Part ii, ch. iii.

†The phraseology of the philosophers was, "living according to nature, and living above nature." The former was the rule for all men, the latter for the philosophers who aimed at perfect virtue.

possible from the body.   Whoever lives in this manner, shall in the present life have converse with God; and when freed from the load of the body, shall ascend without delay to the celestial mansions and shall not need, like the souls of other men, to undergo purgation."*

7. It will be remembered that the Christians adopted the pagan philosophy—of which the teachings of Plato were the basis—and employed it to explain the Christian religion.   It is not surprising, therefore, that they adopted its moral precepts, and by so doing corrupted that reasonable and healthful moral life enjoined upon all alike in the gospel of Jesus Christ.

8. **Celibacy of the Clergy:**—From the same source came the celibacy of the clergy.   It was considered that those who lived in wedlock were more subject to the assaults of evil spirits than those who lived in celibacy; hence those who were appointed to teach and govern others were supposed to be all the better qualified for their work if they had nothing to do with conjugal life.   It was a matter, however, which during the first centuries was not strictly enjoined by any formal regulations of the church; it was left for Pope Gregory VII in the eleventh century to bind such a wicked regulation upon the clergy by express law.   In the third century the most shameful abuses arose out of this doctrine; for men sought to fulfill its requirements with the least violence to their inclinations, and many of those who had taken upon themselves vows of chastity, took to their houses and even to their beds some one of those holy females under like vows of chastity, yet maintained that there was no improper relations between them.   It is but just to say that many bishops condemned this shameful

---

Mosheim's Eccl. Hist., Book I, Cent. i, Part ii, Ch. iii.

practice, but it was some time before the church was rid of it, and the scandal it created, and even when such practices did cease openly, it may well be doubted if they really ceased among those forced into such unnatural conditions.

9. **Deceiving and Lying Accounted Virtues:**—Another evil which went far toward corrupting the church was the idea that to deceive and lie are virtues when religion can be promoted by them. This pernicious doctrine was accepted early in the first centuries and it accounts for the existence and circulation of that great mass of childish fable and falsehood respecting the infancy and youth of Messiah and the miraculous, wonder-working power of the relics of the saints and martyrs, from which the cause of the Christian religion has suffered so much. "If some inquisitive person were to examine the conduct and the writings of the greatest and most pious teachers of this century" (the fourth), writes Dr. Mosheim, "I fear he would find about all of them infected with this leprosy. I cannot except Ambrose, nor Hilary, nor Augustine, nor Gregory Nazianzen, nor Jerome."*

10. **Immoral Condition of the Church in General:**— The wickedness of the clergy in the last centuries, the ambition of the bishops and their imitating in their lives the voluptuousness of princes, we have already noted in section four of part II, and therefore little need be said here further than to remark that those vices very rapidly increased. As time rolled on worldly prosperity seemed to relax the nerves of discipline. "Fraud, envy and malice prevailed in every congregation. The presbyters aspired to the episcopal office, which every day became an object more worthy their ambition. The bishops who contended

---

Mosheim, Book II, Cent. iv, Part ii, Ch. ii.

with each other for ecclesiastical pre-eminence, appeared by their conduct to claim a secular and tyrannical power in the church; and the lively faith which still distinguished the Christians from the Gentiles was shown much less in their lives than in their controversial writings."*

11. Sometimes these struggles for place and power resulted in war and bloodshed. Such was the case in the fourth century when a new pope was to be elected to succeed Liberius [Li-be-ri-us]. One party in Rome was for one Damasus [Dam-a-sus], and another party for Ursicinus [Ur-si-ci-nus]. The contest resulted in a bloody conflict, houses were burned and many lost their lives. In one church alone one morning after the conflict there were found one hundred and thirty-seven corpses to bear witness to the violence of the struggle for what was claimed to be the office of vicegerent of God on earth.

12. **Moral Condition of the Church in the Fourth Century:**—In the fourth century—"If we look at the lives and morals of the Christians—we shall find, as heretofore, that good men were commingled with bad, yet the number of the bad began gradually to increase, so that the truly pious and godly appeared more rare. When there was no more to fear from enemies from without; when the character of most bishops was tarnished with arrogance, luxury, effeminacy, animosity, resentments, and other defects; when the lower clergy neglected their proper duties, and were more attentive to controversies, than to the promotion of piety and the instruction of the people; when vast numbers were induced not by a rational conviction, but by the fear of punishment and the hope of worldly advantage to enroll themselves as Christians, how can it

---

Decline and Fall (Gibbon,) Vol. I, Ch. xvi.

surprise us, that on all sides the vicious appeared a host, and the pious, a little band almost overpowered by them? Against the flagitious and those guilty of heinous offenses, the same rules for penance were prescribed, as before the reign of Constantine. But as the times continually waxed worse and worse, the more honorable and powerful could sin with impunity, and only the poor and the unfortunate felt the severity of the laws."*

13. Moral Condition of the Church in the Fifth Century:—About the middle of the fifth century we have Salvian [Sal-vi-an] saying—"The very church which should be the body to appease the anger of God, alas! What reigns there but disorders calculated to incense the Most High? It is more common to meet with Christians who are guilty of the greatest abominations than with those who are wholly exempt from crime. So that today it is a sort of sanctity among us to be less vicious than the generality of Christians. We insult the majesty of the Most High at the foot of his altars. Men, the most steeped in crime, enter the holy places without respect for them. True, all men ought to pay their vows to God, but why should they seek his temples to propitiate him, only to go forth to provoke him? Why enter the church to deplore their former sins, and upon going forth—what do I say?—in those very courts, they commit fresh sins, their mouths and their hearts contradict one another. Their prayers are criminal meditations rather than vows of expiation. Scarcely is the service ended before each returns to his old practices. Some go to their wine, others to their impurities, still others to robbing and brigandage, so that we cannot doubt that these things had been occupying them while they were in the church. Nor is it

---

Mosheim, Book II, Cent. iv, Part ii, Ch. iii.

the lowest of the people who are thus guilty. There is no rank whatever in the church which does not commit all sorts of crimes."

14. "It may be urged that we are at heart better than the barbarians who oppose us. Suppose this to be granted: we ought to be better than they. But as a matter of fact, they are more virtuous than we. The mass of Christians are below the barbarians in probity. True, all kinds of sins are found among them, but what one is not found among us? The several nations have their peculiar sin; the Saxons are cruel; the Franks perfidious; the Gepidoe inhuman; the Huns, lewd. But we, having the law of God to restrain us, are given over to all these offenses. Then to confine ourselves to the single sin of swearing, can many be found among the faithful who have not the name of Jesus Christ constantly upon their lips in support of their perjuries? This practice, coming down from the higher to the lower classes, has so prevailed that Christians might be deemed pagans. This, although the law of God expressly forbids to take his name in vain. We read this law, but we do not practice it; as a consequence, the pagans taunt us that we boast ourselves the sole possessors of God's law, and of the rules of truth and of what that law enjoins. Christians, indeed, to the shame of Jesus Christ, say they."*

15. In book VI on *The Providence of God*, Salvian continues his arraignment: "We rush from the churches to the theatres, even in the midst of our perils. In Carthage the theatres were thronged, while the enemy were before the walls, and the cries of those perishing outside under the

---

*The above quotation is taken from the third and fourth books on *The Providence* of *God* by *Salvian*, who flourished in the 5th century, a priest of Marseilles, and one who knew whereof he wrote, as he was dealing with affairs of which he was a witness.

sword, mingled with the shouts of the spectators in the circus. Nor are we better here in Gaul (France). Treves [Trevz] has been taken four times, and has only increased in wickedness under her misfortunes. The same state of things exists in Cologne [Ko-lon]—deplorable wickedness among young and old, low and high. The smaller cities have been blind and insensible to the dangers threatening, until they have overwhelmed them. It seems to be the destiny of the Roman empire to perish rather than reform; they must cease to be, in order to cease to be vicious. A part of the inhabitants of Treves, having escaped from the ruins, petitions the emperor for—what? A theatre, spectacles, public shows! A city which thrice overthrown could not correct itself, well deserved to suffer a fourth destruction. * * * Would that my voice might be heard by all Romans! I would cry: Let us all blush, that today the only cities where impurity does not reign, are those which have submitted to the barbarians. Think not, then, that they conquer and we yield by the simple force of nature. Rather let us admit that we succumb through the dissoluteness of our morals of which our calamities are the just punishment."*

16. State of Morals in Centuries Subsequent to the Fifth:—Such was the condition of the Christian church as to morals in the fifth century. It was no better in the sixth or the seventh or the eighth. Indeed the concurrent testimony of all authorities is to the effect that matters moral and spiritual grew gradually worse in these centuries, until darkness covered the earth and gross darkness the people. Of the ninth century Mosheim says: "The ungodly lives of most of those intrusted with the care and

---

Book VI and VII of The Providence of God.—Salvian.

government of the church, are a subject of complaint with all the ingenuous and honest writers of this age.   In the east, sinister designs, rancor, contentions and strife, were every-where predominant.   *   *   *

"In the west, the bishops hung round the courts of princes and indulged themselves in every species of voluptuousness; while the inferior clergy and the monks were sensual, and by the grossest vices corrupted the people whom they were set to reform."*

17.   State of Morals in Tenth Century:—Of the tenth century, Dr. Milner, who wrote his great history for the purpose of maintaining that there had been a succession of pious men since the founding of the church by Messiah, and to "trace the goodness of God taking care of his church in every age by his providence,"† says: "The famous annalist of the Roman Church,‡ whose partiality to the see of Rome is notorious, has, however, the candor to own that this [the tenth century] was an iron age, barren of all good-ness; a leaden age, abounding in all wickedness; and a dark age, remarkable above all other things for the scarcity of writers and men of learning.   Christ was then, as it appears, in a very deep sleep, when the ship was covered with waves; and what seemed worse, when the Lord was thus asleep,

---

*Mosheim, Book III, Cent. ix, Part ii, Chap. ii.

†See Milner's introduction to the first volume of his Church History. It will also be seen in that introduction that Milner wrote his history to counteract the influence that he feared the great work of the too candid Mosheim might exert, viz., to create the impression "That real religion appears scarcely to have had any existence."   Hence the admissions of Dr. Milner to the sad condition of the church in the tenth century have a peculiar significance since he would not admit its corruption unless compelled to by the facts.

‡This is Caesar Baronius, a Catholic historian of the 16th century. His Annales Ecclesiastical comprise twelve volumes and were published in Rome, 1588—1607.   He was a candidate for the papacy in 1605, but failed to secure the election.

there were no disciples, who by their cries, might wake him, being themselves all fast asleep." "Under an allusion by no means incongruous with the oriental and scriptural taste, this writer [Baronius] represents the divine head of the church as having given up the church for its wickedness, to a judicial impenitency, which continued the longer, because there was scarcely any zealous spirits who had the charity to pray for the cause of God upon earth. * * * Infidel Malice has with pleasure recorded the vices and the crimes of the popes of this century. Nor is it my intention to attempt to palliate the account of their wickedness. It was as deep and atrocious as language can paint; nor can a reasonable man desire more authentic evidence of history than that which the records both of civil and ecclesiastical history afford concerning the corruption of the whole church."*

18. The Church Destroyed:—Beyond this century it is not necessary to go. The church of Christ no longer existed in the earth. The persecution of the Jews and the Romans, coupled with the internal dissensions in the church; the rise of false teachers, who brought in damnable heresies; the changing of the character and spirit of the church government; the addition of pagan rites and ceremonies to the doctrines and ordinances of the gospel; the admixture of pagan philosophy with Christian theology; and, finally, the universal departure of the church from that moral life enjoined upon mankind by the precepts of the Christian religion—utterly subverted the religion of Jesus Christ, and destroyed the church which he founded. The

*Milner's Ch. His., Vol. iii, Cent. x, Ch. i. The only thing which seems to console the learned doctor in respect to this terrible condition of the church is that the scripture predicted this awful state, and the truth of scripture was "vindicated by events of all others the most disagreeable to a pious mind."—Ibid.

apostasy of men from that religion and church was complete; and since they did not like to retain God in their hearts, God also gave them up to uncleanness through the lusts of their own hearts. (See notes 1 to 6, end of section.)

NOTES.

1. Admission of the Great Apostasy by Christian Writers:— The church of England in its Homily on the Perils of Idolatry says: "Laity and clergy, learned and unlearned, all ages, sects and degrees have been drowned in abominable idolatry most detested by God and damnable to man for eight hundred years and more."

2. In Smith's Dictionary of the Bible (page 163)—the work is endorsed by sixty-three learned divines and Bible scholars—the following occurs: "We must not expect to see the church of Christ existing in its perfection on the earth. It is not to be found thus perfect, either in the collected fragments of Christendom, or still less in any one of those fragments."

3. John Wesley said that the reason why the extraordinary gifts of the Holy Ghost were no longer to be found in the church (in the dark ages) was "because the love of many waxed cold, the Christians had turned heathens again and only had a dead form left."—(*Wesley's Works, Vol. vii, Sermon* 89, *pages* 26, 27.)

4. Dr. Adam Clark commenting on the fourth chapter of Ephesians —treating church officers and the gifts bestowed upon them—says: "All these officers and the gifts and graces conferred upon them were adjudged necessary by the great head of the church for its full instruction in the important doctrines of Christianity. The same officers and gifts are still necessary, and God gives them, but they do not know their places."

5. Roger Williams (Picturesque America, page 502,) refused to continue as pastor over the oldest Baptist church in America on the ground that there was "no regularly constituted church on earth, nor any person qualified to administer any church ordinance; nor can there be until new apostles are sent by the great head of the church for whose coming I am seeking."

6. Alexander Campbell, founder of the sect of the "Disciples," says: "The meaning of this institution (the kingdom of heaven,) has been buried under the rubbish of human tradition for hundreds of years. It was lost in the dark ages and has never, until recently, been disinterred.—(*Christianity Restored*, page 184.)

REVIEW.

1. What may be learned from the reproofs and admonitions in the writings of the apostles and early Christian fathers?

2. About what time did the notion arise in respect to a double rule of life?

3. What great evil grew out of this erroneous idea?

4. From whence did Christians derive their ideas which demanded the austerities they practiced?

5. Give an account of the origin of monasteries and nunneries.

6. How did the celibacy of the clergy originate?

7. When did it become an express law of the church?

8. What shameful scandal arose from this doctrine in the 3rd century?

9. Under what circumstances were lying and deceiving accounted virtues?

10. What evil grew out of this wicked notion?

11. What can you say of the general moral condition of the church in the early Christian centuries?

12. State the moral condition of the church in the 4th century. In the 5th.

13. What of the moral state of the church subsequent to the 5th?

14. Give the substance of Dr. Milner's admission concerning the moral state of the church in the 10th century.

15. State what several circumstances led to the destruction of the church of Christ.

16. Recount the admissions which noted Christian writers make concerning the apostasy from the Christian religion. (Notes end of section.)

SECTION VIII.

We have considered those events that occurred in the church by which its form and spirit of government were altered, its doctrines corrupted, its ordinances changed, and its truths and powers subverted. We now turn to the scriptures to show that all these things were predicted by the apostles and prophets of God, being foreseen by the Spirit of revelation.

1. **False Teachers to Arise in the Church:**—On the occasion of Paul's last visit to Ephesus, he had the elders assembled, and in the course of his address to them said: "I have not shunned to declare unto you all the counsel of God. Take heed, therefore, unto yourselves, and to all the flock, over which the Holy Ghost hath made you overseers, to feed the church of God which he hath purchased with his own blood. For I know this, that after my departing, shall grievous wolves enter in among you, not sparing the flock. Also of your own selves shall men arise, speaking perverse things to lead away disciples after them."*

2. In his second letter to Timothy, the same apostle again prophesies of the coming of these false teachers: "I charge thee, therefore," said he, "before God, and the Lord Jesus Christ, who shall judge the quick and the dead at his appearing and his kingdom; preach the word; be instant in season, out of season; reprove, rebuke with all long suffering and doctrine. For the time will come when they will not endure sound doctrine; but after their own

*Acts xx: 27-30.

lusts shall they heap to themselves teacners having itching ears; and they [the false teachers] shall turn their ears from the truth, and shall be turned unto fables."*

3. Peter also prophesied the rise of false teachers in the church. In his second epistle, addressed, "to them that have obtained like precious faith," with himself— that is, to the saints; after saying that prophecy in olden time came by men speaking as they were moved upon by the Holy Ghost;† he then remarks—"But there were false prophets also among the people [that is, in ancient Israel], even as there shall be false teachers among you, who privily shall bring in damnable heresies, even denying the Lord that bought them, and bring upon themselves swift destruction. And many shall follow their pernicious ways; by reason of whom the way of truth shall be evil spoken of. And through covetousness with feigned words make merchandise of you; whose judgment now of a long time lingereth not, and their damnation slumbereth not."‡

4. **Hypocrisy and Austerity Predicted:**—Paul also appears to have foreseen the hypocrisy that would creep into the church, together with that useless austerity of life with which men and women would become infatuated, and which, through feigning, became the fountain of so much corruption. He thus speaks of it: "Now the Spirit speaketh expressly, that in the latter times some shall depart from the faith, giving heed to seducing spirits and doctrines of devils; speaking lies in hypocrisy, having their conscience seared with a hot iron; *forbidding to marry,* and commanding to abstain from meats."§

*II Tim. iv: 1-4.
†II Peter i: 21.
‡II Peter ii: 1-3.
§I Tim. iv: 1, 2.

5. The Rise of Anti-Christ Foretold:—Moreover, the Prophet Paul foretold the rise of Anti-Christ before the glorious coming of Messiah to judgment. He plainly foresaw the "falling away"—the long night of spiritual darkness and apostasy that would brood over the world before the coming of the Son of God in the glory of his Father, to reward the righteous, to condemn the wicked. He said of this apostasy:

"Now we beseech you, brethren, by the coming of our Lord Jesus Christ, and by our gathering together unto him; that ye be not soon shaken in mind, or be troubled, neither by spirit nor by word, nor by letter as from us, as that the day of Christ is at hand.*   Let no man deceive you by any means, for that day shall not come except there come a falling away first, and that man of sin be revealed, the son of perdition; 'who opposeth and exalteth himself above all that is called God, or that is worshiped; so that he as God sitteth in the temple of God, showing himself that he is God.   Remember ye not that when I was yet with you I told you these things?   And now ye know what withholdeth that he might be revealed in his time.   For the mystery of iniquity doth already work; only he who now letteth [hindereth] will let [will hinder]† until he be taken out of the way. And then shall that Wicked be revealed, whom the Lord shall consume with the spirit of his mouth, and shall destroy with the brightness of his coming; even him whose coming is

---

*That is, that the day of Messiah's glorious coming is at hand.

†"Letteth" and "let" are the old English equivalents of "hindereth" and "hinder."   The student will remember that Shakespeare makes Hamlet say to those who seek to prevent him following the ghost of his father when beckoned to private interview—"Still am I called. Unhand me gentlemen.   By heaven I'll make a ghost of him that lets me"—i. e., that hinders me.   And Paul, in the St. James translation of Romans, says: "Often times I proposed to come unto you, but was "let [i. e., hindered,] hitherto."   Rom. 1: 13.

after the working of Satan, with all power and signs and lying wonders, and with all deceivableness of unrighteousness in them that perish; because they received not the love of the truth, that they might be saved. And for this cause God shall send them strong delusion, that they should believe a lie; that they all might be damned who believe not the truth, but had pleasure in unrighteousness."*

6. Isaiah's Great Prophecy of the Apostasy:— Isaiah also prophesied of the universal apostasy from the gospel of Christ. After describing the earth as mourning and fading away, together with its haughty people, he said: "The earth also is defiled under the inhabitants thereof, because they have transgressed the laws, changed the ordinance, *broken the everlasting covenant.* Therefore hath a curse devoured the earth, and they that dwell therein are desolate; therefore the inhabitants of the earth are burned, and few men left."†

7. It is sometimes claimed that this prophecy refers to the Mosaic law, and the Mosaic covenant, instead of the gospel of Christ. The answer to such claim is that the prophecy has reference to *an everlasting covenant* that is to be broken; and the Mosaic law, or covenant, never was intended to be an everlasting covenant, while the gospel of Christ is such a covenant. Paul said: "The scripture, foreseeing that God would justify the heathen through faith, preached before the gospel to Abraham. * * * Wherefore then serveth the law [that is, if the gospel was preached unto Abraham, of what use is the law of Moses —the law of carnal commandments—how came it into existence?]   It was added because of transgression, till the seed

---

*II Thes. ii: 1-12.
†Isaiah xxiv: 4-6.

[Christ] should come, to whom the promise was made. * * * Wherefore the law was our schoolmaster to bring us unto Christ, that we might be justified by faith. But after that faith is come, we are no longer under a schoolmaster."*

8. From this it appears that the gospel was preached in very ancient times; that afterwards, because of transgression—doubtless apostasy—the law of Moses was added, or given in the place of the gospel, that it might act as a schoolmaster to bring the people to Christ, that is, prepare them for the gospel. Therefore, when the gospel was introduced by the personal ministry of Messiah, the law of Moses —the carnal law—having served its purpose, was set aside, and the gospel was reinstated. It will be seen, therefore, that the Mosaic law was not an everlasting covenant, but a temporary law, given for a specific purpose, having accomplished which it is supplanted by a more excellent law and covenant. It is clear that Isaiah's great prophecy had no reference to the law of Moses, but to an everlasting covenant which was to be broken, its ordinance changed, its laws transgressed. That covenant is the gospel of Jesus Christ, whose blood is spoken of as the "blood of the everlasting covenant."†

9. Moreover the prophecy ends by saying that in consequence of the transgression of the law, the changing of the ordinance, the breaking of the covenant, "the inhabitants of the earth are burned, and few men left. This predicted calamity did not overtake the people for breaking the Mosaic law. It has not yet taken place. It is a judgment still hanging over mankind for their great apostasy from the gospel of Jesus Christ.

---

*Gal. iii. 8, 19, 24, 25.
†Heb. xiii: 20.

10. John's Vision Foreshadowing the Apostasy:— Among the many revelations given to the Apostle John while a prisoner on the Isle of Patmos was one in which he saw an angel "fly in the midst of heaven, having the everlasting gospel to preach unto them that dwell on the earth, and to every nation, and kindred, and tongue, and people, saying with a loud voice, Fear God and give glory to him, for the hour of his judgment is come: and worship him that made heaven, and earth, and the sea, and the fountains of waters."* From this it is learned that in the hour of God's judgment the gospel will be brought to the earth by an angel, and thence proclaimed to every nation, and kindred, and tongue, and people, a very good evidence that in the "hour of God's judgment" all the world would be without the gospel, or why this restoration at that time and its universal proclamation if the nations at the time indicated already possessed it?

11. Thus through revelation the ancient prophets foresaw the great apostasy from the gospel of Jesus Christ. We who live now, after the great event has occurred, in the light of historical facts, see it no more plainly than did these ancient servants of God through the gift of prophecy. They read the history of it by the light of revelation, we, by the light of history; and the former is a light no less certain than the latter.

REVIEW.

1. By what means were the apostles and still more ancient prophets made acquainted with the great apostasy from the Christian religion?

2. Repeat the several prophecies concerning the rise of false teachers in the church.

---

*Rev. xiv: 6, 7.

3.   Give the passage which predicts the rise of hypocrisy and austerity of life.

4.   In what passage of Paul's writings is the rise of anti-Christ predicted?

5.   What does letteth and let in this passage mean?   Give proof.

6.   State in what way Paul's great prophecy has been fulfilled.

7.   State Isaiah's great prophecy respecting the apostasy.

8.   What objection may be urged to our application of this prophecy?

9.   How would you meet the objection?

10.   What great judgment is still pending over the world because of their wicked apostasy?

11.   What vision given to St. John on Patmos foreshadowed a universal apostasy?

12.   If the gospel from the time it was established on the earth by Messiah's personal ministry had continued with men until now, would there be any necessity for restoring it to the earth in the hour of God's judgment?

13.   Was the fact of the apostasy read by the light of the spirit of prophecy less clear than when by the light of historical facts?

SECTION IX.

1. The Nephite Christian Church:—For nearly two centuries the Nephite Christian church flourished in great prosperity. For that length of time the truth seems to have been preserved in its fullness, and the church in its unity. With the third century, however, began that apostasy which eventually terminated by a complete subversion of the church of Christ on the Western hemisphere.

2. Pride of Wealth and Class Distinctions:—The peace and righteousness of two centuries brought great prosperity and wealth to the Nephite Christians—to the entire western hemisphere; but the commencement of the third century began to develop the fact that pride was pressing fast upon the heels of that prosperity. Up to the commencement of the third century the Nephite Christians had all things common; but early in the third century that order of things was broken up. Class distinctions arose, men began to pride themselves on their fine apparel and jewels. They began to build churches to get gain, and to deny the true church of Christ. Others, professing to be Christians, denied much of that which Messiah taught, and administered that which was sacred to those to whom it had been forbidden, because of unworthiness.

3. The Anti-Christian Church Persecution:—There also arose an anti-Christian church, which persecuted the true church, despising the members thereof because of their humility, and hating them because of the power of God which was with them. Among the twelve apostles whom

Jesus selected from the Nephites three desired that they might remain upon the earth until Messiah should come in his glory. This request was granted them and their bodies were changed that they were not subject to death. They had remained with the church up to the time of which we write, and against them the anti-Christian church was especially embittered. The apostates sought to kill them as the Jews at Jerusalem tried to kill Jesus; they cast them into prison and into dens of wild beasts, but the Lord delivered them from prisons, murders and the wild beasts, and that by the manifestations of his power. Yet the miracles did not convert their ungodly persecutors and the wicked increased rapidly in numbers.

4. Revival of Old Distinctions:—Soon the ancient distinctions of Nephites and Lamanites, which for two centuries had been buried in oblivion, began to be employed to designate the two peoples which gradually began to be formed. The true Christians were called Nephites, and their enemies Lamanites. All the old bitterness which attached to the names in former times was revived.

5. It was but a few years after the apostasy began before the wicked outnumbered the righteous. For a while the name "Nephites" designated the true followers of Messiah, but soon they became as proud and as wicked as the Lamanites, and righteousness was subverted.

6. Revival of Secret Organizations:—The old secret societies were revived for robbery and plunder. Early in the fourth century (320 A. D.) Ammoran, who had charge of the Nephite records, hid them up, revealing the place of their concealment only to Mormon, a lad then ten years of age, giving him a charge to go when he was twenty-four years old and take the plates of Nephi and record on them the things he had witnessed among the people. About the

same time the three Nephite apostles disappeared from among
the people; the church no longer being worthy of their administrations, the Lord took then away. All miracles,
healings, and other spiritual manifestations ceased. Mormon, a historian and a righteous man, remained with them,
but he was forbidden to preach to them. A black pall of
spiritual darkness settled over the land, and the minds of
the people.

7. An Attempt to Reorganize the Church:—Forty
years later, after a series of disastrous wars, by which one
might reasonably expect the Nephites would be humbled
and brought to seek the Lord, an attempt to re-establish
the church was made. Mormon received a commandment to preach repentance and baptism to the people, a
commandment which he willingly obeyed; but all to no
purpose. The people would not repent. They hardened
their hearts against God and made themselves fit only for
destruction.

8. Utter Destruction of the Nephites:—That destruction was not very remote. Towards the close of that
century which witnessed the climax of their wickedness
saw their destruction. By permission of the Lamanites the
Nephites assembled about the hill called by them Cumorah
and prepared for the last great struggle. It took place in
the year 385 A. D., and resulted in the entire destruction of
the Nephite people, except, perhaps, a few who fled south-
ward. Mormon was slain, and his son, the last of the
Nephites, was preserved to record the destruction and
the desolation which followed it, and hid up the records
of the great race which had founded kingdoms and republics upon the western hemisphere, that would vie with
those of Persia, Macedonia or Greece; and cities that in

extent and grandeur must have equalled those of Antioch, Alexandria, Carthage, Tyre or Sidon.

9. **The Reign of Anarchy:**—That civilization was destroyed, the empires and republics were overthrown, government was destroyed, anarchy reigned. The people, chiefly Lamanites, who survived that last terrible conflict about Cumorah, broke up into tribes, each fiercely contending with the other. Cities were laid waste to crumble into shapeless heaps of ruin, with here and there a monument that defied the ravages of time and proudly stood a silent witness of the greatness of the departed race which reared it. Such was the apostasy on the western hemisphere, and such the result which followed it.

REVIEW.

1. For how long did the Nephite Christian church keep the faith?
2. In the 3rd century what occurred?
3. On what were their class distinctions based?
4. State what you can of the rise and course of the anti-Christian church.
5. What of the rise of old distinctions?
6. What old organizations were revived in the 4th century?
7. What attempt was made to reorganize the church?
8. Where were the Nephites destroyed?
9. What followed the destruction of the Nephites?

PART III.

—

THE "REFORMATION."

SECTION I.

1. The Age of Darkness:—We have not found it necessary to our purpose to dwell upon the particular events of ecclesiastical history from the tenth to the sixteenth centuries. Those were the days of spiritual darkness of this earth. The papal power was supreme, and with an iron hand it ruled the nations. Some idea of its arrogance and power may be conjectured from the fact that in the eleventh century* Henry IV, of Germany, the greatest temporal monarch in the world, in that age, stood for three days together in mid-winter, bare headed, and bare footed, and meanly clad, at Canossa (a town in Italy where the pope was temporarily residing), professing himself a penitent in order to obtain absolution from the Roman pontiff, Gregory VII. His offense was persisting to sell ecclesiastical offices in his empire, contrary to the edicts of the pope. (See note 1, end of section.)†

2. The Revival of Learning:—In the latter part of the fifteenth century occurred that event called by historians the "Revival of Learning." The intellectual stupor of Europe had been as profound as spiritual darkness had been dense. But with the close of the fifteenth century, literature, science and art seemed to spring into active life. The invention of gun-powder‡ had completely revolutionized

---

*February, 1070, A. D.

†Subsequently Henry IV made war upon Gregory, drove him from the papal chair into exile, and placed Guibert, archbishop of Ravenna, upon the papal throne. Guibert took the name of Innocent III at his consecration, 1084 A. D.

‡It was invented by *Schwartz* in 1320.

the modes of warfare; the employment of the mariners' compass made ocean navigation less dangerous; the discovery of a new passage to India by the Cape of Good Hope, by Vasco de Gama [Vas-ko-da-ga-ma], and the discovery of America by Columbus, greatly enlarged the commerce of Europe and increased the comforts of life. Painting in oil came into vogue about this time and filled Europe with masterpieces of art; engraving on copper, invented early in the century, multiplied and diffused them. Paper made of linen also came into common use; and, finally, between 1436 and 1452 A. D., printing was invented, which gave to the modern world the intellectual riches of the ancients.

3. In the middle of this century—the fifteenth—Constantinople was taken by the Turks, and with that event the eastern division of the Roman empire fell. The fall of the great capital drove many of the Greeks into Italy. They took with them a greater knowledge of antiquity than that possessed by the western nations, together with numerous manuscripts; and literature from that time may be said to have commenced its splendid career. (See note 2, end of section.) Intellectual pursuits became not only a pleasure, but a passion; "and it may be regarded as a maxim, that wherever the progress of intelligence is a true pleasure, a desire for liberty is soon felt, nor is it long..in passing from the public mind to the state."* It was so in Europe; for the "Revival of Learning" preceded, and there can be no doubt that it did much to produce that struggle for enlarged liberty which convulsed Europe in the following century.

4. **Release of the Masses from Serfdom:**—The masses, moreover, began to be released, to some extent,

---

Guizot Hist. Civilization.

from the serfdom of former times, and to be given some share of civil and political freedom. This change was largely due to the breaking up of the old feudal system of land tenure and service. According to feudal principles, all the land of a country belonged to the king, not as representing the community, but as sovereign feudal lord. Out of this land the king granted portions to his subjects, on condition of their paying him homage and fealty, and rendering him active military service a certain number of days in every year. The estates the king granted to his more immediate and distinguished followers, whom he called his barons, were styled baronies, and were of large extent; the barons in their turn made undergrants to their own retainers, on similar conditions to those imposed upon themselves by the king. The relation between landlord and tenant, though at first merely lifelong, soon came to be regarded as hereditary, the heir becoming entitled on the death of the tenant to occupy his land upon the same terms.*

5. This order of things established a powerful landed aristocracy on the one hand, and a peasant tenantry on the other, whose vassalage was but little removed from absolute slavery. The crusades and the development of a commercial class, living chiefly in the cities, in time wrought the destruction of feudalism.

6. **The Crusades, their Influence on Feudalism and Liberty:**—The crusades were religious wars carried on in the eleventh, twelfth and thirteenth centuries, between the Christian nations of the West and the Mohammedans of the East. It had for ages been looked upon as an act of piety to make a pilgrimage to Palestine and visit the

---

*Smith's Eng. Inst., pages 8, 9.

various places hallowed by the presence of Messiah during his earthly career, especially his sepulchre at Jerusalem. These Christian pilgrims had been respected by the Saracens for centuries; but when the Seljuk Turks captured Jerusalem, towards the close of the eleventh century, the Christians met with insult and cruelty. The western nations, under the fervent preaching of Peter the Hermit, a native of France, who had witnessed the atrocities practiced upon Christians in the Holy Land, were lashed into a fury of resentment against the Turks. Pope Urban II, took up the cause, and advocated wresting the Holy Land from the dominion of the infidels. Europe responded, "God wills it," and preparations were made for the "holy war."

7.   To raise the money necessary to equip and transport their soldiers to the distant East, the barons had to sell their lands, which had the effect of breaking down to a very great extent the feudal system of land tenure, and with it the obligations that it imposed. The direct result of this was to enlarge the liberties of the people. Fo⁻ the same purpose—to raise money for carrying on the holy wars in the East—kings granted to the towns political privileges, a circumstance which also contributed vastly to the progress of popular liberty. Thus the way was prepared for that religious revolution of the sixteenth century known in history as "The Reformation."

8.   **Martin Luther:**—The "Reformation" is usually considered to have begun with the fearless preaching of Martin Luther, against the sale of indulgences, A. D. 1517. Luther was born at Eisleben [Is-la-ben], Germany, A. D. 1483. His father was a miner of Mansfield in the same country. After attending the school of Magdeburg [Mag-de-boorg] and Eisenach [Is-sen-ak], he was sent to

study philosophy and jurisprudence at Erfurt [Er-foort]. Much against the will of his father, he abandoned the pursuit of these studies, and joined himself to the Augustine Eremites, a rigid order of mendicant monks. His good temper, industry and abilities won for him the good opinions of his superiors. In 1508 he was sent by his vicar-general to be professor of philosophy at Wittemburg. While here he applied himself to Biblical theology and soon discovered a wide discrepancy between the religion of the scriptures and that of the church. Two years after becoming a professor at Wittemburg, he made a journey to Rome on some business connected with the Augustine order of monks; and was not a little shocked at the corruption and depravity of the Italian clergy. That visit to Rome did much to dispel the veneration in which he had held the "Holy See," and armed him for his subsequent conflict with it.

9. **Indulgences and their Origin:**—The thing which provoked Luther's opposition to the Church of Rome was the reckless sale of indulgences by the agents of the pope in Germany. The origin of indulgences, according to the learned Schlegel, must be sought in the earliest history of the church. In the first centuries of the Christian era, such Christians as were excluded from the communion of the church on account of their apostasy in the times of persecutions, or on account of other heinous sins, had to seek a restoration to fellowship by a public penance, in which they entreated the brethren to forgive them, frequently standing before the door of the church clothed in the garb of mourning. This punishment was regarded as a sort of "satisfaction" made to the community of saints, and was called by that name—"satisfaction." In the case of aged or infirm Christians this "satisfaction" was sometimes omitted, and this omission was called "indulgence." Originally, therefore,

indulgences were merely the remission of ecclesiastical punishments imposed on grave offenders against church laws.*

10.   It is maintained, however, in the decretal of Pope Clement VI, that "one drop of Christ's blood being sufficient to redeem the whole human race, the remaining quantity that was shed in the garden and upon the cross, was left as a legacy to the church, to be a treasure from whence indulgences were to be drawn and administered by the Roman pontiffs.† The doctrine was held that Messiah had atoned for the eternal punishment of sins, but not for its temporary punishment. The temporary punishment the Catholic Church divided into that of the present life and that of the future life, or of purgatory. It was held that every man who attained salvation, must suffer the temporary punishment of his sins, either in the present world or in the flames of purgatory. It was also held that the priest to whom a man confessed his sins, had the power to adjudge and impose the necessary punishment.

11.   The punishment usually consisted of fastings, pilgrimages, whippings, etc., but people of distinction and wealth were permitted to employ substitutes to receive this punishment; and there were monks ever ready to endure the punishment of the transgressor for a consideration paid in money. This penance was finally changed to paying to the church the money instead of employing monks to endure the punishment. Whoever, for instance, was bound to whip himself with so many stripes each day for several weeks might pay to the church or to the monastery a certain sum of money, or give it a piece of land and then be

---

*It is only fair to Catholics to say that such is their explanation of indulgences now.

†*Maclain's note in Mosheim, Vol. II, Ch. ii.*

released from the penance. As the popes perceived that something might be gained in this way, they assumed to themselves the right of commuting penances for pecuniary "satisfactions," which every bishop had before exercised in his own diocese. At first they released only from the punishments of sin in the present world; but in the fourteenth century they extended this release also to the punishment in purgatory.

12. **The Traffic in Indulgences:**—When such indulgences were to be published, the disposal of them was commonly farmed out. The papal court could not always wait to have the money conveyed from every country of Europe; and there were rich merchants at Genoa, Milan, Venice, and Augsburg, who purchased the indulgences for a particular province and paid to the papal treasury handsome sums for them. Thus both parties were benefitted. The pope came at once into possession of large sums of money; and the farmers did not fail of a good bargain. They were careful to employ skillful hawkers of the indulgences, persons whose boldness and impudence bore due proportion to the eloquence with which they imposed upon the simple people. Yet that this traffic might have a religious aspect, the pope appointed the archbishops of the several provinces to be his commissioners, who in his name, published that indulgences were to be sold, and usually selected the persons to hawk them, and for this service shared the profits with the merchants who farmed them.* (See notes 3 and 4, end of section.)

13. In the beginning of the sixteenth century the sale of indulgences was pushed vigorously and became most

---

*The account here given of the rise and character of indulgences is condensed chiefly from Schlegel, quoted by Murdock in the latter's translation of Mosheim, Vol. III, Book IV, Cent. xvi, Sec. 1, Ch. 1.

offensive. The reason for resorting to this mode of raising revenue was justified by the pope on the plea of completing the church of St. Peter, at Rome, which had been commenced by Julius II.

14. John Tetzel:—The hawker of indulgences who traveled through Germany, where Luther was living, was John Tetzel, a Dominical monk, at once one of the boldest, most eloquent and the most profligate of men. (See note 6, end of section.) His reckless preaching of these papal wares aroused the indignation of Luther, who published ninety-five propositions against the sale of indulgences, in which he even greatly censured the pope for permitting the people to be diverted from Christ.

15. The Indifference of Leo X to the Agitation in Germany:—The dispute which arose between Luther and Tetzel was looked upon at Rome as the wrangle between two monks—Luther was an Augustine monk, Tetzel a Dominican; and it was supposed that the former was jealous because the Dominicans had been preferred for this work of selling indulgences. In addition to assailing Tetzel, Luther wrote a protest to Albert, Archbishop of Mentz and Magdeburg, and was as surprised as he was indignant to learn that the archbishop received of the profits arising from this wretched traffic. His assault upon Tetzel provoked a protracted controversy, a war of pamphlets between himself and Tetzel and his friends, among whom was John Eckius, a theologian of Ingolstadt. The dispute on both sides was more noted for its warmth than for its Christian character.

16. At last Leo X was aroused from his indifference to the controversy that had arisen in Germany, by the emperor, Maximilian I, informing him that the agitation was serious, and that Germany was taking sides in respect to it. He therefore appointed Cardinal Thomas Cajetan, then at the diet of Augsburg, to hear the cause of Luther. The cardinal summoned the monk before him at Augsburg, in October, 1518. They had three interviews, but nothing was accomplished towards reconciliation, as the cardinal treated Luther imperiously, and peremptorily ordered him to submit his judgment to the authority of the pope. This the reformer refused to do until he was convinced of his error, and appealed from the pope ill-informed to the pope better-informed. This took the matter out of the hands of the cardinal.

17. An Appeal to a General Council:—There was a difference between the reformer and the cardinal in their views in respect to authorities appealed to. The latter sought to convince the former of his errors by appealing to the canon law,* and the authority of Lombard;† but Luther refused to admit of any proof except that of the holy scripture, and as the cardinal seems not to have been able to make good his censure of the "Reformer's" doctrines by proofs from the scriptures, Luther appealed to the pope better-informed. But Leo X, the month following (Nov. 9th), issued an edict requiring the church to believe in his power to forgive sins. Learning of this, Luther promptly appealed from the pope to a future council of the whole church.‡

18. Discussion on Free Will:—Meantime the number

---

*The canon law consists of the enactments of the councils and decrees of the popes.

†Peter Lombard, who in the 12th century collected and arranged systematically the theological opinions and decisions of the Latin fathers.

‡In the church of Rome it may be said there were two parties, one of which held that the pope's power was supreme—superior to all other authority in the church; the other maintained that the pope's authority was subordinate to that of a general council of the whole church. The latter party was quite strong in Germany, so that a great many sus-

of points of disagreement between the "Reformer" and the church of Rome increased. In 1519 John Eckius [Eck-ius] challenged Andrew Carolstadt [Karl-stat], a friend and colleague of Luther's, to a discussion on the subject of Free Will, about which there was a disagreement between the "Reformer" and those who thought with him—among whom was Carolstadt—and the adherents of the church of Rome. In this dispute Carolstadt maintained—and of course his were Luther's views—that since the fall, the natural freedom of man is not strong enough to move him to that which is morally good, or to do the will of God. Eckius, on the contrary, insisted that the free will of man produces good works, and not merely the grace of God; that our free will co-operates with divine grace in the production of good works, and that it depends on man's free power, whether he will give place to the operations of grace or will resist them.

19. **Luther and Eckius:**—After this dispute with Carolstadt, Eckius drew Luther—who had been present at the discussion on Free Will—into a public debate on the foundation of the authority of the pope. Eckius maintained the orthodox view that the supremacy of the pope was founded on divine right, that he was the successor of St. Peter and the vicar of Christ. Luther allowed the superiority of the pope over other bishops, but based that superiority on other grounds. He could not deny that the pontiffs had possessed a decided pre-eminence from age to

---

stained Luther in his appeal to a general council. Even Duke George of Saxony favored the calling of such a council. Said he:—"The scandalous conduct of the clergy is a very fruitful source of the destruction of poor souls. There must be a universal reformation; and this cannot be better effected than by a general council. It is therefore the most earnest wish of us all, that such a measure be adopted."—*Milner's Church History, Vol. IV, Ch. v. (Note.)*

age, and therefore he conceived it as his duty not to resist the powers that be. "Unless it had been the will of God," he went on to say, "the pope could never have attained so great and durable a dominion. The whole body of the Christians own themselves to be under the Roman pontiff. This universal consent is a consideration of the greatest weight; the unity of the church should be preserved in everything that is not directly contrary to the word of God."*

20. In all these admissions, however, it will be observed that the "Reformer" placed the supremacy of the pontiffs on human, not divine right. It was based upon tradition, upon human arrangement. To the contention of Eckius that the expressions—"Thou art Peter, and upon this rock I will build my church," "And I will give unto thee the keys of the kingdom"—evinced the supremacy of Peter and his successors; that this was the explanation given by the holy fathers, etc., Luther replied: That even if all the fathers, without exception, had understood the passages in that sense, he would confute them by the authority of St. Paul, and by St. Peter himself, who said that Jesus Christ is the only foundation and corner-stone of the church. And further, if the words "Thou art Peter," etc., be construed strictly then they must be confined to the person of Peter and therefore the authority conveyed by them ceased when that apostle died.†

21. The dispute amounted to nothing except that it widened the breach between the see of Rome and the "Reformer." The latter, while preparing for his discussion with Eckius, had his suspicions aroused that the pope was the very anti-Christ of the New Testament. At the conclusion of the debate, George, Duke of Saxony, said to the disputants, privately, "Whether the pope exists

---

*Milner's Church Hist., Vol. IV, page 405.
†Milner's Church Hist., Vol. IV, ch. iv.

by divine or by human right, he is, however, the pope," and that remark doubtless expressed the sentiments of the papist party.

22. Luther Condemned and Excommunicated:— Eckius hastened to Rome after the discussion at Leipsic [Lip-sik], where, with the assistance of other enemies of Luther, among them Cardinal Cajetan, he urged Leo X to condemn him and his works. This Leo did, by issuing a bull, in which forty-one of his tenets were pronounced heretical; his writings condemned to the flames, and he himself commanded to confess his faults within sixty days, beg the forgiveness of the pope or be excommunicated from the church.

23. This bull of condemnation Luther burned, together with a copy of the pontifical canon law, in the presence of a vast multitude. (See note 6, end of section.) By this act he meant to withdraw from the church of Rome, that the excommunication which was expected to follow might be robbed of its force. About a month later—4th of January, 1521—the second bull of Leo was issued in which the "Reformer" was expelled from the Catholic church for his heresies and for violating the majesty of the pontiff. (See note 7, end of section.)

24. Luther Before the Diet at Worms:—After issuing his bull of excommunication, Leo X called upon the emperor of Germany, Charles V, to vindicate his title to "Advocate and Defender of the Church," by inflicting due punishment upon that "rebellious member, Martin Luther." Charles, however, was under deep obligations to Frederic, the Wise, Elector of Saxony, for his election by the states of Germany to the imperial dignity; and Frederic, being a warm friend of Luther's, and favorable in the main to his doctrines, advised the emperor to take no action against the "Reformer" until he had given him a hearing. This course Charles resolved to follow, and therefore summoned Luther to appear before the diet which assembled at Worms in 1521.*

25. Before this august body the "Reformer" appeared to make answer to the two questions: First, if the books which he had written, the titles of which were read to him, were his; second, if he was prepared to retract those books and their contents, or if he persisted in the opinions he had advanced in them. He acknowledged the books to be his, and in a speech of some length, he explained his motives in writing his books, and refused to retract them. He thus concluded his speech:

26. "I cannot submit my faith either to the pope or to the council, because it is as clear as the day that they have frequently erred and contradicted each other. Unless, therefore, I am convinced by the testimony of scripture, or by the clearest reasoning—unless I am persuaded by means of the passages I have quoted,—and unless they thus render my conscience bound, by the word of God, I cannot and will not retract, for it is unsafe for a Christian to speak against his conscience. **Here I stand, I can do no other, may God help me! Amen!**"

27. Luther was protected by a safe conduct from the emperor—a written guarantee pledging the faith and honor of the empire for his safety for a limited length of time— or doubtless he would have been burned at the stake for his adherence to his doctrines and his defiance of the pope.

---

*The diet was a great council of the German empire, consisting of the princes, provincial rulers and the chief dignitaries of the church. The diet from the 10th century had assumed the right of electing the emperor of Germany, subject to confirmation by the pope, by whom alone he could be crowned. The diet was also usually assembled for the consideration of very important matters pertaining to the empire.

Indeed some members of the diet advised the violation of the safe conduct, as the word of honor given to an heretic, according to the morals of the age, was not binding. Charles V, however, refused to listen to such perfidy. He dismissed Luther to return to Wittemberg in accordance with the terms of his safe conduct; at the same time condemning him as an heretic misled by his own folly. He forbade him on his return to Wittemberg to cause the least disorder among the people, and then promised the representatives of the pope that he would proceed against him and his adherents as contumacious heretics, by excommunication, by interdict and by every means calculated to destroy them.

28. Luther's Confinement at Wartburg:—Prince Frederic, the Wise, fearing that Luther would fall a prey to his enemies, in the storm which he saw gathering about him, had him intercepted on his way back to Wittemberg, by persons in disguise, who carried him to the castle of Wartburg [Wart-berg], where he was concealed ten months. The extremes into which some of his followers went, both in doctrine and in opposition to the Catholics, at last called him from his place of retirement, in order to restrain them and correct the abuses to which some of his doctrines gave birth.

29. Death of Leo X—Demands for a General Council:—The year following the diet at Worms, Leo X died and was succeeded by Hadrain VI. This pontiff, while renewing the demand that the edict of the diet of Worms against Luther and his adherents should be executed, acknowledged the church to be in a lamentable condition and promised a general reformation. The assembled princes at the diet of Nuremberg, before which the demands of Hadrian were presented, thought the time propitious—the emperor Charles was absent in Spain—to insist upon a free council to be held in Germany, to deliberate in the ancient manner on a general reformation of the church. This Hadrian promised to grant, but before it could be assembled he died, having occupied the papal chair but two years and eight months. He was succeeded by Clement VII, who reproved the German princes for neglecting to proceed against Luther and his adherents. The emperor seconded the demands of the pope, and a number of the princes, awed by the united demands of the pope and the emperor, promised to enforce the edict to the extent of their power.

30. Death of Frederic—Distinct Church Founded:— In 1525, Prince Frederic, the Wise, elector of Saxony, and friend of Luther, died. He was succeeded by his brother John. Frederic had ever been an ardent admirer of Luther, but was extremely cautious in giving him any direct assistance. John was of a different temperament. He believed the principles which the "Reformer" taught, but saw quite clearly that they must either be abandoned or the authority of the pope discarded. He resolved upon the latter; and taking matters in his own hands, determined to organize a church altogether distinct from that of Rome. To accomplish this he called upon Luther and Philip Melancthon [Me-lanc-thon] to draw up a formula for public worship, and draft a form of church government in harmony with their principles, fixing the salaries of the clergy, defining their official duties, etc. This the "Reformers" gladly undertook, and shortly afterwards had the pleasure of seeing other German princes pursue the same course that John had taken, and adopt the system of worship they had formulated.

31. The Rupture Between the Pope and the Emperor:—This bold step threatened for a time to disrupt the German empire; for the princes who remained true to the old religion openly consulted together upon the advisability of taking up arms against the Lutherans; and the princes favoring the "Reformers" met to consider the necessity of forming an alliance to resist their enemies. In the midst of these threatening prospects an event happened which was of great advantage to the Lutheran cause, and prevented for the moment any action against them. The Emperor Charles V and Pope Clement VII became open enemies. The pontiff, fearing the increasing power of Charles, had formed an alliance with Francis I, king of France, against him.   This so incensed Charles that he abolished the authority of the pope in Spain, made war upon him in Italy, captured the cities of Rome, besieged the pontiff in his castle of St. Angelo, and subjected him to great indignities.

32.   The Diet at Spire—1529:—The difficulties between Charles and the pope were finally settled, however, and a diet was called at Spire in 1529, in which a majority voted to deprive the princes of Germany of the right to regulate religious matters within their respective territories—a right which a diet held three years before at Spire had granted.   That is, such power was granted pending the settlement of religious difficulties by a free general council.* The diet also declared all changes made in the public religion unlawful.   This action was considered a hardship by those princes who had made such changes, and they protested against the action of the diet and appealed to the emperor.†

---

*Mosheim (Murdock) Vol. III, Book IV, Cent. xvi, Sec. i, Ch. ii.

†The Emperor was not present at this second diet at Spire.   He was absent in Spain.   "They appealed to the emperor, to a future council of the German nation, and lastly to every impartial judge.   For they believed that a majority of votes in a diet could decide a secular question, but not a spiritual or religious question; they appealed to the emperor, not as recognizing him as their judge in a matter of religion, but merely that he might allow their appeal to a council to be valid."— Schlegel.

It was this protest which gave to the dissenting princes, and the followers of Luther generally, the name Protestants.

33. The envoys of the dissenting princes sent to inform Charles of the stand they had taken in relation to the religious controversy in Germany were imprisoned by him, a circumstance which threatened hostility, and the Protestant princes at once took counsel for their safety and sought to form closer alliances with each other for mutual defense. Unfortunately, however, the would-be reformers of religion were not united in doctrine, and the efforts of the princes at union were rendered vain by the disputes of the theologians.

34. **Diet at Augsburg—Protestant Confession of Faith:**—The emperor finally determined to settle this religious controversy within his empire, and appointed a diet to be assembled at Augsburg for that purpose. In order that the faith of the Protestants might be clearly set forth, together with their reasons for separation from the Roman church, Luther and Melancthon, at the instance of the princes who favored their doctrines, drew up a confession of faith, known as the Augsburg Confession. It consisted of twenty-eight articles, twenty-one of which stated the doctrines of the "Reformers," and the other seven stated their reason for withdrawing from the Roman church. These in brief were—Communion in one kind; by which the sacramental cup was denied the laity; imposing celibacy on the clergy; private masses; auricular confession; legendary traditions; monastic vows; and lastly, the excessive power of the church. In respect to this last "abuse," as these several above things are called, they discriminate between civil and ecclesiastical power, and insist that neither should infringe upon the domain of the other.

35. The diet of Augsburg assembled on the 20th of

June, 1530; and after the Confession of Faith was read to the emperor, it was signed by John, Elector of Saxony, four princes of the empire, and the representatives of two imperial cities, Nuremberg [Nu-rem-berg] and Reutlingen [Roit-ling-en].*

36. The friends of the pope at the diet presented a confutation of the Protestant confession, and thereupon the emperor commanded the Protestants to abandon their whole cause of controversy. In reply they protested they were not satisfied with the "confutation," and asked that a copy of it might be given them that they might make answer to it. This the emperor would not grant, nor would he permit an answer to be read before the diet which Philip Melancthon had written out from memory. A number of conferences were held between the leaders of the contending parties with a view to reach an honorable compromise, but they had drifted too far apart, and all hope of reconciliation was lost. At last the emperor issued a decree commanding back to their allegiance to the pontiff the princes and cities that had become alienated from the holy see of Rome, on pain of incurring the vengeance of the emperor. The religious changes made in some of the principalities were censured and the edict of Worms against Luther and his adherents received new force.

37. The League of Smalcald:—Nothing daunted by the unfavorable decree of the emperor, the Protestant princes assembled at Smalcald, and entered into a league among themselves, and made every effort to induce the

---

*Before the diet rose the cities Kempten, Heilbronn, Windsheim and Weisenburg also subscribed; and afterwards many more. It was immediately printed, and soon spread all over Europe, and was translated into various languages. It thus became of great service to the Protestant cause; for it was a very able document and was drawn up in a most judicious manner.—*Murdock.*

kings of England, France, Denmark and other princes to join their confederacy. This movement seriously embarrassed Charles, for he was just on the eve of a war with the Turks, and needed the entire strength of his empire. He therefore entered into negotiations with the Protestant princes, and finally agreed to annul the edict of Worms and of Augsburg, allow the Protestants to regulate religious matters to please themselves until either a council of the church or a diet of the empire should determine what religious principles should be approved and obeyed—the council to be called within six months. Such were the concessions of the emperor. On their part, the Protestant princes were to contribute money for the Turkish war, and acknowledge Ferdinand, brother of the emperor, king of the Romans.*

38. The Truce of Nuremberg:—This treaty of peace being drawn up and accepted in the city of Nuremberg [Nu-rem-berg], was known as the Truce of Nuremberg, and under it the Protestant cause was materially strengthened; for every day men and cities threw off their allegiance to the pope and rejoiced in their new-found freedom.

39. Difficulty in Locating the Council:—The emperor urged the pontiff to call the long-talked-of council which was to settle these unhappy difficulties. But this Clement VII seemed not anxious to do. When he did propose a council it was at places in Italy, and to this the Germans would not consent, as a council held there would be under the influence of the pope; besides, the controversy had arisen in Germany, and there it should be settled. The Protestants also insisted that the decision should be founded solely on the scriptures, a point which required the church of

---

*The Protestant princes had held that the election of Ferdinand to be king of the Romans was contrary to the laws of the empire.

Rome to set aside all the former decisions of her great councils—a thing her pontiffs were in no temper to do, as they considered themselves in the position of a parent having absolute jurisdiction, dealing with a refractory child. Finally, the successor of Clement VII—Paul III—with the approval of the emperor, called a council to meet at Trent, in Austria (in the Austrian Tyrol). But this was not satisfactory to the Protestants, and Charles X, despairing of settling the difficulties by peaceful methods and being urged to it by Pope Paul III, prepared to settle it by resorting to force. While the Catholics and Protestants were preparing for this conflict, Luther whose preaching had begun this agitation died at Eisleben, his native town. (See note 8, end of section.)

40. Reverses of the Protestants:—In the war which followed the Protestants met with severe reverses, and were forced by the emperor to consent to refer the religious controversy to the council of Trent, but it being reported that the plague had broken out in that city the council was broken up, nor could Charles induce the pope to call another immediately (see note 9, end of section); hence it became necessary to formulate a treaty which should bind both parties in respect to religion, pending the convening of a council. This treaty was called "The Interim," and was of course most favorable to the victorious party—the Catholics —and went far towards establishing the old methods of worship.

41. Victory of Protestants—Religious Liberty Secured:—At last the emperor persuaded the pope to reassemble the Council of Trent, and gave notice to the Protestants to attend, promising to use his best endeavor to have everything done in a Christian manner and without passion. But before this council could assemble the Protestant princes revolted, took the emperor by surprise, and forced him into signing a treaty at Paussau, in 1552, which guaranteed religious liberty to the Protestants. This treaty was reconfirmed by the emperor in the diet at Augsburg, 1555. By that treaty all who had accepted the Confession of Augsburg were declared free from all jurisdiction of the Roman pontiff, and his bishops. They were to be permitted to live in peace and the quiet enjoyment of religious liberty. Men were to be left free to join either the Reformed or the Catholic Church, and any person making war upon others, or molesting them because of their religion was to be accounted the public enemy of Germany.

42. Such was the fruit of the great revolution of the sixteenth century in Germany—religious liberty. To that end all the struggles tended, and its result was indeed glorious, worth all the tears and blood it had cost to gain it. But it was not a reformation, if by that is meant the bringing back of primitive Christianity. That the "Reformers" did not do. Indeed they left more truth in the Catholic church than they brought out with them, or found in their speculations after leaving that church, as will be seen by a careful consideration of Protestant doctrines treated in subsequent sections.

NOTES.

1. **The Humiliation of Henry IV**:—It was the fourth day on which he had borne the humiliating garb of an affected penitent, and in that sordid raiment he drew near on his bare feet to the more than imperial majesty of the church, and prostrated himself in more than servile deference before the diminutive and emaciated old man, from the terrible glance of whose countenance, we are told, "the eyes of every beholder recoiled as from the lightning." Hunger, cold and nakedness, and shame, had for the moment crushed the gallant spirit of the sufferer. He wept and cried for mercy, again and again renewing

his entreaties until he had reached the lowest level of abasement to which his own enfeebled heart or the haughtiness of his great antagonist could depress him.   Then, and not till then, did the pope condescend to revoke the anathema of the vatican.—*Sir J. Stephen's Essays On Ecclesiastical Biography.*

2.   **Influence of Greek Literature on the Fifteenth Century:**— The classical school of that period (15th century,) inspired its disciples with admiration, not only for the writings of Virgil and Homer, but for the entire frame of ancient society; for its institutions, its opinions, its philosophy as well as its literature.   Antiquity, it must be allowed, whether as regards politics, philosophy, or literature, was greatly superior to the Europe of the fourteenth and fifteenth centuries.   It is not surprising, therefore, that it should have exercised so great an influence; that lofty, vigorous, elegant and fastidious minds should have been disgusted with the coarse manners, the confused ideas, the barbarous modes of their own time, and should have devoted themselves with enthusiasm, and almost with veneration, to the study of a state of society at once more regular and more perfect than their own.   Thus was formed that school of bold thinkers, which appeared at the commencement of the fifteenth century, and in which prelates, priests and men of learning were united by common sentiment and common pursuits.—*Guizot's Hist. Civilization.*

3.   **Luther on Indulgences:**—I was compelled in my conscience to expose the scandalous sale of indulgences.   I saw some seduced by them into mischievous errors, others tempted into an audacious profaneness.   In a word, the proclaiming and selling of pardons proceeded to such an unbounded licentiousness that the holy church and its authorities became subjects of open derision in the public taverns. There was no occasion to excite the hatred of mankind against priests to a greater degree.   The avarice and profligacy of the clergy had for many years past kindled the indignation of the laity.   Alas! they have not a particle of respect or honor for the priesthood, except what solely arises from fear of punishment.—*Luther.*

4.   **Duke George of Saxony on the Corruption in the Church:** — (Duke George is regarded as a bigoted papist, esteemed by the Roman Catholics as a most sincere and active defender of the faith in his day. His testimony, therefore, to the sale and evils of indulgences, and the corruption of the clergy is the more valuable.   He entirely approved of Luther's condemnation.)   "Indulgences which ought to be obtained by prayer, fastings, benevolence towards our neighbor, and other good works," said the duke, "are sold for money.   Their value is extolled beyond all decency.   The sole object is to gain a deal of money.   Hence the preachers who are bound to set forth truth, teach men nothing but lies and frauds.   They are not only suffered to go on thus, but they are well paid for their fraudulent harangues.   The reason is the more conviction they can produce among their hearers, the more money flows into the chest.   Rivers of scandalous proceedings arise from this corrupt fountain.   The officials of the bishops are equally attentive to scrape money together.   They vex the poor with their censures for great crimes, as whoredom, adultery, blasphemy; but they spare the

rich. The clergy commit the very same crimes, and nobody censures them. Faults which ought to be expiated by prayers and fastings are atoned for by money, in order that the officials may pay large sums to their respective bishops, and retain a portion of the gain for themselves. Neither when a fine is inflicted is it done in a way to stop the commission of the same fault in the future, but rather so that the delinquent understands he may soon do that very thing again, provided he be but ready to pay. Hence all the sacraments are sold for money; and where that is not to be had, they are absolutely neglected."—*Duke George, quoted by Milner, Ch. Hist , vol. IV, p. 568.*

5. **Character of Tetzel:**—He was a profligate wretch, who had once fallen into the hands of the Inquisition in consequence of his adulteries, and whom the elector of Saxony rescued by his intercession. He now cried up his merchandise in a manner so offensive, so contrary to all Christian principles, and so acceptably to the inconsiderate, that all upright men were disgusted with him. * * * He claimed to have power to absolve, not only from all church censures, but likewise from all sins, transgressions, and enormities, however horrid they might be, and even from those of which the pope only can take cognizance. He released from all the punishments of purgatory, gave permission to come to the sacraments, and promised to those who purchased their indulgences, that the gates of hell should be closed, and the gates of paradise and of bliss open to them.—*Schlegel.*

6. **Luther Burning the Pope's Bull:**—On the 10th of December, a placard was posted on the walls of the university of Wittemberg, inviting the professors and students to be present at nine o'clock in the morning, at the eastern gate near the Holy Cross. A great number of doctors and students assembled, and Luther walking at their head, conducted the procession to the appointed place. How many burning piles has Rome erected during the course of ages! Luther resolves to make a better application of the great Roman principle. It is only a few old papers that are to be destroyed; and fire, thinks he, is intended for that purpose. A scaffold had been prepared. One of the oldest masters of arts set fire to it. As the flames rose high into the air, the formidable Augustine, wearing his frock, approached the pile, carrying the Canon Law, the Decretals, the Clementines, the papal Extravagants, some writings by Eckius and Emser, and the pope's bull. Luther held up the bull and said: "Since thou hast vexed the Holy One of the Lord, may everlasting fire vex and consume thee." He then flung it into the flames. Never had war been declared with greater energy and resolution. After this, Luther calmly returned to the city, and the crowd of doctors, professors and students testifying their approval by loud cheers, re-entered Wittemberg with him.—*D'Aubigne's Hist. of the Reformation.*

7. **Excommunication of Luther:**—The excommunication bull was an attack upon the rights of the German churches. For Luther had appealed to an ecclesiastical council; and in consequence of this appeal the pope could no longer have jurisdiction of the case. Hence the number of Luther's friends increased the more after the publication of this bull.—*Schlegel.*

8. The Character of Luther:—Seckendorf * * * defies all
the adversaries of Luther to fix any just censure on his character except what may be ranked under two heads, *viz.*, a disposition to anger,
and an indulgence in jesting. Beyond all doubt the Saxon reformer
was of a choleric temper, and he too often gave way to this constitutional evil, as he himself laments. Neither is it to be denied that he
also too much encouraged his natural propensity to facetiousness.
The monks of his time were in general guilty of the like fault, and often
to so great a degree as very improperly to mix scurrilities with sacred
subjects. Moreover, the vices and follies of those whom Luther opposed, afforded a strong temptation both to the spirit of anger and of
ridicule. For however severe he may be thought in many of his invectives, we are compelled by unquestionable evidence to confess that
his keenest satirical pieces never reached the demerits of those who
ruled the church in that age. But after all that can be said in miti-
gation, it must be owned that a reformer ought to have considered not
so much what they deserved as what became the character he had to
support; *viz.*, that of a serious Christian, zealous for the honor of his
God, displeased with the vices of his clerical brethren, and grieved on
account of the pitiable ignorance of the people, yet more desirous of
curing the prevailing evils than of exposing them.—*Milner.*

9. The Pestilence and the Council of Trent:—The report of a
pestilence was a mere pretense. The Pope Paul III was equally
zealous of the council which had not been disposed in all respects to
govern itself by his prescription, and of the governing power of the
emperor, which he did not wish to see farther increased by the council.
He indeed hated the Protestants, but he did not wish to see the emperor, under color of enforcing the decrees of the council, acquire a
more absolute authority over Germany. He had already withdrawn
his troops from the imperial army; and he now wished to see the council
dispersed. The Spanish members opposed him; but he found means to
prevail.—*Schlegel.*

REVIEW.

1. What centuries may be considered as the age of moral and spiritual darkness?

2. What power was supreme in those ages?

3. Give an instance illustrating the pride and insolence of the popes.
(Note 1.)

4. What was Henry IV's offense?

5. From what period do historians date the "revival of learning?"

6. What several inventions and circumstances contributed to the
intellectual awakening of Europe?

7. What effect did the fall of the eastern division of the Roman
empire have on the west?

8. What was the influence of ancient literature on the west?
(Note 2.)

9. What circumstances led to the enlargement of the liberty of the masses?

10. Describe land tenure under the feudal system.

11. What were the Crusades?

12. Who aroused the nations of western Europe to undertake the Crusades?

13. What effect did the Crusades have on the feudal system of land tenure and liberty?

14. What did this enlarged liberty prepare the people for?

15. What event is usually considered the beginning of the "Reformation?"

16. Give an account of the birth and parentage of Martin Luther.

17. What schools did he attend and with what result?

18. What effect was produced by his visit to Rome?

19. State the origin of indulgences.

20. What doctrine respecting the efficacy of Christ's blood was advanced by Pope Clement VI?

21. What doctrine is held by the Roman Catholic church about the atonement of Christ for sin?

22. Of what did the temporary punishments for sin usually consist —that is, in early times?

23. What changes were made later?

24. Describe the traffic in indulgences.

25. What excuse was made by the pope for the vigorous sale of indulgences in the 16th century?

26. Who hawked indulgences in the part of Germany where Luther lived?

27. What was the character of Tetzel? (Note 5.)

28. In what spirit was Luther's controversy with Tetzel regarded at Rome?

29. What aroused the pope from his indifference?

30. In what way did he meet the difficulty?

31. What course was pursued by Cardinal Cajetan and what was the result?

32. What difference in respect to authorities to be appealed to in the settlement of controversy existed between Luther and the cardinal?

33. What act of Leo X led Luther to appeal to a general council?

34. State what two parties existed in the Roman Catholic church and what their difference.

35. Describe how the controversy on free will arose.

36. State the respective positions of Eckius and Carolstadt in the controversy.

37. What discussion arose between Luther and Eckius after the debate on free will?

38. What position did Eckius take in relation to the supremacy of the pope?

39. What was Luther's position?

40. What was the effect of the discussion?

41.   Relate the circumstance of Luther's excommunication.
42.   How did Luther treat the bull of excommunication?   (Notes 6 and 7.)
43.   State how Luther came to be summoned before the diet at Worms.
44.   What two questions confronted Luther at the diet?
45.   How did he answer them?
46.   By what means was Luther protected from the vengeance of the pope?
47.   What at last called him from his retirement?
48.   Who succeeded Leo X?
49.   What demand was made upon Pope Hadrian by the German princes?
50.   What event prevented the assembling of the council?
51.   What course did Pope Clement VII follow?
52.   How did the death of Frederic, the Wise, and the succession of John, his brother, affect the "Reformation?"
53.   What did John's course threaten to produce?
54.   What circumstance prevented it?
55.   Relate what transpired at the diet at Spire.
56.   By what means did the German emperor decide to settle the religious controversy in his realm?
57.   State what you can of the Augsburg confession of faith.
58.   What unreasonable demand did the emperor make of the Protestants?
59.   What compromise was effected?
60.   What difficulty arose concerning convening the council?
61.   What reverses did the Protestants sustain in the conflict of arms?
62.   What finally resulted from all this agitation?
63.   Give the character of Luther?   (Note 8).

SECTION II.

1. Controversy on the Question of Grace:—It is now for us to consider the principles at issue in the "Reformation." Luther at the first began his opposition to the pope by denouncing indulgences, and there can be no question but he and every other honest Christian had just cause of complaint and indignation against this infamous traffic, and against the church for permitting it. Yet it cannot be denied that there was a wide difference between the doctrine of the Catholic church respecting indulgences (see note 1, end of section) and the things taught by the infamous John Tetzel. This is evident from the fact that Tetzel with other agents of the pope were censured for their over zeal and excesses in dealing in indulgences.* Miltitz, whom the pope had appointed to treat with Luther to bring about his reconciliation with the church, meeting with Tetzel at Leipsic, twice rebuked him with the greatest severity before the bishops of his province, on account of his iniquitous proceedings in the sale of indulgences, and he finally died neglected and alone—"deserted by all the world." (See note 2, end of section.)

2. These abuses in the sale of indulgences and the other corruptions which had crept into the church formed a just cause of complaint; but they were not the true point

---

*Luther himself testifies to this. In the Latin preface to the first volume of his works, the "Reformer" says: "In the year 1517, when I was a young preacher, and dissuaded the people from purchasing indulgences. * * * I felt assured I should have the pope on my side; for he himself, in his public decrees had condemned the excesses of his agents in this business."

at issue in the controversy. Some time before he opposed
indulgences, Luther, if we may believe D'Aubigne [Do-ben-
ya]—had imbibed ideas in respect to the part which the
grace of God takes in the salvation of man that would have
led him to oppose the church of Rome, if the abuses in the
matter of indulgences had never existed. In order that the
student may grasp this subject in its fullness, and the better
understand this controversy between Luther and the Catholic
church, we shall make a careful statement of the facts which
enter into the question of God's grace and the free will of
man.

1. *Power of Deliberation:*—The mind is conscious of
a power of deliberation. Before the intellect passes the
different motives of action, interests, passions, opinions,
etc. The intellect considers, compares, estimates, and
finally judges them. This is a preparatory work which
precedes the act of will.

2. *Liberty, Free Agency or Will:*—When deliberation
has taken place—when man has taken full cognizance of
the motives which present themselves to him, he takes
a resolution, of which he looks upon himself as the author,
which arises because he wishes it, and which would not
arise unless he did wish it—here the fact of agency is shown;
it resides complete in the resolution which man makes after
deliberation; it is the resolution which is the proper act of
man, which subsists by him alone; a simple fact independent
of all the facts which precede it or surround it.

3. *Free Will, or Agency Modified:*—At the same time
that man feels himself free, he recognizes the fact that
his freedom is not arbitrary, that it is placed under the
dominion of a law which will preside over it and influence
it. What that law is, will depend upon the education of
each individual, upon his surroundings, etc. To act in har-

mony with that law is what man recognizes as his duty; it will be the task of his liberty. He will soon see, however, that he never fully acquits himself of his task, never acts in full harmony with his moral law. Morally capable of conforming himself to his law, he falls short of doing it. He does not accomplish all that he ought, nor all that he can. This fact is evident, one of which all may give witness; and it often happens that the best men, that is, those who have best conformed their will to reason, have often been the most struck with their insufficience.

4. *Necessity of External Assistance:*—This weakness in man leads him to feel the necessity of an external support to operate as a fulcrum for the human will, a power that may be added to its present power and sustain it at need. Man seeks this fulcrum on all sides; he demands it in the encouragement of friends, in the councils of the wise; but as the visible world, the human society, do not always answer to his desires, the soul goes beyond the visible world, above human relations, to seek this fulcrum of which it has need. Hence, the religious sentiment develops itself; man addresses himself to God, and invokes his aid through prayer.

5. *Man Finds the Help he Seeks:*—Such is the nature of man, that when he sincerely asks this support he obtains it; that is, seeking it is almost sufficient to secure it. Whosoever feeling his will weak, invokes the encouragement of a friend, the influence of wise councils, the support of public opinion, or who addresses himself to God by prayer, soon feels his will fortified in a certain measure and for a certain time

6. *Influence of Spiritual World on Liberty:*—There are spiritual influences at work on man—the empire of the spiritual world upon liberty. There are certain changes, certain moral events which manifest themselves in man

without his being able to refer their origin to an act of his will, or being able to recognize the author. Certain facts occur in the interior of the human soul which it does not refer to itself, which it does not recognize as the work of its own will. There are certain days, certain moments in which it finds itself in a different moral state from that which it was last conscious of under the operations of its own will. In other words, the moral man does not wholly create himself; he is conscious that causes, that powers external to himself, act upon and modify him imperceptibly*— this fact has been called the grace of God which helps the will of man, while others see in it the evidences of predestination.

3. **The Pelagian View:**—From these facts men arrive at different conclusions. Some regarding only the power of man to deliberate on any proposed course of conduct, and his ability to decide for himself what course he will pursue, ignoring the spiritual influences which operate on him, and taking no account of the aid which comes to man through prayer—believe that man's conduct depends entirely upon his will. " 'Tis in ourselves that we are thus or thus," say they; and hence reject the fact of the grace of God and the influence it exerts on human conduct.

Such was the conclusion arrived at by Pelagius who flourished early in the fifth century. He asserted that human nature is not fallen—that there is no hereditary corruption, and that man having the power to do good has only to will in order to perform. His doctrine has been revised several times. and has drawn to it not a few believers.

---

*The foregoing six statements of fact I have summarized from M. Guizot's excellent work on the *Civilization of Europe.*

4. Catholic View:—Others regarding all the facts elsewhere enumerated—man's power to deliberate, his ability to decide upon his course, his failure to do all that his reason teaches him it is his duty to do, his need of help from a source external to himself, the assistance he can and does obtain through prayer and, lastly, the influence of spiritual forces upon man—leads them to the conclusion that it is through a union of the grace of God and the free will of man that men arrive at last at righteousness. Such was the teaching of the Roman Catholic church.

5. Protestant View:—Others still, looking only upon the influence of the spiritual world on man, and noting how very far short he comes of doing all his reason teaches him it is his duty to do, conclude that man has no power whatsoever to do good of himself, that he can exercise no will to work righteousness, until after the grace of God makes him righteous, and that it is that grace altogether which causes him both to will and to do good works.

6. Luther's Fundamental Doctrine:—Luther belonged to this last-named class. Long before he came to an open rupture with the pope, he taught the doctrine of predestination, and of salvation through faith alone:—"The excellent, infallible, and sole preparation for grace is the eternal election and predestination of God." "On the side of man there is nothing that goes before grace, unless it be impotency and even rebellion." "We do not become righteous by doing what is righteous; but having become righteous we do what is righteous."* "Since the fall of man, free will is but an idle word; and if man does all he can, he still sins mortally." "A man who imagines to arrive at grace by doing all that he is able to do adds sin to

---

*D'Aubigne's Hist. Ref., Vol. I, pages 82, 83.

sin and is doubly guilty." "That man is not justified who performs many works; but he who, without works, has much faith in Christ."* "What gives peace to our consciences is this—by faith our sins are no longer ours, but Christ's on whom God has laid them all; and, on the other hand, all Christ's righteousness belongs to us, to whom God has given it."† Thus taught Luther, and this became the first, the main theological question of the "Reformation." "The point which the 'reformer' had most at heart in all his labors, contests and dangers," says a respectable authority, "was the doctrine of justification by faith alone."‡ (Note 3, end of section.)

7. It is but just to the "Reformer," however, that it should be known that he did not himself reject good works, but on the contrary exhorted men to practice them; but he condemns those who did them with an idea that by them they would be justified, or that they were necessary to salvation. He held also that in order to do good works men must first be justified, and that good works done before justification were even sinful.§

8. **The Mischief of Luther's Doctrine:**—Though Luther did not reject good works, and though he held that justifying faith would produce them, yet his doctrine has been the source of much mischief in the world. When

---

*D'Aubigne's History of the Reformation, Vol. I, Book III, page 119.
†Ibid, page 122.
‡Milner's Ch. Hist., Vol. IV, page 514.

§Men desire to do good works before their sins are forgiven, whilst .t is necessary for sin to be forgiven before men can perform good works. It is not the works that expel sin; but the sin being expelled good works follow. For good works must be performed with a joyful heart, with a good conscience towards God, that is, with remission of sins.— D'Aubigne's Hist. Ref., Vol. 1, page 117. "The works of the righteous themselves would be mortal sins, unless being filled with holy reverence for the Lord, they feared that their works might in truth be mortal sins."—Ibid, page 119.

it was charged by his vicar general, Staupitius, that his doctrines were the delight of debauches, and that many scandalous practices were the consequences of some of his publications, he could not deny the charge, but contented himself by saying, "I am neither afraid of such censorious representations, nor surprised to hear them."* Luther's doctrine of salvation by faith alone, as stated by Melancthon, with his approval, stands thus:

"Man's justification before God proceeds from faith alone. This faith enters man's heart by the grace of God alone."† This leaves man a passive creature in relation to his salvation. He is helpless to procure it; he can do nothing to hasten it; he is helpless; he must wait the divine workings of the grace of God. "As all things which happen," says Melancthon, "happen necessarily, according to the divine predestination, there is no such thing as liberty in our wills."‡ (Note 4, end of section.) Other followers of Luther, among them one Nicholas Amsdorf, went so far as to maintain that good works were a hindrance to salvation.§

9. By denying the existence of human liberty, and maintaining that all things happen necessarily, the "reformers," with Luther at their head, laid themselves open to the charges made by the partisans of the church of Rome, viz.: Their doctrine threw open a door to the most unbounded licentiousness since it furnished men with this defense for the crimes they committed—"We could do no other, our fate did not permit us to do otherwise." By saying that good works were not necessary to salvation, and assisted

---

*Milner's Church Hist., Vol. IV, page 379.
†D'Aubigne's Hist. Ref., Vol. III, page 340.
‡Ibid.
§Mosheim's Eccl. Hist. (Murdock,) Vol. III, page 147 (second edition.)

in no way to procure it, the "reformers" took away the chief incentive to good works, and removed the principal restraint to the doing of evil.

10. Moreover, their doctrine rendered void the ordinances and works required by the gospel; neither repentance nor baptism, nor any other act of obedience to God is essential if salvation is by faith alone. To say that it is a doctrine adverse to the whole tenor of scripture, notwithstanding a few isolated passages depended upon by the "reformers" and their successors to support it, is not necessary here. It is sufficient to remark that it is a doctrine which would render the commandments of God incompatible with the powers and capacity of his creatures; a doctrine which destroys at once the consistency of God, and the moral responsibility of man; and therefore a doctrine most pernicious and dangerous to entertain.   (See note 5, end of section.)

11. **Luther on the Danger of his Doctrine:**—It proved to be so even during the lifetime of Luther; for it led some of his followers to believe that Christ had abolished the moral law; and that Christians, therefore, were not obliged to observe it.* Luther himself saw the danger of his doctrine and thus spoke of it: "If faith be preached, as of necessity it must be, the greater part of mankind will interpret the doctrine in a carnal way, and so understand spiritual liberty as to allow indulgences of the flesh. This we may see in all the ranks of life. All profess themselves to be evangelical; all boast of their Christian liberty; and yet give way to their lusts and passions, for example to covetousness, pride, envy, pleasures, and such like. Who discharges his duty faithfully? Who serves his brother in a true spirit

---

*This doctrine was called *Antinomianism*; many believed it and followed it to its very extremes.

of charity? The disgrace which such conduct brings on the profession of the gospel puts me sometimes so out of temper that I could wish these swine, that tread precious pearls under their feet, were still under the tyranny of the pope; for it is impossible that a people so much resembling those of Gomorrah, should be kept in due subjection by the mild maxims of the gospel of peace."*

12. It counts for nothing that Luther denounced this corrupt state of morals among his followers; it was the legitimate outgrowth of his fundamental doctrine—the doctrine of nearly all Protestants—of justification by faith alone, a faith which man had no part in generating, but which came through the grace of God alone. The tree of his planting produced bitter fruit; it was vain for him to proclaim against the fruit so long as he insisted that it was a good tree on which it grew.

13. **Teaching of the Church of Rome on Justification:**—The Catholic Church at the time, whatever errors in respect to other doctrines it entertained, held that salvation, justification before God, resulted through the exertion of man's free will, aided by the grace of God. It came through a union of faith and works on the part of man, and the rich outpouring of grace on the part of Deity; a doctrine which man is conscious of as operating upon and influencing human conduct, and at once in harmony with the whole tenor of revelation, and consonant with the great facts underlying the free will of man which have been already stated in this section.

14. Unfortunately for the Catholic Church, she did not stop here, but attached too great importance to ex-

---

*From Luther's Commentary on the Epistle to the Galatians, quoted by Milner, Vol. IV, page 520.

ternal marks of repentance, to works of penance—to tears, fastings, mortifications of the flesh, and pilgrimages. Men were required to go barefooted, to wear coarse raiment next their bodies, to become exiles from their homes or to renounce the world and embrace a monastic life. Finally, in the eleventh century, voluntary whippings were added to these other punishments (see note 6, end of section); and men learned to look upon these works of penance as purchasing a forgiveness of sins, and paid little attention to the inward regeneration of the heart. "As confession and penance are easier than the extirpation of sin and the abandonment of vice, many ceased contending against the lusts of the flesh, and preferred gratifying them at the expense of a few mortifications."* Especially did this become the case when the doctrine was promulgated that substitutes could be hired to receive the punishment originally inflicted upon the offender, and monks and priests could be found willing to undergo it for a consideration.

15. The church trusted too much in the works of penance, and did not insist stoutly enough upon repentance— a godly sorrow which worketh a reformation of life. If the "reformers" went to one extreme in attributing man's justification wholly to the act of faith and the grace of God, the Catholic Church went to the other in assigning too much value to works of penance and performances of human invention for the forgiveness of sins.

---

*D'Aubigne's Hist. Ref., Vol. I, page 15.

NOTES.

1. Indulgences to be Accompanied by Amendment of Life:— The doctrine and the sale of indulgences were powerful incentives to evil among an ignorant people. True, according to the church, indulgences could benefit those only who promised to amend their lives, and who kept their word. But what could be expected from a tenet invented solely with a view to the profit that might be derived from it? The vendors of indulgences were naturally tempted for the better sale of their merchandise to present their wares to the people in the most attractive and seducing aspect. The learned themselves did not fully understand the doctrine. All the multitude saw in them was that they permitted men to sin; and the merchants were not over eager to dissipate an error so favorable to their sale.—*D'Aubigne.*

2. Death of Tetzel:— While the proper nuncio (Miltitz) was negotiating a reconciliation in Germany, Tetzel, the wretched subaltern, whose scandalous conduct had so disgraced his employers, met with the reward which frequently awaits the ministers of iniquity. He found himself deserted by all the world. Miltitz in particular had treated him so roughly that this daring and boisterous instrument of papal avarice and extortion actually fell sick, wasted away, and at last died of a broken heart. A dreadful lesson! This unhappy man left the world, as far as appears, destitute of comfort in his own soul, after he had ministered a false peace to thousands.—*Milner.*

3. Luther on Justification by Faith:— I observe that the devil is continually attacking this fundamental article by means of his doctors, and that in this respect he can never cease or take any repose. Well, then, I, Doctor Martin Luther, unworthy herald of the gospel of our Lord Jesus Christ, confess this article, that *faith alone without works justifies before God*; and I declare that it shall stand and remain forever in spite of the emperor of the Romans, the emperor of the Turks, the emperor of the Tartars, the emperor of the Persians—in spite of the pope and all the cardinals, with the bishops, priests, monks and nuns— in spite of kings, princes and nobles, and in spite of all the world and of the devils themselves; and that if they endeavor to fight against this truth they will draw the fires of hell upon their heads. This is the true and holy gospel, and the declaration of me, Doctor Luther, *according to the teaching of the Holy Ghost.—D'Aubigne (Hist. Ref., Vol I., p. 70.)*

4. Effects of Predestination on the Mind:— To what purpose shall I labor in the service of God? If I am predestinated to death, (that is, spiritual death,) I shall never escape from it; and if I am predestined to life, (that is, to salvation, even though I do wickedly;) I shall, no doubt, arrive at eternal rest.—*Raban, quoted by Guizot.*

5. Evil Results of the Doctrine of Justification by Faith Alone:— The serious evil involved in Luther's doctrine of justification by faith without works is perhaps best seen in a quotation from Fletcher, of Madeley, the most able disciple of John Wesley and his successor. Fletcher accuses one Richard Hill, Esq.—who accepted in its widest sense the doctrine of justification by faith alone—with saying: "Even adultery and murder do not hurt the pleasant children, but rather work for their good.   God sees no sin in *believers*, whatever sin they may commit.   My sins might displease God; my person is always acceptable to him * * * It is a most pernicious error of the schoolmen to distinguish sins according to the fact, and not according to the person. Though I blame those who say, let us sin that grace may abound, yet adultery, incest and murder shall, upon the whole, make me holier on earth and merrier in heaven."—*End of Religious Controversy*, p. 90.

6. **The Works in which Catholics Trusted:**—In the eleventh century voluntary flagellations were superadded to these practices (fastings, pilgrimages, etc.); somewhat later they became quite a mania in Italy, which was then in a very disturbed state.   Nobles and peasants, old and young, even children of five years of age, whose only covering was a cloth tied round the middle, went in pairs by hundreds, thousands and tens of thousands, through the towns and villages, visiting the churches in the depth of winter.   Armed with scourges, they flogged each other without pity, and the streets resounded with cries and groans that drew tears from all who heard them.—*D'Aubigne.*

REVIEW.

1.   What difference existed between the teachings of the Catholic church and the conduct of its agents in the matter of indulgences? (Note 1.)

2.   Was the sale of indulgences the chief cause of Luther's revolt from Rome?

3.   What doctrines did Luther entertain which would at last have led him to oppose the Catholic church?

4.   What is the power of deliberation?

5.   Explain what liberty or free agency is.

6.   In what way is man's will or free agency modified?

7.   What is it that convinces man of the necessity of external help to aid his will?

8.   What does man's experience teach him when he seeks external help?

9.   What influence is man conscious of as operating upon him in moral and spiritual affairs?

10.   State the Pelagian view on the subject of grace and free will.

11.   State the Roman Catholic view.

12.   State the Protestant view.

13.   What was Luther's fundamental doctrine?

14.   In what light did Luther hold good works?

15.   What mischief arose out of Luther's doctrine?

16.   What did Luther himself say respecting the danger of his doctrine?

17.   What were the teachings of the Roman church on justification?

18. To what extreme did the church of Rome go in the matter of good works?

19. What was the nature of the works in which Roman Catholics trusted too much? (Note 6.)

20. What influence on morals did the doctrine have that substitutes could be employed to receive punishment for sins?

SECTION III.

1. The Growth of Luther's Rebellion:—The thing most important, the one which drew with it the gravest consequences, and which led to the greatest good produced by the "Reformation," was the rebellion of Luther against the authority of the pope. He did not come out in open rebellion at the first, but arrived at that state by gradual and imperceptible steps. When his opposition to the sale of indulgences met with reproof from the pontiff, he appealed from the pope "ill-informed" to the pope "better-informed." When that pope, better-informed, still held him to be in error and refractory, he appealed to a general, free council of the whole church; but when no heed was taken of this appeal, and Leo, pressed by Eckius, Cajetan and others, excommunicated him, he then answered by burning the pope's bull of excommunication, and stood in open rebellion to the authority of the pontiff. When the pope appealed to Emperor Frederick to make the excommunication of some force by the power of the secular authority vested in him, the emperor, contrary to the protests of the pope's legates, resolved to give the "reformer" a hearing before proceeding against him. Accordingly Luther was summoned before the diet at Worms, where he not only insisted upon having a hearing before a free, general council of the church, but a council that would accept the Bible as the final authority upon the questions at issue between himself and the pontiff.

2. The Catholic Rule of Faith:—This was demanding more than the pope could grant; for the Catholics have never exalted the Bible above the church, but have always held that the scriptures must be accepted as construed by the church, and in the days of Luther the pope was the church. The Catholic rule of faith in respect to the laws by which the church is to be governed is: The word of God, at large, whether written in the Bible or handed down from the apostles by tradition, and as it is understood and explained by the Catholic church."* Besides their rule of faith, which is scripture and tradition, "Catholics acknowledge an unerring judge of controversy, or sure guide in all matters relating to salvation—viz., the church."†

3. This rule employed to interpret the Bible and to settle controversies that might arise, Luther rejected. Writing in defense of his conduct in burning the papal bull of excommunication and the Decretals of the popes, he said: "Let no man's good sense be so far seduced as to reverence the volumes I have burnt, on account of their great antiquity or their high titles. Let every one first hear and see what the pope teaches in his own books, and what abominable, poisonous doctrines are to be found among the sacred, spiritual laws; and then let him freely judge, whether I have done right or not in burning such writings."

4. Among the teachings in the Decretals which Luther help up for special condemnation were the following: (1) "The pope has the power to interpret scripture, and to teach as he pleases; and no person is allowed to interpret in a different way. (2) The pope does not derive from the scripture but the scripture derives from the pope, authority, power and dignity." He then affirms that comparing together the different parts of the canon law, its language amounts to this: "That the pope is God on earth; above

*End of Religious Controversy, page 80.
†Ibid.

all that is earthly or heavenly, temporal or spiritual; that all things belong to the pope; and that no one must venture to say, what doest thou?"*   It was against this arbitrary authority that Luther rebelled.

5. **Attempted Settlement by a General Council:**—At last when through the influence of the emperor, Charles V, the pope consented to appoint a council, a difficulty arose as to where it should be held.   The pope on his part seemed determined to have it assemble in Italy, or in some country where his influence would predominate; the "reformers" were equally determined to submit their cause to no council outside of Germany.   The difficulty had arisen in Germany, they insisted it should be settled by a council in Germany, or by a diet of the empire.   The cause was never fairly tried by a council of the whole church; the revolt against the authority of the pope was sustained by an appeal to arms, as related in section I, Part III, of this work.

6. **Revolution, not Rebellion:**—Had that revolt against the Catholic church been a revolt against legitimate authority it would have been rebellion: but as it was against a usurped—and hence an illegitimate—authority, it was a justifiable revolution.   For in ecclesiastical government, no less than in civil government, if a long train of abuses renders it odious, and those who execute it are tyrannical and usurp authority—which the law of God does not sanction—by which unrighteous dominion is exercised over the minds of men, it is the right of the people to resist such authority, and refuse to sustain those who exercise that unrighteous dominion to please their vanity, or gratify their ambition.

Milner's Church Hist., Vol. IV, page 500.

7. True Position, but a Corrupt Church:—The position that the church, officered by inspired prophets and apostles—men having by virtue of their priesthood and official position a right to the inspiration and revelations of God—the position that the church of Christ so officered, has the right to decide upon all controversies and to determine the meaning of scripture, is, beyond all questioning, a true position   But the difficulty with the Roman Catholic church was that it was no longer the church of Christ, as already proven in Part II of this work.   It had no prophets or apostles, no men who had a right to the revelations of God. The popes and bishops of the church taught that revelation had ceased; and they depended on scripture and tradition alone, interpreted by themselves, for their guide.   The power the church possessed was usurped power merely, the growth of ages.   It had become both arrogant and insolent, and at last intolerable, and when a man was found possessing the courage to resent its presumption and defy it, he found followers to applaud and sanction his act.

8. True Cause of the Reformation:—We cannot ascribe the "Reformation" to accidents and mischances, such for instance as the jealousy of Luther because the sale of indulgences was entrusted to the Dominican monks instead of to the order of Augustine monks, to which he belonged*—we cannot assign the cause of the "Reformation" to this, neither can we go to the other extreme and say that the great revolution of the sixteenth century resulted solely

---

*Such is the cause assigned for the "Reformation" by Catholics: John Milner, the noted Catholic divine, author of "*The End of Religious Controversy*," page 105, says: "As to Martin Luther, he testifies and calls God to witness the truth of his testimony, that it was not willingly (that is, not from a previous discovery of the falsehood of his religion,) but from accident, (namely, a quarrel with the Dominican Friars, and afterwards with the pope,) that he fell into his broils about religion."

from a pure desire to reform the abuses that had arisen in the church or bring back Christianity to its primitive purity. Not a few of the princes that favored 'Luther in his revolt against the pope did so from other motives than those prompted by a desire to reform the church.

9.   Many of the temporal monarchs and princes were jealous of the power exercised within their dominions by the Roman pontiffs, as it lowered the dignity of their own position.   They were tired, moreover, of the assumed right of the pope to enter their dominions, and, under one pretext or another, tax their subjects and thus not only impoverish the people, but reduce the revenue of the temporal rules. It will be found, therefore, that the jealousy, ambition and interest of these princes, and not a desire to establish pure religion, made them factors in the great revolution.   (See note 1, end of section.)

10.   The people also were tired of the dominion asserted over their minds by the papal authority, and were only too glad to escape from that thraldom under any pretext whatsoever.   The preceding century had brought a great intellectual awakening to Europe, and men were no longer content to have questions of fact and belief decided by the authority of the church.   (See note 2, end of section.) They insisted that human reason and individual judgment had a right to investigate and to be satisfied on these questions; and the securing of that freedom was not only the leading principle of the sixteenth century revolution, but its greatest achievement.   (See note 3, end of section.)

11.   **Revolution, not Reformation:**—It is absurd to say that the revolution of the sixteenth century was a reformation, if by that it is meant that it re-established the primitive doctrines of Christianity, purified the morals of the people, or gave birth to a better ecclesiastical govern-

ment. It did nothing of the kind. The "reformers" declaimed against some of the abuses of the Catholic church, such as denying the sacramental cup to the laity, the celibacy of the clergy, the absurdities of the mass, fasts and ceremonies of human invention, the whole system of monkery, and the great usurpation of authority by the church; and consequently did not include any of these abuses—except perhaps the last—in the system of religion they founded. Still their doctrines led them into serious errors and great disorders.

12. Private Interpretation of the Bible and its Effects:—The evils that arose from the doctrine of justification by faith alone, we have already noticed.* The disorders that grew out of the doctrine of private interpretation of scripture is yet to be considered. When Luther refused to longer recognize the authority of the church in matters of doctrine, he still was aware that men would need some authority to decide controversies that would arise, consequently he held up the Bible as the final arbiter of all questions touching faith and morals. But the Bible had to be construed, its meaning made plain, and as each one was left to explain it in his own way, the utmost confusion prevailed. On the great fundamental principle of the Protestants—justification by faith alone—Osiander, a Lutheran, says: "There are twenty several opinions, all drawn from scriptures, and held by different members of the Augsburg, or Lutheran Confession."† When the "reformers" from the several parts of Germany consulted together, and with them the "reformers" from other states met with a view to come to some understanding in respect to religion and

---

*See preceding section.
†*Archdeacon Blackburn's Confessional*, page 16.

modes of worship, it was soon apparent that they were hopelessly divided, not only upon matters unimportant, but also upon fundamental principles. Luther had rejected the authority of the church and set up the tribunal of private interpretation of scripture in its stead. A number of his disciples proceeding on the same principle, rejected some of his doctrines and undertook to prove from the scriptures that he was in error and that the "Reformation" needed reforming.

13. "Carolstadt," says the author of the "End of Religious Controversy," "Zuinglius, Okolampadius, Muncer and a hundred more of his followers, wrote and preached against him and against each other with the utmost virulence, whilst each of them still professed to ground his doctrine and conduct on the written word of God alone. In vain did Luther denounce hell fire against them; in vain did he threaten to return back to the Catholic religion; he had put the Bible into each man's hand to explain it for himself, and this his followers continued to do in open defiance of him, till their mutual contradictions and discords became so numerous and scandalous as to overwhelm the thinking part of them with grief and confusion."* (See note 4, end of section.)

14. **The Multiplication of Sects:**—The division of the "reformers" into numerous sects has ever been a reproach to Protestants, and likewise an evidence of the weakness of their position. Men of different capacities and dispositions examined the Bible; they found it no systematic treatise upon religion and morals, but a miscellaneous collection of inspired writings, dealing with historical events, connected, in the main, with the people

---

End of Religious Controversy, page 100.

of God; prophecies, dreams, revelations, doctrines, and morals; written at different times, to different peoples, and under a great variety of circumstances. In addition to all this, many plain and precious parts have been taken away from it;* other parts have doubtless been purposely changed by designing men;† which, with the imperfections arising from its translation from the original languages in which it was written, has made it an uncertain guide, taken alone, for the church or for individuals; and as Protestants insisted upon the right of private judgment in the interpretation of the Bible, it is not surprising that a great variety of opinions were entertained, or that numerous sects were founded upon them. It was a great evil; much confusion and disorder arose out of it; but it was an evil that could not be avoided. It was one of those periods of time when liberty was a cause of disorder, but the attainment of liberty through that disorder more than outweighed the evils that arose from it.

15. **The Error of the Reformers:**—The great error which the "reformers" made was in not giving full application to their principle of the right of private judgment in matters of religion. They claimed the right to revolt from the Catholic church, to interpret the Bible for themselves, and to found their mode of worship upon their own conceptions of what was required by the revelations of God; but when others differed from them, and desired to exercise the same liberty, the "reformers" were themselves intolerant, and attempted to compel men by force to accept their religious faith and modes of worship. It is this intolerance which is the chief reproach applied to the "Reformation" by

---

*I Nephi xiii: 26, 28-32. See also PartI, Section VI, note 3.
†Ibid.

its enemies, and it must be admitted that it somewhat sullies the glory of its achievements.   (See note 5, end of section.)

NOTES.

1.   **Motives Back of the "Reformation:"**—The Protestant historian, Mosheim, with whom Hume agrees, admits that several of the principal agents in this revolution were actuated more by the impulse of passion and views of interest than by a zeal for true religion. (Maclaine's Mosheim, vol. iv. p. 135.)   He had before acknowledged that King Gustavus introduced Lutheranism into Sweden in opposition to the clergy and bishops, not only as agreeable to the genius and spirit of the gospel, but also as favorable to the temporal state and political constitution of the Swedish dominions.   He adds that Christiern, who introduced the Reformation into Denmark, was animated by no other motives than those of ambition and avarice.   Grotius, another Protestant, testifies that it was sedition and violence which gave birth to the Reformation in his own country—Holland.   The same was the case in France, Geneva and Scotland.   It is to be observed, that in all these countries the Reformers, as soon as they got the upper hand, became violent persecutors of the Catholics.   Bergier defies Protestants to name so much as a town or village in which, when they became masters of it, they tolerated a single Catholic.—*End of Religious Controversy.*   (Note) p. 105.

2.   **Desire for Freedom the Moving Cause in "Reformation":** —The strength of the Protestant party had been derived, both in Germany and England, far less from their superiority in argument, however decisive this might be, than from that desire which all classes, and especially the higher, had long experienced to emancipate themselves from the thraldom of ecclesiastical jurisdiction.— *Hallam's Const. Hist. of Eng.*

3.   **The Cause and Leading Principle of the Reformation:**— In my opinion the Reformation neither was an accident, the result of some casual circumstance, or some personal interests, nor arose from unmingled views of religious improvement, the fruit of Utopian humanity and truth.   It had a more powerful cause than all these; a general cause to which all the others are subordinate.   It was a vast effort made by the human mind to achieve its freedom; it was a new-born desire which it felt to think and judge, freely and independently, of facts and opinions which, till then, Europe received or was considered bound to receive from the hands of authority.   It was a great endeavor to emancipate human reason, and to call things by their right names; it was an insurrection of the human mind against the absolute power of spiritual order.   Such, in my opinion, was the true character and leading principle of the Reformation. * * * Not only was this the re-

sult of the Reformation, but it was content with this result. Whenever this was obtained no other was sought for; so entirely was it the very foundation of the event, its primitive and fundamental character! * * * I repeat it; whenever the Reformation attained this object, it accommodated itself to every form of government and to every situation.—*Guizot.*

4. **Unhappy Divisions Among "Reformers":**—Capito, minister of Strasburg, writing to Forel, pastor of Geneva, thus complains to him: "God has given me to understand the mischief we have done by our precipitancy in breaking with the pope. The people say I know enough of the gospel. I can read it for myself. I have no need of you." In the same tone Dudith writes to his friend Beza: "Our people are carried away with every wind of doctrine. If you know what their religion is today, you cannot tell what it will be tomorrow. In what single point are those churches which have declared war against the pope agreed amongst themselves? There is not one point which is not held by some of them as an article of faith, and by others as an impiety!" In the same sentiment, Calvin, writing to Melancthon, says: "It is of great importance that the divisions which subsist among us should not be known to future ages: for nothing can be more ridiculous than that we who have broken off from the whole world, should have agreed so ill among ourselves from the very beginning of the Reformation."—*End of Religious Controversy, Page* 101.

5. **The Reproach of the "Reformation":**—What were the reproaches constantly applied to the "Reformation" by its enemies? Which of its results are thrown in its face, as it were, unanswerable? The two principal reproaches are, first, the multiplicity of sects, the excessive license of thought, the destruction of all spiritual authority, and the entire dissolution of religious society; secondly, tyranny and persecution. "You provoke licentiousness," it has been said to the "Reformers": "you produce it; and, after being the cause of it, you wish to restrain and repress it. And how do you repress it? By the most harsh and violent means. You take upon yourselves, too, to punish heresy, and that by virtue of an illegitimate authority."—*Guizot.*

REVIEW.

1. What was the matter of chief importance in the Reformation?
2. Describe the growth of Luther's conflict with the pope.
3. Describe the Catholic rule of faith.
4. What demands contrary to that rule did Luther make?
5. What difficulty arose in respect to settling the controversy by an appeal to a general council?
6. What can you say of the revolt of Luther to the Catholic church authority?
7. What can you say of the right of the true Church of Christ to settle controversies and determine the meaning of scripture?

8.   Why was the Catholic church unqualified to render decisions on such matters?

9.   What several causes are assigned for the "Reformation" by Catholics and Protestants respectively?   (Note.)

10.   What was the true cause?

11.   What several considerations aided the "Reformation"?

12.   Was the religious movement of the 16th century a reformation or a revolution?

13.   What can you say of the evils which arose from the private interpretation of the Bible?

14.   What caused the multiplication of sects among the Protestants?

15.   What makes the Bible an insufficient guide in matters of faith and worship?

16.   What was the great error of the Reformers?

SECTION IV.

1. The Reformation in Switzerland:—So far we have considered this sixteenth century revolution as it affected the German empire alone. It was not confined, however, to that country. As a matter of fact, the so-called "Reformation" began in Switzerland before it did in Germany. Ulrich Zwingle, born in Wildhausen, Canton of St. Gall, Switzerland 1484, attacked many of the errors of the Catholic Church, before Luther began his opposition.

2. In 1516, Zwingle openly declaimed against many Catholic abuses, such as monastic vows, pilgrimages, worship of relics and indulgences. He also taught that the Bible was the only standard of religious truth. In 1518, one Samson came into Switzerland, to sell indulgences. The year following Zwingle opposed him and drove him from Zurich. Four years later the Swiss "Reformer" was accused of heresy by adherents of the Roman pontiff, and brought before the council of Zurich. He presented sixty-seven doctrinal propositions before the council which he agreed to defend by the scriptures against all opposers. The council before which his cause was tried decided that the controversy must be settled by an appeal to the Bible, and Zwingle triumphed. At the conclusion of the hearing the council decreed that the "Reformer" should be allowed to teach as he had formerly done, unmolested; and that no preacher in the canton should teach any doctrine he could not prove by the Bible. The year following—1524—the council "reformed" the public worship; that is, they adopted the principles and methods of worship proposed by Zwingle.

3. In 1531, the Catholics in the surrounding cantons attacked Zurich, and early in the battle, Zwingle, while leading the Protestant forces, was slain, his body hacked to pieces and afterwards burned. (See note 1, end of section.)

4. **Jonn Calvin:**—Zwingle was succeeded in the leadership of the Swiss "Reformers" by John Calvin, a talented but austere man, a native of Noyon, France. (See note 2, end of section.) He more than any other man—Luther excepted—influenced the character of the Protestant churches. He held many views that were at variance with those of Zwingle. The latter taught that civil rulers possessed absolute power in religious matters, and subjected the ministers altogether to their authority. Calvin held that the church should be free and independent of the state; that it should govern itself by its own officers whom the church and not the state should appoint; he limited the power of the state over the church to giving it external protection. Zwingle recognized a gradation of officers in the Christian church; Calvin held that all were equal. Suitable persons appointed and ordained with the consent of the members of the church, constituted, in his theory of church government, a legitimate ministry to preach the gospel and administer the sacraments. But for the government of the church a number of men were chosen by the people from among the most venerable and respectable of the congregation. These men were called presbyters or elders. They were all equal in authority, and even the preaching minister was in no sense superior to them in office.

5. The elders of a single church or congregation convened in council constituted the church session; councils

composed of representatives from the several churches in a province, constituted synods or consistories; while a general council composed of elders from all the churches was known as the general assembly. The elders in these several councils were all regarded as equal in authority and had full power to enact laws relating to religious matters and to establish the discipline of the church. Such is the order of church government founded by Calvin, and known as Presbyterianism.

6. **Difference of Opinion on the Eucharist:**—As already stated in a previous section, the Catholics maintained that in the eucharist, the bread and the wine, were converted by consecration into the very body and blood of Messiah. Zwingle maintained that the bread and wine were symbols merely of Christ's flesh and blood, employed to call to mind his death, and the blessings procured to man by that death. Calvin stood between these two extremes, as also did Luther, and while they disagreed with Catholics, and would not concede that the bread and wine were changed to the *very* body and blood of Christ, neither would they concede that the bread and wine were *merely*, symbols, but insisted upon a sort of spiritual presence. That is, they held that the saints in the exercise of faith in partaking of the sacrament, do become united in a certain mystic way with Christ, and from this union received an increase of spiritual life.

7. **Predestination:**—Another thing in which Calvin differed from Zwingle was in relation to the celebrated doctrine of an absolute decree of God respecting the salvation of men. Calvin emphasized the doctrines of Luther and Melancthon in regard to the part which the grace of God takes in the salvation of men; and perhaps carried it further than they would have done, certainly further than

Zwingle did. On this point Calvin taught that God had elected some persons from all eternity to everlasting life; and had appointed others to everlasting punishments; and that for this he had no other ground except his own pleasure, or his most free and sovereign will. This is the doctrine of predestination.

8. **The Spread of Calvin's Doctrines:**—It was some time before the Swiss could be brought to accept these doctrines, so at variance with or not found in the teachings of Zwingle. Yet by the perseverance and the high reputation for learning and piety of Calvin they were very generally accepted in Switzerland; and after him, such was the success of his pupils, that large bodies of Protestants in other nations accepted his doctrines. Especially was this the case in France, England, Scotland, and even in Germany.

9. **The "Reformation" in France:**—In France, though in the main her people adhered to the Catholic church, the "Reformation" found its most faithful adherents, and there they suffered the most violent persecutions. The Protestants were opprobriously called Huguenots [Hu-ge-nots] the origin of the appellation is uncertain. Among these French Protestants were men of high character, and not a few bishops of the church. The king and the magistrates, however, protected the ancient religion by the sword, by penal inflictions; and a large number of pious and good people were put to death, among them not a few of the nobility. (See notes 3 and 4, end of section.)

10. **The "Reformation" in Sweden:**—In Sweden the "Reformation" made rapid headway. Its doctrines were introduced into that country by Olaus Peri, whose zeal for the cause was warmly seconded by the king, Gustavus Vasa, who while an exile in Lubec, during the

revolution of 1523, learned something of the "reformed" religion. For some time before 1523 Sweden had been ruled by Danish kings; but in that year, in consequence of the tyranny practiced by Christiern II, of Denmark, a revolution was inaugurated by Gustavus Vasa, which ended in Christiern being driven from Sweden. Gustavus was chosen king in his stead. While prejudiced in favor of the "reformed" religion, he acted with great moderation. He invited learned Protestants from Germany whom he directed to instruct his people in the Bible and the Protestant faith. The Bible translated by Olaus Petri he caused to be published and disseminated. In 1526, a great discussion on religion was held at Upsal at the instance of the king, between Olaus Petri and Peter Gallius, a Roman Catholic. Gallius seems to have been so far defeated, even in his own estimation, that in the year following, in the assembly of the states at Westeras, he recommended the "reformed" religion of Luther to the representatives of the nation. After a long discussion, and much opposition from the bishops, it was finally harmoniously decreed that the "reformed" religion should be introduced. From that time until now the power of the pope in Sweden has been prostrated. (See note 5, end of section.)

11. **Denmark:**—In Denmark the "reformation" was not accomplished so happily. Christiern, whose authority, as we have seen, was overthrown in Sweden, sought to establish the "reformed" religion in Denmark, but more from a desire to deprive the bishops of their power, and confiscate their property, than from a right zeal for true religion. In 1520 he invited Martin Reynhard, a disciple of Carolstadt, to Denmark, and made him professor of theology at Copenhagen. Reynhard stayed about a year. When he left the king sent for Carolstadt. He remained

but a short time; and then the king invited Luther himself
to come, but the "reformer" would not accept the invitation. All these failing him, the king set about the work of
"reformation" himself, but as he was a tyrant, his people
conspired against him, and banished him from the kingdom, in 1523. He was succeeded by his uncle, Frederic,
Duke of Holstein and Sleswick.

12. Frederic was as anxious as Christiern had been
to see the "reformed" religion established in Denmark,
but he was more prudent than his nephew. He permitted
the leaders among the Protestants to teach publicly the doctrines of Luther, and in time these raised up a strong following. In 1527 the king procured a decree from the senate,
at the diet of Odensee, giving religious liberty to the people.
By this decree the Danes were left free to embrace the new
religion, or continue members of the Catholic Church, as
they saw proper. The successor of Frederic—Christian III
—went further than this, however, in the interest of the
"Reformation." He stripped the bishops of their odious
power, confiscated the church property, much of which,
however, he restored to the original owners, from whom
it had been obtained, it is alleged, by base arts. He called
John Bugenhagius from Wittemburg, and with his assistance
regulated the religious affairs of his realm by making the "reformed" the established religion of his kingdom. The
action of Christian III seems harsh, but a circumstance
which mitigates, if it does not destroy the harshness of his
measures, was the insufferable arrogance, pride and power of
the bishops, which was a constant menace to the power of
the monarch, and did much to eclipse his glory. (See note
6, end of section.)

13. Holland:—Perhaps from being contiguous to Germany, the Netherlands—Belgium and Holland—soon par-

took of the spirit of the "Reformation"—the desire to be free. The writings of Luther were early received and widely read by the Netherlanders. This alarmed the Catholics who, in 1552, established the Inquisition there and persecuted with great vigor all who accepted the doctrines of the "reformers." It is estimated that in those provinces which, taken together, constituted the Netherlands, in the reign of Charles V alone—from 1519 to 1552—not less than 50,000 persons lost their lives in consequence of their defection from the church of Rome. But notwithstanding this severe persecution, adherents to the Protestant faith increased. The tyranny of their oppressors seemed to increase the boldness of the people in clamoring for the rights of conscience; and towards the close of the sixteenth century, seven of the provinces successfully revolted against the Duke of Alva, viceroy of the Catholic monarch, Phillip II, of Spain. These revolting provinces formed the Dutch Republic, and in a short time became the most formidable maritime power in the world. They suffered the most and wrought the most in behalf of the liberty of conscience, the freedom of commerce, and the liberty of the state. It is said by one historian that "In freedom of conscience they were the light of the world."* It is well known that for many years their land was the asylum for the oppressed, especially for those persecuted for their religion.

14. **England:**—The "Reformation" in England took on a different aspect to what it did in the other countries. When Luther began his assault upon the church of Rome, the English monarch, Henry VIII, appeared as a champion on the side of the Roman pontiffs. He wrote a book against Luther in defense of the seven sacraments of the Catholic

---

*Bancroft.

Church, which met with such favor in the eyes of the pope, that he conferred upon Henry the title of "Defender of the Faith." Henry's book appeared in 1522. Soon after this the king began to question the legality of his marriage with Catherine of Aragon.

15. Catherine had been the wife of the king's deceased brother, Arthur; and a marriage with a deceased brother's widow was regarded as contrary to the law of God.* Henry therefore applied to the pope for the annulment of his marriage, since his "conscience" would not permit him to cohabit longer with his deceased brother's wife. The conduct of the king, however, was such as to give strong ground to the belief that it was his love for Anne Boleyn, an English lady of high birth, and not conscientious scruples as to the lawfulness of his marriage with Catherine. The queen's beauty had faded and some disease, it is said, had rendered her person less agreeable. Still, to do Henry justice, it must not be concealed that his father had scrupled the legitimacy of the marriage; a foreign court had made it an objection to intermarriage with his children by his wife; and the people of England very generally entertained fears respecting the succession to his crown, and these political considerations doubtless had their influence.† Still it will not be denied that after the king had fallen in love with Anne Boleyn, his love for her and not political considerations, or religious scruples, was the incentive that prompted him to seek a divorce.

16. **The Rupture with the Pope:**—The pope, Clement VII, evaded a direct answer to Henry's appeal. Catherine

---

*It must appear remarkable that such an idea could become prevalent since it is provided in the law of God to ancient Israel that the brother should marry the deceased brother's widow.—Deut. xxv:5; 6: 9, 10.

†Hume's Hist. of England vol. iii, ch. xxx.

was the aunt of Charles V, and perhaps Clement feared that he would offend that monarch—to whom he looked to suppress the "Reformation" in Germany—if he granted the divorce. Henry, impatient of these enforced delays, consulted the universities of Europe, and as most of them pronounced marriage with a deceased brother's wife unlawful, he divorced Catherine without the consent of the pope. A quarrel ensued between the king and the pontiff, which resulted in the former casting off the authority of the latter, and the pope excommunicated the king. In 1533 Henry was declared head of the British church and Defender of the Faith, by the English parliament. He thereupon ejected the monks from their possessions, disposed of their property at his own good pleasure, and abolished *in toto* the authority of the pope in England.

17. No other country in all Europe was so well prepared for the Sixteenth Century Revolution as England. A century and a half before either Luther or Zwingle were heard of, John Wycliffe proclaimed against the corruption and abuses of the Catholic Church, denounced the pope as Anti-Christ,* and preached against the doctrine of transubstantiation. He also translated the scriptures and circulated them among the common people. Two years before his death, however, he was summoned before a church council by which, notwithstanding he defended himself with great ability, many of his doctrines were condemned, and he himself was restricted in his ministry to the parish of Lutterworth, in Leicestershire, where he died. (See note 7, end of section.) His teachings, however, had made a deep impression upon his countrymen, and he left many followers,

---

*On one occasion he declared the pope to be "The proud, worldly priest, Rome, the most cursed of clippers and purse-kervers (cutpurses)."

who were called by their opponents, Lollards. The Lollards were a proscribed sect in England, and as they avoided persecution, but little was heard of them. Still they cherished the doctrines of their leader, and transmitted them to their children; so that when Luther and the other continental "reformers" began their work, there were many in England who sympathized with them; and when Henry VIII considered it to his interests to revolt against the authority of the pope, he found large numbers of his people not only ready to support him in casting off that authority, but anxious to go much further in that revolt than the king desired. (See note 6, end of section.) They had viewed the rupture between the king and the pope with deep satisfaction; but they were soon to learn that the defection of the monarch was not to bring religious liberty to England, or establish there the doctrines of Wycliffe or Luther. It was but a change of masters that had taken place, and the king was as despotic as the pope. (See note 9, end of section.) Although Henry had thrown off the authority of the pontiff, he would tolerate but few changes in the forms and ceremonies of religion. More changes were introduced in the reign of Edward VI, the son of Henry VIII, by Jane Seymore; and still more in the reign of Elizabeth, his daughter by Anne Boleyn.

18. **The Puritans:**—But these changes came far short of satisfying the English Protestants, who were called Puritans. They demanded almost a complete abolition of the rites and ceremonies of the Roman Church, which they denounced as idolatrous. The most of them favored the Presbyterian form of church government, or a still simpler method which would recognize each congregation as a complete church within itself. Those who contended for this more simple form of church government

were called Independents. The Puritans were frequently
rude and clamorous in their demands for further reformation; and on their part the adherents of the established
religion were intolerant, and persecuted to imprisonment,
exile or death the Puritans. (See note 10, end of section.)

19. The "Reformation" in Scotland:—All things considered, the "Reformation" in Scotland—that is the overthrow of the authority of the pope—was accomplished with
as little trouble as it was in England; and accompanied
by less injustice to Catholics. In Scotland, as in England,
the doctrines of Wycliffe had many silent adherents, and
such was the frame of the popular mind, that only the leadership of bold men was needed to make a successful revolt
against the authority of the pope. That leadership was
found in John Knox.* Knox was thirty-eight years of age
when he openly declared himself a Protestant, and began
his work of "reform." About three years later Cardinal
Beaton, a proud, arrogant man, and the head of the Catholic
church in Scotland, was assassinated. His castle—St.
Andrews—was taken possession of by the band of nobles
and others who had murdered him, and it became for a time
the stronghold of Protestantism. To this place Knox re-
paired, and there in the parish church of St. Andrews,
first became famous as a preacher. In a short time, however,
the fortress was surrendered, and Knox was sent to the
French galleys a prisoner. After two years he was set at
liberty, and allowed to depart for England, where he lived
for years, on terms of intimacy with Cranmer and other
English "reformers." On the accession of Queen Mary,†

---

*Knox was born in the year 1505, near Haddington, Scotland. Died
at Edinburgh, 1572.

†Daughter of Henry VIII and Catherine of Aragon. She was a
bigoted Catholic; married Philip II of Spain, also a Catholic.

Knox retired to Germany and Switzerland, residing chiefly in the latter place, where he learned and became attached to both the doctrines and form of church government taught by Calvin.

20. In 1559, political necessity compelled the government in Scotland to become more lenient towards the nobles favoring the "Reformation," and Knox returned to Scotland, where his impassioned denunciations of the idolatry of the mass and of image-worship aroused the pent up enthusiasm of the people. Indeed the people went far beyond what Knox intended; riots ensued, churches and monasteries were destroyed, and the whole country, already suffering the evils of civil war, was plunged into greater disorder. At last, through the assistance of Queen Elizabeth, of England, a truce was proclaimed, and a parliament chosen to settle the troubles. The parliament met in 1560, and its deliberations resulted in the overthrow of the old religion, and the establishment of the "Reformed church," based on the doctrines and church polity of Calvin. In the midst of the harshness which attended the overthrow of the old religion, there was a singular instance of moderation which will be looked for in vain in other countries where the "Reformation" succeeded. According to Hallam, it was agreed in the settlement made by the parliament of 1560, "That the Roman Catholic prelates, including the regulars, should enjoy two-thirds of their revenues as well as their rank and seats in parliament; the remaining third being given to the crown, out of which stipends should be allotted to the Protestant clergy."* "Whatever violence may be imputed to the authors of the Scots Reformation," continues Mr. Hallam, "this arrangement seems to display

---

* *Hallam's Const. Hist. England, p.* 812.

a moderation which we would vainly seek in our own"*—
the English "Reformation."

21. Unfortunately, as in England, after the authority
and religion of the pope were overthrown in Scotland, the
religious difficulties were far from settled. A controversy
arose between the church and the crown on the subject of
authority. It will be remembered that Calvin insisted that
the church should be independent of the state,† and nowhere
was it so strenuously insisted upon as in Scotland; not only
did it demand of the secular authority freedom from inter-
ference, but assumed the right to reprove the king and his
court, and that, too, in no guarded language. In 1854,
Andrew Melville was summoned before the king's council,
to give an account of some seditious language employed by
him in the pulpit against the court. He declined the jurisdiction of the council on the ground that he was responsible
only to the church for such language; and the king could not
judge of the matter without violating the immunities of the
church.‡

22. The king and council, however, did not hesitate
to declare the supremacy of the secular power, and thus
was begun a controversy which, united with the attempts
on the part of the sovereigns and parliament to restore
the Episcopal form of church government, led to violent
persecutions on the part of the secular authority, and to
heroic resistance on the part of the people of Scotland.
In that protracted struggle, prosecuted by both parties
with varying fortunes, the people were at last successful;

---

* *Hallman's Const. Hist. England, p.* 812.

†Ante this Section, ¶ 4, John Calvin.

‡Precedents for such an immunity it would not have been difficult
to find; but they must have been sought in the archives of the enemy
[*i. e.,* in the Catholic Church]. It was rather early for the new republic
to emulate the despotism she had overthrown.— *Hallam, Hist. of Eng.*

though their victory was not secured for them until the Stuart line of monarchs were driven out of Scotland and England by the revolution of 1688, which dethroned James II of England and VII of Scotland, and placed William, Prince of Orange, and Mary, his wife, on the British throne.

23. **The Discovery of America—Its Influence on Liberty:**—It is significant that about the time of the "Revival of Learning" in Europe, America was discovered by Columbus, led hither by the inspiration of God. (Note 11, end of section.) Between this struggle for liberty in the Old World and the discovery of the New, there was doubtless a providential connection. God knew there could be but a stunted growth of the tree of liberty in the Old World, hence he opened the way for it to be planted in a land more congenial to its growth. The whole continent of America is a land consecrated by the decrees of Almighty God to Liberty, and the people who inhabit it are assured by that same decree of their freedom.* Hence when a fullness of liberty was denied the Puritans in England, they fled to America, and here found room for the planting of colonies where they could enjoy the liberty denied them in the Old World, and the founding of the New England colonies (now the New England States within the United States of America) was the result.

24. **Catholics Seek Liberty in America:**—Nor were the Puritans the only ones who sought liberty in the New World. Even the Catholics came; for they, no less than the Puritans, were persecuted in England. Sir George Calvert, whose title was Lord Baltimore, a Roman Catholic, desiring to establish a colony in America that would be a place of refuge for persecuted Catholics, obtained a charter for that

---

*Book of Mormon, Ether, ch. 11:7-13.

territory comprised within the boundary lines of the State of Maryland. Before the charter was signed, Sir George died; but it was made out to his son Cecil, who carried out his father's designs. The charter granted to Lord Baltimore was unlike any which had hitherto passed the royal seal, in that it secured to all who should settle in the colony, religious liberty. That is, Christianity was the recognized religion, made so by the law of the land, but no preference was given to any sect or party.

25. **Puritan Intolerance:**—Unfortunately all the colonies were not founded in the same liberal spirit as Maryland. The Puritans themselves seemed not to have learned toleration by the persecutions they had suffered; but, on the contrary, when they found themselves possessed of power, they forgot right and persecuted all those not of their own way of thinking. This led to the founding of other colonies where greater religious liberty was granted; such as Pennsylvania, settled by the Quakers; Rhode Island, by Roger Williams, a Baptist, driven by Puritan intolerance from Massachusetts.

26. Common dangers, however, taught these colonists toleration. They were surrounded by hordes of savages, against whom they were compelled frequently to combine. The wars between the French and the English extended to their respective settlements in America, and this circumstance drove the English colonists together and taught them toleration. They were driven into a still closer union by the oppression of England, and forgot their religious differences in the presence of the great danger of losing all their freedom, civil as well as religious. When they had achieved their independence, and necessity and experience taught them that a national government—an indissoluble union of the colonies—must be formed, wisdom clearly

suggested that the chief cornerstone of the new temple of liberty must be religious freedom.   Hence in the constitution which they adopted, freedom to worship God according to the dictates of conscience is guaranteed.   (See note 12, end of section.)

27.   **The Hand of God Manifested:**—If in the rise of the great Roman Empire we see the hand of God preparing the way for the introduction of the gospel under the personal administration of the Son of God, that under the protection of that great government the apostles of Messiah might visit every land and deliver the glad tidings of great joy—if in this the land of God is visible—and we have acknowledged it was (see note section II, paragraph 13)—it is equally clear that the meaning of this sixteenth century revolution, which we have been considering, together with the subsequent founding of a great republic in the New World, pledged to the maintenance of religious liberty—it is clearly the meaning of all this that God was preparing the day for a restoration of the gospel—the ushering in of the Dispensation of the Fullness of Times.   (See note 13, end of section.)   That revolution of the sixteenth century was the first glimmerings of the dawn which heralded the approaching day; the light became clearer in America on the establishment of religious liberty under the constitution of the United States; the sun rose when the Lord introduced the **Dispensation of the Fullness of Times** by revealing himself and his Son Jesus Christ to the Prophet Joseph Smith, early in the spring of 1820.

NOTES.

1.   **Zwingle:**—Zwingle discovered the corruptions of the church of Rome at an earlier period than Luther.   Both opened their eyes gradually, and altogether without any concert; and without aid from each

other. But Zwingle was always in advance of Luther in his views and opinions; and he finally carried the Reformation somewhat farther than what Luther did. But he proceeded with more gentleness and caution, not to run before the prejudices of the people; and the circumstances in which he was placed did not call him so early to open combat with the powers of the hierarchy; Luther, therefore, has the honor of being the first to declare open war with the pope, and to be exposed to persecution. He also acted in a much wider sphere. All Germany, and even all Europe, was the theatre of his operations. Zwingle moved only in the narrow circle of a single canton of Switzerland. He also died young, and when but just commencing his career of usefulness. And these circumstances have raised Luther's fame so high that Zwingle has almost been overlooked.—*Murdock.*

2. **Calvin::**—John Calvin was born in the year 1509; and in his studies connected law with theology, studying the former at the command of his father, and the latter from his own choice; and from Melchior Valmar, a German and professor of Greek at Bourges, he acquired a knowledge of the evangelican ["Reformed"] doctrines. After the death of his father, he devoted himself wholly to theology, and publicly professed the reformed doctrine, which he spread in France with all diligence. His name soon became known in Switzerland as well as in France; and Farell and Viret [two Swiss "Reformers"] besought him, as he was traveling through Geneva, to remain there and aid them in setting up the new church. But in the year 1538, great dissension arose in Geneva; and Calvin and his assistant, Farell, severely inveighed from the pulpit against the conduct of the council, which resolved to introduce the ceremonies agreed on at Bern, in the ordinances of baptism and the Lord's supper, and to reject those which these ministers wished to have adopted: and the consequence was, that Calvin and Farell were banished from the republic. * * * But in the year 1541, at the pressing and repeated invitation of the Genevans, he returned to them again, and there officiated with great perseverance, zeal, prudence and disinterestedness, till his death in 1564. His great talents and virtues were shaded by the love of control, by a want of tenderness, and by a passionate vigor against the erring.—*Schlegel.*

3. **The "Reformation" In France:**—France was the first country where the Reformation that commenced in Germany and Switzerland, very soon and under the severest oppressions, found many adherents. No country seems to have been so long and so well prepared for it as this: and yet here it met the most violent opposition; and nowhere was it later, before it obtained legal toleration. Nowhere did it occasion such streams of blood to flow; nowhere give birth to such dreadful and deadly civil wars. And nowhere have state policy, court intrigue, political parties and the ambition of greatness had so powerful an influence on the progress and fortunes of the reformation, as in France.— *Schroeckh.*

4. **Massacre on St. Bartholomew's Eve:**—During the civil wars which desolated France from the year 1560 up to the edict of Nantes— which secured religious toleration from the Protestants, 1598—oc-

curred the massacre of St. Bartholomew's eve. A peace was concluded in 1570, by which toleration was granted the Protestants. The terms of the treaty were enforced with much apparent zeal by the French court, for the purpose, as Protestant writers claim, of lulling the Protestants into security preparatory to their assassination by order of the king. The bloody scene began at midnight of the 22nd of August, 1572. The signal for the beginning of the massacre was the tolling of the great bell of the palace. The scene of blood and murder continued for three days. During which time five hundred noblemen and about six thousand other Protestants were butchered in Paris alone. Orders were dispatched to all parts of the empire for a similar massacre everywhere. More than thirty thousand—some say seventy thousand—perished by the hands of the royal assassins; and the pope ordered a jubilee throughout Christendom.—*Murdock.*

5. **The Decision to Introduce the "Reformed" Religion into Sweden:**—This decision was the effect specially of the firmness and resolution of the king [Gustavus Vasa], who declared publicly that he would rather resign his crown and retire from the kingdom, than rule over a people subjected to the laws and authority of the Roman pontiff, and more obedient to their bishops than to their king.—*Mosheim*

6. **The Danish and Swedish Bishops Stripped of Power:**— Violent measures were adopted, and the bishops, against their wills and their efforts to the contrary, were deprived of their honors, their prerogatives and their possessions. Yet this reformation [?] of the clergy in both those northern kingdoms, was not a religious, but a mere civil and secular transaction; and it was so necessary that it must have been undertaken if no Luther had arisen. For the bishops had by corrupt artifices got possession of so much wealth, so many cattle, such revenues and so great authority, that they were far more powerful than the kings, and were able to govern the whole realm at their pleasure; indeed they had appropriated to themselves a large portion of the patrimony of the kings and of the public revenues. Such therefore was the state both of the Danish and the Swedish commonwealths in the time of Luther, that either the bishops, who shamefully abused their riches, their prerogatives and their honors must be divested of the high rank they held in the state, and be deprived of their ill-gotten wealth, or the ruin of those kingdoms, the irreparable detriment of the public safety and tranquility, and the sinking of their kings into contempt, with an utter inability to protect the people, must be anticipated.—*Mosheim.*

7. **Wycliffe:**—John Wycliffe, the greatest of all the "Reformers before the Reformation," was born in 1324, and is supposed to have been a native of the parish of Wycliffe, near the town of Richmond, Yorkshire. He studied at Oxford, but little is known of his university career. Wycliffe appears to have been a man of simple faith and of earnest and manly courage. He made a strong impression upon his age; an impression that was not effaced at the time of the "Reformation." The Lollards, as his disciples were called, were to be found, not only among the poor, but in the church, the castle and even the throne, Wycliffe died in the year 1384.

8. England Prepared for the "Reformation":—No revolution has been more gradually prepared than that which separated one half of Europe from the communion of the Roman see; nor were Luther and Zwingle any more than occasional instruments of that change which, had they never existed, would at no great distance of time been effected under the names of some other reformers. At the beginning of the sixteenth century, the learned, doubtfully and with caution, the ignorant with zeal and eagerness, were tending to depart from the faith and rites which authority prescribed. But probably not even Germany was so far advanced on this course as England. Almost a hundred and fifty years before Luther, nearly the same doctrines as he taught had been maintained by Wycliffe, whose disciples usually called Lollards, lasted as a numerous though obscure and proscribed sect, till aided by the confluence of foreign streams, they swelled into the Protestant church of England. We hear, indeed, little of them during some parts of the fifteenth century, for they generally shunned persecution; and it is chiefly through records of persecution that we learn of the existence of heretics. But immediately before the name of Luther was known, they seem to have become more numerous, or to have attracted more attention; since several persons were burned for heresy, and others abjured their errors in the first years of Henry VIII's reign. Some of these, as usual among ignorant men, engaging in religious speculation, are charged with very absurd notions; but it is not so material to observe their particular tenets as the general fact that an inquisitive and sectarian spirit had begun to prevail.— *Hallam's Const. Hist. Eng.*

9. Henry VIII and His Revolt Against Rome:—Soon after Henry was declared by Parliament the only supreme head on earth of the church of England, the authority of the pope was finally abolished, and all tributes paid to him were declared illegal. But although the king thus separated from the church of Rome, he professed to maintain the Catholic doctrine in its purity, and persecuted the reformers most violently; so that while many were burned as heretics for denying the doctrines of Catholicism, others were executed for maintaining the supremacy of the pope. As therefore the earnest adherents of both religions were equally persecuted and equally encouraged, both parties were induced to court the favor of the king, who was thus enabled to assume an absolute authority over the nation, and to impose upon it his own doctrines as those of the only true church. * * * When news of these proceedings reached Rome, the most terrible fulminations were hurled by the pope against the king of England, whose soul was delivered over to the devil, and his dominions to the first invader; all leagues with Catholic princes were declared to be dissolved—his subjects were freed from their oaths of allegiance, and the nobility were commanded to take up arms against him. But these missives, which half a century before would have hurled the monarch from his throne and made him a despised outcast among his people, were now utterly harmless. The papal supremacy was forever lost in England.— *Marcus Wilson, Hist. U. S. Appendix to Voyage and Discoveries, p.* 153.

10. The Puritans:—The Puritan party professing to derive their doctrines directly from the scriptures, were wholly dissatisfied with the old church system, which they denounced as rotten, depraved and defiled by human inventions, and they wished it to undergo a thorough reform, to abandon everything of man's device, and adopt nothing, either in doctrine or discipline, which was not directly authorized by the word of God. Exceedingly ardent in their feelings, zealous in their principles, abhorring all formalism as destructive of the very elements of piety, and rejecting the regal as well as papal supremacy, they demanded in place of the liturgical service, an effective preaching of the gospel, more of the substance of religion, instead of what they denominated its shadows; and so convinced were they of the justness of their views and the reasonableness of their demands, that they would listen to no considerations which pleaded for compromise or delay.—*Marcus Wilson, Hist. U. S. Appendix Voyage and Discoveries, p.* 157.

11. Columbus Inspired of God:—And it came to pass that I looked and beheld many waters; and they divided the Gentiles from the seed of my brethren. And it came to pass that the angel said unto me, Behold the wrath of God is upon the seed of thy brethren. And I looked and beheld a man among the Gentiles who was separated from the seed of my brethren by the many waters; and I beheld the Spirit of God, that it came down and wrought upon the man; and he went forth upon the many waters, even unto the seed of my brethren who were in the promised land. And it came to pass that I beheld the Spirit of God, that it wrought upon other Gentiles; and they went forth out of captivity upon the many waters: * * * [and] I beheld many multitudes of the Gentiles upon the land of promise.— *Nephi's Vision, Book of Mormon, Ch. xiii:*10-14.

12. Religious Liberty in the Constitution:—The parts of the United States Constitution which secure religious freedom are the clause in article vi, which says: "No religious test shall ever be required as a qualification to any office or public trust under the United States;" and the first Amendment which says: "Congress shall make no law respecting an establishment of religion or prohibit the free exercise thereof." Respecting these two clauses in the Constitution, Judge Story remarks: "We are not to attribute this prohibition of a national religious establishment to an indifference to religion in general, and especially to Christianity (which none could hold in more reverence than the framers of the Constitution), but to a dread by the people of the influence of ecclesiastical power in matters of government; a dread which their ancestors brought with them from the parent country, and which unhappily for human infirmity, their own conduct, after their emigration, had not, in any just degree, tended to diminish. It was also obvious, from the numerous and powerful sects existing in the United States, that there would be perpetual temptations to struggles for ascendency in the national councils, if any one might thereby hope to found a permanent and exclusive national establishment of its own; and religious persecutions might thus be introduced, to an extent utterly subversive of the true interests and good order of the Republic. The most effectual mode of suppressing the evil, in the view of the

people, was to strike down the temptations to its introduction."—
Story's Comments on the U. S. Constitution.

**13. Hand of the Lord in the Establishment of the United
States Government:**—That the hand of Almighty God was in the
work of founding the Government of the United States is plainly declared in one of the revelations to Joseph Smith: "It is not right that
any man should be in bondage one to another. And for this purpose
have I established the constitution of this land, by the hands of wise
men whom I raised up unto this very purpose, and redeemed the land
by the shedding of blood." (*Doc. and Cov., Sec. ci,* 79, 80.) Nor are
thoughtful historians blind to the fact that the hand of God has had
much to do with those revolutions which finally produced the great
Republic of the New World. Commenting on the war of the American
Revolution, Marcus Wilson says: "The expense of blood and treasure
which this war cost England was enormous; nor, indeed, did her European antagonists suffer much less severely. The United States was the
only country that could look to any beneficial results from the war, and
these were obtained by a strong union of opposing motives and principles, unequalled in the annals of history. France and Spain, the arbitrary despots of the Old World, had stood forth as the protectors of
an infant republic, and had combined, contrary to all the principles
of their political faith, to establish the rising liberties of America. They
seemed but as blind instruments in the hands of Providence, employed
to aid in the founding of a nation which should cultivate those Republi-
can virtues that were destined yet to regenerate the world upon the
principles of universal intelligence, and eventually to overthrow the
time-worn system of tyrannical usurpation of the few over the many."
Marcus Wilson, Hist. U. S. Appendix, Revolutionary Period.

REVIEW.

1. Was the "Reformation" confined to Germany?
2. When did the "Reformation" first begin?
3. Who was the leader of the movement in Switzerland?
4. State what you can of the "Reformation" in Switzerland under
Zwingle.
5. What fate befell the young "Reformer"?
6. State the chief difference in methods of work between Luther
and Zwingle. (Note 1.)
7. Who succeeded in the leadership of the "Reformation" in
Switzerland?
8. Where and when was Calvin born?
9. State the points of difference in the views of Calvin and Zwingle.
10. Describe the Presbyterian system of church government.
11. Give a sketch of the life and character of Calvin. (Note 2.)
12. State the several views of the "Reformers" in respect to the
Eucharist.

13.   What difference existed between Calvin and Zwingle on the subject of predestination?

14.   What can you say of the spread of Calvin's doctrine?

15.   Describe the "Reformation" in France.

16.   What can you say of the persecution of the Protestants in France?   (Note 3.)

17.   Give a description of the massacre of St. Bartholomew's eve.

18.   State what you can of the "Reformation" in Sweden.

19.   Tell how the "Reformation" in Sweden was accomplished.

20.   On what ground can the king and people of Sweden and Denmark be justified in stripping the Catholic bishops of their power and wealth?   (Note 5.)

21.   Give an account of the "Reformation" in Holland.

22.   What was the attitude of Henry VIII of England at the beginning of the "Reformation" in Germany?

23.   What title did his defense of the Roman Catholic sacraments secure for him?

24.   What circumstance was it that afterwards estranged Henry from the pope?

25.   What was the conduct of Pope Clement VII in this controversy?

26.   What course did Henry adopt?

27.   What resulted from the king's conduct?

28.   How did the friends of the "Reformation" in England receive the rupture of the king and pope?

29.   Did the rupture between king and pope help the "Reformation" in England?

30.   What were the "Reformers" in England called?

31.   What were the demands of the Puritans in respect to religion? (Note 8.)

32.   When denied religious liberty in England to what country did the Puritans go?

33.   What influence on liberty did the discovery of America have?

34.   What can you say of the inspiration of Christopher Columbus? (Note 9.)

35.   What people besides Puritans sought religious liberty in the new world?

36.   Give an account of the settlement of Maryland.

37.   What can you say of Puritan intolerance?

38.   What circumstances taught them, at least, partial toleration?

39.   What power was working in all those changes which brought freedom to man?   (Note 11.)

40.   What was the object of enlarging the liberties of mankind?

PART IV.

THE RESTORATION OF THE GOSPEL.

SECTION I.

1. The Dispensation of the Fullness of Times:—
By a dispensation, in connection with the work of God,
we mean "the opening of the heavens to men, the bestowing
of the Holy Priesthood with all its powers upon them, and
the organization and building up of the church of Christ
upon the earth, for the salvation of all who will obey the
gospel."* By the Dispensation of the Fullness of Times
we mean the last dispensation, the one in which all things,
in Christ, whether in heaven or in earth, shall be gathered
together in one;† a dispensation which will include all other
dispensations—one which will encompass all truth. As the
rivers of the earth all eventually find their way to the ocean
and empty into it, so all former dispensations will run into,
and become part of the Dispensation of the Fullness of
Times, in which the work of God, in respect to the salvation
of man and the redemption of the earth, will be consummated.‡   (See note 1, end of section.)

2. Birth and Parentage of Joseph Smith:—Joseph
Smith, the man whom God appointed to stand at the head
of the Dispensation of the Fullness of Times, and be the
great Prophet, Seer, Revelator and President thereof, was
born in the year of our Lord 1805, on the 23rd of December,
in Sharon, Windsor [Winsor] County, State of Vermont.
His father's name was Joseph‡ Smith, and his mother's
maiden name Lucy Mack. Joseph and Lucy Smith had

Jaques' Catechism, page 77.
†God having made known unto us   *   *   * that in the dispensation of the fullness of times, he might gather together in one all things
in Christ, both which are in heaven, and which are on earth; even in
him   (Ephesians i:9, 10.)
‡Note 2, end of section.

nine children, six sons and three daughters. The sons in the order of their age were Alvin, Hyrum, Joseph, Samuel Harrison, William, Don Carlos; the daughters, Sophronia, Catherine, Lucy.

3. The parents of the prophet were of humble origin and poor, having to labor with their hands, hiring out by day's work, and otherwise to obtain a livelihood for their large family. In consequence of their poverty, they could give their children but very limited opportunities for attending school; yet Joseph learned to read, to write, and had some knowledge of the rudimentary principles of arithmetic.

4. When Joseph was ten years of age, his father moved from the State of Vermont to that of New York, settling in Palmyra, Ontario County.* Four years later the family moved from Palmyra to Manchester, in the same county.

5. **Religious Agitation:**—While the Smith family lived in Manchester, when Joseph was in his fifteenth year, there was an unusual excitement on the subject of religion. It began with the Methodists, but soon became general among all the sects, and union revival meeetings, in which all sects took part were held in the vicinity of Manchester township, in Palmyra. The Smith family, being by nature religiously inclined became interested in these meetings, and several of them, viz., Joseph's mother, his brothers Hyrum and Samuel Harrison, and his sisters Lucy and Sophronia, were converted to the Presbyterian faith. Joseph's own mind was much wrought up by this religious agitation, and at one time he became somewhat partial to the Methodist persuasion.

6. He was greatly perplexed, however, by the strife among

_____

*Ontario County has since been divided, and the north part of it, in which Palmyra is located, is now called Wayne County.

the sects, and the divisions which existed. The Presbyterians were opposed to the Methodists and Baptists; and these last named sects, though not agreeing with each other, were equally opposed to the Presbyterians. Why should the church of Christ be split up into fractions? Is God the author of confusion? Would he teach one society to worship one way, and administer one set of ordinances; and then teach another society quite a different system of worship, and another set of principles and ordinances different from those taught the first? Such were the questions Joseph Smith frequently asked himself when he reflected upon the confusion he witnessed.

7. In the midst of the war of words and tumult of opinion that accompanied this agitation, Joseph would often say to himself, "What is to be done? Who of all these parties are right?"

8. **Joseph Smith's First Prayer and Vision:—** While floundering in the midst of these difficulties he came to the following passage in the first chapter of the Epistle of James:

"If any of you lack wisdom, let him ask of God, that giveth to all men liberally and upbraideth not; and it shall be given him."

This passage impressed him with great force. It was the voice of God to him. If any man lacked wisdom he did; and here was counsel given directly how to obtain it, with a promise that he should receive it and not be unbraided for asking. He at last decided to follow the divine injunction.

9. It was in the morning of a beautiful, clear day, early in the spring of eighteen hundred and twenty, that Joseph put his resolution into effect. He selected a place in a grove near his father's house for that purpose. It was his

first attempt to pray vocally, and he was somewhat timid; but finding himself alone he knelt down and began to offer up the desires of his heart to the Lord. He had scarcely began to pray when he was seized by some power which threw him violently to the ground, and it seemed for a time that he was doomed to sudden destruction. It was no imaginary power, but some actual being from the unseen world. His tongue for a time was bound that he could not speak; darkness gathered about him; but exerting all his powers he called upon God to deliver him out of the hands of his enemy, and at the very moment he was ready to give up in despair and abandon himself to destruction, he beheld a pillar of light immediately over his head descending towards him. Its brightness was above that of the sun at noon-day, and no sooner did it appear than he was freed from the enemy which had held him bound.

10. When the light rested upon him he beheld within it two personages standing above him in the air, whose brightness and glory defy all description, but they exactly resembled each other in form and features. One of them, pointing to the other said:

"*Joseph, this is My Beloved Son, hear Him.*"

11. Joseph's purpose in calling upon the Lord was to learn which of the sects was right, that he might know which to join. As soon, therefore, as he gained his self-possession, he addressed these questions to the personage to whom he was directed. To his astonishment he was told that none of the sects were right, and that he must join none of them. He was further told by the person who addressed him, that all their creeds were an abomination in his sight; that those professors were all corrupt; that they drew near to him with their lips, but their hearts were far from him; that they taught for doctrine the command-

ments of men; that they had a form of godliness, but denied the power of God. And he was commanded the second time to join none of them.

12. There were many other things which Jesus said to Joseph on this occasion, but the prophet never · recorded them further than to say that he received a promise that the fullness of the gospel would at some future time be made known to him.

13. **The Importance of the Vision:**—This revelation is of vast importance:

First, it dispels the vagaries that men had conjured up in respect to the person of Deity. Instead of being a personage without body, parts or passions, it revealed the fact that he had both body and parts, that he was in the form of man, or, rather, that man had been made in God's image.*

Second: It clearly proves that the Father and Son are distinct persons, and not "one person," as the Christian world believes. The oneness of the Godhead, so frequently spoken of in scripture, must therefore relate to oneness of sentiment and agreement in purpose.

Third: It swept away the rubbish of human dogma and

---

*While the Prophet Joseph in describing this first great vision refers to the Lord and His Son Jesus Christ as two glorious personages without giving at that time any particular description of their persons, it is clear that they were in the form of men. Teaching the church the character of the Godhead some years later, the prophet said: "God himself was once as we are now, and is an exalted Man and sits enthroned in yonder heavens. That is the great secret. If the vail was rent today and the great God who holds this world in its orbit, and who upholds all worlds and all things by his power, was to make himself visible—I say if you were to see him today, you would see him like a man in form—like yourselves, in all the person, image and very form as a man, for Adam was created in the very fashion, image and likeness of God, and received instruction from and walked and talked, and conversed with him, as one man talks and communes with another."— *Journal of Discourses, Vol. VI*, page 3. All which means that the personage referred to was and is as the Christ was and is

tradition that had accumulated in all the ages since Messiah's personal ministry on earth, by announcing that God did not acknowledge any of the sects of Christendom as his church, nor their creeds as his gospel.   Thus the ground was cleared for the planting of the truth.

Fourth: It showed how mistaken the Christian world was in claiming that all revelation had ceased—that God would no more reveal himself to man.

Fifth: The vision created a witness for God on the earth: a man lived who could say to some purpose that God lived and that Jesus was the Christ, for he had seen and talked with them.   Thus was laid the foundation for faith.   We shall see anon, how the foundation was broadened.

14.   The Interval of Three Years:—For three years after this first vision, Joseph received no other visitation or revelation; and as he had been forbidden to join any of the religious sects then existing he stood alone.   It was a period of severe trial.   A few days after his first vision, he related the circumstance to a Methodist minister who had been active in the religious agitation before mentioned.   To the lad's surprise he treated his story with the utmost contempt; and declared it to be from the devil, as the Lord gave no revelations in these days, those things having ceased with the apostles.   Making his vision public brought upon him the ridicule and indignation of the whole neighborhood, especially of the ministers.   In this trying period of three years, according to his own statement, he was guilty of some youthful follies; but he was true to God, and continued in the face of all opposition to maintain that he had received a revelation from him.

15.   The First Visit of Moroni:—On the 21st of September, 1823, having retired for the night, he betook himself to prayer to obtain the forgiveness of his sins, and a manifestation that would enable him to know his standing before the Lord. While thus engaged the room began to be filled with light, and presently a personage appeared by his bedside, standing in the air. (See note 3, end of section.) This personage said that he was a messenger sent from the presence of God, and that his name was Moroni. He announced to Joseph Smith that the Lord had a work for him to do; and that his name would be had for good and evil among all nations.

16. **The Book of Mormon:**—The angel informed Joseph of the existence of the Book of Mormon, a record engraven upon gold plates, giving an account of the ancient inhabitants of the American continent and their origin. He said, also, that this record contained the everlasting gospel as taught by the Savior to the ancient inhabitants of this Western hemisphere. Deposited with the record was a Urim and Thummim, consisting of two stones fastened in silver bows, attached to a breast-plate. The Lord' had prepared this instrument for the purpose of translating the record. A vision of the hill where the sacred plates were hidden was given to the prophet.

17. **Ancient Prophecies Quoted by Moroni:**—After relating these things, the angel began quoting from the prophecies of the Old Testament. He first quoted part of the third chapter of Malachi;* and then the fourth chapter. The first verse of the fourth chapter he quoted as follows: "For, behold, the day cometh that shall burn as an oven; and all the proud, yea, and all that do wickedly shall *burn as stubble; for they that come shall burn them,*

---

*Most likely the first part of the third chapter, as that relates to the coming of a messenger to prepare the way for the glorious coming of Messiah. (See Mal. iii: 1-6.)

saith the Lord of hosts; that it shall leave them neither root nor branch." The fifth and sixth verses he quoted— "Behold, I will *reveal unto you the priesthood by the hand of* Elijah, the prophet, before the coming of the great and dreadful day of the Lord. And he shall *plant in the hearts of the children, the promises made to the fathers, and the hearts of the children shall turn to their fathers; if it were not so, the whole earth would be utterly wasted at his coming."**

18. Moroni also quoted the eleventh chapter of Isaiah, and said the predictions in it were about to be fulfilled. They relate to the glorious restoration of the house of Israel from their long dispersion, and the reign of peace and rightousness on the earth. He quoted also the twenty-second and twenty-third verses of the third chapter of Acts: "For Moses truly said unto the fathers, a prophet shall the Lord your God raise up unto you of your brethren, like unto me; him shall ye hear in all things whatsoever he shall say unto you. And it shall come to pass, that every soul which will not hear that prophet, shall be destroyed from among the people." Moroni explained that the prophet here spoken of was Jesus Christ; but the day when they who would not hear his voice should be cut off from among the people had not yet come, but it would soon come.

19. The angel quoted from the twenty-eighth verse to the end of the second chapter of Joel; and said that it was soon to be fulfilled. It predicts the outpouring of God's Spirit upon all flesh; the signs in the heavens and the earth which are to precede the glorious coming of Messiah; and

---

Pearl of Great Price, page 51, (1921 edition.) The words in *Italics* indicate the difference between the passages as quoted by Moroni and as they stand in our English version of the Bible. The student should compare the passages as quoted above with the Bible and mark how superior is the angel's rendering of them.

foretells the safety which shall be found in Mount Zion and Jerusalem in those troublous times

20. The Warnings of Moroni:—After making these and other explanations the light within the room seemed to condense about the person of the angel and he departed. Shortly, however, he returned and repeated what he had said on his first appearance, and again withdrew. To Joseph's astonishment he appeared the third time and again repeated his message.

21. In his first appearance that eventful night, the angel told Joseph that when he obtained the plates containing the record of the ancient inhabitants of America, together with the breast-plate and the Urim and Thummim—the full time for them to be given to him had not then arrived—he was to show them to no person except those to whom he would be commanded to show them. He was told that if he violated his commandment he would be destroyed. At his third appearing that same night the angel cautioned Joseph, saying that Satan would try to tempt him, in consequence of the poverty of his father's family, to obtain the plates for the purpose of getting rich. This he forbade him, saying that he must have no other object in view in getting the plates but to glorify God, and must be influenced by no other motive than that of building up his kingdom.

22. The Fourth Appearance of Moroni:—The whole night was consumed in these interviews with the angel. In the morning of the day following, Joseph went to his usual labors, but was so exhausted and faint that he found himself unable to pursue them. His father, who was laboring with him, observing that he was ailing, directed him to go home. In attempting to climb the fence out of the field where he was working, his strength entirely failed him and he fell unconscious to the ground. When he became conscious, the angel who had visited him the night before was standing by him calling his name. He repeated again the things of the night before, and commanded Joseph to go and tell his father of them. This he did, and his father testified that they were of God, and counseled his son to be obedient to the heavenly vision.

23. Cumorah and Its Treasures:—Joseph went immediately to the hill Cumorah* where the ancient record was hidden. So vivid had been his vision of the place the night before that he had no difficulty in recognizing it. (See note 4, end of section.)

24. On the west side of the hill Cumorah, not far from the top, under a stone of considerable size, lay the plates, deposited in a stone box. Removing the soil from around the edges of the stone box with the aid of a lever, he raised it up and to his joy beheld the plates, the Urim and Thummim and breast-plate, just as described by the angel. He was about to take these treasures from the box when the messenger of the previous night again stood before him, and told him again that the time for bringing them forth had not yet arrived, and would not until four years from that date. The angel instructed him to come to that place in just one year from that time and he would meet with him, and that he would continue to do so until the time for obtaining the plates for translation had come. Accordingly at the end of each year Joseph went to the place appointed, and every time met the same heavenly messenger, who gave him instruction and intelligence in respect to the work of the Lord, and how the Christ's kingdom was to be conducted in these last days.

---

*That was the name of the hill among the Nephites. The Jaredites, a still more ancient people, called it Ramah.

25. Translation and Publication of the Book of Mormon:—On the 22nd of September, 1827, the plates, together with the Urim and Thummim and breast-plate, were given into the hands of Joseph Smith by the angel Moroni, with a strict charge to keep them safe, saying that he [Joseph,] would be held responsible for them; that if he should carelessly let them go, through any neglect of his, he would be cut off; but if he would use his best endeavors to preserve them, they should be protected. He soon learned the necessity of the strict charge given to him by Moroni, for no sooner was it learned that he had the plates than every kind of device, not even omitting that of violence, was employed to wrest them from him. He guarded them safely, however, and in the midst of much persecution and many difficulties, succeeded by the help of the Lord and the assistance of Martin Harris, a well-to-to farmer; Oliver Cowdery, a young school teacher, who acted as his scribe in much of the work of translation, and the Whitmer family—with this assistance he succeeded in completing the translation, and finally published the work in the year 1830.

26. The Witnesses:—In the course of the work of translation, Joseph and those assisting him learned from the record itself that it would be hidden from the eyes of the world, that the eyes of none might behold it except Three Witnesses that should see it by the power of God—besides him to whom the record would be given to translate—and a few others who should view it that they might bear witness of the work of God to the children of men.*

27. Oliver Cowdery, David Whitmer, and Martin Harris desired to become the three witnesses named, and

*Book of Mormon, II Nephi, 27.

obtained that privilege from the Lord. Some time in June, 1829, the promise that they should have a view of the plates, the Urim and Thummim and breast-plate was fulfilled. The angel Moroni appeared unto them, exhibited to them those sacred things, and commanded them to bear witness of their existence to the world. This they did, and their testimony is published upon the fly-leaf of all editions of the Book of Momon.

28. The plates were exhibited by Joseph Smith to eight other witnesses, whose testimony and names are also published on the fly-leaf of all editions of the Book of Mormon.

NOTES.

1. **The Fullness of Times:**—Now the thing to be known is, what the fullness of times means, or the extent and authority thereof. It means this, that the dispensation of the fullness of times is made up of all the dispensations that have ever been given since the world began, until this time. Unto Adam first was given a dispensation. It is well known that God spake to him with His own voice in the garden, and gave him the promise of the Messiah. And unto Noah also was a dispensation given. * * * And from Noah to Abraham, and from Abraham to Moses, and from Moses to Elias, and from Elias to John the Baptist, and from them to Jesus Christ, and from Jesus Christ to Peter, James and John, the apostles all having received their dispensation by revelation from God to accomplish the great scheme of restitution, spoken by all the holy prophets since the world began, the end of which is, the dispensation of the fullness of times in which all things shall be fulfilled that have been spoken of since the earth was made.— *History of the Church, Period I.*

2. **The Name of Joseph Foretold:**—The Book of Mormon contains a remarkable prophecy by Joseph, the favorite son of Jacob, by which the name of the Prophet Joseph Smith and of his father were foretold. The Prophet Lehi, who, it will be remembered, left Jerusalem six hundred years B. C., and who was acquainted with the Jewish scriptures, says, in blessing his son Joseph: "For Joseph (the one sold into Egypt by his brother) truly testified saying: A seer shall the Lord my God raise up, who shall be a choice seer unto the fruit of my

loins. * * * Behold that seer will the Lord bless; and they that seek to destroy him shall be confounded. * * * And his name shall be called after me (Joseph;) and it shall be after the name of his father. And he shall be like unto me; for the thing which the Lord shall bring forth by his hand by the power of the Lord shall bring my people unto salvation."—*II. Nephi, ch. iii.*

3. **Description of Moroni:**—He had on a loose robe of most exquisite whiteness. It was a whiteness beyond anything earthly I had ever seen; nor do I believe any earthly thing could be made to appear so exceedingly white and brilliant; his hands were naked and his arms also, a little above the wrist; so, also, were his feet naked, as were his legs a little above the ankles. His head and neck were also bare. I could discover that he had no other clothing on but this robe, as it was open, so that I could see into his bosom. Not only was his robe exceedingly white, but his whole person was glorious beyond description, and his countenance truly like lightning.—*Joseph Smith, Pearl of Great Price*, p. 49

4. **Description of Cumorah:**—As you pass on the mailroad from Palmyra, Wayne County, to Canandaigua, Ontario County, New York, before arriving at the little village of Palmyra, you pass a large hill on the east side of the road. Why I say large, is because it is as large, perhaps, as any in that country. The north end rises quite suddenly until it assumes a level with the more southerly extremity, and I think I may say, an elevation higher than at the south, a short distance, say half or three-fourth of a mile. As you pass towards Canandaigua it lessens gradually, until the surface assumes its common level, or is broken by other smaller hills or ridges, water-courses and ravines. I think I am justified in saying that this is the highest hill for some distance round, and I am certain that its appearance, as it rises suddenly from a plain on the north, must attract the notice of the traveler as he passes by. The north end, (which has been described as rising suddenly from the plain) forms a promontory without timber, but covered with grass. As you pass to the south you soon come to scattering timber, the surface having been cleared by art or wind; and a short distance further left, you are surrounded with the common forest of the country. It is necessary to observe that even the part cleared, was only occupied for pasturage; its steep ascent and narrow summit not admitting the plough of the husbandman with any degree of ease or profit. It was at the second mentioned place, where the record was found to be deposited, on the west side of the hill, not far from the top down its side; and when myself visited the place in the year 1830, there were several trees standing—enough to cause a shade in summer, but not so much as to prevent the surface being covered with grass, which was also the case when the record was found.—*Oliver Cowdery*, in *Messenger and Advocate*, 1834.

5. **Analysis of the Book of Mormon:**—

1. *The Construction of the Record:*—The Book of Mormon is an abridgment made from more extensive records kept by the ancient civilized people of America—chiefly by the people known in the Book of Mormon

as Nephites. The abridgment, for the most part, is made by one Mormon, a Nephite prophet, who was born 311 A. D., and slain by his enemies in the year 400 A. D. The parts which are not his abridgment are the first 122 pages (edition of 1921,) which bring us to the "Words of Mormon," page 122, and from page 472 to the end of the volume—50 pages. This latter part of the record was made by Moroni, the son of Mormon, who was also the one who hid up the plates containing his father's and his own abridgment, in the year 421 A. D.; and who, having been raised from the dead, revealed the existence of these plates to Joseph Smith.

The first 122 pages are a verbatim translation from what are known as the "smaller plates" of Nephi—we will explain: The first Nephi, who left Jerusalem with a small company of people led out from that city by his father, Lehi, 600 B. C., and who afterwards became their leader, prophet, and their first king—made two sets of plates, on which he proposed engraving the history of his people. On the "larger" of these two sets he engraved an account of his father's life, travels, prophecies, etc., together with his genealogy; and upon them also he recorded a full history of the wars and contentions of his people, as also their travels, and an account of the cities they founded and colonies they established. These larger plates were preserved in the care of succeeding kings, or judges of the republic when the kingdom was transformed into a republic; and, in a word, upon them was written a full history of the rise and fall of the nations which existed in America, from the landing of this colony from Jerusalem to 400 A. D., a period of nearly one thousand years.

It is quite evident that as these plates were transmitted from king to king, or from one ruling judge of the republic to another, or given into the possession of successive prophets, that each recorded the historical events of his own day, and gave to such account his own name—hence Mormon found in these "larger plates" of Nephi, The Book of Lehi, the Book of Mosiah, the Book of Alma, the Book of Helaman, etc.

Furthermore, it happened that there were colonies from time to time that drifted off into distant parts of the land and became lost for a season to the main body of the people; and there were missionary expeditions formed for the conversion of the Lamanites; and these parties, whether missionary or colonial, generally kept records; and when these colonists or missionary parties were found, or returned to the main body of the people, their records were incorporated within the main record, being kept by the historian—hence there was, sometimes, a book within a book, and the current of events was interrupted to record the history of these detached portions of the people, or some important missionary expedition.

Mormon, when abridging these plates of Nephi, gave to each particular division of his abridgment the name of the book from which he had taken his account of the events recorded—hence in Mormon's abridgment, the Books of Mosiah, Alma, Helaman and III and IV Nephi. He also, in some instances, at least, followed the sub-divisions we have alluded to, hence we have the Record of Zeniff within the Book of Mosiah (page 152); the account of the church founded by the first Alma (page 178); and the account of the missionary expeditions of the sons of Mosiah to the Lamanites within the Book of Alma (page 237.)

2. *Complexity of the Literary Structure of the Book:*—Again we caution the student to remember that the Book of Mormon is, for the most part, an abridgment from the "larger plates" of Nephi; but it is quite evident that Mormon frequently came to passages upon the plates of Nephi which pleased him so well that he transcribed them verbatim upon the plates containing his abridgment. An example of this will be found beginning on page 136, in the second line of the ninth paragraph, and ending with page 142—the words of King Benjamin to his people. The words of King Benjamin are also renewed on page 142, in the second line of the fourth paragraph, and continue to the close of the chapter. There are many such passages throughout Mormon's abridgment.

In addition to this, Mormon frequently introduces remarks of his own by way of comment, warning, prophecy or admonition, and since there is nothing in the text, neither quotation marks nor a change of type, to indicate where these comments, or what we might call annotations, begin or end, they are liable to confuse the reader—a difficulty that we hope will be obviated by this caution. So much for Mormon's abridgment.

Now to consider the part of the work which was done by his son, Moroni. This is from page 472 to the end of the volume. He closes up the record of his father, Mormon, and then gives us an abridgment of the twenty-four plates of Ether, which were found in North America by the people of Limhi, in the second century B. C., and then concludes his work with notes on the manner of ordaining priests and teachers, administering the sacrament of the Lord's supper, baptism, spiritual gifts, together with a sermon and some of his father's letters. In his abridgment of the record of the Jaredites, the peculiarity of mixing up his comments, admonitions and prophecies with his narrative, is even more marked than in the abridgment of Mormon, therefore the reader will need to be doubly on his guard.

3. *How the "Smaller Plates" of Nephi came to be attached to Mormon's Abridgment:*—We have already said that the first 132 pages of the Book of Mormon were not a part of Mormon's abridgment. Those pages are a verbatim translation of the "smaller plates" of Nephi, and became connected with Mormon's abridgment in this manner: Mormon had abridged the "larger plates" of Nephi as far as the reign of King Benjamin, and in searching through the records which had been delivered to him, he found the "smaller plates" of Nephi. They contained a brief history of events connected with the departure of Lehi and his colony from Jerusalem to their landing in America, and thence down to the reign of this King Benjamin—covering a period of about 400 years. These plates were made by Nephi, that upon them might be engraven an account of the ministry of the servants of God, among his people, together with their prophecies and teachings. They contain, in other words, an ecclesiastical history of the Nephites, while the "larger

plates" of Nephi contained a political or secular history of the same people.   (I Nephi ix; xix: 1-5.)

Mormon was particularly well pleased with the contents of these "smaller plates" of Nephi, because upon them had been engraven so many prophecies concerning the coming and mission of the Messiah; and instead of condensing the history recorded on them into an abridgment, he took the plates themselves and attached them to the abridgment of Nephi's "larger plates."   "And this I do for a wise purpose," says Mormon, "for thus it whispereth me according to the Spirit of the Lord which is in me."   (Words of Mormon, page 132 N. E.)   Nephi also, in speaking of these "smaller plates," says, "the Lord hath commanded me to make these plates for a wise purpose in him, which purpose I know not."   (I Nephi ix:5.)

4.   *The Wise Purpose:*—By Mormon attaching these "smaller plates" of Nephi to his own abridgment of Nephi's "larger plates," it will be observed there was a double line of history of the Nephites for about 400 years, and the wisdom of this arrangement is seen in the following circumstances.   When Joseph Smith had translated the first part of Mormon's abridgment—amounting to 116 pages of manuscript, he listened to the importunities of Martin Harris, who was giving him some assistance in the work of translating, and who desired to show that portion of the work to his friends.   The result was the manuscript was stolen from Harris; the plates of the Book of Mormon were taken from Joseph by the angel, and for a season he lost his power to translate. After a time, however, he was permitted to go on with the work, but the Lord made it known to him that it was the design of those into whose hands the 116 pages of manuscript had fallen to wait until he had translated that part again, and then by changing the manuscript in their possession, would bring it forth and claim that he could not translate the same record twice alike; and thus they would seek to overthrow the work of God.

But the heavenly messenger commanded Joseph Smith not to translate again the part he had already translated, but instead thereof he should translate the "smaller plates" of Nephi, and that account was to take the place of Mormon's abridgment up to the latter days of the reign of King Benjamin. (Doc. and Cov., Sec. 10.) Thus it is that we have the "Words of Mormon," beginning on page 132, explaining how the "smaller plates" of Nephi came into his possession and attached to the plates containing the record he himself was making, and connecting the historical narrative of the "smaller plates" of Nephi with his own abridgment of Nephi's "larger plates."   The "Words of Mormon," interrupting as they do the history of the Nephites, have caused no little confusion in the minds of unthoughtful readers; but after it is understood that they are merely the link connecting the ecclesiastical history engraven on the "smaller plates" of Nephi to Mormon's abridgment of the "larger plates of Nephi," and that they take the place of the first part of Mormon's record, the difficulty will disappear.

5.   *Difference in the Literary Style of the "Smaller Plates" and Mormon's Abridgment:*—One thing we cannot forbear to mention, and that

is, in the parts of the Book of Mormon translated from the "smaller plates" of Nephi, we find none of those comments or annotations mixed up with the record that we have already spoken of as being peculiar to the abridgment made by Mormon—a circumstance, we take it, which proves the Book of Mormon to be consistent with the account given of the original records from which it was translated. The value of this fact appears if we stop to consider how destructive to the claims of the book it would be if the peculiarity of Mormon's abridgment were found in that part of the book which claims to be a verbatim translation of the "smaller plates" of Nephi. There will be found, however, in this translation direct from the "smaller plates" of Nephi, as also in Mormon's abridgment, extracts from the old Jewish Scriptures—especially from the writings of Isaiah—this is accounted for by the fact that when Lehi's colony left Jerusalem, they took with them copies of the books of Moses and the writings of the prophets, and the record of the Jews down to the commencement of the reign of Zedekiah, all of which were engraven on plates of brass (see I Nephi v: 10-13,) and the Nephite historians transcribed passages from these sacred records into their own writings.

6. *The Transcribed Passages:*—There are a few suggestions about these transcribed passages which may be valuable to the student, as they furnish an indirect evidence of the truth of the Book of Mormon. The Nephites having transcribed passages from the brass plates they carried with them from Jerusalem into their records, in many cases where such passages occur in the Book of Mormon, and corresponding passages are found in our English Bible, it will be seen by the reader that so far we have two translations of the writings of the old Hebrew prophets, and a number of variations occur; and where this occurs it will be found on comparison that the passages in the Book of Mormon are stronger and more in keeping with the sense sought to be expressed by the prophet than the corresponding passages and chapters in the Bible. As a proof of this I ask the student to compare I Nephi xx and xxi with Isaiah xlvii and xlix.

In some instances there are sentences, in the Book of Mormon version of passages from Isaiah, not to be found in our English version, as witness the following:

Book of Mormon.	Bible.
O house of Jacob, come ye and let us walk in the light of the Lord; *yea, come, for ye have all gone astray, every one to his wicked ways.*—*II Nephi xii:* 5.	O house of Jacob, come ye, and let us walk in the light of the Lord.—*Isa. ii:* 5.

In other instances it will be found that the sense of the passages is different, and that the passages in the Book of Mormon best accord with the sense of the whole:

Book of Mormon.	Bible.
Therefore, O Lord, thou hast forsaken thy people, the house of Jacob, because they be replenished from the east, and hearken unto soothsayers like the Philistines, and they please themselves in the children of strangers.—*II Nephi xii*: 6.	Therefore hast Thou forsaken Thy people the house of Jacob, because they be replenished from the east, and *are* soothsayers like the Philistines, and they please themselves in the children of strangers.—*Isa. ii*: 6
Their land is also full of idols they worship the work of their own hands, that which their own fingers have made: and the mean man boweth not down, and the great man humbleth himself not, therefore, forgive him not.—*II Nephi xii*: 8, 9.	Their land also is full of idols; they worship the work of their own hands, that which their own fingers have made: and the mean man boweth down, and the great man humbleth himself: therefore, forgive them not.—*Isa. ii*: 8, 9.
Thou hast multiplied the nation, and increased the joy: they joy before thee according to the joy in harvest, and as men rejoice when they divide the spoil.—*II Nephi xix*: 3.	Thou hast multiplied the nation, and not increased the joy: they joy before Thee according to the joy in harvest, and as men rejoice when they divide the spoil.—*Isa. ix*: 3.

Observe, too, the difference in the clearness of the following passages:

Book of Mormon.	Bible.
And when they shall say unto you, seek unto them that have familiar spirits, and unto wizards that peep and mutter; should not a people seek unto their God? for the living to hear from the dead?—*II Nephi xviii*: 19.	And when they shall say unto you, seek unto them that have familiar spirits, and unto wizards that peep, and that mutter; should not a people seek unto their God? for the living to the dead?—*Isa. viii*: 19.

Again, the English translators of the Bible, in order to make the sense of various passages more clear, inserted here and there, words of their own; which are always written in *Italics*, that the reader might know what words have been inserted by the translator, and for which he will find no equivalent in the original text. It is worthy of note that in those transcribed passages from the brass plates into the Book of Mormon, in almost every instance, the words in the Book of Mormon version are different to those substituted by the translators of the common English Version; or are left out, as follows:

Book of Mormon.	Bible.
What mean ye? Ye beat my people to pieces, and grind the faces of the poor.—*II Nephi ixii*: 15.	What mean ye *that* ye beat my people to pieces, and grind the faces of the poor?—*Isa. iii*: 15.

The above is a case where the inserted word of the translator, which I have written in *Italics*, is omitted, and to my mind the passage as it stands in the Book of Mormon is the stronger and more beautiful. Here is a passage where different words are used than those inserted by the translators:

Book of Mormon.	Bible.
Say unto the righteous, that it is well with them; for they shall eat the fruit of their doings.	Say ye to the righteous, that *it shall be* well *with him*: for they shall eat the fruit of their doings.
Woe unto the wicked! for they shall perish; for the reward of their hands shall be upon them. —*II Nephi xiii*: 10, 11.	Woe unto the wicked; *it shall be ill with him*: for the reward of his hands shall be given him.— *Isa. iii*: 10, 11.

I think it will be readily conceded that the above passage as it stands in the Book of Mormon is much superior to the version given in our common Bible.

7. *A Means of Testing the Truth of the Book of Mormon:*—One suggestion more I would make to the readers of the Book of Mormon: That is, that they read it prayerfully with a real desire to know if it is of God. If they will peruse it with that desire in their hearts, I am sanguine that the Spirit of God which searches all things, yea, the deep things of God, will bear witness to their understanding that the book is of divine origin, and they will have a witness from God of its truth. Such a promise in fact, is contained within the book itself. When Moroni was closing up the sacred record previous to hiding it up unto the Lord until the time should come for it to be revealed as a witness for God, he engraved the following passage on the plates as words of counsel to those into whose hands the record should fall:

"And when ye shall receive these things" [i. e., the things written in the Book of Mormon,] "I would exhort you that ye would ask God the Eternal Father, in the name of Christ, if these things are not true; and if ye shall ask with a sincere heart, with real intent, having faith in Christ, he will manifest the truth of it unto you by the power of the Holy Ghost; and by the power of the Holy Ghost ye may know the truth of all things." (Moroni x: 4, 5.)

Here, then, is a means by which every person into whose hands the Book of Mormon falls may find out for himself, not from human testimony, not from the deductions of logic, but through the power of the

Holy Ghost, whether the Book of Mormon is of divine origin or not. This test must be final, either for or against it, to every individual who complies with the conditions enjoined by Moroni. Those conditions are, that they into whose hands the record falls shall inquire of God with a sincere heart, with real intent, and having faith in Christ; and to those who so proceed he promises without equivocation that they shall receive a manifestation of its truth by the power of the Holy Ghost. Therefore, if these directions are complied with faithfully and honestly, and the manifestation follows not, then they may know it is not of God. If the manifestation comes, of course the divine origin of the book is confirmed, for the Holy Ghost would not confirm by any manifestation of its power an imposition.

REVIEW.

1. What is a dispensation in connection with the work of God?

2 In what does the dispensation of the fullness of times differ from other dispensations?

3. State where and when the Prophet Joseph was born.

4. What was the condition and standing of the prophet's parents?

5. State what you can about the movements of the Smith family until its settlement in Manchester township.

6. What occurred in Manchester when the prophet was in his fifteenth year?

7. What influence did this religious revival have on the Smith family?

8. What reflections did it give birth to in the boy Joseph?

9. What circumstances was it that decided the course of Joseph?

10. Describe the first great vision Joseph received.

11. What sectarian vagary is dispelled by this vision?

12. What were the prophet's subsequent teachings relative to the personage of God? (Note.)

13. What does the vision teach in respect to the Father and Son being distinct persons?

14. What great truth respecting the character of the creeds and sects of Christendom is learned from the vision?

15. What did it prove in regard to the false idea that God would give no more revelation to man?

16. What other important thing did this first vision accomplish?

17. How long was it after the prophet received his first vision before any other revelation was given him?

18. How was Joseph's announcement that he had received a revelation from God treated by the ministers?

19. What can you say of the prophet's conduct during the above mentioned interval of three years?

20. Give an account of Moroni's first visit to the Prophet Joseph.

21. Give a description of Moroni. (Note 3.)

22.   What ancient record did Moroni reveal the existence of?

23.   Enumerate the several ancient prophecies of the Bible quoted by Moroni.

24.   What cautions did Moroni give Joseph before finally leaving him?

25.   Relate Moroni's fourth appearance to Joseph.

26.   Give an account of Joseph's first visit to Cumorah.

27.   By what name was this same hill known among the Jaredites?

28.   Give a description of Cumorah.

29.   What arrangements for future visitations did Moroni make with Joseph?

30.   When were the plates of the Book of Mormon together with the Urim and Thummim given into the possession of Joseph?

31.   What individuals and family rendered Joseph valuable assistance while translating the Book of Mormon?

32.   How many especial witnesses were raised up to the Book of Mormon?

33.   State how the Book of Mormon was constructed.

34.   Describe the complexity of the structure of the Book of Mormon.

35.   How did the "smaller plates" of Nephi come to be attached to Mormon's abridgment of the larger plates?

36.   For what wise purpose were they attached to Mormon's abridgment?

37.   What difference in style of composition is noticeable between these "smaller plates" and Mormon's abridgment?

38.   What can you say of the transcribed passages from the brass plates into the Book of Mormon?

39.   What direct means exists for testing the truth of the Book of Mormon?

SECTION II.

1. **The Restoration of the Aaronic Priesthood:**—
While engaged in the work of translating the Book of Mormon, Joseph Smith and Oliver Cowdery found reference made in the record to baptism for the remission of sins; and on the 15th of May, 1829, they went into the woods to inquire of the Lord about it.   While thus engaged a messenger from heaven descended in a cloud of light and announced himself to be John, the same that is called the Baptist,* in the New Testament. He placed his hands upon the heads of Joseph and Oliver and ordained them to the Aaronic Priesthood.†   He explained that this priesthood held the keys of the ministration of angels, the gospel of repentance and of baptism for the remission of sins, but had not the power of laying on hands for the gift of the Holy Ghost. He promised them also that the priesthood he then conferred upon them should never be taken again from the earth, until the sons of Levi offer an offering unto the Lord in righteousness.   (See note 1, end of section.)

2.   John stated that he was acting under the direction of Peter, James and John, who held the keys of the Mel-

---

*This messenger was a resurrected personage.   It will be remembered that John the Baptist was beheaded by Herod Antipas before the crucifixion of the Lord; and that after the resurrection of Messiah, "the graves were opened; and many bodies of the saints which slept arose, and came out of the graves after his" (Christ's) "resurrection, and went into the holy city, and appeared unto many." (Matt. xxvii: 52, 53.)   As John the Baptist was one of the most worthy of the saints, and a martyr for righteousness, it is but reasonable to conclude that he was most likely among the number resurrected immediately after the resurrection of Jesus.

†For the words of the angel see Doc. and Cov., sec. xiii.

chisedek Priesthood, which he said would in due time be conferred upon them. He then commanded Joseph to baptize Oliver, and afterwards Oliver to baptize Joseph.* After their baptism they were both filled with the spirit of prophecy and predicted many things concerning the rise and progress of the work. The angel also commanded them to each re-ordain the other to the Priesthood—Joseph to first ordain Oliver, and afterwards Oliver to ordain Joseph. To this commandment they were obedient, and thus the Aaronic Priesthood, the power from God which gives the right to those who receive it to preach repentance and administer baptism for the remission of sins, was restored to men.

3. For a season, doubtless in order to avoid persecution, which constantly increased in bitterness, Joseph and Oliver kept their baptism and ordination to the Aaronic Priesthood a secret; but as men's minds were wrought upon to inquire after the truth, they at last let it be known that they had received authority to baptize for the remission of sins, and a number of people received the ordinance at their hands.

4. **Restoration of the Melchisedek Priesthood:**— Some time in June, 1829,† the promise made by John the Baptist to Joseph and Oliver, at the time he conferred the Aaronic Priesthood upon them—*viz.*, that they should receive the higher or Melchisedek Priesthood was ful-

---

*These baptisms were, of course, by immersion. The Savior when teaching the Nephites how to baptize, said: "Ye shall go down and stand in the water, and   *   *   *   these are the words ye shall say, calling them by name, saying—Having authority given me of Jesus Christ, I baptize you in the name of the Father, and of the Son, and of the Holy Ghost. Amen. And then shall ye immerse them in the water, and come forth again out of the water." (III Nephi xi: 23-26.) It was this passage which led Joseph and Oliver to inquire of the Lord about baptism with the result stated in the text.

†*See Cannon's Life of Joseph Smith,* p. 73.

filled.   This Priesthood was conferred upon them by Christian Apostles Peter, James and John, probably in the wilderness, between Harmony, Susquehanna County, and Colesville, Broome County, on the Susquehanna River.* (See note 2, end of section.)   It is quite evident from the prominence given to these three apostles in the New Testament, that they held the keys of this Priesthood; and that of the three Peter was the chief.   To him the Lord said: "I will give unto thee the keys of the kingdom of heaven; and whatsoever thou shalt bind on earth shall be bound in heaven; and whatsoever thou shalt loose on earth shall be loosed in heaven."†   It was eminently proper therefore that these three apostles should be the ones to restore to the earth the Melchisedek Priesthood by conferring the apostleship upon Joseph and Oliver.

5.   As after receiving their ordination under the hands of John the Baptist they were required to re-ordain each other, so after receiving the apostleship under the hands of Peter, James and John they re-ordained each other, Joseph first re-ordaining Oliver, and afterwards accepting re-ordination at his hands.‡

6.   The power and authority of this Melchisedek Priesthood (see note 3, end of section), is to hold the keys of all the spiritual blessings of the church, and those holding it have the privilege of receiving the mysteries of the kingdom of heaven—they have the right to have the heavens opened unto them—to commune with the general assembly and church of the First Born, and to enjoy the communion and presence of God the Father and Jesus the Mediator of the

---

*Doc. and Cov., sec. cxxviii: 20; also article by Joseph F. Smith on Restoration of the Melchisedek Priesthood. Contributor, Vol X, p. 310.
†Matt, xvi: 19.
‡Cannon's Life of Joseph Smith, p. 73.

new covenant.* Hence, clothed with this power, Joseph Smith and Oliver Cowdery were authorized to organize the Church of Christ in the earth.

7. **The Organization of the Church of Christ:**— In all things, however, the two young men waited for direction from the Lord, and hence did not undertake to organize the church until he commanded them. It was in obedience to a commandment from the Lord, therefore, that they appointed the sixth day of April, 1830, as the time to organize the church. Six persons† who had been baptized, and a few of their friends, met at the house of Peter Whitmer, Sen., in Fayette township, Seneca County, in the State of New York, to effect that organization. The meeting was opened by solemn prayer, after which, according to previous commandment, the prophet Joseph called upon the brethren present to know if they would accept himself and Oliver Cowdery as their teachers in the things of the kingdom of God; and if they were willing that they should proceed to organize the church according to the commandment of the Lord. To this they consented by unanimous vote. Joseph then ordained Oliver an Elder of the Church of Jesus Christ;‡ after which Oliver ordained Joseph an Elder of the said church. The sacrament was administered and those who had been previously baptized were confirmed members of the church and received the Holy Ghost by the laying on

---

*Doc. and Cov., sec. cvii: 18, 19.

†Their names were Joseph Smith, Oliver Cowdery, Hyrum Smith, Peter Whitmer, Jr., Samuel H. Smith and David Whitmer. There were a number of others who had been baptized, but as six persons were sufficient to fill the requirements of the laws of the State of New York in respect to organizing religious societies, the church was organized with that number.

‡The words "of Latter-day Saints," were not used until some time after April 26, 1838, when they were added by revelation from the Lord. (Doc. and Cov., sec. cxv.)

of hands. Some enjoyed the gift of prophecy, and all rejoiced exceedingly. (See note 4, end of section.)

8. While the church was yet assembled a revelation was received from the Lord,* directing that a record be kept in the church, and that in it Joseph be called a seer, a translator, a prophet, an apostle of Jesus Christ, an elder of the church; and the church was commanded to give heed to all his words and commandments which he should receive from the Lord, accepting his word as the word of God in all patience and faith. On condition of their doing this, the Lord promised them that the gates of hell should not prevail against the church; but on the contrary he would disperse the powers of darkness from before them and shake the heavens for their good.

9. **The Voice of God and the Voice of the People in Church Government:**—Thus the church was organized; and in that organization we see the operation of two mighty principles—the voice of God; the consent of the people. At the time that Joseph and Oliver received instruction to ordain each other to be elders of the church, they were told to defer their ordination until such time as would be practicable to get their brethren who had been and who would be baptized assembled together; for they must have the sanction of their brethren before they ordained each other elders of the Church; and their brethren must decide by vote whether they would accept them [Joseph and Oliver] as spiritual† teachers. Thus, notwithstanding Joseph and Oliver had been ordained apostles under the

---

**See Doc. and Cov., sec. xxi.*

†The revelation giving these instructions was given in the chamber of Peter Whitmer, Sen., and is the "voice of God in the chamber of old father Whitmer," alluded to in the letter of Joseph to the church under date of Sept. 6, 1842, contained in sec. cxxviii of the Doc. and Cov.

hands of Peter, James and John, and had doubtless re-ordained each other as already stated,* yet when it came to being ordained *elders of the Church*,† and made the spiritual leaders of it, it must be done by the common consent of the church; and thus early we see enforced that law which says: "All things shall be done by common consent in the church, by much prayer and faith."‡ But no sooner was the church organized than a prophet, a seer, a translator, is appointed and the church commanded to give heed to his words, and to receive them as coming from the mouth of of the Lord himself. Here in the very inception of the church organization is clearly established the great truth, the grand principle, that in the government of the church there is to be a union of the voice of God and the consent or voice of the people. Not *vox populi, vox Dei*;§ nor *vox Dei, vox populi*;‖ but *vox Dei et vox populi*.¶

10. **Revelation on Church Government and Discipline:**—Previous to the organization of the church, a very important revelation was given—in fact it was the revelation which pointed out the date on which the church was to be organized**—which teaches many important truths and points out the duties of the members of the church and also the duties of the officers of the church—so far as

---

*See also note page 326.

†It is the law of the church that "no person is to be ordained to any office in this church, where there is a regularly organized branch of same, without the vote of that church." (Doc. and Cov., sec. xx: 65.)

‡*Doc. and Cov.*, sec. xxvi.

§The voice of the people is the voice of God.

‖The voice of God is the voice of the people.

¶The voice of God *and* the voice of the people.

**This revelation is the one found in sec. xx., Doc. and Cov. The Prophet Joseph precedes it in his history with these remarks: "Among many other things of the kind [spiritual manifestations,] we obtained of Him the following, by the spirit of prophecy and revelation, which, not only gave us much information, but also pointed out to us the pre-

the officers of the church at that time had been given.   That
revelation announces the following doctrines:—

I.   Of the Existence of God:—There is a God in heaven
who is infinite and eternal from everlasting to everlasting—
unchangeable; the framer of heaven and earth and all things
which are in them.

II.   Of the Creation and Fall of Man:—God created
man, male and female, after his own image, and in his own
likeness created he them.   He gave them commandment
that they should love and serve him, and that he should be
the sole object of their worship.   But by the transgression
of these holy laws man became sensual and devilish—fallen
man.

III.   Of Jesus Christ:—The Almighty God gave his
Only Begotten Son as a ransom for fallen man, as it is
written of him in the scriptures.   He suffered temptations,
but gave no heed to them; he was crucified, died, and rose
again the third day; he ascended into heaven to sit on the
right hand of his Father, to reign with Almighty power according to the will of God.   As many as believe on him and
are baptized in his holy name, enduring in faith to the end
—shall be saved.   Not only those who believe after he came
in the flesh; but all those who from the beginning believed
in the words of the holy prophets, who testified of him in all
things.

IV.   Of the Holy Ghost and the Trinity:—The Holy
Ghost beareth record of the Father and of the Son—is
God's witness.   The Father, Son and Holy Ghost con-

---

cise day upon which, according to His will and commandment, we should
proceed to organize His church once again here upon the earth."
Then followed the revelation above referred to. History of the Church
Vol. I, ch. vii.

stitute the Holy Trinity—one God or grand Presidency of heaven and earth, infinite, eternal.

V. Of Justification and Sanctification:—Justification and sanctification come through the grace of God, and are just and true principles. That is, the grace of God supplies the means or conditions of justification and sanctification, and it is for man to apply those means of salvation. The means or conditions of justification and sanctification are that men love and serve God with all their might, mind, and strength. That would lead them to exercise faith in God, repentance of sin and baptism for the remission of sins, laying on of hands for the Holy Ghost, and the pursuit of a godly life and conversation—the old conditions of salvation.*

VI. Of Falling from Grace:—It is possible for men to fall from grace and depart from the living God, therefore the saints are admonished to take heed and pray always, least they fall into temptation. Even those who are sanctified are cautioned to take heed.

VII. Of Baptism:—All who humble themselves before God, and desire to be baptized and come forth with broken hearts and contrite spirits, and witness before the church that they have truly repented of all their sins, and are willing to take upon them the name of Jesus Christ, having a determination to serve Him to the end, and truly manifest by their works that they have received of the spirit of Christ unto the remission of their sins—shall be received by baptism into the church.†

---

*See part I.

†Subsequently when some persons desired to join the church without baptism at the hands of the elders, having been baptized by the ministers of other churches, the Lord said: "All old covenants have I caused to be done away in this thing, and this is a new and everlasting covenant, even that which was from the beginning. Wherefore,

No person, however, can be received into the church of Christ, unless he has arrived unto the years of accountability* before God, and is capable of repéntance.

VIII. Of the Manner of Baptism:—The person who is called of God, and has authority from Jesus Christ to baptize, shall go down into the water with the person who has presented him or herself for baptism, and shall say—calling him or her by name—"having been commissioned of Jesus Christ, I baptize you in the name of the Father, and of the Son, and of the Holy Ghost. Amen."† Then shall he immerse him or her, and come forth again out of the water.

IX. Of Confirmation:—Confirmation into the church follows baptism and is performed by the laying on of hands, by those who have authority in the church. The Holy Ghost is imparted in the same manner and at the same time —one ordinance. There is no form of exact words given for confirming persons into the church and imparting the Holy Ghost; but judging from the forms given for baptism, administering the sacrament, etc., a simple form would be most proper. But whatever other words are used, the following should not be omitted: I confirm you a member of the Church of Jesus Christ of Latter-day Saints; and say unto you, receive ye the Holy Ghost. Those officiating would

---

although a man should be baptized an hundred times, it availeth him nothing, for you cannot enter in at the straight gate by the law of Moses neither by your dead works. For it is because of your dead works that I have caused this last covenant and this church to be built up unto me even as in days of old. Wherefore enter ye in at the gate, as I have commanded, and seek not to counsel your God." Doc. and Cov., Sec. xxii.

*Eight years is fixed as the age of baptism for children. Doc. and Cov. Sec., lxviii: 27.

†These are the same words given to the Nephites, except that the opening clause in the Book of Mormon is, "Having authority given me of Jesus Christ" (III Nephi xi: 25,) and that means the same as "Having been commissioned of Jesus Christ," etc.

of course be careful to do this in the name of Jesus Christ, or their administration would be of none effect.

X. *Of the Duties of Members:*—It is the duty of the members of the church to manifest righteousness by "a Godly walk and conversation;" to abstain from ill feeling toward each other, neither indulging in lying, back-biting nor evil speaking. It is also their duty to pray vocally and in secret. They are required to meet together often to partake of bread and wine in remembrance of the Lord Jesus, which is to be administered by the elder or priest* in the following manner: kneeling with the church he consecrates the emblems of the body and blood of Christ in these words:

Blessing on the Bread.

"O God, the Eternal Father, we ask thee in the name of thy Son Jesus Christ to bless and sanctify this bread to the souls of all those who partake of it, that they may eat in remembrance of the body of thy Son, and witness unto thee, O God, the Eternal Father, that they are willing to take upon them the name of thy Son, and always remember him, and keep his commandments which he has given them, that they may always have His Spirit to be with them. Amen."

Blessing on the Wine.†

"O God, the Eternal Father, we ask thee in the name of thy Son Jesus Christ to bless and sanctify this wine to the

---

*All officers in the church holding higher authority than those named would, of course, have authority to administer the sacrament.

†A few months after the organization of the church, *viz.*, early in the month of August, 1830, when the Prophet Joseph left his house in Harmony, Penn., for the purpose of procuring wine to administer the

souls of all those who drink of it, that they may do it in remembrance of the blood of thy Son, which was shed for them; that they may witness unto thee, O God, the Eternal Father, that they do always remember him, that they may have his Spirit to be with them.   Amen."

XI.   Of the Duties of Saints Respecting Children:—Every member of the church having children is required to bring them to the elders, before the church, who are to lay their hands upon them and bless them in the name of Jesus Christ. *

---

sacrament to a few saints visiting him at his home—he had gone but a short distance when he was met by a heavenly messenger and received the revelation contained in the Doc. and Cov. sec. xxvii, a portion of which is as follows: "Listen to the voice of Jesus Christ, your Lord, your God and your Redeemer, whose word is quick and powerful. For behold I say unto you, that it mattereth not what ye shall eat or what ye shall drink when ye partake of the sacrament, if it so be that ye do it with an eye single to my glory, remembering unto the Father my body which was laid down for you and my blood which was shed for the remission of your sins; wherefore, a commandment I give unto you, that ye shall not purchase wine, neither strong drink of your enemies; wherefore you shall partake of none except it is made new among you; yea, in this my Father's kingdom, which shall be built up on the earth." This revelation is the authority the Church of Jesus Christ of Latter-day Saints has for using water instead of wine in the sacrament.

*It must be remembered that this revelation was given before the church was organized; at that time there were a number who had been baptized, and who had children not old enough to be baptized, and had not yet been blessed of the elders. This commandment therefore was directed more especially to them, but applies, of course, to people placed in like circumstances. Subsequently, in November, 1831, the Lord said: "Inasmuch as parents have children in Zion, or in any of her Stakes which are organized, that teach them not to understand the doctrine of repentance, faith in Christ, the Son of the living God, and of baptism and the gift of the Holy Ghost by the laying on of hands when eight years old, the sin be upon the heads of the parents; for this shall be a law unto the inhabitants of Zion, or in any of her Stakes when organized; and their children shall be baptized for the remission of sins when eight years old and receive the laying on of hands, and they shall also teach their children to pray and walk uprightly before the Lord." (Doc. and Cov. sec. lxviii:25-28.)

XII.   Duties of Officers—Elders:—Elders have authority to preside over meetings and conduct them as prompted by the Holy Ghost.   They also have authority to teach and expound the scriptures; to watch over the church; to baptize; to lay on hands for the bestowal of the Holy Ghost; confirm those baptized, members of the church; administer the sacrament, and ordain other elders and also priests, teachers, and deacons.

—*Priests:*—It is the duty of priests to preach, teach, and expound the scripture; to visit the home of each member and exhort them to pray vocally and in secret and attend to all duties.   They may also baptize and administer the sacrament, ordain other priests, teachers and deacons, take the lead of meetings when no elder is present, and in a general way assist the elder; but they have no authority to lay on hands for the gift of the Holy Ghost or for confirmation in the church.

—*Teachers:*—The teacher's duty is to always be with the church, watch over and strengthen it; to see that there is no iniquity in it, and that the members thereof meet together often and all do their duty.   Teachers may warn, expound, exhort, teach and invite all to come unto Christ, and take the lead of meetings when no elder or priest is present; but they have not the authority to baptize, administer the sacrament or lay on hands.

—*Deacons:*—Deacons are appointed to assist the teachers

---

*The term "elder" is both a general and a specific title.   That is, it may be applied to an apostle or a seventy; as, for instance, in the revelation under consideration (Doc. and Cov. sec. xx.), it is said: "An apostle is an elder," etc.   We shall see also further on that it is the name of a specific office in the Church; that ninety-six elders constitute a quorum; that they constitute a standing ministry in the Stakes of Zion; and that they have authority to do all that is enumerated in the text above.

in the performance of their duties. They may also warn, expound, exhort, teach and invite all to come unto Christ, but like teachers have no authority to baptize, administer the sacrament, or lay on hands.

XIII. Conferences:—The several elders comprising the church of Christ are to meet in conference once in three months, or from time to time as the said conference shall appoint, to do whatever church business is necessary. It is the duty of the several branches of the church to send one or more of their teachers (or other representatives) to attend the conferences of the church, with a list of the names of those who joined the church since the last conference, that a record of the names of the whole church may be kept by one who shall be appointed to that work; and the names of those who are expelled from the church are also to be sent up to the conferences, that their names may be blotted out of the general record of the church. Members removing from the church where they reside are to take a letter certifying that they are regular members in good standing, and that when signed by the regular authorities of the church from whence they move is to admit them into the fellowship of the Saints in the church to which they go.

Such is the plan of government and discipline contained in the revelation given just previous to the organization of the church; and in it one may observe the outlines of that more complete organization of the church which will be treated more fully in another section. The above was sufficient for the church in its infancy.

11. Commencement of the Public Ministry:—On Sunday, the 11th of April, 1830, the first public discourse was preached. It was delivered by Elder Oliver Cowdery, at the house of Peter Whitmer, in Fayette. After the services six persons were baptized. Thus began the public ministry of the church.

12. First Miracle in the Church:—In this same month of April the first miracle in the church was performed. It occurred in this manner: The Prophet Joseph went on a visit to Mr. Joseph Knight, at Colesville, Broome County, New York. This gentleman had rendered the prophet some timely assistance while translating the Book of Mormon, and he was anxious that Mr. Knight and his family should receive the truth. While in Mr. Knight's neighborhood the prophet held a number of meetings. Among those who regularly attended was Newel Knight, son of Joseph Knight. He and the prophet had many serious conversations on the subject of man's salvation. In the meetings held the people prayed much, and in one of the aforesaid conversations with the prophet, Newel Knight promised that he would pray publicly. When the time came, however, his heart failed him, and he refused, saying that he would wait until he got into the woods by himself. The next morning when he attempted to pray in the woods, he was overwhelmed with a sense of having neglected his duty the evening before in not praying in the presence of others. He began to feel uneasy and continued to grow worse both in mind and body, until upon reaching home his appearance was such as to alarm his wife. He sent for the prophet, who, when he came, found Newel in a sad condition and suffering greatly. His visage and limbs were distorted and twisted in every shape imaginable. At last he was caught up off the floor and tossed about most fearfully. The neighbors hearing of his condition came running in. After he had suffered for a time, the prophet succeeded in getting him by the hand when immediately Newel spoke to him, saying he knew he was possessed of the devil and that the prophet had power to cast him out. "If you know I can, it shall be done," replied the prophet; and then impulsively he rebuked Satan and commanded him to depart from the man. Immediately Newel's contortions stopped, and he spoke out and said he saw the devil leave him and vanish from sight.

13. "This was the first miracle which was done in this church, or by any member of it," writes the prophet; "and it was done not by man, nor by the power of man, but it was done by God, and by the power of godliness; therefore let the honor and praise, the dominion and the glory, be ascribed to the Father, Son and Holy Spirit, for ever and ever. Amen."

14. **The First Conference:**—The first conference of the church was held the first day of June, 1830. About thirty members were in attendance, besides a number of unbaptized believers and others anxious to learn. The sacrament was administered, a number who had been baptized were confirmed, and brethren were called and ordained to various offices of the Priesthood. The time was spent in prayer, singing, instruction and exhortation. The Holy Ghost was abundantly poured out upon the Saints. Some prophesied, and others were wrapped in heavenly vision, until their bodily strength was exhausted. When restored they shouted Hosannah to God and the Lamb, and related the glorious things they had seen and felt while in vision. (See note 4, end of section.) Thus the ministry of God's servants began to be confirmed by the signs and the gifts of the Holy Ghost following those who believed.

15. **Errors of the Saints:**—It would be unreasonable to suppose that the members of the church fell into no errors. Some time in the summer of 1830, while the prophet was still living in Harmony, Penn., and Oliver Cowdery

was with the Whitmer family in New York, he received a
letter from Oliver informing him that he [Oliver] had discovered an error in one of the revelations, and added: "I
command you in the name of God to erase these words
[having named the passage] that no priestcraft be among
us."* The prophet wrote immediately asking by what
authority Oliver took it upon himself to command him to
alter or erase, to add to, or diminish a revelation or commandment from Almighty God. Joseph followed his letter
in a few days, and was grieved beyond measure to find that
the whole Whitmer family sustained Oliver in the position
he had taken. By labor and perseverance, however, he convinced them that they were in error and the difficulty was
settled.

16. Scarcely had this trouble subsided when another
arose. In the month of August, 1830, in consequence
of persecution having grown extremely bitter in Harmony
and vicinity, the prophet removed with his family to Fayette,
New York, at the invitation of the Whitmers, to live with
them. On arriving there he learned that Hyrum Page was
in possession of a stone which he called a seer stone, and
through which he was receiving revelations for the church
in respect to the up-building of Zion, church government,
etc. The Whitmers and the inconstant Oliver accepted
these revelations and much harm was being done. A conference was to convene on the first of September, but before
it assembled the prophet inquired of the Lord and obtained
a revelation on the subject which was directed more especially
to Oliver Cowdery.† In regard to the subject in hand, it
contained the following: Oliver was to be heard by the

---

*The closing phrases of paragraph 37, sec. xx, Doc. and Cov.,
are what Oliver objected to—"And truly manifest by their works that
they have received of the Spirit of Christ unto the remission of sins."
†Doc. and Cov. sec. xxviii.

church in all things whatsoever he taught by the Comforter, concerning the revelations and commandments; and if led by the Comforter to teach by way of commandment, he had permission to do it; "But thou shalt not write by way of commandment," said the Lord to him, "but by wisdom. And thou shalt not command him who is at thy head and at the head of the church." No one was to receive commandments and revelations in the church, that is for the church, except Joseph the prophet; for the Lord had given him the keys of the mysteries and revelations, until he appointed unto the church another in his stead. Oliver was commanded to take Hyrum Page aside by himself and tell him that the revelations which he had written from that stone were not of the Lord, but that Satan had deceived him, and they must be given up, for he had not been appointed to receive revelations neither would any one be appointed contrary to the church covenants, which provided that all things must be done in order and by common consent of the church.

17. During the conference the subject of the revelations from Hyrum Page's seer stone was discussed, and after much consideration, the whole church, including Hyrum Page, renounced the stone and all things connected with it; and the church was made to understand more clearly that there is but one on the earth at a time who is authorized to receive the word and commandment of the Lord for the Church.*

---

*Doc. and Cov. xxviii and sec. xliii:1-6.

NOTES.

1. The Visitation of John the Baptist:—On a sudden, as from the midst of eternity, the voice of the Redeemer spake peace to us, while the vail was parted and the angel of God came down clothed with glory, and delivered the anxiously looked for message, and the keys of the gospel of repentance! What joy! what wonder! what amazement! While the world was racked and distracted—while millions were groping as the blind for the wall, and while all men were resting on uncertainty, as a general mass, our eyes beheld, our ears heard. As in the blaze of day; yes, more—above the glitter of the May sunbeam which then shed its brilliancy over the face of nature! Then this voice, though mild, pierced to the center, and his words, "I am thy fellow servant," dispelled every fear. We listened, we gazed, we admired! 'Twas the voice of an angel from glory, 'twas a message from the Most High! And as we heard we rejoiced, while His love enkindled upon our souls, and we were wrapt in the vision of the Almighty! Where was room for doubt? Nowhere; uncertainty had fled, doubt had sunk more more to rise, while fiction and deception had fled forever! * * * Think for a moment what joy filled our hearts, and with what surprise we must have bowed (for who would not have bowed the knee for such a blessing when we received under his hand the holy Priesthood as he said, "Upon you my fellow servants, in the name of Messiah, I confer this Priesthood and this authority, which shall remain upon earth, that the sons of Levi may yet offer an offering to the Lord in righteousness."—*Oliver Cowdery, Hist. of the Ch. Vol. I, Ch. 5—footnote p. 42.*

2. Melchisedec Priesthood Restored:—We canot fix the exact date when the Melchisedec priesthood was restored, but it occurred sometime between the 15th of May, 1829, and the 6th of April, 1830. We can approximate within a few months of the exact time, but no further, from any of the records of the church. Joseph, the Prophet, designates the place where their ordination took place, in his address to the saints, written September 6th, 1842, as follows: "Again what do we hear? * * * the voice of Peter, James and John in the wilderness, between Harmony, Susquehanna County, and Colesville, Broome County, on the Susquehanna River, declaring themselves as possessing the keys of the Kingdom and of the Dispensation of the Fullness of Times." And in a revelation given September, 1830, referring to Joseph and Oliver, the Lord said, in reference to partaking again of the sacrament on the earth, that the "hour cometh that I will drink of the fruit of the vine with you on the earth, and with Moroni, * * * and also with Elias, * * * and also with John, the son of Zacharias, * * * and also with Peter, James and John whom I have sent unto you, by whom I have ordained you and confirmed you apostles and especial witnesses of my name." It would appear from the instructions given in the revelation, dated June, 1829, [Doc. and Cov. sec. xviii], that the apostleship had been conferred on Joseph Smith, Oliver Cowdery, and David Whitmer. If this supposition is correct, it reduces the period of uncertainty when this glorious event actually took

place to a few weeks, or from the middle of May to the end of June.—
Joseph F. Smith, Contributor, vol. 10, *p.* 310.

3. Why the Higher Priesthood is Called After Melchisedek:—
There are in the church two Priesthoods * * * Why the first is
called the Melchisedek Priesthood, is because Melchisedek was such a
great high priest. Before his day it was called the *Holy Priesthood,
after the order of the Son of God*; but out of respect or deference to the
name of the Supreme Being, to avoid the too frequent repetition of his
name, they, the church, in ancient days called that Priesthood after
Melchisedek, or the Melchisedek Priesthood.—*Doc. and Cov. Sec. cvii.*
Changing the name of the priesthood did not change the nature of the
thing—it is still the "Priesthood after the order of the Son of God."

4. Visions at the First Conference of the Church:—Among
those who received visions was Newel Knight, who was so completely
overcome by the power of the spirit that he had to be laid on a bed,
being unable to help himself. "By his own account of the transaction,"
says the Prophet, "he could not understand why we should lay him on
the bed, as he felt no sensibility of weakness. He felt his heart filled
with love, with glory, and pleasure unspeakable, and could discern all
that was going on in the room; when all of a sudden a vision of futurity
burst upon him. He saw there represented the great work which
through my instrumentality was yet to be accomplished. He saw
heaven opened, and beheld the Lord Jesus Christ, seated at the right
hand of the majesty on high, and had it made plain to his understanding that the time would come when he would be admitted into His
presence to enjoy His society for ever and ever."

REVIEW.

1. Relate the circumstances which led to the restoration of the
Aaronic Priesthood.

2. What explanation did the angel make concerning this Priesthood?

3. What reason have you for believing that John the Baptist would
be among the resurrected saints spoken of by Matthew? (Note.)

4. Under whose direction did John say he was acting?

5. What promise did he make to them about the Melchisedek
Priesthood?

6. What commandment did the angel then give to Joseph and
Oliver?

7. How were these baptisms performed? (Note.)

8. What commandment did the angel give in relation to re-ordination?

9. What course did Joseph and Oliver pursue after their ordination?

10. About what time was the Melchisedek Priesthood restored?
(Note 2.)

11. By whom and in what locality was it restored?

12. What made it especially appropriate that these three apostles should restore that Priesthood?

13. What is the power or authority of the Melchisedek Priesthood?

14. What particular power did this Priesthood give to Joseph and Oliver?

15. When was the church organized?

16. How many persons effected the organization?

17. Were six persons all who had been baptized up to that date— 6th of April, 1830?

18. Relate the circumstances connected with the organization of the church.

19. What was the organization then called?

20. When was the phrase "of Latter-day Saints," added as a part of the name of the church?

21. What spiritual manifestations were experienced at the organization of the church? (Note 4.)

22. What important revelation was given immediately after the church was organized?

23. What two great principles are seen operating at the organization of the church?

24. What can you say of the union of these two principles in church government?

25. What revelation is it that commanded the organization of the church? (Note.)

26. State what that revelation says upon the existence of God.

27. —Of the creation of man:

28. —Of Jesus Christ:

29. —Of the Holy Ghost:

30. —Of justification and sanctification:

31. —Of falling from grace:

32. —Of baptism:

33. —Of the manner of baptism:

34. —Of confirmation:

35. —Of the duties of members:

36, —Of the duties of parents respecting their children: (Note.)

37. —Of the duties of officers—elders: (Note.)

38. —Of priests:

39. —Of teachers:

40. —Of deacons:

41. —Of conferences.

42. In what manner did the public ministry of the church begin?

43. Relate the first miracle performed in the church.

44. When was the first conference of the church held, and what occurred?

45. What error did Oliver Cowdery and the Whitmer family fall into?

46. How was Hyrum Page deceived by Lucifer?

47. What great principle concerning revelations to the church was brought out by these errors?

SECTION III.

1. First Mission to the Lamanites:—At the conference held in Fayette, New York, September, 1830, the first mission to the Lamanites was appointed. In the revelation* which corrected the evils introduced by Hiram Page's "seer stone," Oliver Cowdery was appointed to a mission to the Lamanites [American Indians]; and before the conference was adjourned another revelation as given appointing Parley P. Pratt, Peter Whitmer, Jr., and Ziba Peterson to accompany him. Great promises are contained in the Book of Mormon concerning the Lamanites, and the elders at that conference hoped that the time had come for their fulfillment. (See note 1, end of section.)

2. *En route* for their field of labor—the western part of the State of Missouri—the elders of the Lamanite mission stopped at Kirtland, in the north-eastern part of Ohio. Here they found a society of reformed Baptists, sometimes called "Campbellites," after Alexander Campbell, the chief founder of the new sect. Their pastor was Sidney Rigdon. Elder Parley P. Pratt had formerly been a member of this sect, and he presented to his former co-religionists the Book of Mormon, and with his associates preached the fullness of the gospel to them, which, finally, Mr. Rigdon and nearly all his congregation accepted.

3. The Lamanite mission continued. its journey westward, and in mid-winter reached the city of Independence, in the western borders of Missouri. Crossing the

---

Doc. and Cov., sec. xxviii.

frontier, several meetings were held with the Delaware Indians, which had the effect of arousing the jealousy of the sectarian missionaries among them. Such was their influence with the Indian agents that they succeeded in getting the elders banished from the territory. Returning to Independence, they sent one of their number, Parley P. Pratt, to report their labors to the prophet.

4. **The First Commandment to Gather:**—In December, 1830, the Lord gave a revelation* to the church in New York, requiring the Saints in that State to move into Ohio by the time Oliver Cowdery returned from his mission to the Lamanites. This is the first direct commandment to the church to gather together. During the winter of 1830-31, the Saints obeyed this commandment, the most of them settling in Kirtland. The Prophet Joseph and his family arrived there about the first of February, 1831. Before the coming of the New York Saints there was a church at Kirtland of about one hundred members, most of whom had been drawn from the Campbellite sect.

5. **The First Bishops of the Church:**—On the 4th of February, 1831, the Lord by revelation† commanded that Edward Partridge should be "appointed by the voice of the church, and ordained a bishop." Edward Partridge was a merchant in Kirtland, of whom the prophet said: "He was a pattern of piety, and one of the Lord's great men, known by his steadfastness and patient endurance to the end;" and of whom the Lord said, in the revelation appointing him bishop—"His heart is pure before me, for he is like unto Nathaniel of old, in whom there is no guile." He was required to give up his business of merchant, and devote all

---

*Doc. and Cov., sec. xxxvii.
†Doc. and Cov., sec. xli.

his time in the labors of the church. He was not to be the only bishop in the church, however, as in the November following (1831), the Lord said: "There remaineth * * * other bishops to be set apart unto the church, to minister even according to the first."* In December of that year, Newel K. Whitney was appointed a bishop over the church in Kirtland and vicinity (see note 2, end of section); while Edward Partridge was bishop in Zion and the regions round about.

6. **The Bishopric:**—Although nothing is said in the revelation which appointed Edward Partridge bishop about the rights and powers of his office in the church, yet here, doubtless, will be the most proper place to speak of bishops in respect to their rights and authority.

I. The bishopric is the presidency of the Aaronic Priesthood;† and since that Priesthood has most to do with administering the "outward ordinances, the *letter* of the gospel,"‡ the bishops will find their chief employment in the temporal affairs of the church. Indeed the Lord plainly says: "The office of a bishop is in administering all temporal things."§ By ministering in temporal things we mean attending to the tithing, caring for the poor, and when the law of consecration shall be observed by the church, the bishops will receive the consecrations, settle people on their possessions, divide their inheritances unto them,|| keep the Lord's store house, etc. (See note 3, end of section.)

II. The bishops are also to be judges among the people, to sit in judgment on transgressors, to hear testimony and

---

Doc. and Cov. sec. lxviii.
†*Doc. and Cov., sec. cvii*: 15.
‡*Ibid, verse* 20.
§*Ibid, verse* 68.
|| *Doc. and Cov., sec. lviii*:17.

give decisions according to the laws of the kingdom which are given by the prophets of God.* The bishop's court is the first court of record in the church; that is, a record is kept of the trial and preserved; whereas in any investigation of difficulties that may be had before the teachers or others, no record is kept. An appeal lies from the bishop's courts to the high council having jurisdiction. For want of a better expression we may say there are several kinds of bishops; first, the general presiding bishop of the church; second, traveling bishops; third, local or ward bishops. †

III.   Presiding Bishop of the Church:—This bishop is the President of the Aaronic Priesthood throughout the church; he has a jurisdiction over all other bishops, priests, teachers and deacons; and a general supervision of the temporal affairs of the church, subject, of course, to the counsel of the Presidency of the Melchisedek Priesthood. Of right this bishop should be the first-born among the sons of Aaron; "For the first-born holds the right of the presidency over this [the Aaronic] Priesthood, and the keys or authority of the same. No man has a legal right to this office, to hold the keys of this priesthood, except he be a literal descendant and the first-born of Aaron." ‡ But before the first-born among the literal descendants of Aaron can legally officiate in this calling, he must first be designated by the First Presidency of the Melchisedek Priesthood; second, he must be found worthy

---

*Doc. and Cov., sec. lviii: 15-18.   Ibid, sec. cvii: 72-75.

†There are bishops holding different positions: Bishop Partridge was a general bishop over the land of Zion; while Bishop Whitney was a general bishop over the Church in Kirtland, Ohio, and also over the eastern churches until afterwards appointed as presiding bishop. * * * There are also ward bishops, whose duties are confined to their several wards. * * * There are also bishop's agents, such as Sidney Gilbert (he was Bishop Partridge's agent in Zion, Missouri), and others. *Items on Priesthood* by the late President *John Taylor.*

‡Doc. and Cov., sec. lxviii: 17, 18.

of the position, and that includes his capacity to fill the office with ability, honor and dignity; third, he must be ordained under the hands of the First Presidency of the Melchisedek Priesthood.* But by virtue of the decree concerning the right of the Priesthood descending from father to son, the first-born of the sons of Aaron may claim their anointing, if at any time they can prove their lineage or do ascertain it by revelation from the Lord under the hands of the First Presidency.† A literal descendant of Aaron when appointed as above described, may act without counselors, except in a case where a President of the High Priesthood after the order of Melchisedek is tried. In that event he is to be assisted by "twelve counselors of the High Priesthood."‡ But when no literal descendant of Aaron can be found, as a High Priest of the Melchisedek Priesthood has authority to officiate in all the lesser offices, he may officiate in the office of bishop; provided he is called, set apart and ordained unto that power under the hands of the First Presidency of the Melchisedek Priesthood, and is assisted by two other high priests as counselors.§ This bishop, whether a descendant of Aaron or a high priest appointed to officiate in that calling, cannot be tried or condemned for any crime save before the First Presidency of the church. If he be found guilty on testimony that cannot be impeached, he is to be condemned.|| These are the powers, prerogatives and privileges of the Presiding Bishop of the church.

---

*Doc. and Cov., sec. lxviii: 20.

†Doc. and Cov., sec. lxviii: 21.

‡And inasmuch as a President of the High Priesthood shall transgress, he shall be had in remembrance before the common council of the church, who shall be assisted by twelve counselors of the High Priesthood; and their decision upon his head shall be an end of controversy concerning him. (Doc. and Cov., sec. cvii: 82, 83.)

§Doc. and Cov., sec. lxviii: 19.

|| Doc. and Cov., sec. lxviii: 22-24.

IV. Traveling Bishops:—These are bishops appointed to preside as such over large districts of country in which there are a number of branches of the church, and among which they would be expected to travel, to set in order temporal affairs and preside over those holding the Aaronic Priesthood. Newel K. Whitney when called to preside over the church at Kirtland and the regions round about was a traveling bishop, and best illustrates this order of bishops. Some eight or ten months after his ordination he was called upon by the Lord to travel among all the churches of the east, searching after the poor, to administer to their wants by humbling the rich and the proud."* He was also sent to the cities of New York, Albany and Boston, to warn the inhabitants thereof of judgments to come and to preach the gospel.

V. Local or Ward Bishops:—By local bishops we mean those ordained and set apart to preside over a single ward or branch of the church; and whose jurisdiction is strictly limited to that ward or branch. Both traveling and local bishops must either be high priests or literal descendants of Aaron. If the latter, then from among the first-born of the sons of Aaron.† In the event of their being descendants of Aaron, they would possess the same privileges in their sphere as the presiding bishop does in his; that is, they could act without counselors, but must be found worthy men designated and ordained by the First Presidency of the church, or by their direction. If high priests appointed to act in these bishoprics, then they must be designated and

---

*Doc. and Cov., sec. lxxxiv: 112.

†I think a careful reading of sec. lxviii of the Doc. and Cov., will justify this conclusion—that not only the office of presiding bishop of the church should be filled by the first-born of the sons of Aaron, but that the traveling and local bishops also, so far as can be, should be chosen from among the first born of the sons of Aaron. The following

set apart by the same authority as literal descendants of Aaron, and assisted by two counselors who are also high priests. They would form the presidency over the Aaronic Priesthood in the districts over which they preside, have an oversight of all the temporal concerns thereof, and in addition to that act as the common judge in that ward or district assigned to them.

7. **Zion:**—The Book of Mormon prophecies predict the founding of a glorious city upon the American continent to be called New Jerusalem, or Zion. (See note 4, end of section.) * It was but natural, therefore, that the first elders of the church should be anxious to learn where it was to be built and seek to find it. The Book of Mormon, while clearly predicting that the city will be established, fails to give its location. In March, 1831, however, the Saints were commanded to gather up their riches that they might purchase an inheritance that the Lord promised to point out to them some time in the future, the New Jerusalem—"a city of refuge, a place of safety for the Saints of the Most High†—Zion. In June, 1831, a conference convened at Kirtland, and the Lord called twenty-eight elders to go through the Western States by different routes, two by two, preaching by the way, baptizing by water and the laying on of hands by the water side.‡ They were to meet in

---

passage seems especially clear on the question: "There remaineth hereafter, in the due time of the Lord, other bishops to be set apart unto the church, to minister even according to the first; wherefore they shall be high priests who are worthy, and they shall be appointed by the first presidency of the Melchisedek Priesthood, except they be descendants of Aaron, and if they be literal descendants of Aaron, they have a legal right to the bishopric, if they are the first-born among the sons of Aaron." Sec. lxviii: 14-16.

*Book of Ether, ch. xiii, and III Nephi, ch. xx.
†Doc. and Cov., sec. xlv.
‡Doc. and Cov., sec. lii.

Western Missouri to hold a conference, and if faithful the Lord promised to reveal to them the place of the city of Zion.

8. About the middle of July the Prophet Joseph and a number of these brethren arrived at Independence, meeting with Oliver Cowdery and his associates—the mission to the Lamanites. A few days afterwards a revelation was received* declaring Missouri to be the land which God had appointed for the gathering of the Saints, the land of promise, the place of the city of Zion, Independence being the "center place." The site of the temple which the Lord has decreed shall be built in this generation, upon which his glory shall rest, and in which the sons of Moses and of Aaron shall offer an acceptable offering to the Lord—was declared to be a short distance west of the court-house. On the morning of the 3rd of August, 1831, the Prophet Joseph, with the other elders that had arrived at Independence, met at the temple site and dedicated it as the place for the building of a temple. (See notes 5 and 6, end of section.)

Meantime a company of Saints known as the Colesville Branch—from their having lived at Colesville, Broome County, New York,—had arrived in Missouri, and having received instructions to purchase the lands in the regions round about Zion, they secured a tract of land in a fertile prairie some ten or twelve miles west of Independence, in Kaw township, not far from the present location of Kansas City. On the 2nd of August—the day preceding the dedication of the temple site—in the settlement of the Colesville Saints, the first log was laid for a house, as the foundation of Zion. The log was carried by twelve men in honor of the Twelve Tribes of Israel; and Elder Sidney Rigdon conse-

---

*Doc. and Cov., sec. lvii.

crated and dedicated the land of Zion for the gathering of the Saints.   (See note 7, end of section.)

9.   **The Law of Consecration:**—It is said of the early Christian saints that they "were of one heart and of one soul; neither said any of them that aught of the things which he possessed was his own; but they had all things common."* It was doubtless a desire to imitate this condition of affairs which led the followers of Sidney Rigdon, at Kirtland, to establish the "common stock" plan of living.   That is, the whole community attempted to live together as one family, having all things in common.   Nearly all the "family" joined the church; and when the Prophet Joseph settled in Kirtland, about the 1st of February, 1831, he persuaded them to abandon that plan of living, for the more perfect law of the Lord."†   The more perfect law was the law of consecration.

10.   Preparations for the introduction of this law was first made by the appointment of a bishop, who should have authority to administer in temporal things.   The bishop was called by revelation on the 4th of February, 1831.‡ On the 9th of the same month the Lord in a revelation gave the first instructions about the law of consecration.§   From

---

*Acts iv : 32.

†The branch of the church in this part of the Lord's vineyard (Kirtland,) which had increased to nearly one hundred members, were striving to do the will of God so far as they knew it, though some had strange notions, and false spirits had crept in among them.   With a little caution and some wisdom, I soon assisted the brethren and sisters to overcome them.   The plan of "common stock," which had existed in what was called "the family," whose member generally had embraced the everlasting gospel, was readily abandoned for the more perfect law of the Lord, and the false spirits were easily discerned and rejected by the light of revelation.—*Joseph Smith*, Hist. of the Ch. Vol. I, Ch. xiii.

‡*Doc. and Cov., sec. xli.*
§*Doc. and Cov., sec. xiii.*

that and subsequent revelations we summarize the following in relation to that law:

I. The person desiring to make the consecration brings his possessions to the bishop and delivers them unto him—consecrates them unto the Lord, giving them up absolutely, with a deed and a covenant that cannot be broken.*

II. The person so consecrating his possessions, whether they be much or little, if it be a full consecration, has claim upon the bishop for a stewardship out of the consecrated properties of the church, an inheritance for himself and his family,† from the management of which, by industry and economy—for this law contemplates industry and economy on the part of those who embrace it‡—they may obtain a livelihood. But the possessions consecrated are the Lord's, or else the consecrations are vain, and the whole proceedings farcical.§ The inheritance given to the individual is given to him as his stewardship, of which he must render an account unto the bishop.|| The steward is responsible for his stewardship in time and in eternity unto the Lord.¶ The stewardships are to be secured to those to whom they are given by

---

*Doc. and Cov., sec. xlii: 30-32.

†Doc. and Cov., sec. xlii: 32.

‡In the very revelations in which the first instructions on the subject of consecration and stewardship are given the Lord says: "Let all thy garments be plain and their beauty the beauty of the work of thine own hands. * * * Thou shalt not be idle, for he that is idle shall not eat the bread nor wear the garments of the laborer." (Doc. and Cov., sec. xliii: 40-42.)

In a subsequent revelation, referring to the inhabitants of Zion who were living under this law of consecration, the Lord said: "And the inhabitants of Zion, also, shall remember their labors, inasmuch as they are appointed to labor in all faithfulness, for the idler shall be had in remembrance before the Lord." (Doc. and Cov., sec. lxviii: 30.

§Doc. and Cov., sec. civ: 54-57.

||Doc. and Cov., sec. lxxii: 2-8.

¶Doc. and Cov., sec. civ.

a written deed, that they may not be deprived of their inheritance.*

III. After men have received their stewardships the income from them, over and above that which is needful for the support of themselves and their families, is also to be consecrated unto the Lord and taken to the Lord's store house to be distributed to the poor to supply stewardships to those who have not yet received them, to purchase lands for the public benefit, to build houses of worship, temples, etc., etc.†

IV. In the event of any steward needing means to improve his stewardship, or for any other righteous purpose, he has a claim upon the Lord's store house, and so long as he is in full fellowship with the church, and is a wise and faithful steward, on application to the treasurer of the general fund, he is to be supplied with that which he needs; the treasurer, of course, being accountable to the church for his management of the general fund, and subject to removal in the event of incompetency or transgression.‡

V. Each steward is independent in the management of his stewardship. He must pay for that which he buys; he can insist on payment for that which he sells. He has no claim upon the stewardship of his neighbor; his neighbor has no claim upon his stewardship; but both have claim, as also have their children—when they shall become of age and start in life for themselves§—upon the surplus in the Lord's store house to aid them in the event of their needing

---

*Doc. and Cov., sec. li: 4-5.

†Doc. and Cov., sec. xlii: 33-35.

‡Doc. and Cov., sec. civ: 70-77.

§"All children have claim upon their parents for their maintenance until they are of age. After that they have claim upon the church, or in other words, upon the Lord's store house, if their parents have not assistance.* The various churches, or branches of the church, are each to be independent in the management of their respective store houses,† subject of course to a general supervision of the Presiding Bishop of the church and of the First Presidency thereof.

11. **Reflections:**—Such is the law of consecration and stewardship given to the church as early as the first and second year of its existence in this last dispensation; under which law, and under no other, the Saints are to build up the Zion of God, the New Jerusalem upon this continent.‡ The law is designed to humble the rich and the proud and raise the poor and the lowly,§ that men might be equal in temporal possessions according to their families, their circumstances, their wants and their needs.‖ There is enough in the earth and more than enough¶ to supply the necessities and the reasonable luxuries desired by man if the wealth created by his industry was but more equally distributed. The plan which the Lord has revealed to accomplish this, however, does not aim at the destruction of the individuality of men. It makes no attempt to control men in the detail management of their stewardships, or the disposal of their time, or to set taskmasters over them, but only to control and dispose of the surplus arising from their labors in the management of their respective stewardships.

---

wherewith to give them inheritances. And the store house shall be kept by the consecrations of the church, and widows and orphans shall be provided for as also the poor." (Doc. and Cov., sec. lxxxiii: 4, 6.)

*Sec. xlii: 53-54. And you are to be equal, or in other words, you are to have equal claims on the properties for the benefit of managing the concerns of your stewardships, every man according to his wants and needs inasmuch as his wants are just. (Doc. and Cov., sec. lxxxii: 17.)

†*Doc. and Cov., sec. li*: 10, 13, also verse 18, which says the law laid down in verses 10, 13, shall be an example to all churches.

‡*Doc. and Cov., sec. cv*: 1-5, *also sec. lviii*: 35-36.

§*Doc. and Cov., sec. xlii*: 39.

‖*Doc. and Cov., sec. li*: 3.

¶*Doc. and Cov., sec. civ*: 15-17.

12.   In consequence of the unsettled state of the church arising from the persecutions and drivings inflicted upon the Saints during the time they were settling in Missouri, coupled with their inexperience, their pride, covetousness, greed and disobedience, they failed to live up to the requirements of the law of consecration, and in 1838 the lesser law of tithing was given, and has obtained in the Church unto this day. This law of tithing requires that the Saints pay one-tenth of their income annually.   This is the law of tithing now in force in the church.*

NOTES.

1.   Promises to the Lamanites:—Then shall the remnant of our seed know concerning us, how that we came out from Jerusalem, and that they are descendants of the Jews.   And the gospel of Jesus Christ shall be declared among them; wherefore they shall be restored unto the knowledge of their fathers, and also to the knowledge of Jesus Christ, which was had among their fathers.   And then shall they rejoice; for they shall know that it is a blessing unto them from the hand of God; and their scales of darkness shall begin to fall from their eyes; and many generations shall not pass away among them, save they shall be a white and delightsome people.—Prophecy of Nephi, Nephi II, ch. xxx.

2.   Newel K. Whitney's Appointment to be Bishop:—Though in natural gifts few men were better qualified for such a position, he nevertheless distrusted his ability, and deemed himself incapable of discharging the high and holy trust.   In his perplexity he appealed to the prophet: "I cannot see a bishop in myself, Brother Joseph; but if you say it's the Lord's will, I'll try." "You need not take my word alone," answered the prophet, kindly, "go and ask Father for yourself." Newel felt the force of this mild rebuke, but determined to do as he was advised and seek to obtain the knowledge for himself.   His humble, heartfelt prayer was answered.   In the silence of night and the solitude of his own chamber, he heard a voice from heaven: "Thy strength is in me."   The words were few and simple, but for him they had a world of meaning.   His doubts were dispelled like the dew before the dawn.

Doc. and Cov., sec. cxix.

He straightway sought the prophet, told him he was satisfied and was willing to accept the office to which he had been called.—*Orson F. Whitney.*

3. **The Sphere of the Aaronic Priesthood:**—The lesser Priesthood is a part of or an appendage to the greater, or the Melchisedek Priesthood, and has power in administering outward ordinances. The lesser or Aaronic Priesthood can make appointments for the greater, in preaching, can baptize, administer the sacrament, attend to the tithing, buy lands, settle people on possessions, divide inheritances, look after the poor, take care of the properties of the church, attend generally to temporal affairs, act as common judges in Israel and assist in ordinances of the temple, under the direction of the greater or Melchisedek Priesthood. They hold the keys of the administering of angels and administer in outward ordinances, *the letter of the gospel* and the baptism of repentance for the remission of sins. *Items on Priesthood. John Taylor.*

4. **Zion:**—The word Zion is variously employed: "This is Zion, the pure in heart." (Doc. and Cov.) In this instance the word refers to a people who are declared to be the pure in heart. In the south part of Jerusalem is a hill frequently spoken of in Jewish scriptures as Zion, or Mount Zion. Then Enoch the seventh from Adam gathered the righteous and built a city, "that was called the city of Holiness, even Zion." The Lord in speaking to Enoch about the great events to take place in the last days, in which He would come to the earth in His glory, said He would with righteousness and truth sweep the earth as with a flood to gather His elect to "an holy city * * * and it shall be called Zion, a new Jerusalem." The Nephite prophet, Moroni, tells us that Ether in vision saw the days of the coming of the Son of Man, and that "he spake concerning a new Jerusalem upon this land (America)" that was to be built up unto the remnant of the seed of Joseph. (Ether xiii.) Jesus also after his resurrection, when he visited the Nephites on the American continent, told them that he would establish them upon this land, and if the Gentiles would not harden their hearts, but would repent of their sins, they should be included in the covenant, and should assist in building up the city of Zion or New Jerusalem (III Nephi xx.) The word Zion, then, is applied to a people; it is the name of a hill in the south part of Jerusalem; it is the name of a city built by Enoch and his people; it is to be the name of a city built in the last days by the saints of the Most High upon the continent of America.—*Roberts Missouri Persecutions.*

5. **Western Missouri (1831):**—It was a country whose richness and fertility of soil far surpassed anything which they (the saints,) had ever before seen. It was a country abounding with springs and rivulets of the purest kind of water, whose crystal streams flowed in luxuriant abundance in almost every grove and prairie. A great variety of the most excellent timber bordered upon the rivers and watercourses. These shady and delightful groves were from one to three miles in width, extending many miles in length, while the rich rolling prairies, covered with a gorgeous profusion of wild flowers of every

varied hue, lay spread around among the intervening groves. Their grassy surfaces extending for miles, presented the delightful appearance of a sea of meadows. It was a new country; but few inhabitants had as yet formed settlements within its borders. These consisted principally of emigrants from the southern states.—*Orson Pratt.*

6. **The Temple Site:**—Taking the road running west from the court house for a scant half mile, you come to the summit of a crowning hill, the slope of which to the south and west is quite abrupt but very gradual toward the north and east. * * * This is the temple site. It was upon this spot on the third day of August, 1831, that Joseph Smith, Sidney Rigdon, Edward Partridge, W. W. Phelps, Oliver Cowdery, Martin Harris and Joseph Coe and another person whose name I cannot learn, for there were eight in all—men in whom the Lord was well pleased, assembled to dedicate this place as the temple site in Zion. The eighty-seventh psalm was read. Joseph (the prophet) then dedicated the spot where is to be built a temple on which the glory of God shall rest. Yea the great God hath so decreed it, saying "Verily, this generation shall not all pass away until an house shall be built unto the Lord, and a cloud shall rest upon it, which cloud shall be even the glory of the Lord, which shall fill the house. * * * And the sons of Moses, and also the sons of Aaron shall offer an acceptable offering and sacrifice in the house of the Lord, which house shall be built unto the Lord in this generation upon the consecrated spot as I have appointed." (Doc. and Cov., sec. lxxxiv: 5, 31.)—*Roberts Missouri Persecutions.*

7. **The Founding of Zion:**—Thus the work of building up Zion commenced, and though the commencement was humble in the extreme, the final result shall be the erection of a city that shall be the crowning glory of the whole earth; a city from which shall go forth the law of the Lord unto all nations, for is it not written: "Out of Zion shall go forth the law? (Isaiah ii.) It shall be a city of refuge, for the Lord has said: "Every man who will not take up his sword against his neighbor, must needs flee to Zion for safety." The wicked will consider her inhabitants terrible, while the righteous out of every nation will come into it with songs of everlasting joy in their hearts. (Doc. and Cov., sec. xlv.)—*Roberts Missouri Persecutions.*

REVIEW.

1. When and under what circumstances was the first mission appointed to the Lamanites?

2. What important circumstance occurred in the experience of the Lamanite mission en route for the west?

3. What success attended the mission to the Lamanites?

4. When was the first commandment given to the Church to gather?

5. To what place did the Church first gather?

6. Who was the first Bishop in the Church?

7. What was his character?

8. State what you can of the sphere of labor belonging to the bishopric.

9. What can you say of bishops as judges in Israel?

10. How many kinds of bishops are there?

11. Tell what you can of the authority, rights and powers of the Presiding Bishop of the church.

12. What difference exists in respect to a bishop who is a literal descendant of Aaron and one who holds the office by virtue of being a High Priest?

13. Is being a descendant of the first-born among the sons of Aaron all sufficient to qualify a man to be a bishop?

14. What is the exception to the rule that a bishop who is a literal descendant of Aaron can act without counselors?

15. Describe traveling bishops.

16. Give an example of such a bishop in the church.

17. What is meant by local bishops?

18. Describe their power and jurisdiction.

19. How did the first Elders of the church learn that Zion was to be built in America?

20. What various significations are attached to the word Zion? (Note 4.)

21. What circumstances led a number of the Elders to western Missouri?

22. What was revealed to them there?

23. Where is Zion located?

24. Describe the land of Zion. (Note 5.)

25. What promises are made respecting a temple in that land? (Note 6.)

26. What caused the people in Kirtland before they heard the Gospel to have all things in common?

27. What course did Joseph Smith take relative to this subject? (Note.)

28. In what way were the people prepared for the introduction of the law of consecration?

29. Describe the law of consecration and stewardship.

30. What purposes are designed to be accomplished in the law of consecration?

31. What circumstances prevented the successful operation of this law in Missouri?

SECTION IV.

1. Persecution:—From the very commencement the work of the Lord in these last days met with the most violent opposition. No sooner did Joseph Smith declare that he had received a revelation from God than it brought upon him the ridicule and wrath of many who heard of it. The stream of hatred grew broader and deeper as the work progressed. Joseph himself endured many vexatious persecutions, and those who believed in his teachings were doomed to share them. The first general persecution of the church, however, occurred in Missouri.

2. The people among whom the Saints settled on the western frontiers of the United States, in Jackson County, Missouri, were ignorant, jealous, bigoted, and superstitious. They were also given to Sabbath-breaking, drunkenness, profanity, horse racing and gambling. It will be seen at once, therefore, that there could be but little fellowship between them and the Saints. (See note 1, end of section.) Moreover, they were principally from the Southern states, and slaveholders; and as the Saints were from the "free" states of the north, they were inclined to be suspicious of them. It was an easy matter, therefore, for demagogues to persuade the Missourians that it was the design of the Saints to supplant them in the possession of the country.

3. Expulsion of the Saints from Jackson County:— The Saints themselves were not as prudent as they should have been. Many boasted that God would destroy the wicked and give their possessions as inheritances unto the righteous. Many more failed to live up to the moral pre-

cepts of the gospel, and were disobedient to the counsels of
the Lord. This gave the wicked great power over them, and
the result was that the jealousy and wrath which had been
burning for some time in the hearts of the old settlers finally
broke out into deeds of violence. Almost the entire population about Independence arose and drove the Saints from the
county under circumstances of the utmost cruelty.* Twelve
hundred people were driven from their possessions, and
about two hundred of their homes and one grist mill were
burned. This was in the fall and winter of 1833-34. (See
note 2, end of section.)

4. **Zion's Camp:**—The exiled Saints found a temporary
abode in Clay County—the next county north of Jackson—
and in the meantime the Lord commanded the Prophet
Joseph to gather up the strength of the Lord's house—the
young and middle-aged men in the church—for the purpose
of going to the assistance of their brethren in Missouri, and
to redeem Zion.† In the spring of 1834, therefore, about one
hundred and fifty of the brethren from the churches in the
Eastern States assembled at New Portage, Ohio, about
fifty miles from Kirtland; and this number was increased to
about two hundred by the time the camp reached Missouri.
They took with them money to purchase lands, food and
clothing to assist their destitute brethren, and it was also
the determination of the camp to help their exiled friends
maintain their possessions when the governor of Missouri
re-instated them upon their lands.‡ But *en route* to Missouri

---

*For a detailed account of this event and the causes leading up to it,
see the author's work on the "Missouri Persecutions."

†*Doc and Cov.*, sec. *ciii.*

‡Daniel Dunklin, Governor of Missouri, agreed to call out the militia
of the state and re-instate the exiles on their lands; but he claimed that
he had no authority to keep a force under arms to protect them after
they were restored. Hence the coming of Zion's camp to so strengthen
the brethren that they could hold their own against the mob when once
placed back in their homes.

the brethren did not live up to the requirement made of the camp. Some of them were disobedient, even rebellious, towards the Prophet, and the Lord was not well pleased with them.

5. As the camp approached Jackson County it was met by delegations inquiring into their designs for approaching Jackson County. Various reports had been spread abroad in respect to their intentions, and some of them were of a character to create alarm. In order to correct these false reports the brethren made the following statement:

"In the first place it is not our intention to commit hostilities against any man, or set of men; it is not our intention to injure any man's person or property except in defending ourselves.   *   *   *   It is our intention to go back upon our lands in Jackson County by order of the executive of the state, if possible. We have brought our arms with us for the purpose of self-defense, as it is well known to almost every man of the state, we have every reason to put ourselves in an attitude of defense, considering the abuse we have suffered in Jackson County. We are anxious for a settlement of the difficulties existing between us, upon honorable and constitutional principles."*

6. The brethren also made a proposition to submit their losses to a committee of impartial arbitrators, and another to buy out those of the old settlers who could not live with them. But before matters were brought to an investigation and adjustment the Lord in a revelation to the prophet,† gave instructions which led to the abandonment of any attempt at that time to redeem Zion.

7. The Lord in this revelation declared that Zion might

Missouri Persecutions.
†*Doc. and Cov., sec. cv.* The revelation was given on Fishing River, Missouri.

have been redeemed by that time, had it not been for the transgressions of his Saints. They had not been obedient to the requirements made of them. They had withheld their means, and in their hearts had said concerning the Saints in Zion, "Where is their God? Behold he will deliver them in time of trouble, otherwise we will not go up unto Zion, and we will keep our moneys." Besides these evidences of a want of faith, they lacked that unity required by the law of the celestial kingdom, and it is only through the observance of that law that Zion can be redeemed. The Lord, therefore, commanded the elders to wait a season for the redemption of Zion, until the Saints should obtain more experience, learn obedience, and until means could be raised to purchase all the lands in Jackson County that could be purchased and also in the surrounding counties; and until the Lord's army had become very great, and sanctified before him. And when this was done the Lord promised to hold his people guiltless in taking possession of that which was their own; and they should possess it forever. He had permitted the elders composing the camp to come thus far, for a trial of their faith; and now he had prepared a great endowment for them in the house which he had commanded to be built in Kirtland. Those who could stay in Missouri were to do so, but those who had left their families in the east were at liberty to return. In obedience to the commandment to await for a season the redemption of Zion, the Camp of Zion was disbanded early in the morning of the 25th of June. A number remained in Missouri, but the most of the camp returned to the east.

8. Relieved now of the immediate responsibility of redeeming Zion, the brethren who returned from Missouri and the churches in the east devoted their attention to building up Kirtland as a "Stake" of Zion, and completing the

temple, the foundation of which had been laid about a year before.* The declaration of the Lord in that revelation given on Fishing River, Missouri, to the effect that he had prepared a great endowment for the faithful elders in the house which he had commanded them to build in Kirtland, hastened the work, as they were anxious to receive those spiritual blessings.

9. **High Councils:**—Meantime the Lord had given many important revelations in respect to the Priesthood and the organization of the church. In February, 1834 —a few months previous to Zion's Camp starting for Missouri—the First High Council of the Church was organized. This council was appointed by revelation for the purpose of settling important difficulties that might arise in the church, and which could not be settled in the bishops' courts to the satisfaction of the parties.

10. The High Council is composed of Twelve High Priests, presided over by one or three presidents, as circumstances may determine. The High Council cannot act unless seven of its members are present; but seven have the power to appoint other high priests to act temporarily in the place of absent councilors. Whenever a High Council is organized, the twelve members draw lots for their places. Those who draw the even numbers—two, four, six, eight, ten, twelve— are to stand in behalf of the accused; those drawing the odd numbers in behalf of the accuser. In every case the accused has a right to half the council to prevent injury or injustice. The councilors who represent the accused and accuser respectively, do not become partisans bent on winning their case irrespective of its righteousness or justice;

---

*The corner stones of the Kirtland temple were laid on the 23rd of July, 1833.

on the contrary every man is to speak according to equity and truth; and aside from that is merely to see that each party to the issue involved has justice accorded him, and that he be not subjected to insult or injury. (Note 3, end of section.)

11. Whenever the council convenes to act on any case, the twelve councilors are to consider whether it is very difficult or not. If it be not a difficult case, then only two of the councilors, one for the accused and accuser respectively, are appointed to speak. But if the case is accounted difficult, then four are appointed to speak; if still more difficult, six; but in no case are more than six to speak. In all cases both the accuser and the accused are to have the privilege of speaking for themselves, after the evidence is all in and the councilors appointed to speak have all spoken.

12. The evidence all in, the speakers for the accused and the accuser having spoken, as also the accused and the accuser, the president gives a decision according to the understanding he has of the case and calls upon the twelve councilors to sustain it by vote. But should the councilors who have not spoken, or any one of them, discover an error in the decision of the president, they have the right to manifest it and the case has a re-hearing. If after a careful re-hearing, additional light is thrown upon the case, the decision is altered accordingly. "But in case no additional light is given, the first decision stands, the majority of the council having power to determine the same."* Such are the general outlines of the organization of a High Council and the manner of procedure before it. (Notes 4 and 5, end of section.)

13. **Different Kinds of High Councils:**—There are

---

*Doc. and Cov., sec. cii, verse 22.

three kinds of High Councils in the church.   They are similar in organization, and the manner of procedure is practically the same before them all, but they differ in authority and jurisdiction.

I.   The Traveling High Council:—This Council consists of the Twelve Apostles of Jesus Christ.   They are a traveling, presiding high council; and, laboring under the direction of the First Presidency of the Church, they have the right to build up the church, and regulate all the affairs of the same in all the world.*   Whenever they sit as a High Council, there is no appeal from their decisions—that is, they can only be called in question by the general authorities of the church in the event of transgression. †

II.   The Standing High Councils at the Stakes of Zion:— The church is divided into branches or wards with appropriate officers; and these branches, wards, and settlements of the Saints are grouped for convenience into "Stakes of Zion."   In each Stake there is a Standing High Council, limited in its jurisdiction to the affairs of that particular Stake where it is located.

III.   Temporary High Councils:—The   high   priests abroad, that is, outside of the organized Stakes of Zion, whenever the parties to a difficulty, or either of them request it, and the high priests abroad deem the case of sufficient importance to justify such action, are authorized to organize a Temporary High Council to try the case, appointing one of their own number to preside over the council during its continuance.   Otherwise the council is to be organized after the pattern and proceed in the same manner as those at the Stakes of Zion.   "It shall be the duty of said

---

*Doc. and Cov., sec. cvii: 23-33.
†Doc. and Cov., sec. cii: 30-32, also sec. cvii: 32.

council to transmit immediately a copy of its proceedings, with a full statement of the testimony accompanying their decision, to the High Council of the seat of the First Presidency of the Church. Should the parties, or either of them, be dissatisfied with the decision of said council, they may appeal to the High Council of the seat of the First Presidency of the Church, and have a re-hearing, which case shall then be conducted according to the former pattern written, as though no such decision had been made."*

14. **Organization of the Quorum of Twelve Apostles:**—As early as June, 1829, the Lord revealed that there would be twelve especial witnesses or apostles called to preach the gospel to the nations of the earth. But it was not until several months after the prophet returned from the Zion's Camp expedition that such a quorum was organized. In the month of February, 1835, however, a general conference was called, and the three especial witnesses to the Book of Mormon selected the men—under the inspiration of the Holy Ghost, for they were appointed to that mission by revelation—who were to constitute the quorum of the Twelve Apostles† or Especial Witnesses.

15. **Organization of Quorums of Seventies:**—In the same month—February, 1835—the first quorum of seventies was organized by the Prophet Joseph and his two counselors and others. Shortly afterwards the second quorum was also organized. These quorums, as would be inferred from their being called "seventies' quorums," consist of seventy men. Seven presidents preside over each quorum, and the first Seven Presidents—the presidents of the first quorum—

---

*Doc. and Cov., sec. cii: 26, 27.

†Their names were Lyman E. Johnson, Brigham Young, Heber C. Kimball, Orson Hyde, David W. Patten, Luke S. Johnson, Wm. E. McLellin, John F. Boynton, Wm. B. Smith, Parley P. Pratt, Thomas B. Marsh, Orson Pratt.

preside over all the quorums of seventy in the church.

16. About a month after the organization of these quorums—28th of March, 1835—a revelation was given,[*] in which the duties of the apostles and seventies are made clear, as well as the duties of other officers.[†] We have now, however, reached a point in the historical development of the Church of Christ in the New Dispensation, where we can consider it as a system of ecclesiastical government; and to that consideration the next section is devoted.

---

[*]*Doc. and Cov., sec. cvii.*

[†]The circumstances under which this revelation (contained in section cvii, Doc. and Cov.) was given are highly interesting; they are as follows: On the afternoon of the 28th of March the twelve met in council and had a time of general confession. "On reviewing our past course," writes Orson Hyde and Wm. E. McLellin, clerks of the meeting, "we are satisfied, and feel to confess also, that we have not realized the importance of our calling, to that degree that we ought; we have been light minded and vain, and in many things done wrong—*wrong.* For all these things we have asked the forgiveness of our Heavenly Father; and wherein we have grieved or wounded the feelings of the Presidency, we ask their forgiveness. The time when we are about to separate is near, and when we shall meet again, God only knows; we therefore feel to ask of him whom we have acknowledged to be our Prophet and Seer, that he inquire of God for us and obtain a revelation (if consistent) that we may look upon it when we are separated, that our hearts may be comforted. Our worthiness has not inspired us to make this request, but our unworthiness. We have unitedly asked God our Heavenly Father to grant unto us through his Seer, a revelation of his mind and will concerning our duty the coming season, even a great revelation, that will enlarge our hearts, comfort us in adversity and brighten our hopes amidst the power of darkness." (Mill. Star, vol. xv., p. 245.) The revelation which was given in answer to this request is one of the most splendid contained in the Book of Doctrine and Covenants.

NOTES.

1.   Character of the Old Settlers in Jackson County:—Speaking of his arrival in Independence and meeting with Oliver Cowdery and other brethren there, the Prophet Joseph says: "It seemed good and pleasant for brethren to meet together in unity. But our reflections were great, coming as we had from a highly cultivated state of society in the east, and standing now upon the confines and western limits of the United States, and looking into the vast wilderness of those that sat in darkness; how natural it was to observe the degradation, leanness of intellect, ferocity and jealousy of a people that were nearly a century behind the time and to feel for those who roamed about without the benefit of civilization, refinement or religion; yea, and to exclaim in the language of the prophets, 'when will the wilderness blossom as a rose? When will Zion be built up in her glory, and where will thy temple stand, unto which all nations shall come in the last days?' " *Missouri Persecutions—Roberts.*

2.   Persecution in Jackson County:—The month of November, 1833, was big with important events for the members of the Church in Jackson County. That month witnessed the expulsion of twelve hundred American citizens from their homes, and from the lands which they had purchased from the general government. The events of that month branded the sovereign state of Missouri with an infamy that will cling to her as long as the name is remembered on earth or in heaven; and when her officials of that period shall stand before the bar of God, blood will be found on their ministerial vestments—it will be the stain, too, of innocent blood! * * * Early in the spring the mob burned the houses belonging to the Saints. According to the testimony of Lyman Wight (*Times and Seasons* for 1843, p. 264,) two hundred and three dwelling houses and one grist mill were so destroyed.—*Missouri Persecutions—Roberts.*

3.   Fair Dealing in High Councils:—The council should try no case without both parties being present, or having had an opportunity to be present; neither should they hear one party's complaint before his case is brought up for trial; neither should they suffer the character of any one to be exposed before the high council without the person being present and ready to defend him or herself; that the minds of the councilors be not prejudiced for or against any one whose case they may possibly have to act upon.—*Joseph Smith, Hist., under date of July 11, 1840.*

4.   Order in High Councils:—In ancient days councils were conducted with strict propriety; no one was allowed to whisper, be weary, leave the room or get uneasy in the least until the voice of the Lord by revelation, or the voice of the council by the spirit was obtained. * * * It was understood in ancient days that if one man could stay in the council, another could; and if the President could spend his time, the members could also.—*Joseph Smith, Hist, under date of Feb. 12, 1834.*

5. Just Judgment Demanded in High Councils:—No man is capable of judging a matter in council unless his own heart is pure; and we frequently are so filled with prejudice, or have a beam in our own eye, that we are not capable of passing right decisions. * * * Our acts are rendered, and at a future day they will be laid before us; and if we should fail to judge right, and injure our fellow beings, they may be there perhaps, and condemn us. There they are of great consequence, and to me the consequence appears to be of force beyond anything which I am able to express.—*Joseph Smith, Hist., under date of Feb.* 12, 1834.

REVIEW.

1.   What can you say of the opposition which the work of God has met with in these last days?

2.   Where did the first general persecution of the church begin?

3.   What was the character of the people in western Missouri? (Note.)

4.   Relate the expulsion of the saints from Jackson County.

5.   What event brought Zion's camp into existence?

6.   Relate its history.

7.   What prevented Zion's camp from redeeming Zion?

8.   When was the first High Council organized?

9.   For what purpose are such councils organized?

10.   Describe the organization of the High Council.

11.   What are the privileges of the accused and accuser before the council?

12.   What rule obtains as to the decision of the president of the council?

13.   What is to be the course of the High Council in respect to deportment, fair dealing and judgment?   (See notes 3, 4 and 5.)

14.   How many kinds of high councils are there?

15.   Describe each.

16.   When did the Lord first reveal that there would be a quorum of Twelve Apostles called?

17.   When and in what manner were the members of this quorum selected?

18.   When were seventies quorums first organized?

19.   State what you can concerning the presidency of the seventies' quorums.

SECTION V.

1. Priesthood:—Priesthood is power which God gives to man, by which man becomes an agent of God; an authorized officer in his kingdom, with the right and power to teach the laws of the kingdom, and administer the ordinances by which foreigners and aliens are admitted to citizenship. It gives man the right and power to act in God's stead,—thus: If a man endowed with the proper degree of the priesthood takes one who believes the gospel and baptizes him for the remission of sins in the name of the Father, Son and Holy Ghost, the act of that authorized servant of God is just as valid as if the Lord Jesus Christ himself did it, and remission of sins will follow. So also if an authorized servant of God lays on hands to impart the Holy Ghost, the Holy Ghost will be given, inasmuch as all is done as the law of the Lord directs. So in preaching, exhorting, warning; whether it be by God's own voice, or the voice of his servants, it is the same.* Man through receiving the priesthood becomes God's agent; and the Lord is bound to recognize the ministrations of his agents so long as they act in accordance with the terms by which they hold that agency. Such is priesthood.

2. Spirit of Government by the Priesthood:—The government of the priesthood is exercised through the channels of love, knowledge and righteousness. The rights of the priesthood are inseparably connected with the powers of heaven, and the powers of heaven can only

---

*Doc. and Cov,. sec. i: 38.

be controlled upon the principles of righteousness.* No power can or ought to be maintained by virtue of the priesthood, only by persuasion, by long-suffering, by gentleness and meekness and by love unfeigned; by kindness and pure knowledge, which shall greatly enlarge the soul without hypocrisy and without guile; reproving betimes with sharpness, when moved upon by the Holy Ghost, and then showing forth afterwards an increase of love, lest those reproved esteem those reproving as enemies.† Such is the *spirit* of government under the priesthood: it may be summed up in this: men are to be taught correct principles and then be governed by them.‡

3.   The Church:—From the gospel and the priesthood comes the church. The church is the medium through which the gospel is promulgated—by which it is made known among the children of men, and administered. It is the system of government by which those who accept the gospel are controlled in things religious.   It is the government of

---

*Doc. and Cov., sec. cxxi: 36.

†Doc. and Cov. sec. cxxi: 41-44.   These views from the revelations of the Lord to Joseph Smith are in strict accord with the teachings of Jesus Christ to the twelve apostles among the Jews.   To them he said: "Ye know that the princes of the Gentiles exercise dominion over them, and they that are great, exercise authority upon them.   But it shall not be so among you; but whosoever will be great among you, let him be your minister; and whosoever will be chief among you, let him be your servant; even as the Son of Man came not to be ministered unto but to minister, and to give his life a ransom for many."   (Matt. xx. 25-28.)   Peter it would seem remembered the spirit of these instructions, as years afterwards we have him saying to those set to govern the churches: "Feed the flock of God which is among you, taking the oversight thereof, not by constraint, but willingly; not for filthy lucre, but of a ready mind; neither as being lords over God's heritage, but being ensamples unto the flock."   (I Peter v: 2, 3.)

‡This it appears is the view Joseph Smith took of the subject.   Replying to a question of Judge Stephen A. Douglas, how he governed so easily so large a people as the saints were at Nauvoo, the prophet replied, "I teach them correct principles and they govern themselves."

God on earth pertaining to religious affairs. The Lord hath clothed it with his authority, which is his power; and it hath authority not only to teach the gospel, but to execute its laws, and inflict the penalties attached to a violation thereof—at least so far as dealing with the membership of transgressors is concerned; as for other penalties that will fall upon the violators of divine law, the Father hath reserved that to himself, and will in his own time and way vindicate his own laws, having due regard to the relative claims of justice and mercy. The authority of the church comes from the priesthood, and may be said to be the collected authority of all the quorums of the priesthood combined—the aggregation of God's authority in the earth, in relation to things religious. Such is the church.

4. **"Divisions" of the Priesthood:**—In the church of Christ there are two grand divisions of priesthood; or rather its powers are grouped under two great heads—for all priesthood comes from God, is power from him, and therefore cannot properly be regarded as two different priesthoods.* The two divisions of priesthood are named respectively the Melchisedek Priesthood† and the Aaronic Priesthood.‡ The Melchisedek Priesthood ministers more especially in spiritual things; it holds the keys of all the spiritual blessings of the church, is entitled to receive the mysteries of the king-

---

*In answering the question: Was the Priesthood of Melchisedek taken away when Moses died, the Prophet Joseph said: "All priesthood is Melchisedek, but there are different portions or degrees of it. The portion which brought Moses to speak with God face to face was taken away; but that which brought the ministry of angels remained." (*Hist. of Joseph Smith. See also Doc. and Cov., sec. cxii: 4, 5.*

†The reasons for calling this first division the Melchisedek Priesthood are given in note 3, section ii of Part IV.

‡The reason for calling the second division the Aaronic Priesthood, is because it was a priesthood conferred upon Aaron, the brother of Moses, and his sons after him. It is a division of the priesthood which belongs of right to the house of Aaron. (See Doc. and Cov. sec. cvii: 13, 14.)

dom of heaven, to commune with the church of the First Born, and enjoy the communion and presence of God the Father, and his Son Jesus Christ.* The Aaronic Priesthood ministers more especially in temporal things; it holds the keys, however, of the ministering of angels and the baptism of repentance for the remission of sins.†

5. **Officers of the Priesthood:**—The officers of the Melchisedek Priesthood are Apostles, Seventies, Patriarchs, High Priests, Elders. The officers of the Aaronic Priesthood are Bishops, Priests, Teachers, Deacons. Of necessity there are presidents, or presiding officers growing out of, or appointed from among those who are ordained to the several offices in these two priesthoods.‡

6. **Presidencies in the Melchisedek Priesthood—First Presidency:**—Since of necessity there are presiding officers growing out of the priesthood, there is a president appointed from the High Priesthood to preside over that priesthood. He is called President of the High Priesthood of the Church; or, the "Presiding High Priest over the High Priesthood of the Church."§ This President of the High Priesthood also presides over the whole church; he is a seer, a revelator, a translator and a prophet, having all the gifts of God which he bestows upon the head of the church.‖ Two other High Priests,¶ associated with the President of

---

*Doc. and Cov. sec. cvii: 18-19.
†Doc. and Cov., sec. cvii: 20.
‡Doc. and Cov., sec. cvii: 21.
§Doc. and Cov., sec. cvii: 65-66.
‖Ibid, verse 91, 92.
¶It must be remembered by the student that apostles are also high priests. (Doc. and Cov. Sec. 84:63.) In fact the apostleship circumscribes all priesthood, hence it happens that some men who have not been directly ordained high priests, but who were apostles, have acted in the quorum of the first presidency of the church. Brigham Young did so.

the High Priesthood as counselors, all being appointed and ordained to that office, and upheld by the confidence, faith and prayer of the church, form the quorum of the First Presidency of the Church;* and they preside over all quorums, over Zion and all the Stakes thereof; over all wards and branches and missions of the Church in all the world. The president in his quorum is to be like unto Moses,† therefore he is the prophet and law-giver unto the church—the mouth-piece of God unto it.

7. **The Traveling Presiding High Council:**—The Twelve Apostles, or special witnesses of the name of Christ in all the world, are a traveling, presiding High Council, and have the power to officiate in the name of the Lord, under the direction of the First Presidency of the church, to build up the church and regulate all the affairs of the same in all nations. In all large branches of the church, or the Stakes of Zion, they are authorized to ordain patriarchs, as they may be designated unto them by revelation; it is the duty of the Twelve also to ordain and set in order all other officers in the church. These Twelve Apostles form the second general presiding quorum in the church, and are equal in authority and power to the quorum of the First Presidency.‡

8. **The Presiding Quorum of Seventy:**—The Seventy are appointed to act in the name of the Lord under the direction of the Traveling High Council in building up the Church and regulating all the affairs of the same in all nations.§ The First Quorum of Seventy is presided over by seven presidents, and the senior of the seven—that is, the senior by ordination, not by age—presides over

---

*Doc. and Cov., sec. cvii: 22.
†Ibid, verse 91.
‡Doc. and Cov., sec. cvii: 23, 24, 33, 39, 58.
§Doc. and Cov., sec. cvii: 34.

the six. This quorum is equal in authority to the Traveling High Council—the quorum of the Twelve Apostles.* In addition to presiding over the First Quorum of Seventy —to which quorum they belong—the First Seven Presidents were authorized in the beginning to choose other seventy, besides the first, until seven times seventy had been chosen—if the labor in the ministry required it†— and preside over them. Each quorum has its council of seven presidents; but the First Seven Presidents preside over all these quorums and all their presidents. The seventies are special witnesses for the Lord in all the world,‡ and are especially chosen to preach the gospel abroad; the responsibility of declaring the great message of God unto the world rests upon them particularly, laboring, of course, under the direction of the Twelve; and the Twelve are to call upon the Seventy "instead" of any others, when they have need of assistance to fill the calls for preaching and administering the gospel.§

9. We have spoken of these three quorums being equal in authority; but every decision made by either of them, in order to make such decision of the same power or validity one with the other, must be by unanimous voice of the respective quorums; that is, every member in each quorum must be agreed to its decisions, or such decisions are not entitled to the same blessings as the decisions of the quorum of the First Presidency. When circumstances render it

---

*Doc. and Cov., sec. cvii, verses 25, 26.

†Up to the present date—1925—there have been two hundred and fifteen quorums of seventy organized. The Prophet Joseph Smith said that this choosing of seventies was to go on—if the labor in the vineyard required it—"even until there are one hundred and forty and four thousand thus set apart for the ministry."

‡Doc. and Cov, sec. cvii.

§Doc. and Cov., sec. cvii: 38.

impossible to be otherwise, a majority may form a quorum.*
The decisions of these quorums of course are to be made in
righteousness, in holiness and lowliness of heart.   If so made
there is no appeal from their decision; but in case that any
decision of these quorums is made in unrighteousness, it
may then be brought before a general assembly of the several
quorums of the priesthood which constitute the spiritual
authorities of the church.

10. Patriarchs:—These officers hold the keys of
blessings in the church.   The order of this priesthood was
confirmed to be handed down from father to son, and rightly
belongs to the literal descendants of the chosen seed, to
whom the promises were made.†   There is one general and
a number of local patriarchs in the church.   The first is
Patriarch to the whole church, and he may minister in any
branch or Stake in it, his jurisdiction in blessing the people
being co-extensive with the church.   He holds the keys of
the patriarchal blessings upon the heads of all the Lord's
people.   And whomsoever he blesses shall be blessed, and
whomsoever he curses shall be cursed; and whatsoever he
binds on earth shall be bound in heaven; and whatsoever he
looses on earth shall be loosed in heaven.‡   He holds the
sealing blessings of the church, "even the Holy Spirit of
promise," whereby men are sealed up unto the day of redemption; that they may not fall, notwithstanding the hour
of temptation that may come upon them.§   The local
patriarchs referred to above are patriarchs appointed and
ordained by the Apostles to hold and exercise the powers of
giving patriarchal blessings to the Saints within the branches

*Doc. and Cov., sec. cvii: 27, 28.
†Doc. and Cov. sec. cvii: 39-41.
‡Doc. and Cov., sec. cxxiv: 91-93.
§Ibid, verse 124.

and Stakes of Zion in which they are appointed to minister in this calling, but they are not to minister outside of their respective districts. Hence they are local patriarchs. They possess the same powers in blessing within the district where they are appointed to labor as the general patriarch of the church in his wider sphere.

11. **High Priests:**—The quorums of High Priests are designed to qualify those who shall be appointed standing presidents over different Stakes in Zion, and abroad.* They may travel and preach the gospel if they choose, for High Priests have power to preach and administer all the ordinances of the gospel; but their calling is more especially to preside. To them belongs the sphere of presidency in the government of the church. From these quorums, so far as the most suitable men can be found in them, are chosen men to act as bishops—where no literal descendant of Aaron can be found—the bishops' counselors; Presidents of Stakes and their counselors; and also High Counse ors. When men more suitable for these positions are found in other quorums of the priesthood, then they are ordained High Priests, and appointed to the presiding positions enumerated. In every Stake there is a High Priests' quorum, presided over by a president and two counselors. There is no specific number necessary to form a quorum of High Priests, the quorum includes all High Priests within a Stake or branch where it exists, be they many or few. The quorum organization is for convenience, for discipline, and for training its members in the art of government. Since to the High Priests belongs the sphere of government; we know of no position in the church which calls for higher qualities of heart and mind

---

*Doc. and Cov., sec. cxxiv: 133-136.

than that of High Priests. It is an office that requires the combination of wisdom and executive ability, a combination the rarest among men. The world has had untold thousands of learned men and orators, and multitudes of men with special great gifts; but it has had comparatively few blessed with that combination of gifts which make men successful rulers; and yet those qualities which make men rulers are the qualities to be looked for and developed in High Priests.

12. **Elders:**—Elder is the lowest office in the Melchisedek Priesthood. It is an office that is an appendage to the Melchisedek Priesthood.* Yet the Elder has the power to preach the gospel, baptize, lay on hands for the Holy Ghost, administer the Sacrament, and preside when there is no High Priest present. Indeed the Elder has a right to officiate in the High Priest's stead when there is no High Priest present.† Ninety-six Elders constitute a quorum.‡ The quorum is presided over by a president and two counselors, whose duty it is to instruct them in the duties of their office. There may be any number of quorums of Elders in a branch or stake of Zion, as there is no limit whatsoever in the revelations. The Elders constitute a standing ministry in Zion and her Stakes.§ They are not under obligations to travel abroad as the Seventies are; but may be called upon to preside from time to time as circumstances may require.‖

---

*Doc. and Cov., sec. lxxxiv, verse 29.
†Doc. and Cov. sec. cvii: 11.
‡Doc. and Cov., sec. cvii: 89.
§Doc. and Cov., sec. cxxiv: 137.
‖Doc. and Cov., sec. cvii: 89, 90. Ibid, sec. cxxiv: 140. For further information on duties of elders see sec. ii, Part IV, of this work.

13. **Presidencies in the Aaronic Priesthood:**—The Aaronic Priesthood, as already remarked,* has to do more especially with the temporal affairs of the Church; and the general presidency of it is the presiding bishopric of the Church. The local bishops in like manner preside over the Aaronic Priesthood within their respective districts. The powers, rights, duties and responsibilities of the bishops have been treated at some length in Section III, Part IV, under the caption **The Bishopric,** and to the paragraphs in that division the student is directed.

14. **Priests:**—Forty-eight Priests of the Aaronic order of Priesthood constitute a quorum. The president of this quorum is to be a bishop, for that is one of the duties of his calling to sit in council with this quorum and teach the members thereof their duties.† There is no limit to the number of quorums of Priests in the church; there may be such a quorum in every ward or branch.

15. **Teachers:**—Twenty-four Teachers constitute a quorum. They are presided over by a president and two counselors, who are to teach them the duties of their office.‡

16. **Deacons:**—Twelve Deacons form a quorum. The quorum is presided over by a president and two counselors, who are to instruct them in the duties of their office.§ The offices of Teacher and Deacon are appendages‖ to the Aaronic Priesthood, as the office of Elder and Bishop are appendages to the Melchisedek Priesthood.¶ What is

---

*See section iii, Part IV.

†See section ii, Part IV, under caption *Priests* for explanation of their duties and powers.

‡For explanation of the duties and powers of teachers see caption *Teachers*, section ii, Part IV.

§For explanation of their duties see caption *Deacons*, section ii, Part IV.

‖*Doc. and Cov., sec. lxxxiv:* 30.

¶*Doc. and Cov., sec. lxxxiv:* 29.

meant by "appendage" to the priesthood is an addition to the regular quorums of the priesthood. When so added they become part of the organization but in a subordinate way. The Elders may assist High Priests in their duties when called upon, and may officiate in their stead when there is no High Priest present; but when the High Priest is present the Elder has no right to act in his stead except when called upon. The Teacher may assist the Priest in his duties, as the Deacon may assist the Teacher in his duty,* but in that event the lesser quorums act in subordination to the ones they are authorized to assist. They were quorums added to the regular organization of the priesthood, when the duties were so multiplied that the higher and regular quorums could not discharge them. By creating these "appendages" to the priesthood men could be called into requisition whose wisdom and experience would not justify placing upon them *all* the authority with the accompanying responsibility of the higher offices of the priesthood.

17.   **Territorial Divisions of the Church:**—The church in relation to the territory it occupies, for convenience in government, is divided into Stakes of Zion, wards and branches.

I.   Stakes:—A Stake of Zion is a division of the church territorially that embraces several wards and branches. There is no set number of wards or branches necessary to constitute a Stake. That is arranged according to convenience. The Stake is presided over by a president, who is a High Priest, assisted by two other High Priests as counselors. They constitute the Presidency of the Stake, and preside over the whole Stake and the organizations in that Stake much in the same way that the President of the Church

---

*Doc. and Cov., sec. xx: 38-59.

presides over the entire church; but is subject of course to the general authorities of the church.

In each Stake is a Standing High Council, over which the Presidency of the Stake preside. The President alone, or either one of his counselors, may preside over the Council when circumstances render it impossible or inconvenient for more than one of the Presidency to be present. This forms the highest judicial tribunal in the Stake.

One or more Patriarchs are appointed to confer upon the people patriarchal blessings within each Stake.

The High Priests are organized into a quorum with a presidency over them as already explained.*

The Elders are organized into one or more quorums, according as they are numerous enough for one or a number of quorums;† and with the High Priests constitute the standing ministry in the Stake.

II. Wards:—The Stakes are divided into ecclesiastical wards, presided over by a Bishopric, consisting of a Bishop aided by two High Priests as Counselors, unless the Bishop is a literal descendant of Aaron, in which event he has authority to act as Bishop without counselors.‡ The Bishopric has a direct general presidency over the quorums of the lesser priesthood in his ward, and presides even over those holding the Higher Priesthood as *members* of his ward; but not over the quorums of the Higher Priesthood as quorums. The Bishopric of a ward, like the Bishopric of the church, has to do chiefly with temporal affairs; but in nearly all cases, in fact, so far as we know, in all cases at present in the church, the Bishops are high priests acting in that capacity; and since in acting as bishops they do not lose

---

*See caption *High Priests* this section.
†See caption *Elders* this section.
‡See *Bishopric*, sec. iii, Part IV.

their position as high priests they have a right to minister in both temporal and spiritual affairs. It may be well to remark, however, in passing, that wherein bishops do take the lead in spiritual concerns they do so by virtue of the High Priesthood which they hold, which is the proper authority to act in spiritual matters.

The ward officers consist of a quorum of Priests, of Teachers and of Deacons. Their powers and duties have already been explained.* They labor under the direction of the bishop, and are the standing ministers within the ward, to be with and watch over the church to see that each member thereof does his duty and that no iniquity is allowed to creep into the church, to corrupt it. At present in many wards there are not enough men to fill up the quorums of the lesser priesthood, and members of the High Priesthood are frequently found officiating as teachers, etc.

Each ward is divided up into teachers' districts, and two teachers appointed to take charge of each district, and visit every family and member within it, to see that all are doing their duty; that they live, so far as may be, in peace with all men; that they are prayerful; diligent in attending public worship; and that they are honest, sober and hold no hardness of mind or heart against their neighbors.

III. Branches:—Branches are organizations established chiefly out in the world where there are no regularly organized stakes. The elders while abroad on missions in order to preserve in the faith those who receive the gospel, organize branches, set apart elders or priests to preside, and also ordain as many other elders, priests, teachers and deacons

---

*See caption *Of the Duties of Officers, Priests, Teachers, Deacons.*

to assist the president of the branch as may be deemed necessary. These officers discharge the same duties in a branch that they would in a fully organized ward; branches are also sometimes organized in outlying districts of large wards where there are not enough people to justify a complete ward organization, and yet the district is too far removed from the ward to permit the members living there to enjoy the advantages of the adjacent ward organization. In such an event the branch is usually placed under the care of the neighboring ward.

18. Helps in Government:—In addition to these regular and direct means of ecclesiastical government in the church, there are also "helps in government," or appendages to the church organization. The chief of these are:

I. Female Relief Societies:—A women's association organized in each ward to relieve the poor in their distress, and visit the sick and afflicted. Also to afford a means of self culture and spiritual development to the members.

II. Sunday Schools:—In every ward also is a Sunday School, in which the young are taught in the gospel and educated in church discipline.

III. Y. M. and Y. L. M. I. Associations:—In nearly all wards also are Young Men's and Young Ladies' Mutual Improvement Associations for the instruction of the young in religion, science, history and literature; and, in fact, in all things that tend to the development and refinement of the mind of man; but the main object of these organizations is to establish the young of both sexes in a knowledge of the truth of the gospel.

IV. Primary Associations:—Primary Associations are ward organizations for juveniles too young to be connected with the Improvement Associations; and were established to train the young in such moral precepts and conduct as are suitable to their years.

19. **The Church Judiciary System:**—So long as men are imperfect just so long will difficulties and misunderstandings arise among them. And these things will beget bitterness of feeling, enmities and animosities unbecoming those striving to be Saints; and hence the church must be purged of these things. Moreover, although man by nature is a religious creature, he is prone to be forgetful of religious duty; and unless a wholesome church discipline be enforced he is liable to become neglectful of his religious obligations. To settle difficulties, then, which may arise between members on the one hand, and to enforce church discipline on the other, there exists in the church an ecclesiastical judiciary system, that is most admirably adapted to answer the purposes for which it exists.

20. First, as to the settlement of difficulties arising between members of the church. The law of the Lord requires that if a brother or sister offend another, the one offended should go alone to the one who gave offense and tell him his fault; if he repents and seeks forgiveness, and makes restitution, then the one offended must forgive his brother and become reconciled. In the event of the offender being stubborn and impenitent; or maintaining that he has done no wrong, then the one aggrieved should take others with him, one or more,* and in their presence, and with whatever assistance they can render, seek justice of and reconciliation with his brother. If the offender refuse to make restitution or become reconciled to his brother, then the

---

*When the difficulty arises in a regularly organized ward the most suitable persons to engage in such business would be the teachers of the respective parties, and this is usually the course followed.

matter may be taken to the bishop's court for settlement.*
Here the matter is put on trial, the statements of the respective parties received, and the testimony of witnesses
admitted and a decision rendered by the bishop according
to his understanding of the case.

21.   In the event of either party being dissatisfied with
the bishop's decision, they may appeal to the High Council
of the Stake.   But if either or both of them neither take an
appeal to the High Council nor comply with the bishop's
decision, then they stand in danger of losing their fellowship
in the church, for if men will not respect the decisions of the
ecclesiastical courts, then the officers thereof must vindicate
their decisions and make the courts respected by punishing
those who would treat them with contempt.

22.   If the case be appealed to the High Council of
the Stake, it is heard on its merits in the manner already
described in section IV, Part IV, under the caption **High
Councils**, which see.   The parties or either of them may
appeal to the First Presidency of the Church, who will
direct in what manner the case shall be disposed of; but the
parties must abide that decision or lose their standing in
the church.

23.   Now as to those who neglect their duties; who
do not so much offend against individuals as against the
church, by failing to live up to the regulations it prescribes
for its members.   It is especially the duty of the teachers,
priests and bishopric to labor very assiduously to preserve
their people in the faith, and by patient watchfulness; by
teaching and admonition; by warning and reproof, when
necessary, keep alive the spirit of the gospel in the hearts of

*See on this method of settling difficulties Matt. xviii: 15-17.   **Doc.
and Cov.** sec. xlii: 88-91.   Book of Mormon III Nephi xii: 23-25.

the Saints. If, however, in spite of all these efforts to preserve the church members in an active performance of their
duties men will grow careless and transgress the law of the
Lord, they are amenable to the church courts and may be
tried for their fellowship. In that case they would have the
same rights in the courts and quorums of the church, and
the same rights of appeal as in the case of difficulty between
members.

24. The only real punishment which is within the power
of the church to inflict is to disfellowship or excommunicate
its members. In the former case the offender is merely suspended from the privileges of church communion; this
punishment may be inflicted by the bishop, until satisfaction is made by the offender. In the latter case—excommunication—the person absolutely loses his membership
in the church, together with all the priesthood he holds; and
if he ever regains a standing it will be by baptism and confirmation as at the first.

25. Of course to those who hold lightly their standing
in the church, suspension of fellowship, or excommunication has no especial terror; but to the man of faith, whose
full hopes of eternal life with all its advantages stand or fall
with his standing in the church of Christ, no greater punishment can threaten him. He remembers that the Lord
hath said: "Woe unto them who are cut off from my church,
for the same are overcome of the world.* And, again:
"Inasmuch as ye are cut off by transgressions, ye cannot
escape the buffetings of Satan, until the day of redemption." †
The punishment, then, of excommunication is a serious one
in the estimation of the faithful; and since man in his im-

---

*Doc. and Cov. sec. 1: 8.
†Doc. and Cov. sec. clv: 9.

perfect state is influenced to righteousness by his fear of punishment, as well as by his hope of reward, the punishment of excommunication has a wholesome effect in preserving the discipline of the church.

26. Conferences of the Church:—There are two general conferences of the church each year, one convening always so as to include the 6th of April, and the other convening so as to include the 6th of October. Conferences are convened every three months in all the stakes of Zion; and in the respective wards once a year. The chief purposes of holding these conferences, aside from the giving of instructions by the general authorities, who are usually present, is to sustain by vote the officers of the church. The principle of common consent operating in the church government has already been explained;* and it only remains to say that the means by which this "common" consent is expressed— voting to sustain those proposed for the several offices— virtually amounts to an election. The elective principle in government or in societies is not only carried out by direct means; it may be carried out by indirect means. It is just as much a fact under the form of popular acceptance as of popular choice.† It is in the form of popular acceptance that the elective principle exists in the church.

27. Reflections:—If a good system for the organization and administration of authority, and an equally good system for the security of liberty is the test of a good plan of government, then this ecclesiastical government we have described must be recognized as of the very highest order. It is elaborate in organization, but simple in its operations. There is in it a most excellent assemblage of means to transmit the will of the central power into all departments of the

---

*See section ii, Part IV, paragraphs 8, 9.
†*Guizot's Hist. Civilization.*

society; and, on the other hand, an equally efficient assemblage of means for transmitting the response of the society to the central organized power. And as the whole government exists by the common consent of the church members, and elections by popular acceptance are frequent, the liberties of the people composing the church are secured. Where these facts exist, the highest order of government must result. And we may say, in conclusion, that the formation of a free ecclesiastical government on so extensive a scale is one of the most interesting problems of humanity. "It requires such refined prudence [to form such a government], such comprehensive knowledge, and such perspicacious sagacity, united with such almost illimitable powers of combination, that it is nearly in vain to hope for qualities so rare to be congregated in a solitary mind.* Indeed it is in vain to hope for these powers in an uninspired mind. It is a task too difficult for mere human ingenuity. And when it is remembered that Joseph Smith's knowledge of government and history in his early life was exceedingly limited; and that this system of church government was given piecemeal—as will be seen by its gradual development as portrayed in this work†—it is absurd to accredit it to a mere youth's native ingenuity. It was not a system marked out in theory and then organized. On the contrary, line was given upon line, precept upon precept. An officer was given today and his duties explained; another given at another time, when the development of the work required his services, and his duties explained. After a lapse of years men began to discover that these fragments of government constituted a most elaborate yet simple system—a consistent

---

*Remarks of Disraeli on the formation of government in his *Vindication of the English Constitution*.
†That is Part IV of this work.

whole, based on the highest and truest principles of government; a system that while it was suited to the conditions of the church in the earlier years of its existence, yet is capable of answering the needs of the organization should it be so expanded as to fill the earth.   This is a fact as astonishing to the world as it is gratifying to the Saints.   The church is its own witness that the mind which fashioned it is divine.   It is too great in its organization, and yet too simple in its administration to be the creation of an uninspired mind, especially of a mind so narrow in its knowledge and inexperienced in affairs related to government as that of Joseph Smith.   No, neither the hand of man nor the mind of man created it; it came from God, and bears the impress of its divine creation.

REVIEW.

1.   What is priesthood?
2.   What is the spirit of the government by the priesthood?
3.   For what was the church instituted?
4.   What powers and authority appertains unto it?
5.   How is the Priesthood divided?
6.   Why was the higher priesthood named after Melchisedek? (Note 3.)
7.   What are the powers of the Melchisedek Priesthood—of the Aaronic?
8.   Enumerate the officers of the respective priesthoods.
9.   What constitutes the First Presidency of the Church?
10.   What are the rights and powers of the First Presidency?
11.   What are the rights and powers of the Twelve Apostles?
12.   What is the mission and calling of the Seventies?
13.   What are the duties and the special calling of the Patriarchs?
14.   What are the powers and special duties of the High Priests—of Elders?
15.   What can you say of Presidencies in the Aaronic Priesthood?
16.   What are the privileges and duties of Priests?—of Teachers?—of Deacons?
17.   What is the significance of "appendage" in connection with priesthood?
18.   What can you say of the territorial divisions of the church?

19. Describe the Stake organization—the organization of the ward —of the branch.

20. What institutions are recognized as helps in government?

21. What can you say of the church judiciary system?

22. State how difficulties are to be settled in the church.

23. What are the means of punishment legitimately within the right of the church to exercise?

24. What can you say of the effectiveness of church punishment?

25. What regular conferences are held by the church?

26. What can be said of the church as an ecclesiastical system of government?

SECTION VI.

Having paused to consider the church as a system of ecclesiastical government, it now remains for us to return to the historical development of the work of the Lord as connected with the dispensation of the fullness of times.

1. **The Kirtland Temple:**—During the winter of 1835-36 the temple at Kirtland was completed. This was the first temple built by the church in this dispensation. It was a stone structure, eighty by sixty, and fifty feet to the square. At the front was a tower one hundred and ten feet high. There were two main halls fifty-five by sixty-five feet; four vestries in the front, two on each floor. There was also an attic, divided into five rooms. During the winter of 1835-6, a high school was conducted in Kirtland by H. M. Hawes, Professor of Greek and Latin,* and the rooms in the attic were used as class rooms and for the meetings of the various quorums of the priesthood. (See note 1, end of section.)

2. **Dedication of the Temple:**—On Sunday, the 27th of March, 1836, the temple was dedicated with imposing ceremonies, beginning early in the morning—eight o'clock —and continuing all day. As all the Saints could not be admitted at once, the Thursday following, March 31st, the ceremonies were repeated. The service consisted of singing,

---

*Besides the classic, there was an English department that included a course in common and higher mathematics, geography, English grammar, reading and writing. Hebrew was taught by Professor Seixas, a Jew, and the Elders made considerable progress in that language. These items are interesting as showing that "Mormonism" is not and was not even in the beginning of its career, opposed to education as many have claimed.

prayer, preaching, prophesying, speaking in tongues, sustaining the several officers of the church by votes of acceptance and confidence, the offering of a special dedicatory prayer,* partaking of the Lord's Supper, rendering the grand shout of Hosanna,† etc.   The Spirit of the Lord was poured out in great power upon the Saints, and spiritual manifestations were abundant.

3.   **Spiritual Manifestations in the Temple:**—Frederick G. Williams, Counselor in the First Presidency, testified that while Elder Rigdon was making the opening prayer, an angel entered the window, and took a seat between himself and Patriarch Joseph Smith, father of the prophet, and remained there during the prayer.

David Whitmer, one of the three especial witnesses to the Book of Mormon, also saw angels in the house.

Apostle Brigham Young gave a brief address in tongues.

Apostle David W. Patten, interpreted the address, and gave an exhortation in tongues himself.

At a meeting in the evening George A. Smith—afterwards an Apostle and Counselor to President Brigham Young—arose and began to prophesy, when a noise was heard like the sound of a rushing mighty wind, which filled the temple, and all the congregation simultaneously arose, being moved upon by an invisible power; many began to

---

*The prayer will be found in the Doc. and Cov. sec. cix.   It was given by revelation to the prophet.

†The shout of hosanna consists in the whole congregation shouting with all the strength of their voices—accompanying it with the waving of handkerchiefs—these words: **Hosanna! Hosanna! Hosanna! to God and the Lamb! Amen! Amen! Amen!** Those who have witnessed this shout of praise and gladness to God by a large congregation of saints, will never forget the power and heavenly influence that accompanies it.

speak in tongues, and prophesy; others saw glorious visions. The Prophet Joseph saw that the temple was filled with angels, which fact he declared to the congregation. The people of the neighborhood came running together—hearing an unusual sound within, and seeing a bright light like a pillar of fire resting upon the temple—and were astonished at what was transpiring.

Wednesday night—30th March—while the meeting in the temple was in charge of the Twelve Apostles, the brethren continued exhorting, prophesying and speaking in tongues all night. The Savior made his appearance to some, while angels ministered to others, and it was a Pentecost and an endowment long to be remembered.*

4. **Restoration of the Keys of Former Dispensations:**—Sunday, the 3rd of April, one week following the first dedication services, there was a series of most glorious visions and revelations given in the temple. After the sacrament was administered to the congregation, the curtains dividing the main hall were dropped and the Prophet Joseph and Oliver Cowdery retired into the pulpit and bowed in solemn and silent prayer. After prayer, they both beheld the Lord Jesus Christ standing upon the breastwork of the pulpit. He announced himself as the First and the Last, the one who liveth and the one who was slain—their advocate with the Father. He declared his acceptance of the temple, and promised to appear unto his servants and speak unto them with his own voice, if the Saints would but keep his commandments, and not pollute the temple, the fame of which he declared should spread to foreign lands. †

---

*For the foregoing account of spiritual manifestations see *Hist. of the Church, Vol. II*, pp. 426-7-8.

†*Doc. and Cov. sec. cx.*

5. The Appearing of Moses:—After this vision closed, the heavens were again opened and Moses appeared before them and committed unto them the keys of the gathering of Israel from the four quarters of the earth and the leading of the ten tribes from the land of the north.*

6. The Appearing of Elias:—Then Elias appeared and committed the dispensation of the gospel of Abraham, saying that in them and in their seed all generations after them should be blessed.

7. The Appearing of Elijah:—As soon as the above vision closed, another opened before them, and Elijah the Prophet, who was taken to heaven without tasting death, stood before them, and said that the time had fully come which Malachi had spoken of, saying, that before the great and dreadful day of the Lord should come, he, Elijah, would be sent to turn the hearts of the fathers to the children, and the children to the fathers, lest the whole earth be smitten with a curse.† "Therefore," said Elijah to Joseph and Oliver, "the keys of this dispensation are committed into your hands, and by this ye may know that the great and dreadful day of the Lord is near, even at the doors."‡

NOTES.

1. Inner Courts of Kirtland Temple:—There was a peculiarity in the arrangement of the inner court which made it more than ordinarily impressive—so much so that a sense of sacred awe seemed to rest upon all who entered; not only the Saints but strangers also manifested a high degree of reverential feeling. Four pulpits stood one above another, in the center of the building, from north to south, both on the east and west ends; those on the west for the presiding officers of the Melchisedek Priesthood, and those on the east for the Aaronic: and

*Doc. and Cov. sec. cx.
†Mal. iv: 5, 6.
‡Doc. and Cov. sec. cx.

each of these pulpits was separated by curtains of white painted canvas, which were let down and drawn up at pleasure. In front of each of these two rows of pulpits was a sacrament table for the administration of that sacred ordinance. In each corner of the court was an elevated pew for the singers, the choir being distributed into four compartments. In addition to the pulpit curtains, were others, intersecting at right angles, which divided the main ground-floor wall into four equal sections, giving to each one half of one set of pulpits.—*Eliza R. Snow.*

REVIEW.

1. When was the Kirtland Temple completed?
2. Give a description of it. (Note 1.)
3. For what were the attic rooms used?
4. What branches were taught in the temple school? (Note.)
5. Describe the dedicatory services.
6. State what spiritual manifestations occurred during the dedicatory services.
7. Describe the vision of the Savior given to the Prophet Joseph and Oliver Cowdery in the temple.
8. Relate the appearing of Moses—of Elias—of Elijah.

SECTION VII.

The appearing of Moses in the Kirtland Temple and his restoring the keys for the gathering of Israel, marks the inauguration of a mighty work within the work of God, in this dispensation, and gives a reality to many of the predictions of the ancient prophets. To fully comprehend this great work it will be necessary to call the attention of the student to Israel, and a brief outline of their history.

1. Who Are Israel:—The children of Israel are the descendants of Abraham through the loins of Isaac and Jacob, taking their name, however, from the last-named patriarch, whose name was changed by an angel of the Lord from Jacob to Israel, which means a prince of God. Unto Jacob by four wives were born twelve sons—the heads of the Twelve Tribes of Israel. Joseph, Jacob's son by his wife Rachel, being his father's favorite son, was hated by his brethren, and without the father's knowledge was sold to Egyptian merchants, who carried him into their own country. His cruel brethren rent his clothing and stained it in blood, then taking it to their father represented that his son had been destroyed by a wild beast.

The Lord, however, was with Joseph in Egypt, and gave him favor in the eyes of the rulers of that land, until he became second in authority in the kingdom. Having been warned in a dream of an approaching famine, some years before it took place, Joseph, as chief minister in Egypt, laid up in store an abundance of corn, so that while famine distressed surrounding countries there was plenty of corn in Egypt, and thither the sons of Israel went to purchase food. Joseph revealed his identity to his brethren, became reconciled to them, and sent for his father and all attached to his household—about seventy souls in all—to come to him and take up their abode in Egypt. This the aged patriarch did, and ended his days there.

2. Israel Enslaved:—Some time after Joseph's death, there arose a king who knew him not, and observing that the Israelites were likely to become more numerous than the Egyptians—since they did not murder their offspring either before or at birth, as many among the Egyptians did— this monarch enslaved them and placed task masters over them, and by oppression and the destruction of their male offspring sought to prevent their increase. Finally the Lord raised up Moses and delivered them from bondage amid a splendid display of his Almighty power, and eventually settled them in the land of Canaan—the land he had promised unto Abraham as an inheritance—where they became a mighty nation.   (See note 1, end of section.)

3. Revolt of the Ten Tribes:—As a nation the Israelites reached the zenith of their splendor under the reign of David and his son Solomon. At the death of the latter, 975 B. C., the kingdom was divided. Ten tribes revolted against the oppression of Solomon's successor, his son Rehoboam, and formed the kingdom of Israel, choosing for their king Jeroboam, the son of Nebat, one of Solomon's servants. The new king—a man of great valor—established his capital at Shechem [Shek-em,] but fifty years afterwards it was removed to Samaria.

4. The Captivity of Israel—The Lost Tribes:—This kingdom of Israel continued its existence for about two hundred and fifty, years. In that time the people may be said to have departed wholly from the paths of righteousness, becoming drunken, licentious and idolatrous. So the Lord gave them up and Shalmaneser, a noted Assyrian king, made war upon them, utterly overcame them and led them captives into Assyria. From thence the Lord led many of them away into the north country, where, no man knoweth, and hence they are denominated the "Lost Tribes." Our reason for saying they were led away into the north is to be found in the fact that many predictions of the prophets plainly declare that they shall come from the land of the north, a great company, etc.;* and it must be manifest that they cannot come from the land of the north unless they are there. Messiah, when he visited the Nephites after his resurrection, plainly told them that the other tribes of the house of Israel—meaning the ten tribes—the Lord had led away out of the land;† and he also announced his intention of visiting them, and commanded the Nephites to make a record of it that a knowledge of the existence of these "other tribes" might be made known unto the Gentiles when the Nephite records should be revealed to them. These "other tribes," Messiah spoke of, he declared not to be of the land of America, nor of the land of Jerusalem, "neither in any parts of that land round about whither I have been to minister."‡

5. The Apocryphal writer Esdras, in relating one of his visions describes one of the great characters that figured in those visions as calling unto himself a peaceful people. "Those," said the angel sent to interpret the vision, "are the tribes which were carried away captives out of their own land in the time of Oseas (Hosea) the king, whom Salmanaser, the king of the Assyrians, took captive, and crossed

---

*See pages 397-8-9.
†*Book of Mormon, III Nephi xv*: 12-20.
‡*Book of Mormon, III Nephi xvi*: 1-5.

them beyond the river; so were they brought into another land. But they took counsel to themselves, that they would leave the multitude of the heathen, and go forth unto a further country where never man dwelt, that they there might keep their statutes, which they never kept in their own land. And they entered in at the narrow passage of the River Euphrates. For the Most High then showed them signs, and stayed the springs of the flood till they were passed over. For through the country there was great journey, even of a year and a half, and the same region is called Arsareth (or Ararah). Then dwelt they there until the latter time, and when they come forth again, the Most High shall hold still the springs of the river again, that they may go through; therefore sawest thou the multitude peaceable."*

6. Whatever doubt may be entertained respecting the writings of Esdras, it cannot be denied that in respect to the Ten Tribes and what became of them he is in harmony with the statement made by Jesus to the Nephites, *viz.*, that the Lord had led them away out of the land. The Most High, according to Esdras, showing them signs by staying the springs of the flood of the Euphrates, as he will do when the time comes for them to return.† He is also in harmony with the prophets who predict the return of Israel in the last days from the land in which they have been hidden by the Lord.‡ (See note 2, end of section.)

7. **The Samaritans:**—The country inhabited by the kingdom of Israel—the north half of Palestine—was taken possession of by people sent from Babylon, Persia and other countries by the Assyrian king, and these strangers, inter-

---

II Esdras xiii.
†Compare with Isaiah xi: 15, 16.
‡See prophecies quoted p. 397-8.

marrying with the few Israelites remaining in the land, after the main body of the people had been led away into captivity, became the mixed people called Samaritans, so heartily despised by the Jews.

8. **The Kingdom of Judah:**—In the civil dissensions which divided the Israelites at the death of Solomon, the tribe of Benjamin remained loyal to Judah, and may be said to have almost lost its identity in the kingdom which with Judah he formed after the revolt of the ten tribes. It was a stormy career that the kingdom of Judah experienced after the said revolt. It was subject in turn to the Egyptians, Assyrians, and Babylonians. In consequence of treachery to the last named power, Nebuchadnezzar, king of Babylon, about 586 B. C.,* besieged Jerusalem, reduced the city to the utmost extremity, captured the king, put out his eyes and led him and most of the Jews captive to Babylon. The walls of the city were thrown down, the temple rifled of its sacred vessels and the city left desolate to be inhabited by strangers. The captivity of the Jews in Babylon lasted about seventy years.† The Babylonians in the meantime had been overcome of the Persians, under Cyrus the Great, who in the first year of his reign permitted the Jews to return and rebuild the city and its walls.

9. The Jews, however, never wholly regained their independence. Being located between Syria and Egypt, their country was held in subjection as a province to one or the other of them according as now one and now the other was successful in the unhappy wars which broke

---

*I do not state this date definitely because authorities differ in respect to it; some fixing it at 588, others at 590, and still others as in the text. The difference, which is not material, arose no doubt from some giving the date at which the king of Babylon began his siege and others when it ended.

†Fifty-six according to some historians.

out between those nations. Finally Palestine became a
province of Rome, but the people were allowed the freedom
to worship God according to the teachings of Moses and their
prophets.   This was their condition at the birth and during
the lifetime of Messiah.*

10.   About forty years after the crucifixion of the Christ,
the Jews foolishly rebelled against the Roman authority,
which brought on a terrible war.   During the siege of Jerusalem, which lasted six months, over one million of the
wretched inhabitants, according to Josephus, perished of the
famine.   The remainder were either driven into exile or
sold into slavery.   The city was razed to the ground, the
temple destroyed, and in their eager search for gold the Romans tore up the very foundation, and ploughed up the site,
so that literally there was not left one stone to stand upon
another that was not thrown down.†   Since the destruction
of their city and the overthrow of their nation, the Jews have
been scattered among all nations, despised, hated, oppressed,
until all the evil that was prophesied of by Moses concerning
them‡—when they should turn away from God and his law
—came upon them.   (See note 3, end of section.)

11.   Miscellaneous Dispersions:—Besides the tribes
of Israel that were thus dispersed, there were families of
various tribes whom the Lord led away at different times
into distant lands.   Such as the family of Lehi, of the
tribe of Manasseh; and that of Ishmael, of the tribe of
Ephraim; both of which families, together with one Zoram
—of what tribe he was is not known—the Lord led to the
continent of America.   The Lord also led to the same land

*See Part I, p. 27.
†Matt. xxiv:2.
‡Deut. xxviii:15-68.   The student should read this passage in Deuter-
onomy.   It is without exception the most terrible warning and prophecy
on record.   Yet terrible as it is, it hath all overtaken Israel.

a colony that departed from Jerusalem immediately after its destruction by King Nebuchadnezzar, in the sixth century B. C., among whom was one Mulek, one of the sons of King Zedekiah, whose people founded the city of Zarahemla, and afterwards united with the Nephites.

12. **The Blood of Israel Sprinkled Among All Nations:**—The Jews since the destruction of their city and nation by the Romans, have been scattered among all nations, but they have succeeded in a remarkable manner in preserving their identity as a distinct people. Still it is not to be doubted that there are instances where Jews have married and inter-married with the Gentiles among whom they lived, and these lost their identity as Israelites, and thus the blood of Israel, unrecognized, is in the veins of many supposed to be Gentiles.

13. The tribes of Israel sent into Babylon, Assyria and the surrounding countries in like manner intermingled their blood with the people of those nations. Moreover, there are good reasons to believe that in that exodus of the ten tribes from Assyria to the north, many became discouraged and stopped by the way. Others unable to prosecute the journey also abandoned the expedition, and these that thus "halted," uniting and intermarrying with the original inhabitants of the land where they "halted," constituted those prolific races that over-ran the western division of the Roman Empire.

14. In this manner the blood of Israel has been "sprinkled" almost among all the nations of the earth, until the word of the Lord which says, "I will *sift* the house of Israel among all nations,"* has been literally fulfilled.

15. **The Gathering of Israel:**—Notwithstanding Israel

---

*Amos 1x:8, 9.

and Judah have thus been scattered, their temple destroyed and their chief city trodden down of the Gentiles, the remnant of this favored people of God, according to the promises of the Lord, are to be gathered together again and established upon the lands promised to their forefathers. The keys necessary for the inauguration of this work were given to the Prophet Joseph by Moses on the occasion, as we have seen, of his appearing to him and to Oliver Cowdery in the Kirtland Temple, and the work of the gathering of Israel has begun. I think it proper here to give some of the passages of scripture which promise this gathering.

16. **From the Bible:**—"Hear the word of the Lord, O, ye nations, and declare it in the isles afar off, and say, He that scattered Israel will gather him, and keep him as a shepherd doth his flock. For the Lord hath redeemed Jacob, and ransomed him from the hand of him that was stronger than he. Therefore they shall come and sing in the height of Zion, and shall flow together to the goodness of the Lord for wheat and for wine, and for oil, and for the young of the flock and of the herd: and their soul shall be as a watered garden, and they shall not sorrow any more at all."*

"Therefore, behold the days come, saith the Lord, that it shall no more be said, the Lord liveth that brought up the children of Israel out of the land of Egypt; but the Lord liveth that brought up the children of Israel from the land of the north, and from all the lands whither he had driven them: and I will bring them again into their land that I gave unto their fathers."†

---

*Jeremiah xxxi:10-12. See also verses **7, 8, 9.**
†Jeremiah xvi:14, 15.

"And it shall come to pass in that day* that the Lord shall set his hand again the second time to recover the remnant of his people, which shall be left from Assyria, and from Egypt, and from Pathos, and from Cush, and from Elam, and from Shinar, and from Hamath, and from the islands of the sea. And he shall set up an ensign for the nations, and shall assemble the outcasts of Israel, and gather together the dispersed of Judah from the four corners of the earth. The envy also of Ephraim shall depart, and the adversaries of Judah shall be cut off. Ephraim shall not envy Judah, and Judah shall not vex Ephraim. * * * And there shall be an highway for the remnant of his people, which shall be left from Assyria; like as it was to Israel in the day that he came up out of the land of Egypt."†

"Turn, O backsliding children, saith the Lord; for I am married unto you: and I will take you one of a city, and two of a family, and I will bring you to Zion: and I will give you pastors according to my own heart, and they shall feed you with knowledge and understanding. And it shall come to pass when ye be multiplied and increased in the land in those days, saith the Lord, they shall say no more the ark of the covenant of the Lord: neither shall it come to mind. * * * At that time they shall call Jerusalem the throne of the Lord; and all the nations shall be gathered unto it, to the name of the Lord, to Jerusalem. * * * In those days the house of Judah shall walk with the house of Israel, and they shall come together out of the land of the

---

*See the verses preceding this quotation for an explanation of the time of this occurrence, (Isaiah xi:1-10.) This is one of the passages quoted to Joseph Smith by the angel Moroni, who said also that "it was about to be fulfilled." See Pearl of Great Price, p. 51.

†Isaiah xi:10-12, 16.

north, to the land that I have given for an inheritance unto your fathers."*

17. From the Book of Mormon:—"But behold thus saith the Lord God: when the day cometh that they [the Jews—see context] shall believe in me, that I am Christ, then have I covenanted with their fathers that they shall be restored in the flesh, upon the earth, unto the lands of their inheritance. And it shall come to pass that they shall be gathered in from their long dispersion, from the isles of the sea, and from the four parts of the earth; and the nations of the Gentiles shall be great in the eyes of me, saith God, in carrying them forth to the lands of their inheritance."†

18. From the Doctrine and Covenants:—"And the Lord, even the Savior, shall stand in the midst of his people, and shall reign over all flesh. And they who are in the north countries shall come in remembrance before the Lord, and their prophets shall hear his voice, and shall no longer stay themselves, and they shall smite the rocks, and the ice shall flow down at their presence. And an highway shall be cast up in the midst of the great deep. Their enemies shall become a prey unto them, and in the barren deserts there shall come forth pools of living water; and the parched ground shall no longer be a thirsty land. And they shall bring forth their rich treasures unto the children of Ephraim, my servants. And the boundaries of the everlasting hills shall tremble at their presence. And there shall they fall down and be crowned with glory, even in Zion, by the hands of the servants of the Lord, even the children of Ephraim; and they shall be filled with songs of everlasting joy. Be-

---

*Jeremiah iii:15-19.
†Book of Mormon, II Nephi x:7, 8. See also I Nephi x:14. II Nephi vi:8-11, and also Book of Jacob v. This last reference especially should be studied.

hold, this is the blessing of the Everlasting God upon the tribes of Israel, and the richer blessing upon the head of Ephraim and his fellows. And they also of the tribe of Judah, after their pain, shall be sanctified in holiness before the Lord to dwell in his presence day and night, for ever and for ever."* (See note 4, end of section.)

19. The Preparatory Work to the Return of the Ten Tribes:—This is enough in a general way upon the return of the Ten Tribes from the north and the return of the Jews to Jerusalem. Yet there is another part of this work of gathering Israel that calls for our attention. We have described the manner in which the blood of Israel has been sprinkled among the Gentile nations. The people in whose veins that blood runs must be gathered as well as the Jews and the Ten Tribes; for the promise of gathering extends to all the children of Israel, in all the countries whither they have been scattered. Moreover, it would seem that the Ten Tribes are to come to Zion and sing in the heights thereof, and there be crowned with glory by the hands of the servants of the Lord, the children of Ephraim.† The gathering of Israel scattered among the Gentile nations will have made considerable progress, and Zion will be built up before the Ten Tribes will be brought from the north. This work of gathering Israel from among the Gentile nations is the work that the Church of Jesus Christ is now engaged in. The Lord has revealed the location of Zion;‡ it has been dedicated for the gathering together of his people Israel. Even the temple site is known and dedicated, and the sure word of God given that the temple shall be built in this

---

*Doc. and Cov., sec. cxxxiii:25-35.
†Doc. and Cov., sec. cxxxiii:32.
‡See page 342-3, this work.

generation.* The enemies of the church drove the Saints away from the consecrated land, it is true†—this in 1833; but their absence will only be temporary, the time will come when they will return and fulfill all that the Lord hath decreed in relation to Zion and its redemption.

20. Meantime they are building up stakes of Zion in the Rocky Mountain valleys, and on the Pacific slope; and in this way are fulfilling predictions of the ancient prophets. Isaiah hath it written, that "In the last days the house of the Lord shall be established in the tops of the mountains, and all nations shall flow unto it. And many people shall go and say, Come ye and let us go up to the mountain of the Lord, to the house of the God of Jacob, and he will teach us of his ways, and we will walk in his paths: for out of Zion shall go forth the law and the word of the Lord from Jerusalem."‡

21. It is remarkable how minutely the Latter-day Saints are fulfilling the terms of this prophecy:

I. They are building the temples of God in the tops of the mountains, so that the house of the Lord is truly where Isaiah saw it would be.

II. The Saints engaged in this work are people gathered from nearly all the nations under heaven, so that all nations are flowing unto the house of the Lord in the top of the mountains. (See note 5, end of section.)

III. The people who receive the gospel in foreign lands joyfully say to their relatives and friends: Come ye, and let us go up to the house of the Lord, and he will teach us of his ways and we will walk in his paths.

---

*See p. 343.

†For the particulars of the persecution which resulted in the banishment of the saints from that land, the student is referred to the author's work on the *Missouri Persecutions*.

‡Isaiah ii:2, 3.

22. The manner in which the Saints are gathered, one here and one there, one from this city and one from another, fulfills the prophecy of Jeremiah, who, in speaking of this great gathering of Israel, represents the Lord as saying: "I will take you one of a city, and two of a family, and I will bring you to Zion; and I will give you pastors according to mine heart, which shall feed you with knowledge and understanding."*

23. The student should be informed how it is we know the Saints are of the house of Israel. First, they fulfill the terms of the prophecies written about the gathering of Israel by the ancient prophets, as seen above; second, the patriarchs of the church, ordained and set apart to that calling by the apostles, in giving blessings to the Saints declare them to be of the house of Israel, and mainly of the tribe of Ephraim. (See note 6, end of section.)

24. Object of Gathering:—Another object of this gathering of the people of God from among the Gentile nations—which with their wickedness, spiritual blindness, and confusion constitute Babylon—is that they may not partake of the sins of Babylon, and that they might escape the judgments and plagues decreed by God against the wickedness thereof. The Apostle John prophesies of this. In those visions given to him on the Isle of Patmos, showing him things that would take place in the future, he heard a voice from heaven saying: "Come out of her [that is out of Babylon], my people, that ye be not partakers of her sins, and that ye receive not of her plagues, for her sins have reached unto heaven and God hath remembered her iniquities. * * * Therefore shall her plagues come in one day, death and mourning and famine; and she shall be

---

*Jeremiah iii:14, 15.

utterly burned with fire; for strong is the Lord God who judgeth her."* The Saints are gathering out of Babylon that they may escape these threatened judgments.

NOTES.

1. **Settlement of Israel in Canaan:**—Of the twelve tribes of Israel, nine and a half were located to the west and two and a half to the east of the Jordan. Into this region they had been led by Joshua, Moses being only permitted to catch a distant glimpse of the promised land. After the death of Joshua, followed the period of Judges, which lasted about five centuries. The last of the judges was Samuel, who, when the people demanded a king, anointed Saul—1095, B. C.—*Anderson's Gen. Hist.*

2. **The Departure of the Ten Tribes for the North:**—They [the ten tribes] determined to go to a country "where never man dwelt," that they might be free from all contaminating influences. That country could only be found in the North. Southern Asia was already the seat of comparatively ancient civilizations, Egypt flourished in northern Africa, and southern Europe was rapidly filling with the future rulers of the world. They had, therefore, no choice but to turn their faces northward. The first portion of their journey was not, however, north; according to the account of Esdras, they appear to have at first moved in the direction of their old home, and it is possible that they originally started with the intention of returning thereto, or probably in order to deceive the Assyrians, they started as if to return to Canaan, and when they crossed the Euphrates, and were out of danger from the hosts of the Medes and Persians, then they turned their journeying feet toward the polar star. Esdras states that they entered in at the narrow passage of the river Euphrates, the Lord staying the springs of the flood until they were passed over. The point on the river Euphrates at which they crossed would necessarily be in its upper portion, as lower down would be too far south for their purpose. The upper course of the Euphrates lies among lofty mountains near the village of Pastash; it plunges through a gorge formed by precipices more than a thousand feet in height and so narrow that it is bridged at the top; it shortly afterwards enters the plain of Mesopotamia. How accurately this portion of the river answers to the description of Esdras of the "Narrows," where the Israelites crossed !—*Reynolds' Are We of Israel, pp.* 26-27.

3. **Final Overthrow of Judah:**—According to Josephus (The Wars of the Jews vi:9, 3) 1,100,000 men fell in the siege of Jerusalem

------

*Rev. xviii:4-8.

by Titus, and 79,000 were captured in the whole war. Of the latter number, the greater part was distributed among the provinces, to be butchered in the amphitheaters or cast to wild beasts; others were doomed to work as public slaves in Egypt; only those under the ages of seventeen were sold into private bondage. An equally dreadful destruction fell upon the remains of the nation, which had once more assembled in Judea, under the reign of Hadrian (A. D. 133), which Dion Cassius concisely relates. By these two savage wars the Jewish population must have been effectually extirpated from the Holy Land itself, a result which did not follow from the Babylonian captivity. Afterwards a dreary period of fifteen hundred years' oppression crushed in Europe all who bore the name of Israel, and Christian nations have visited on their head a crime [the crucifixion of Messiah] perpetrated by a few thousand inhabitants of Jerusalem, who were not the real forefathers of the European Jews. Nor in the east has their lot been much more cheering. With a few partial exceptions, they have ever since been a despised, an oppressed and naturally a degraded people; though from them have spread light and truth to the distant nations of the earth.—*Biblical Literature (Kitto) vol I, p.* 39.

4. **All Nations Flowing Unto the House of the Lord:**—One of the features in the celebration of Pioneer Day—24th of July, 1880, the fiftieth anniversary of the day the company of Pioneers entered Salt Lake Valley, 1847—was to have represented the various nationalities composing the population of Utah. A man and a woman of each nation from which people had been gathered by the proclamation of the gospel were selected as the representatives of their nationality, each pair bearing the national colors of their country. They occupied a platform in the Tabernacle during the services, and after a historical sketch of the introduction of the gospel in the various nations was read by Orson Pratt, the representatives of the nations arose and President John Taylor said: "I wish to state to the congregation that the Lord commanded his servants to go forth to all the world to preach the gospel to every creature. We have not yet been to *all* the world, but here are *twenty-five* nations represented today, and we have thus far fulfilled our mission."

5. **The Latter-day Saints of Israel:**—The set time was come for God to gather Israel, and for his work to commence upon the face of the whole earth; and the elders who have arisen in this church and kingdom are actually of Israel. Take the elders who are in this house [the old Tabernacle in Salt Lake City] and you can scarcely find one out of a hundred but what is of the house of Israel. * * * Will we go to the Gentile nations to preach the gospel? Yes, and gather out the Israelites wherever they are mixed among the nations of the earth. * * * Ephraim has become mixed with all the nations of the earth, and it is Ephraim that is gathering together. It is Ephraim that I have been searching for all the days of my preaching, and that is the blood which ran in my veins when I embraced the gospel. If there are any of the other tribes of Israel mixed with the Gentiles we are also searching after them.—*Brigham Young. From a Discourse preached April 8th,* 1855.

REVIEW.

1. What great work did the visit of Moses to the Kirtland Temple inaugurate?

2. Who are Israel?

3. Give a sketch of the history of Israel to the revolt of the ten tribes.

4. How came the ten tribes to revolt?

5. Give an account of the fall of the kingdom of·Israel.

6. Why are the ten tribes called the "lost tribes?"

7. What evidence have you that they are in the North?

8. Give the evidence to be found in the words of Jesus to the Nephites.

9. What statement does the Apocryphal writer Esdras make respecting the ten tribes?   (Note 2.)

10. Who were the Samaritans?

11. What tribes formed the kingdom of Judah?

12. Give an outline of the history of Judah to the birth of Messiah?

13. What befell Judah about thirty years after the crucifixion of Messiah?   (Note 3.)

14. What can you say of miscellaneous dispersions?

15. How came the blood of Israel "sprinkled" among all nations?

16. What promises are made to scattered Israel?

17. Quote the several passages from the Bible which predict the gathering of Israel.

18. Quote the passages from the Book of Mormon.

19. What progress has been made in the preparatory work of the gathering of Israel?

20. What prophecies are the Saints minutely fulfilling in gathering together in the mountains?   (Note 4.)

21. How do we know that the Latter-day Saints are of Israel? (Note 5.)

22. For what object are the Saints gathering from Babylon?

SECTION VIII.

1. Salvation for the Dead:—The appearing of Elijah the prophet, in the Kirtland Temple on the 3rd of April, 1836, was the introduction of another great work connected with the redemption of the human race. That work is Salvation for the Dead, the keys of which were given to the Prophet Joseph Smith by Elijah, on the occasion of the appearing mentioned above. That event was an epoch in the history of this great dispensation. It began a revolution in the eschatology (es-ca-tol-o-ji)* of the Christian world. Up to that time—1836—it was universally believed by orthodox Christians that the souls of men who died without conversion to the Christian religion, were everlastingly lost. It was believed that the application of the Gospel of Jesus Christ was limited to this life; and those who failed, through whatever cause, to obtain the benefits of the means of salvation it affords, are for ever barred from such benefits. "If the tree fall toward the south, or toward the north, in the place where the tree falleth, there it shall lie;"† and they argued from this that in whatever state a man died so he remained. If he died in a state of justification, his salvation was assured; but if not, then justification, and consequently salvation, was forever beyond his hope.

2.   This sectarian doctrine which does so much violence to the justice of God—since it closes the door of salvation against so many millions of God's children through no other

*Treats of death, resurrection, immortality, the end of the world, final judgment, and the future state of man.
†Eccl. xi.

circumstance than that they never so much as heard of the gospel of Jesus Christ, and therefore could not either believe or obey it—arose, first, through a misconception of the doctrine of eternal punishment with which the wicked are threatened in the scriptures; and, second, through a very narrow conception of the sure mercies of God.

3. **Christian Dogma of Eternal Judgment:**— Christians believed that to receive eternal punishment was to be punished eternally. This popular Christian error was corrected in a revelation to Martin Harris through Joseph Smith, even before the church was organized.* In that revelation it is explained that God is "Endless," that is one of his names; as also is "Eternal" one of his names.

"Therefore, eternal punishment is God's punishment; Endless punishment is God's punishment."

In other words, the punishment that will overtake the wicked is Eternal's punishment; Endless's punishment. But Christians, mistaking the *name of punishment* for the sign of its duration, taught that men were punished eternally for the sins committed in this life. Then, again, God's punishment is eternal; that is, punishment always exists; it is eternal as God is, but the transgressor receives only so much of it, endures it only so long, as may be necessary to satisfy the reasonable claims of justice, tempered with mercy. Then, when the insulted law is vindicated, the offender is released from the punishment. But as "the bars survive the captive they enthrall;" as the prison remains after the transgressor has served his time in it; so in God's government, the punishment eternally remains after transgressors have satisfied the claims of justice, and are relieved from its pains and penalties. But the punishment remains to vindicate the

---

*The revelation was given March, 1830; *Doc. and Cov. sec. xix.*

law of God whenever it shall be broken. But men read—
"He that believeth not [the gospel] shall be damned,"*
and they were taught to believe that men were damned to
all eternity—that they were consigned forever to the flames
of hell without hope of relief.† (See note 1, end of section.)

4. One would think that anything like right conceptions
of the attributes of justice and mercy, as they exist in God,
would lead men to the rejection of the horrible dogma of
eternal punishment as taught by orthodox Christianity.
But if that be not sufficient then the scriptures themselves
refute it, as will appear in the following paragraphs:

5. Preaching to the Spirits in Prison:—From a

---

*Mark xvi:16.

†The so-called early fathers of the church, Justin Martyr, Clement,
of Alexandria, Tertullian and Cyprian all taught that the fire of hell
is a real material flame, and that the wicked were punished in it eternally. Augustine in the fifth century stated the same doctrine with
great emphasis and argued against those who sought to modify it.
(See *Augustine's City of God.* Part II, book xx, and xxi.)

Thomas Aquinas (A-kwi-nas) of the mediaeval school of theologians,
rising head and shoulders above divines of his day, teaches in his *Sum-
ma Theologia*, that the fire of hell is of the same nature as ordinary fire,
though with different properties; that the place of punishment though
not definitely known is probably under the earth. He also taught that
there was no redemption for those once damned, their punishment is
to be eternal.

Coming to more modern times, we read in the Westminster Confession of Faith—adopted in the seventeenth century by the Puritan
party in England—the following on the subject (ch. xxxiii): "The
wicked who know not God, and obey not the Gospel of Jesus Christ,
shall be cast into eternal torment and be punished with everlasting
destruction from the presence of the Lord and from the glory of His
power." Question twenty-nine of the larger catechism and the answer
to it are as follows: "What are the punishments of sin in the world to
come. Ans. The punishments of sin in the world to come are everlasting separation from the comfortable presence of God, and most
grievous torment in soul and body, without intermission, in hell fire
forever." The Westminster Confession and the larger catechism are
still the standards of the Presbyterian churches. Indeed the above
expresses the orthodox Christian faith, from the second and third centuries until the present time.

remark made in the writings of the Apostle Peter,* we learn that after Messiah was put to death in the flesh "He went and preached to the spirits in prison, which sometime [aforetime] were disobedient, when once the long-suffering of God waited in the days of Noah." During the three days, then, that Messiah's body lay in the tomb at Jerusalem, his spirit was in the world of spirits preaching to those who had rejected the preaching of righteous Noah. The Christian traditions no less than the scriptures teach that Jesus went down into hell and preached to those there held in ward. (See note 2, end of section.)

6. Not only is the mere fact of Messiah's going to the spirit-prison stated in the scripture, but the purpose of his going there is learned from the same source. "For this cause was the gospel preached also to them that are dead, that they might be judged according to men in the flesh, but live according to God in the spirit."† This manifestly means that these spirits who had once rejected the counsels of God against themselves, had the gospel again preached to them, and had the privilege of living according to its precepts in the spirit life, and of being judged according to men in the flesh, or as men in the flesh are judged; that is, according to the degree of their faithfulness to the precepts of the gospel.

7. Naturally the question arises why was the gospel preached to the spirits in prison who had once been disobedient if there were no means by which it could be applied to them for their salvation? We can scarcely suppose that Messiah would preach the gospel to them if it could do them no good. He did not go there to mock their sufferings, or

---

*I Peter iii:18-21. ,
†I Peter iv:6.

to add something to the torture of their damnation by explaining the beauties of that salvation now forever beyond their reach! Such a supposition would at once be revolting to reason, insulting to the justice of God, and utterly repugnant to the dictates of mercy!

8.   Following that question comes another: If the gospel is preached again to those who have once rejected it, how much sooner will it be presented to those who have never heard it, who have lived in those generations when the gospel and the authority to administer its ordinances were not in the earth? Seeing that those who once rejected the offer of salvation had it presented to them again—after paying the penalty of their first disobedience—it would seem that those who lived when it was not upon the earth, or who when it was upon the earth perished in ignorance of it, will much sooner come to salvation.

9.   Of the things we have written, this is the sum: (1) The gospel was preached by Messiah to the spirits in prison who had rejected the teachings of Noah; therefore there must be some means through which its precepts and ordinances may be applied to them.   (2) If the gospel can be made available to those who once rejected the proffered mercies of God, its privileges will much sooner, and doubtless more abundantly, be granted to those who died in ignorance of it.

10. Baptism for the Dead:—The manner in which the ordinances of the gospel may be administered to those who have died without receiving them is hinted at by Paul. Writing to the Corinthians on the subject of the resurrection, —correcting those who said there was no resurrection—he asks: "What shall they do which are baptized for the dead, if the dead rise not at all? Why are they then baptized for

the dead?"* In this the apostle manifestly referred to a practice which existed among the Christian saints of the living being baptized for the dead, and argues from the existence of that practice that the dead must rise, or why the necessity of being baptized for the dead. Though this is the only passage in the New Testament, or in the whole Bible, that refers directly to the subject of baptism of the dead, yet of itself it is sufficient to establish the fact that such a principle was known among the ancient saints. (See notes 3 and 4, end of section.)

11. From the revelations of God to the church in this dispensation the following may be learned: Elijah, in fulfillment of ancient prophecy, appeared unto Joseph Smith and Oliver Cowdery, and delivered to them those keys or powers of the priesthood which give to the living the right to do a work for the salvation of the dead. As a consequence the hearts of the children are turned to the fathers; and of course, since the fathers in the spirit world through the preaching of the gospel learn that it is within the power of their children to do a work for them, their hearts are turned to the children, and thus the predicted result to follow Elijah's mission is fulfilled.

12. The work that the living may do for the dead is that of attending to outward ordinances—baptisms, confirmations, ordinations, washings; anointings and sealings— all being appointed by revelation and the direction of the Lord, and all sealed and ratified by the power of the priesthood of God, which has power to bind on earth and in heaven. It is required that all baptisms and other ordinances of the gospel performed for the dead be attended to in houses— and more properly in temples—specially dedicated for holy

---

*I Cor. xv:29.

purposes. Those ordinances are to be faithfully recorded by those who see and hear them performed,* that there may be valid testimony that the work has been done. These ordinances attended to on earth by the living, and accepted in the spirit world by those for whom they are performed, will make them a potent means of salvation to the dead and of exaltation to the living, since they become in very deed "saviors upon Mount Zion."

This work that can be done for the dead enlarges one's view of the gospel of Jesus Christ. One begins to see indeed that it is the "everlasting gospel;" for it runs parallel with man's existence both in this life and in that which is to come. It vindicates the character of God, for by it we may see that justice and judgment, truth and mercy are in all his ways. (See note 5, end of section.)

13. **Different Degrees of Glory:**—Closely associated with the subjects treated in the foregoing paragraphs of this section, is the subject of the Different Degrees of Glory. Nothing is more clearly stated in holy writ than that men will be judged and rewarded according to their works.† And as their works vary in degree or righteousness so will their rewards vary, and so will they have bestowed upon them different degrees of glory according as their works shall merit and their intelligence be capable of comprehending. Messiah said to his disciples: "In my Father's house are many mansions: if it were not so I would have told you. I go to prepare a place for you; * * * that where I am there ye may be also."‡ Still it is commonly held among Christian sects that he who attains heaven partakes immediately of the highest glories; while he who misses heaven

---

*Doc. and Cov. sec. cxxvii and cxxviii.
†Rom. ii:6-12. I Cor. iii:8. II Cor. v:10. Rev. ii:23. Rev. xx:12.
‡St. John xiv:1-3.

goes direct to hell and partakes of all its miseries forever.* Yet nothing is clearer than the fact that there are different heavens spoken of in scripture and different degrees of glory. When Solomon dedicated the temple he had builded, he exclaimed in his prayer—"Behold the heaven and heaven of heavens cannot contain thee; how much less this house which I have builded!" † Paul in writing to the Corinthians says "I knew a man in Christ about fourteen years ago * * * such an one caught up to the *third* heaven. And I knew such a man * * * how that he was caught up into Paradise, and heard unspeakable words, which it is not lawful for a man to utter." ‡

14. Reasoning on the resurrection, the last writer quoted says: "There are also celestial bodies, and bodies terrestrial; but the glory of the celestial is one, and the glory of the terrestrial is another. There is one glory of the sun, another glory of the moon, and another glory of the stars: for as one star differeth from another star in glory, so also is the resur-

---

*An exception must be made in the case of the Roman Catholic Church. Catholics do not believe that all Christians at death go immediately into heaven, but on the contrary "believe that a Christian who dies after the guilt and everlasting punishment of mortal sins have been forgiven him, but who, either from want of opportunity or through his negligence, has not discharged the debt of temporal punishment due to his sin, will have to discharge that debt to the justice of God in purgatory." "Purgatory is a state of suffering after this life, in which those souls are for a time detained, which depart this life after their deadly sins have been remitted as to the stain and guilt, and as to the everlasting pain that was due to them; but which souls have on account of those sins still some temporal punishment to pay; as also those souls which leave this world guilty only of venial [pardonable] sins. In purgatory these souls are purified and rendered fit to enter into heaven, where nothing defiled enters." The quotations in the above are from *Catholic Belief*, by Bruno, D. D. of the Catholic church. As all works of the Catholic church accessible to me have nothing on the different degrees of glory, I conclude that Catholic teaching is that they who attain unto heaven are all equal in glory.

†I Kings viii:27.

‡II Cor. 12:2-4.

rection of the dead."* In all this, however, the great subject is but vaguely hinted at. For a full understanding of it we are indebted to a revelation given to Joseph Smith, February 16th, 1832. From that revelation we summarize the following:†

15. The Celestial Glory:—They who receive the testimony of Jesus, that believe on his name and are baptized after the manner of his burial; that by keeping the commandments they might be washed and cleansed from all sin, and receive the Holy Ghost by the laying on of hands by those having authority; who overcome by faith, and are sealed by the Holy Spirit of Promise—these become the church of the First Born. They are they into whose hands the Father hath given all things—they are priests and kings, who have received of God's fullness, and of his glory; they are priests of the Most High, after the order of Melchisedek, which is after the order of the Son of God—therefore they are Gods, even the Sons of God. All things are theirs, whether life or death, or things present, or things to come, all are theirs, and they are Christ's, and Christ is God's. They

---

*I Cor. xv:40-42.

†The circumstances under which the revelation was given are these: The Prophet Joseph and Sidney Rigdon were engaged in revising the Jewish scriptures. When they came to St. John, ch. v:29—speaking of the resurrection of the dead, concerning those that should hear the voice of the Son of Man and come forth, instead of reading in the text of our common English Bibles—"And shall come forth; they that have done good, unto the resurrection of life; and they that have done evil, unto the resurrection of damnation," the following was given to them by the Spirit: "And shall come forth, they who have done good in the resurrection of the just, and they who have done evil in the resurrection of the unjust." This reading of the passage caused them to marvel as it was given to them by inspiration; and while they pondered on this thing the Spirit of God enveloped them, and they saw the Lord Jesus Christ and those different glories which men will inherit, an account of which is given in the text. The vision is recorded in Doc. and Cov., sec. lxxvi.

shall overcome all things; they shall dwell in the presence of God and Christ forever and forever; they are they whom Christ will bring with him when he shall come in the clouds of heaven to reign on the earth over his people; they have part in the resurrection of the just; their names are written in heaven, where God and Christ dwell; they are just men made perfect through Jesus the mediator of the new covenant; these are they whose bodies are celestial, whose glory the sun in heaven is spoken of as typical—they inherit the celestial glory, they see as they are seen and know as they are known.

16. **The Terrestrial Glory:**—The terrestrial glory differs from the celestial glory as the light of the moon differs from the light of the sun. These are they who died without law, and also they who are the spirits of men in prison, whom the Son visited, and preached the gospel unto them, that they might be judged according to men in the flesh, who received not the testimony of Jesus in the flesh, but afterwards received it. These are they who are honorable men of the earth, who were blinded by the craftiness of men. These are they who receive of God's glory but not of his fullness. They may enjoy the presence of the Son but not of the presence of the Father; these are they who are not valiant in the testimony of Jesus, therefore they obtain not the crown over the kingdom of God.

17. **The Telestial Glory:**—The telestial glory differs from the terrestrial, as the light of the stars differs from the light of the moon. The inhabitants of the telestial glory are those who neither received the gospel of Christ in the flesh nor the testimony of Jesus in the spirit world. These are they who are thrust down to hell, and will not be redeemed from the devil until the last resurrection, when Christ shall have finished his work. These are they who are

of Paul and of Apollos, and of Cephas; some of Christ and some of John, some of Moses and some of Elias; but received not the gospel nor the testimony of Jesus. These are they who will not be gathered with the Saints, to be caught up unto the church of the First Born, and received into the cloud.   These are liars and sorcerers and adulterers, and whoremongers, and whosoever loves and makes a lie.   They suffer the wrath of God on earth and the vengeance of eternaɩ fire; but they will be judged every man according to his works, and receive according to his works, his own dominion, in the mansions which are prepared; and they shall be servants of the Most High,* but where God and Christ dwell they cannot come, worlds without end.   They of the Telestial Glory enjoy neither the presence of the Father nor the Son, but receive the ministration of angels, and of the Holy Ghost, for even they of the Telestial Glory are accounted heirs of salvation.   The Prophet Joseph and Sidney Rigdon in their vision saw that the inhabitants of the telestial glory were as innumerable as the stars in the firmament of heaven, or as the sand upon the sea shore—and they heard the voice of God saying—"These all shall bow the knee and every tongue shall confess to Him who sits upon the throne forever and ever; for they shall be judged according to their works, and every man shall receive according to his own works, his own dominions, in the mansions which are prepared, and they shall be servants of the Most High, but where God and Christ dwell they cannot come, worlds without end."

18. Degrees Within the Three Great Kingdoms of Glory:—These are the three great general divisions of

---

*"Servants of God, but not Gods nor the sons of God," remarks Apostle Orson Pratt in his foot note on the passage from which this is condensed. *Doc. and Cov. sec. lxxvi*:112.

glory in the world to come, but within these great divisions are subdivisions or degrees. The Prophet Joseph taught that in the celestial glory there are three heavens or degrees.* Of the telestial glory it is written: "And the glory of the telestial is one, even as the glory of the stars is one, for as one star differs from another star in glory even so differs one from another in glory in the telestial world."† From this it is evident that there are different degrees of glory within the celestial and telestial glories; and though we have no direct authority for the statement, it seems but reasonable to conclude that there are different degrees of glory in the terrestrial world also. It appears but rational that it should be so, since the degrees of worthiness in men are almost infinite in their variety; and as every man is to be judged according to his works, it will require a corresponding infinity of degrees in glory to mete out to every man that reward of which he is worthy, and that also which his intelligence will enable him to enjoy.

19. Progress Within and From Different Degrees of Glory:—The question of advancement within the great divisions of glory—celestial, terrestrial, and telestial; as also the question of advancement from one sphere of glory to another, remains to be considered. In the revelation from which we have summarized what has been written here, in respect to the different degrees of glory, it is said that those of the terrestrial glory will be ministered unto by those of the celestial; and those of the telestial will be ministered unto by those of the terrestrial—that is, those of the higher glory minister to those of a lesser order of glory. We can conceive of no reason for all this administration of the higher to the

---

*Doc. and Cov., sec. cxxxi:1.
†Doc. and Cov., sec. lxxvi.

lower, unless it be for the purpose of advancing our Father's children along the lines of eternal progression. Whether or not in the great future, full of so many possibilities now hidden from us, they of the lesser glories after education and advancement within those spheres may at last emerge from them and make their way to the higher degrees of glory until at last they attain to the highest, is not revealed in the revelations of God, and any statement made on the subject must partake more or less of the nature of conjecture.

20. But if it be granted that such a thing is possible, they who at the first entered into the celestial glory—having before them the privilege also of eternal progress—have been moving onward, so that the relative distance between them and those who have fought their way up from the lesser glories, may be as great when the latter have come into the degrees of celestial glory in which the righteous at first stood, as it was at the commencement; and thus between them is an impassable gulf which time cannot destroy. Thus: those whose faith and works are such only as to entitle them to inherit a telestial glory, may arrive at last where those whose works in this life were such as to entitle them to entrance into the celestial kingdom—they may arrive where these *were*, but never where they *are*. But if it be granted that the chief fact about Intelligences is that they have power to add fact to fact and thus build up knowledge, and through knowledge have wisdom, and thus make progress; and if to such intelligences there is granted *eternal life—immortality* —then it is useless to postulate any limitations for them; for in the passing of even a few thousands of millions of years, even if progress be very slow—there will come a time when these intelligences—men and women of even the telestial glory—may become very acceptable characters, and very important personages.

21. Sons of Perdition:—There is a class of souls with whom the justice of God must deal, which will not and cannot be classified in the celestial, terrestrial or telestial glories. They are the sons of perdition. But though they will not be assigned a place in either of these grand divisions of glory, the revelation from which we have drawn our information respecting man's future state, describes the condition of these sons of perdition so far as it is made known unto the children of men. It also informs us as to the nature of the crime which calls for such grievous punishment.

22. The sons of perdition are they of whom God hath said that it had been better for them never to have been born; for they are vessels of wrath, doomed to suffer the wrath of God, with the devil and his angels in eternity. Concerning whom he hath said there is no forgiveness in this world nor in the world to come. These are they who shall go away into everlasting punishment, with the devil and his angels, and the only ones on whom the second death shall have any power; the only ones who will not be redeemed in the due time of the Lord, after the sufferings of his wrath. He saves all the works of his hands except these sons of perdition; but they go away to reign with the devil and his angels in eternity, where their worm dieth not, and the fire is not quenched, which is their torment. The end thereof, the place thereof no man knoweth. It has not been revealed, nor will it be revealed unto man, except to them who are made partakers thereof. It has been partially shown to some in vision, and may be shown again in the same partial manner to others; but the end, the width, the height, the depth and the misery thereof they understand not, nor will any one but those who receive the terrible condemnation.

23. Such the punishment: now as to the crime that merits it. It is the crime of high treason to God, which pulls down on men this fearful doom. It falls upon men who know the power of God and who have been made partakers of it, and then permit themselves to be so far overcome of the devil that they deny the truth that has been revealed to them and defy the power of God. They deny the Holy Ghost after having received it. They deny the Only Begotten Son of the Father after the Father hath revealed him, and in this crucify him unto themselves anew, and put him to an open shame. They commit the same act of high treason that Lucifer in the rebellion of heaven did, and hence are worthy of the same punishment with him. Thank God, the number who commit that fearful crime is but few. It is only those who attain to a very great knowledge of the things of God that are capable of committing it, and the number among such are few indeed who become so recklessly wicked as to rebel against and defy the power of God.* But when such characters do fall, they fall like Lucifer, never to rise again; they get beyond the power of repentance, or the hope of forgiveness.

NOTES.

1. **The Sectarian Dogma of Eternal Punishment:**—There is nothing more obnoxious to a reasonable mind, a loving heart, a soul susceptible to the relative claims of justice and mercy, than the Presbyterian and other old ecclesiastical school doctrines of an eternal, material, unchanging hell of fire and torment in which the unregenerate are doomed to suffer the implacable wrath of an unrelenting Deity forever and forever, worlds without end.   *   *   *   And it is not true. It was not and is not a doctrine of Christ. It sprang from the gloom-clothed brains of cloistered monks and heretic burning priests, bearing not a vestige of the sacred authority vested in the apostles and their immediate associates. It is redolent of the *Auto de fe*, and stamped

---

*Those desiring to verify the statements of the text will consult with care Heb. vi:4-8 and Doc. and Cov., sec. lxxvi:25-48.

with the bloody seal of apostate papal Rome. It breathes of vengeance instead of justice, and banishes sweet mercy from the economy of heaven. It makes God more cruel than the most inhuman mortal. It is a libel on the Almighty and a fruitful cause of atheism, irreverence and doubt.—*C. W. Penrose, now* (1924) *First Counselor in the First Presidency of the Church of Jesus Christ of Latter-day Saints.*

2. Messiah Preaching to the Spirits in Prison:—In the second and third centuries every branch and division of the Christian church, so far as their record enables us to judge, believed that Christ preached to the departed; and this belief dates back to our earliest reliable sources of information in the former of these two centuries.—*Christ's Mission to the Under World,* (Huidekoper), Fourth Edition, p. 49.

As Christ died for us, and was buried, so also is it to be believed, that he went down into hell.—*Articles of Religion—Church of England —Art. III, Book of Common Prayer, p.* 311.

These "spirits in prison" are supposed to be the holy dead. • • • The most intelligent meaning suggested by the context is, however, that Christ by his spirit preached to those who in the time of Noah, while the Ark was a preparing, were disobedient, and whose spirits are now in prison, abiding the general judgment. The prison is doubtless hades, but what hades is must be determined by other passages of scripture; and whether it is the grave or hell, it is still a prison for those who yet await the judgment day.—*Cyclopedia Biblical Literature (Kitto), p.* 798.

3. Baptism for the Dead:—While not maintaining the view that there is such a thing as a living man being baptized for one who is dead, the writer in *Biblical Literature (Kitto),* expresses these views: "From the wording of the sentence [why then are they baptized for the dead?] the most simple impression certainly is, that Paul speaks of a baptism which a living man receives in the place of a dead one. This interpretation is particularly adopted by those expounders with whom grammatical construction is of paramount importance, and the first thing to be considered." This view is also upheld by Ambrose among the early Christian writers; and by Erasmus, Scaliger, Grotius, Calixtus among the moderns; and still more recently by Augusti Meyer, Billroth and Ruckert. De Wette considers this the only possible meaning of the words.

4. Epiphanius, a writer of the fourth century, in speaking of the Marcionites, a sect of Christians to whom he was opposed, says: "In this country—I mean Asia—and even Galatea, their school flourished eminently; and a traditional fact concerning them has reached us, that when any of them had died without baptism, they used to baptize others in their name, lest in the resurrection they should suffer punishment as unbaptized (*Heresies xxviii:*7). This proves beyond controversy the fact that vicarious baptism for the dead was practiced among some sects of the early Christians. Another fact proves it still more emphatically than this statement by Epiphanius. The Council of Carthage, held A. D. 397, in its sixth canon, forbids the administration of baptism and holy communion for the dead; why should this canon be formed against these practices if they had no existence among the Christians of those days?—*Roberts, The Gospel, pages* 245-7, *5th Edition.*

REVIEW.

1.   What great work did Elijah's visit to the Kirtland Temple introduce?

2.   What was the Christian belief previous to this in respect to those who died without conversion to the Christian religion?

3.   Through what cause did this error arise?

4.   Explain the meaning of "Eternal" punishment—"Endless" punishment.

5.   What scripture teaches that Jesus preached to the spirits in prison?

6.   For what purpose was the gospel preached to those who once rejected it?

7.   If the gospel was preached again to those who once rejected it, what may we conclude in respect to those who never heard it in this life?

8.   By what means is the gospel made available to those who died without a knowledge of it, or who hearing, rejected it?

9,   Give an exposition of baptism for the dead.   (Notes 3 and 4.)

10.   What is the scriptural doctrine in relation to the future rewards of men?

11.   What is the orthodox Christian view in respect to those who attain unto heaven?

12.   In what does the Catholic view differ from that of the Protestant?   (Note, p. 412.)

13.   What evidences in the scripture can you quote to prove that there are different kingdoms or degrees of glory in heaven?

14.   Say what you can of the celestial glory.

15.   Describe as far as you can the terrestrial glory.

16.   In what does the telestial glory differ from the terrestrial?

17.   What class of people inherit the telestial glory?

18.   What can you say of degrees within the three great kingdoms of glory?

19.   What can you say of progress within and from the different degrees of glory?

20.   What can you say of the sons of perdition and their punishment?

21.   What is the nature of their sin?

22.   What of the number of those who commit it?

SECTION IX.

1. The Break up at Kirtland:—The keys of knowledge respecting the great doctrines treated in the last two sections were received in the Kirtland temple; and for a time it appeared that the Saints would long enjoy the blessings of their temple and the communion and instruction of heavenly messengers. But not so. With prosperity which attended the saints there, came pride, envyings, jealousies and heart-burnings. Their temporal prosperity existed but a brief period. It was carried away by the wave of financial disaster which swept over the United States in 1837. Then came financial embarrassment, accompanied with charges and counter-charges of fraud and dishonesty. Apostasy among men high in authority was rife. Several of the Twelve Apostles went down in those dark days, and became bitter enemies to the Prophet Joseph. To such an extent did the spirit of apostasy prevail that it became murderous; and the prophet and a number of his most devoted friends had to flee from Kirtland for their lives. (See note 1, end of section.)

2. The Founding of Far West—Expulsion From Missouri:—Meantime the Saints in Missouri who were driven from Jackson County, in the latter part of 1833, removed from their temporary locations in Clay County, and settled in the new county of Caldwell, where they founded the city of Far West. It was to Far West that the Prophet Joseph and other church leaders fled when compelled to leave Kirtland. But there was little rest for the church in Missouri; persecution was threatened before the prophet arrived, and his presence only seemed to hasten the impending storm. In the autumn of 1838 it broke upon the church in all its fury, and during that winter the entire church was expelled from the State by order of its Governor, Lilburn W. Boggs. (See note 2, end of section.)

3. **The Rise of Nauvoo:**—While the Saints were being expelled from the State, the Prophet Joseph and several other leading Elders were imprisoned in Liberty Jail, Clay County, Missouri, having been betrayed into the hands of their enemies by the treachery of false brethren. They were held on false charges of "murder, arson and treason." They finally made their escape from their enemies and joined the body of the church, which had found a temporary resting place in the city of Quincy and vicinity, in Illinois. Shortly afterwards they settled at Commerce, in Hancock County, in the same State. The church purchased several large tracts of land at this place of Dr. Galland, a Mr White, Hubbard, Wells, Hotchkiss, and others; and soon from the wilderness and bogs of Commerce—(see note 3, end of section)—rose the city of Nauvoo—meaning The Beautiful; "Carrying with it also," says the Prophet Joseph, "the idea of rest."

4. Although both Joseph and the Saints saw some of their happiest days in Nauvoo, there was not much "rest" for them there, especially for the former. The toil and anxiety of founding a city, establishing manufactures, publishing a paper, and converting the surrounding prairie country into fields and gardens; sending the Apostles to preach the gospel in foreign lands, being all the time tormented by their enemies in Missouri and Illinois, kept the church, and especially the Prophet Joseph, harrassed during the whole time they remained in Nauvoo. Here the translation of the Book of

Abraham was published. (See note 4, end of section.) A magnificent temple was constructed in which to carry on the work of salvation for the dead, and in which the living could receive those washings and anointings, endowments and sealings, necessary to prepare them for their entrance into and their exaltation in heaven.

5. **Celestial Marriage Introduced:**—It was in Nauvoo also that the prophet introduced Celestial Marriage,—the marriage system which obtains in celestial worlds. It consists of the eternity of the marriage covenant, that is, the marriage covenant between a man and his wife is made for time and all eternity, and being sealed by that power of the priesthood which binds on earth and in heaven, the covenant holds good in heaven as well as on earth; and by reason of it men will have claim upon their wives, and wives upon their husbands, in and after the resurrection. Celestial marriage may also include a plurality of wives.

6. **Eternity of the Marriage Covenant:**—This new marriage system—new at least to this generation—completely revolutionized the ideas of the Saints in respect to the marriage institution. In common with the Christian sects, they had regarded marriage vaguely as an institution to exist in this world only; and married their wives as other Christians did and now do—until death shall them part. But by the revelation which the prophet made known at Nauvoo, they learned that in celestial spheres the marriage covenant exists eternally, and that the pleasing joys of family ties and associations coupled with the power of endless increase, contributes to the happiness, power and dominion of those who attain to the celestial glory. What a revelation was here! Instead of the God-given power of pro-creation under the law of God being one of the things that is to pass away, it is one of the chief means of man's

exaltation and glory in that great **Eternity,** which like an
endless vista stretches out before him! Through it man
attains to the glory of the endless increase of eternal lives,
and the right of presiding as priest, patriarch and king,
over his ever increasing posterity. Instead of the commandment—"Be fruitful, multiply and replenish the earth,"
being an unrightous law, it is one by means of which the
race of Divine Beings is perpetuated, and is as holy and
pure as the commandment, "Repent and be baptized."
Through that law, in connection with an observance of
all the other laws of the gospel, man will yet attain unto
the power of the Godhead,* and like his Father—God—

---

*It may sound like sacrilege in modern ears to speak of man becoming
as God. Yet why should it be so considered? Man is the offspring of
Deity, he is of the same race, and hath within him—undeveloped, it is
true—the faculties and attributes of his Father. He hath also before
him an eternity of time in which to develop both the faculties of the
mind and the attributes of the soul—why should it be accounted a
strange thing that at last the Child shall arrive at the same exaltation
and partake of the same intelligence and glory with his Father? If
Jesus Christ, "being in the form of God, thought it not robbery to be
equal with God" (Philippians ii:6), why should it be thought blasphem-
ous to teach that men by faith and righteousness in following the counsels of God shall at last become like him, and share in his power and
glory, being as God, even a son of God? I grant you the height from
our present position looks tremendous; yet it is not impossible of attainment, since we have eternity in which to work. Stand by the cradle
of a new-born babe and contemplate it. Within that little body of
organized pulp—with eyes incapable of distinguishing objects; legs unable to bear the weight of its body—without the power of locomotion;
hands over whose movement it hath no control; ears that hear but cannot distinguish sounds; a tongue that cannot speak—yet within that
little helpless tabernacle what powers lie dormant! Within that germ
in the cradle are latent powers which only require time for their unfolding to astonish the world. From it may come the man of profound
learning who shall add something by his own wisdom to the sum total
of human knowledge. Perhaps from that germ shall come a profound
historian, a poet or eloquent orator to sway the reason and passions of
men, and guide them to better and purer things than they have yet
known. Or a statesman may be there in embryo; a man whose wisdom
shall guide the destiny of the state or perhaps with God-like power rule
the world! If from such a germ as this in the cradle may come such an

his chief glory shall be to bring to pass the eternal life and happiness of man.

7. **Plurality of Wives:**—Celestial marriage, as already observed, may include a plurality of wives. This was as great an innovation as marriage for eternity. It came in conflict with the education and tradition of the Saints, and the sentiments of the age. Still God had commanded it through his prophet, and though their prejudices—the outcropping of their traditions—revolted against it, the faithful to whom it was revealed resolved to obey it.

8. It was in 1831 that plural marriage was first made known to Joseph Smith. In that year he was engaged in revising by inspiration the Jewish Scriptures;* and observing with what favor the Lord regarded the early patriarchs, and many of the kings and prophets of the Jews who had a plurality of wives, he inquired of God how it was he justified them in that thing. The Lord in answer revealed the law of celestial marriage. But the time had not come for the Saints to enter into its practice, and hence the prophet kept what had been revealed to him locked up a secret in his own breast, with the exception of saying to one or two of his most confidential friends that plural marriage was, within certain limits and restrictions, a correct principle. (See note 4, end of section.) In 1841

---

unfolding of power as we see in the highest and noblest manhood, may it not be, that taking that highest and noblest manhood as the germ, that from it may come, under the guiding hand of our Father in heaven, a still more wonderful unfolding, until the germ of highest and noblest manhood shall develop into a Deity! The distance between the noblest man and the position of a God is greater than that between the infant in the cradle and the highest development of manhood; but if so, there is a longer time—eternity—in which to arrive at the result; and a God and heavenly influences instead of the human parent and earthly means to bring to pass the necessary development.—*Roberts.*

Mill. Star, Vol. xiv, p. 114.

the prophet introduced the practice of this principle into the church by taking to himself plural wives.* He also taught the principle to a number of the leading elders and they obeyed it.

NOTES.

1. **Prosperity and Disaster which Overwhelmed the Church at Kirtland:**—Speculation was rife all over the United States at that time, [1837] and the Saints did not escape the contagion. They started a banking institution, engaged in mercantile pursuits and land speculation. For a time they were prosperous and wealth rapidly accumulated among them. Sidney Rigdon declared, in a burst of enthusiasm, that the glory of the latter-days was now being ushered in, and that Zion would soon become the glory of the whole earth; when the Lord for silver would bring gold; for iron, brass; and for stones, iron. But a wave of financial disaster swept over the entire country. Banking institutions went down before it; thousands of merchants were hopelessly ruined; and in the general disaster Kirtland did not escape. Like the inhabitants of other towns her people were overwhelmed with financial embarrassment. "Distress, ruin and poverty," says Elder Taylor, "seemed to prevail. Apostates and corrupt men were prowling about as so many wolves seeking whom they might devour. They were oppressive, cruel, heartless; devising every pretext that the most satanic malignity could invent to harass the Saints. Fraud, false accusation and false swearing, vexatious law suits, personal violence, and barefaced robbery abounded. They were truly afflicted, persecuted and tormented."—*Life of John Taylor, p. 52.*

---

*On the 12th of July, 1843, at the request of Hyrum Smith, the revelation as now contained in the book of Doctrine and Covenants was written from the dictation of the Prophet Joseph, by Elder William Clayton, at that time the Prophet's scribe. The same day a copy of the revelation was made for Bishop Newel K. Whitney, by Joseph C. Kingsbury. Emma Smith, the first wife of the Prophet, obtaining the revelation as first written out by Wm. Clayton, in a moment of jealousy, destroyed it. Bishop Whitney's copy, however, was preserved and from it the revelation, afterwards published in the Doctrine and Covenants, was printed. It will be observed by the student from the revelation itself that the principle of plural marriage was known and practiced before the writing and publishing of the revelation on the 12th of July, 1843.

2. Persecution of the Saints in Missouri:—This brings us to the close of our story of the Missouri Persecutions. We have seen a people start out under the direction of the Lord to build up the city of Zion to his holy name; but who, through their disobedience and failure to observe strictly those conditions upon which the Lord promised them success in accomplishing so great and glorious a work, were driven entirely from the State where that city is to be founded. We have seen a proud, sovereign State, with a constitution that guaranteed the largest possible religious and civil liberty to its citizens, ignore the spirit and letter of that constitution; shamelessly violate the laws passed in pursuance of it; and the officers of the State, from the chief executive down, combine to destroy the Saints of God, or drive them from the State; in accomplishing which, they were guilty of the most cruel barbarity. It is no palliation of their offense to say that the Saints had not strictly kept the commandments of God. Their offenses were against the laws of God rather than the laws of man. So far as the State of Missouri was concerned, she was not justified in trampling on her own constitution and laws, and committing outrages that would bring to the cheek of a savage the blush of shame. It was a case where offenses must needs come, but woe, woe, unto them by whom they come!—*Missouri Persecutions—Roberts.*

3. Commerce, Afterwards Nauvoo:—The place was literally a wilderness. The land was mostly covered with trees and bushes, and much of it was so wet that it was with the utmost difficulty a footman could get through, and totally impossible for teams. Commerce was unhealthful, very few could live there; but believing that it might become a healthful place by the blessing of heaven to the Saints, and no more eligible place presenting itself, I considered it wisdom to make an attempt to build up a city.—*Joseph Smith.*

4. The Book of Abraham:—The rolls of papyrus filled with Egyptian characters and hieroglyphics, from which Joseph translated the Book of Abraham, came into his possession in the following manner: In 1831 the celebrated French traveler, Antonio Sebolo, penetrated Egypt as far as the ancient city of Thebes, under a license procured from Mehemet Ali—then Viceroy of Egypt—through the influence of Chevalier Drovetti, the French Consul. Sebolo employed four hundred and thirty-three men for four months and two days, either Turkish or Egyptian soldiers, paying them from four to six cents a day per man. They entered the Catacombs near ancient Thebes, on the seventh of June, 1831, and procured eleven mummies. These were shipped to Alexandria, and from there the great traveler started with his treasures for Paris. But en route for the French capital, Sebolo put in at Trieste, where he was taken sick, and after an illness of ten days, died. This was in 1832. Previous to his death he willed his Egyptian treasures to his nephew, Michael H. Chandler, who was then living in Philadelphia, Pennsylvania, but whom Sebolo believed to be in Dublin, to which city he ordered the mummies shipped. Mr. Chandler ordered the mummies forwarded to New York from Dublin where he took possession of them. Here the coffins for the first time were opened, and in them was found two rolls of papyrus covered with engraving. While still in the customs house, Mr. C. was informed by a gentleman, a stranger to him, that no one in the city could translate the characters; but was referred to Joseph Smith, who, the stranger informed him, possessed some kind of gift or power by which he had previously translated similar characters. Joseph Smith was then unknown to Mr. C. The mummies were shipped to Philadelphia; and from there Mr. C. traveled through the country, exhibited them and the rolls of papyrus, reaching Kirtland in July, 1835, and the Saints purchased some of the mummies and the two rolls of papyrus, one of which was the writing of Abraham and the other of Joseph, who was sold into Egypt. The Book of Abraham has been translated and published, at least in part. [See Pearl of Great Price. Elder George Reynolds has published a work on this subject, "The Divine Authenticity of the Book of Abraham," which should be carefully studied by every Elder in Israel.]

   5.   **The Establishment of Plural Marriage:**—The principle of plural marriage was first revealed to Joseph Smith in 1831, but being forbidden to make it public, or to teach it as a doctrine of the gospel, at that time, he confided the facts to only a very few of his intimate associates. Among them were Oliver Cowdery and Lyman E. Johnson, the latter confiding the fact to his traveling companion, Elder Orson Pratt, in the year 1832. And this great principle remained concealed in the bosoms of the Prophet Joseph Smith and the few to whom he revealed it, until he was commanded, about 1842, to instruct the leading members of the priesthood, and those who were most faithful and intelligent, and best prepared to receive it—in relation thereto; at which time, and subsequently until his martyrdom, the subject, in connection with the great principles of baptism, redemption and sealing for the dead, became the great theme of his life; and as the late President George A. Smith repeatedly said to me and others—"The prophet seemed irresistibly moved by the power of God to establish that principle not only in theory, in the hearts and minds of his brethren, but in practice also, he himself having led the way."—*Joseph F. Smith,* (*President of the Church.*)

REVIEW.

1.   What appeared to be the prospects of the Saints at Kirtland?
2.   What influence did wealth have upon them?
3.   What did the great apostasy at Kirtland result in?
4.   State what you can about the founding of Far West.
5.   What effect did the presence of the Prophet Joseph have in Missouri?
6.   Tell what you can of the expulsion from Nauvoo.
7.   Where did the church find a temporary resting place after its expulsion from Missouri?
8.   Where did the church next settle?
9.   What is the meaning of the word "Nauvoo?"

10.   What can you say of Nauvoo being a place of rest to the Prophet Joseph and the Saints?

11.   Enumerate the several things which employed the attention of the Prophet and the Saints at Nauvoo.

12.   Where was celestial marriage introduced?

13.   What is celestial marriage?

14.   In what light was celestial marriage looked upon by the Saints?

15.   What was the effect of this principle upon their minds?

16.   Is it sacrilege to believe that man may become like his Father—God?   (See foot note p. 425.)

17.   What besides marriage for eternity may celestial marriage include?

18.   When was the rightfulness of plural marriage first made known to the Prophet Joseph?

19.   About what time was this principle introduced into the church?

20.   Under what circumstances and on what date was the revelation on celestial marriage written out?   (Foot note, also note 5.)

SECTION X.

1. **Martyrdom of the Prophets:**—The relentless persecution which had followed the Prophet Joseph Smith ever since he first announced that he had received a revelation from God, culminated at last in his and his brother Hyrum's martyrdom, at Carthage Jail, Hancock County, Illinois, on the 27th of June, 1844. Religious prejudices and political jealousies, combined with the treason of wicked apostates from the church in Nauvoo, are the forces which led to this sad result. The two brothers were murdered in Carthage prison while awaiting trial on a false charge of treason against the State of Illinois. They were under the immediate protection of the officers of the State, the Governor thereof having only the day before pledged the honor of the State for their protection. Notwithstanding all this, a mob of from one to two hundred surrounded the prison where they were confined, forced the door, killed the Prophet Joseph and his brother Hyrum, and severely wounded Elder John Taylor, who, with Willard Richards, was a voluntary inmate of the prison with the brothers Smith.* Willard Richards was unhurt.

2. The martyrdom of the prophet has an importance second only to the crucifixion of Messiah; for in his martyrdom he sealed his testimony with his blood, and thenceforth it is made binding on all the world. "For where a testament is, there must also of necessity be the death of

*For a full account of this terrible tragedy the student is referred to the Life of Joseph Smith, by Geo. Q. Cannon, ch. lxvi; and the Life of John Taylor, by the writer of this book, ch. xiii, xiv, xv.

the testator. For a testament is of force after men are dead; otherwise it is of no strength at all while the testator liveth."* The Dispensation of the Fullness of Times doubtless required a testimony such as Joseph Smith bore to the world, to be sealed with his blood, else the tragedy at Carthage would be without meaning.

3. **The Twelve Apostles Succeed in Presidency:—** After the death of the Prophet Joseph, the Twelve—the quorum standing next to the First Presidency, and as we have seen, equal in authority to that quorum—took charge of the affairs of the church. Sidney Rigdon, who was a counselor in the First Presidency, pressed his claims to be recognized as the "guardian," or interim President of the church, but he was rejected by the Saints, and the Twelve were sustained, for the time being, as the presiding quorum in the church.†

4. **Expulsion from Illinois:—** When the enemies of the Saints in Illinois saw that the killing of the prophet did not destroy the church, they agitated the question of driving the saints from the State, and such was the influence of the mob, and such the cowardice and weakness of the State officials, that they were entirely successful in the undertaking. The Saints were compelled to leave the State under circumstances of the utmost cruelty, sacrificing very much of their property, the city they had founded, and the temple they had built.

5. **Flight to the West—Why.—** When compelled to leave Illinois, the Saints turned their faces westward. The

---

*Heb. ix:16, 17.

†The subject of "Succession in the Presidency of the Church" is a subject of deep importance, and those who desire to enter minutely into the consideration of it should consult the author's work of that title, a book of 120 pages.

country west of the Missouri was unoccupied, except by wandering tribes of Indians, and they might look for that peace in the vast wilderness of the west which had been denied them in the Christian civilized States of the East. But what caused them to look to the west for an abiding place—even more than the fact that the west was unoccupied —was the frequent predictions of the Prophet Joseph that the Saints would yet remove to the valleys of the Rocky Mountains, and there become a great people. (See note 1, end of section.) Here, too, in the tops of the Rocky Mountains they could fulfill better than anywhere else the predictions of the ancient prophets. (See note 2, end of section.)

6. **Arrival in Salt Lake Valley:**—Westward, therefore, they turned their faces; the Pioneer company—consisting of one hundred and forty men and three women— crossed the plains in 1847, arriving in Salt Lake Valley on the 24th of July of that year. They made their encampment on the present site of Salt Lake City, and soon afterwards laid off the city and began the erection of permanent homes.

7. **Re-organization of the First Presidency:**—At Winter Quarters, December 5, 1847, the First Presidency of the church was re-organized. Brigham Young was nominated and sustained as the President, with authority to choose his two counselors. He selected Heber C. Kimball and Willard Richards for first and second counselors, respectively, and they were unanimously sustained by the church.

8. **Brigham Young:***—Brigham Young acted as the President of the church for thirty years—for thirty-three

---

*President Brigham Young was born in Whitingham, Windham County, Vermont, June 1, 1801. He was baptized into the Church April 14th, 1832, and immediately afterwards ordained an Elder.

years, if the three years that the quorum of the Twelve
(of which he was president,) acted as the presiding quorum
of the church, be counted. In the course of these thirty-
three eventful years this truly great man conducted the
exodus of the Saints from Nauvoo; led them across the wide
extended plains which form the eastern slopes of the Rocky
Mountains; established them in Salt Lake and surrounding
valleys, located and laid out many of their settlements, and
taught them not only the moral precepts of the gospel, but
how to produce from the elements, sterile as they then seemed
to be, the necessaries and comforts of life. Through his
wisdom—God-given—he laid the foundation of the present
commonwealth of Utah. Just previous to his death he
organized the settlements of the church into Stakes of Zion,
as we now know them, and set in order the various quorums
of the priesthood.

9. President Young was a natural leader among men—
a master spirit. His genius especially manifested itself
in his ability to organize and govern men. He had not
only been the President of the Church and the first Governor of Utah, but he was also the friend of the people.
In times of trial and sorrow they turned to him for comfort;
in times of danger they looked to him to direct their action;
in times of perplexity they went to him for the word of the
Lord; and Brigham Young, full of inspired wisdom, never
failed them in any of these things. (See note 3, end of
section.)

10. The Twelve Again Presiding:—At the death of
President Brigham Young, August 25, 1877, the quorum
of the Twelve Apostles again became the temporary presiding quorum of the church, with John Taylor at their head.
(See note 4, end of section.) The quorum of the Twelve
continued to act as the presiding quorum of the church until

the October conference of 1880, when the First Presidency was again organized.   John Taylor was chosen President, and he selected George Q. Cannon for his First, and Joseph F. Smith for his Second Counselor.

11. John Taylor—His Administration:—President John Taylor came to the high office of President of the Church late in life, in his seventy-second year.   He joined the church in his early manhood, in 1836, and two years later was ordained into the quorum of the Twelve Apostles.   He was a trusted friend of the Prophet Joseph, and was in prison with him when he was martyred, and he himself was wounded nigh unto death.   He had been prominent in all leading events of the church from the time he was ordained an apostle until he became the President thereof.   He was a man of wide experience, profound judgment, and unwavering integrity.   (See note 5, end of section.)   He entered upon the performance of his high duties with a zeal and vigor only to be expected of a younger man.   He was careful to set in order the several quorums of the priesthood, and insist upon each man doing his duty.   The seven years of his administration as President of the Church will be remembered as among the most eventful in the history of the church. It was during those years that the judicial crusade was inaugurated by the United States and most vigorously carried on against the Saints for the suppression of plural marriage.

12. Wilford Woodruff—His Administration:—President Taylor died on the 25th of July, 1887, and once more the quorum of the Twelve Apostles became the presiding quorum of the church.   They continued to act in that capacity, with Wilford Woodruff as President, until April 7, 1889, when the First Presidency was again reorganized, with Wilford Woodruff as President.   He retained the counselors of the late President Taylor, George Q. Cannon and Joseph F. Smith, as his counselors.

13. The persecution which the United States had inflicted upon the church on the pretext of suppressing plural marriages culminated in 1890 in the discontinuance of the practice of that principle. It may be well here to enumerate those circumstances which led to the above result. It has already been stated how plural marriage was introduced and practiced in Nauvoo. After the church settled in Salt Lake Valley it was publicly proclaimed as a doctrine of the church in 1852. The practice of it then was public, the whole church —and at that time the members of the church comprised nearly the whole community—approving the principle, which was at once recognized as a proper religious institution.

14. **Enactments of Congress Against Plural Marriage:**—For ten years the practice in Utah of this system of marriage met with no opposition from the United States. But in 1862 a law was enacted by Congress to punish and prevent the practice of polygamy in the Territories of the United States.* The penalties affixed were a fine, not to exceed five hundred dollars, and imprisonment not to exceed five years. For twenty years, however, the law remained practically a dead letter. It was claimed by the Saints that it was an infringement of the religious liberty guaranteed by the Constitution † of the United States, since it prohibited the free exercise of religion. For twenty years no pronounced effort was made by the general government to enforce the law. In 1882, however, the law enacted twenty

*The first anti-polygamy law was approved July 1st, 1862.
†"Congress shall make no law respecting an establishment of religion, or prohibiting the free exercise thereof."—*Amendments to the Constitution, Article I.*

years before was supplemented by what is known as the Edmunds Law. In addition to defining the crime polygamy—for which it retained the same penalties as the law of 1862—the Edmunds law also made the "cohabiting" with more than one woman a crime, punishable by a fine not to exceed three hundred dollars, and by imprisonment not to exceed six months. This law also rendered persons who were living in polygamy, or who believed in its rightfulness, incompetent to act as grand or petit jurors; and also disqualified all polygamists for voting or holding office. This law of 1882 was supplemented by the Edmunds-Tucker law— enacted in 1887—which made the legal wife or husband, in case of polygamy or unlawful cohabitation, a competent witness, provided the accused consented thereto; it also enlarged the powers of United States commissioners and marshals, and required certificates of all marriages to be filed in the office of the Probate Court. The violation of this last provision was a fine of one thousand dollars, and imprisonment for two years. The law disincorporated the church, and ordered the Supreme Court to wind up its affairs, and take possession of the escheated property.

15. The laws were rigorously enforced by the United States officials, special appropriations being made by Congress to enable them to carry on a judicial crusade against the Saints. Some of the prominent church officials were driven into retirement; others into exile. Homes were disrupted; family ties were rent asunder. Upwards of a thousand men endured fines and imprisonment rather than be untrue to their families. Every effort of the government to deprive the people of what was considered their religious liberty was stubbornly contested in the Courts until the decision of the Supreme Court of the United States was obtained. While some of the proceedings of the courts in

Utah in enforcing the anti-polygamy laws were condemned, the laws were sustained as constitutional. The court also held that the first amendment to the Constitution, which provides that Congress shall not prohibit the free exercise of religion, cannot be invoked against legislation for the punishment of plural marriages. Meantime government was relentless, and still more stringent measures than those already enacted were threatened.

16. **Discontinuance of Plural Marriages:**—In the midst of these afflictions and threatening portents President Wilford Woodruff besought the Lord in prayer and the Lord inspired him to issue the manifesto which discontinued the practice of plural marriages. At the semi-annual conference in October following, the action of President Woodruff was sustained by a unanimous vote of the conference, and plural marriages are discontinued in the church. (See notes 6, 7, 8, end of section.)

17. **Laying of the Cap-Stone of the Salt Lake Temple:**—One of the most pleasing and at the same time one of the most important events in the history of the church during the administration of President Woodruff, was laying the cap-stone of the Salt Lake Temple, on the 6th of April, 1892. It was laid by President Woodruff amid the rejoicing of thousands of the Saints; and a resolution was adopted to complete the sacred edifice and dedicate it on the 6th of April, 1893—forty years from the time the cornerstone thereof was laid, and this was done.

18. **Lorenzo Snow's Administration:**—President Wilford Woodruff died September 2, 1898, and Lorenzo Snow, on the 13th of the same month, was sustained by the quorum of the Twelve Apostles, President of the Church, and at the general conference of the Church following—October 9th,

the action of the Apostles was ratified by vote of the assembled Saints.

19. Joseph F. Smith's Administration:—President Lorenzo Snow died October 10, 1901, and was succeeded by Joseph F. Smith, son of Hyrum Smith, the brother of the Prophet Joseph Smith, and who shared in the imprisonment and in the martyrdom of the Prophet at Carthage Prison, Illinois. President Smith's administration began on the 17th of October, 1901, and continued through seventeen years, until the 19th of November, 1918, on which day he died.

20. Heber J. Grant's Administration:—President Joseph F. Smith was succeeded in the Presidency of the Church by Heber J. Grant. He was designated as the President by the Apostles' Quorum on the 23rd of November, 1918. An epidemic of influenza prevailing in Utah in the spring of 1919, prevented the usual annual general conference of the church from convening, and confirmation of the action of the Quorum of the Twelve in the appointment of Heber J. Grant as President of the Church, was delayed until the convening of a special general conference of the Church held on the first of June, 1919. Heber J. Grant is now (November, 1924) President of the Church.

21. The Growth and Present Status of the Church: —Since the Saints settled in the valleys of the Rocky Mountains—1847—the Church has been making steady growth in numbers and territorial expansion. According to the official statistics for January, 1922, the church has a membership in the organized stakes of Zion of 441,472; and 107,331 in the various missions, a total of 548,803.

As a people the Saints are thriving and prosperous, and are continually extending their settlements throughout the intermountain region, from the Province of Alberta, Canada, in the north, to the northern states of Old Mexico, and along the Pacific coast. In the main the Saints gathered in the western parts of the United States are an agricultural people; and 75 per cent of the whole church membership own their own homes.

The foreign work of the church occupies much of the attention of the presiding authorities. Recognizing that a dispensation of the gospel has been committed unto the church, and that it cannot escape condemnation if it fails to make proclamation to the world of the truths committed to it, the Elders of Israel have been devoted in the work of foreign propaganda. Missions have been established in the following countries, and tens of thousands from these nations have been brought to the gathering place of the church: the United States (nine missions,) Great Britain, France, Germany, Holland, Belgium, Denmark, Sweden, Norway, Finland, Russia, Hindustan, Iceland, Italy, Switzerland, Jersey Island, Malta, Cape of Good Hope, Mexico, Canada, among a number of Indian tribes in the Western States and territories of the United States, Sandwich Islands, Samoa, Friendly Islands, Australia, New Zealand, Turkey, Palestine, Empire of Japan, and the republic of Guatemala, Central America. The proclamation of the gospel in these lands is much, but it is not all that the church hopes to achieve in the work of her foreign ministry. It is regarded as the mission of the church to continue this proclamation of the gospel until the commandment given to her in the commencement of her existence shall have been complied with, viz: that this "Gospel of the Kingdom" shall be proclaimed to every nation, and kindred, and tongue, and people, until it shall have been preached as a witness in all the world, "and then shall the end come."*

---
*Matt. 24:14.

22. The Work for the Dead:—The church is also devoting much of its energies in the work for the dead. In order that this work more especially might be done, six temples have been erected, four in Utah, one in Canada, one in Hawaii; and there is one in course of erection in the State of Arizona. In these temples the faithful Saints are doing a noble work for their ancestors, as well as a very important work for the living.

23. The New Dispensation of the Gospel a Preparatory Work:—The work of God, as revealed through the Prophet Joseph Smith has a peculiar significance to this generation, it is essentially a preparatory work; its direct mission is to prepare for the glorious coming of the Son of God to reign over the earth. Nothing can be more explicitly stated in the scripture than the fact that the Son of God will come to the earth in the glory of his Father, to reward the righteous with a resurrection from the dead, and to establish his kingdom in power, bringing in a reign of peace, liberty and righteousness. In proof of this let the student consider the following scripture:

I. Promise of Messiah's Glorious Return:—And when he had spoken these things, while they beheld, he was taken up; and a cloud received him out of their sight. And, while they looked steadfastly toward heaven as he went up, behold two men (angels,) stood by them in white apparel; which also said, Ye men of Galilee, why stand ye gazing up into heaven? This same Jesus, which is taken up from you into heaven, shall so come in like manner as ye have seen him go into heaven."*

"For the Son of man shall come in the glory of his Father,

*Acts 1:9-11.

with his angels; and then he shall reward every man according to his works."*

II. Messiah to Come to Judgment:—"For if we believe that Jesus died, and rose again, even so them also which sleep in Jesus will God bring with him. For this we say unto you by the word of the Lord, that we which are alive and remain unto the coming of the Lord, shall not prevent them which are asleep. For the Lord himself shall descend from heaven with a shout, with the voice of the archangel, and with the trump of God, and the dead in Christ shall rise first; then we which are alive and remain shall be caught up together with them in the clouds, to meet the Lord in the air; and so shall we ever be with the Lord." †

"And to you who are troubled rest with us, when the Lord Jesus shall be revealed from heaven with his mighty angels, in flaming fire, taking vengeance on them that know not God, and that obey not the gospel of our Lord Jesus Christ; who shall be punished with everlasting destruction from the presence of the Lord, and from the glory of his power; when he shall come to be glorified in his saints, and to be admired in all them that believe (because our testimony among you was believed,) in that day." ‡ But of the day and hour of Messiah's coming no man knoweth. §

III. The World to be Warned of Coming Judgments:—To a number of elders in Kirtland, in 1832, who had been called to the ministry, the Lord gave these instructions, and, of course, they apply to all elders called to the same ministry:—"Teach ye diligently and my grace shall attend you, that you may be instructed more perfectly in theory

---

*Matt. xvi:27.
†I Thess. iv:14-17.
‡II Thess. 1:7-10.
§Luke xii:40. II Peter iii:10. Doc. and Cov., sec. xlix: 607.

in principle, in doctrine, in the law of the gospel, in all
things that pertain unto the kingdom of God that is ex-
pedient for you to understand. * * * That ye may be
prepared in all things when I shall send you again to magnify the calling whereunto I have called you, and the mission
with which I have commissioned you. Behold I sent you
out to testify and warn the people, and it becometh every
man who is warned to warn his neighbor. Therefore they
are left without excuse, and their sins are upon their own
heads. * * * Therefore, tarry ye, and labor diligently,
that you may be perfected in your ministry to go forth among
the Gentiles for the last time, as many as the mouth of the
Lord shall name, to bind up the law and seal up the testimony, and to prepare the Saints for the hour of judgment
which is to come; that their souls may escape the wrath of
God, the desolation of abomination which awaits the wicked
both in this world and the world to come. * * * Abide
ye in the liberty wherewith ye are made free; entangle not
yourselves in sin, but let your hands be clean, until the Lord
comes; for not many days hence and the earth shall tremble
and reel to and fro as a drunken man, and the sun shall hide
his face, and shall refuse to give light, and the moon shall be
bathed in blood, and the stars shall become exceeding angry,
and shall cast themselves down as a fig that falleth from off
a fig tree.

"And after your testimony cometh wrath and indignation
upon the people; for after your testimony cometh the testimony of earthquakes, that shall cause groanings in the midst
of her, and men shall fall upon the ground, and shall not be
able to stand. And also cometh the testimony of the voice
of thunderings, and the voice of lightnings, and the voice
of the waves of the sea heaving themselves beyond their
bounds. And all things shall be in commotion; and surely

men's hearts shall fail them; for fear shall come upon all people; and angels shall fly through the midst of heaven, crying with a loud voice, sounding the trump of God, saying, Prepare ye, prepare ye, O inhabitants of the earth; for the judgment of our God is come; behold and lo! the bridegroom cometh, go ye out to meet him."*

IV. The Coming of the Kingdom of God from Heaven:— "Hearken, and lo, a voice as of one from on high. * * * Prepare ye the way of the Lord, make his paths straight. The keys of the kingdom of God are committed unto man on the earth, and from thence shall the gospel roll forth unto the ends of the earth, as the stone which is cut out of the mountains without hands shall roll forth, until it has filled the whole earth; yea, a voice crying—Prepare ye the way of the Lord, prepare ye the supper of the Lamb, make ready for the Bridegroom; pray unto the Lord, call upon his holy name; make known his wonderful works among the people; call upon the Lord, that his kingdom may go forth upon the earth, that the inhabitants thereof may receive it, and be prepared for the days to come, in which the Son of Man shall come down from heaven, clothed in the brightness of his glory, to meet the kingdom of God which is set up on the earth.'†

V. A Prayer:—"Wherefore may the kingdom of God go forth, that the kingdom of heaven may come, that thou, O God, mayest be glorified in heaven so on earth, that thy enemies may be subdued; for thine is the honor, power and glory, forever and ever. Amen."‡

22. **Conclusion:**—Such then is the work of God in the great Dispensation of the Fullness of Times—a pre-

---

*Doc. and Cov., sec. lxxxviii:78-92.
†Doc. and Cov., sec. lxv.
‡Ibid.

paratory work for the glorious coming and reign of Messiah.
It is the gospel of Jesus Christ restored to the earth through
the ministration of angels to Joseph Smith and others whom
the Lord called to the work.   In it are found all the principles, ordinances, authorities, powers, gifts, graces, callings
and appointments necessary to accomplish the eternal salvation of the living and of the dead—it is the *fullness* of the
gospel; and has or will gather into it all that has ever been
revealed concerning the redemption of the earth and the
human race.   This great work of God, as we have seen, contemplates the gathering of Israel and the restoration of the
"lost tribes;" the return of the Jews to Palestine and to
Jerusalem, which city they will rebuild; the redemption of
the Lamanites and the building of a glorious city upon the
American continent to be called Zion; the advent of Messiah
in power and glory to reign in righteousness over the earth
for a thousand years, with all the ancient Saints and those
of modern days who are worthy.   It contemplates the final
redemption of the earth, and teaches that it will become
a celestial sphere, the abode of resurrected celestial beings
forever.   This work of God accepts and includes within
its boundary lines all truth.   It is progressive and is destined to become the religion of the age.   Within it is scope
for all the intelligence that shall flow unto it.   It does not,
as some have supposed, thrive best where ignorance is most
profound; nor does it depend upon superstition for its
existence or perpetuity; but it possesses within itself principles of native strength that will enable it to weather every
storm, outlive all hatred born of ignorance and prejudice,
and will yet prove itself to be what indeed it is—the power of
God unto salvation, to all those who believe and obey it.

NOTES.

1. Prophecy that the Saints Would Remove to the West:—
I passed over the river to Montrose, Iowa, in company with General
Adams, Colonel Brewer and others, and witnessed the installation of the
officers of the Rising Sun Lodge of Ancient Order of Masons, at Montrose, by General James Adams, deputy Grand Master of Illinois.
While the deputy Grand Master was engaged in giving the requisite
instructions to the Master-elect, I had a conversation with a number of
the brethren in the shade of the building on the subject of our persecutions in Missouri, and the constant annoyance which has followed us
since we were driven from that state. I prophesied that the Saints
would continue to suffer much affliction and would be driven to the
Rocky Mountains, many would apostatize, others would be put to
death by their persecutors, or lose their lives in consequence of exposure
or disease, and some of you will live to go and assist in making settlements and build cities and see the Saints become a mighty people in
the midst of the Rocky Mountains.—*Joseph Smith's Journal for 6th
of August*, 1842.

2. Why the Church Came West:—"Many living witnesses can
testify that we proposed moving to California [Then a general name for
the great West, including what is now Utah] leaving the land of our oppression, preaching the gospel to the Lamanites, building up other
temples to the living God, establishing ourselves in the far distant West.
The cruel and perfidious persecutions that we endured tended to hasten
our departure, but did *not* dictate it. It jeopardized our lives, property
and liberty, but was not the cause of our removal. Many a time have
I listened to the voice of our beloved prophet, while in council, dwell
on this subject with delight; his eyes sparkling with animation, and his
soul fired with the inspiration of the Spirit of the living God. It was a
theme that caused the bosoms of all who were privileged to listen, to
thrill with delight; intimately connected with this were themes upon
which prophets, patriarchs, priests and kings dwelt with pleasure and
delight; of them they prophesied, sung, wrote, spoke and desired to see,
but died without the sight. My spirit glows with sacred fire while I
reflect upon these scenes, and I say, O Lord, hasten the day ! Let Zion
be established ! Let the mountain of the Lord's house be established
in the tops of the mountains !"—a thing, I may add—and which he
plainly intimates—could not have been done had the Saints remained
in Nauvoo. The Saints did not come to the Rocky Mountain valleys
because they were compelled to by their enemies, but came here because
it was their destiny to come; because the Lord would have them here;
and because there were problems to work out in connection with the
work of God which could be worked out nowhere else.—*Life of John
Taylor, p.* 179.

3. Character of Brigham Young:—Brigham Young was colon-
izer, statesman, philosopher, philanthropist, reformer, prophet-leader,
priestly-king, an honest man, God's noblest work! * * * His
greatness shines forth in conduct and leadership and colonization and

Katy First Ward

July 22, 2012
Sacrament Meeting

Presiding ……………......……….. Bishop John Ravenberg

Conducting …………………….…… Lee Prince

Organist ……………………....…… Sister Brenda Curtis

Chorister ……………………..…… Sister Heather Mathews

Reverence Children ………………. By Invitation

Welcome

Opening Hymn #36 ….....… *"They, the Builders of the Nation"*

Invocation …………………….………..…… By Invitation

Sacrament Hymn #185 ……….. *"Reverently and Meekly Now"*

Administration of the Sacrament
By the Priesthood

Speaker ……………………………………....…… Abi Bero

Speaker ……………………………....……... Jay Holcomb

Speaker …………………………..…............ Cindy Holcomb

"Come Thou Fount of Every Blessing"
Sung by Ryan Allred, Accompanied by Brenda Curtis and
Spencer Fairwell of the Katy 4th Ward

Speaker ……………....…,,,,,,,,,,,,,,,,,,.………,,,.....… JJ Holcomb

Closing Hymn #30 ……………..…….. *"Come, Come, Ye Saints"*

Benediction …………..………………..…………. By Invitation

KATY FIRST WARD LEADERSHIP

Bishop	John Ravenberg
1st Counselor	Mike Turner
2nd Counselor	Lee Prince
Exec. Secretary	Loren Roundy
Ward Clerk	Ted Hawkes
High Priest Gp.L.	Mike Skye
Elders Quorum	Andrew Hyde
Primary	Amie Gillett
Relief Society	Tara Fulmer
Sunday School	Aaron Lauritzen
Young Men	Jay Holcomb
Young Women	Brittany Filetti
Ward Missionary	Kevin Sommerfeldt

TO CONTACT MISSIONARIES SERVING IN KATY 1ST WARD:

CALL 832–578-7166

This is the phone number to reach the missionarie
who have been assigned to serve in our ward

Katy First Ward

Katy Stake, Katy, Texas

2012 Katy First Ward Meeting Schedule

2:00 pm – 3:05 pm   Sacrament Meeting

3:15 pm - 4:00 pm   Sunday School
3:15 pm - 4:00 pm   Primary

4:10 pm - 5:00 pm   Priesthood
                                      Relief Society
                                      Young Women

July 22, 2012

Announcements

Announcements to be included in the bulletin, about upcoming events, should be e-mailed to Norman Patrick no later than noon on Saturday. Norm's e-mail is norwalpat@aol.com

Katy First Ward

Katy Stake, Katy, Texas

2012 Katy First Ward Meeting Schedule

2:00 pm – 3:05 pm   Sacrament Meeting

3:15 pm - 4:00 pm   Sunday School
3:15 pm - 4:00 pm   Primary

4:10 pm - 5:00 pm   Priesthood
                                     Relief Society
                                     Young Women

July 22, 2012

Announcements

Announcements to be included in the bulletin, about upcoming events, should be e-mailed to Norman Patrick no later than noon on Saturday. Norm's e-mail is norwalpat@aol.com

Katy First Ward

July 22, 2012
Sacrament Meeting

Presiding ………………......……….. Bishop John Ravenberg
Conducting ……………………....….. Lee Prince
Organist ……………………....…… Sister Brenda Curtis
Chorister ……………………..……. Sister Heather Mathews
Reverence Children ……………….. By Invitation

Welcome

Opening Hymn #36 …...… *"They, the Builders of the Nation"*

Invocation ……………………….……....… By Invitation

Sacrament Hymn #185 ……….. *"Reverently and Meekly Now"*

Administration of the Sacrament
By the Priesthood

Speaker ……………………………….....…… Abi Bero

Speaker ……………………………....……... Jay Holcomb

Speaker ………………………..…............ Cindy Holcomb

"Come Thou Fount of Every Blessing"
**Sung by Ryan Allred, Accompanied by Brenda Curtis and
Spencer Fairwell of the Katy 4th Ward**

Speaker ……………...…,,,,,.,,,,,,,,,,……….,,,.…... JJ Holcomb

Closing Hymn #30 …………….…... *"Come, Come, Ye Saints"*

Benediction ………….……..………...………... By Invitation

KATY FIRST WARD LEADERSHIP

Bishop	John Ravenberg
1st Counselor	Mike Turner
2nd Counselor	Lee Prince
Exec. Secretary	Loren Roundy
Ward Clerk	Ted Hawkes

High Priest Gp.L.	Mike Skye
Elders Quorum	Andrew Hyde
Primary	Amie Gillett
Relief Society	Tara Fulmer
Sunday School	Aaron Lauritzen
Young Men	Jay Holcomb
Young Women	Brittany Filetti
Ward Missionary	Kevin Sommerfeldt

TO CONTACT MISSIONARIES SERVING IN KATY 1ST WARD:

CALL 832–578-7166

This is the phone number to reach the missionaries who have been assigned to serve in our ward

Katy First Ward

Katy Stake, Katy, Texas

2012 Katy First Ward Meeting Schedule

2:00 pm – 3:05 pm	Sacrament Meeting
3:15 pm - 4:00 pm	Sunday School
3:15 pm - 4:00 pm	Primary
4:10 pm - 5:00 pm	Priesthood
	Relief Society
	Young Women

July 22, 2012

Announcements

Announcements to be included in the bulletin, about upcoming events, should be e-mailed to Norman Patrick no later than noon on Saturday. Norm's e-mail is norwalpat@aol.com

Katy First Ward

July 22, 2012
Sacrament Meeting

Presiding ……………..…....………. Bishop John Ravenberg

Conducting ……………………...….. Lee Prince

Organist ……………………...…… Sister Brenda Curtis

Chorister ………………………..…. Sister Heather Mathews

Reverence Children ……………….. By Invitation

Welcome

Opening Hymn #36 …..… *"They, the Builders of the Nation"*

Invocation ……………………….…...… By Invitation

Sacrament Hymn #185 ……….. *"Reverently and Meekly Now"*

Administration of the Sacrament
By the Priesthood

Speaker ……………………………....…… Abi Bero

Speaker ……………………....……... Jay Holcomb

Speaker ……………………..…........... Cindy Holcomb

"Come Thou Fount of Every Blessing"
Sung by Ryan Allred, Accompanied by Brenda Curtis and
Spencer Fairwell of the Katy 4th Ward

Speaker …………….....,,,,..,,,,,,,,,,,,………,,,…..… JJ Holcomb

Closing Hymn #30 …………..….. *"Come, Come, Ye Saints"*

Benediction ……….……..……….…..……….. By Invitation

KATY FIRST WARD LEADERSHIP

Bishop	John Ravenberg
1st Counselor	Mike Turner
2nd Counselor	Lee Prince
Exec. Secretary	Loren Roundy
Ward Clerk	Ted Hawkes

High Priest Gp.L.	Mike Skye
Elders Quorum	Andrew Hyde
Primary	Amie Gillett
Relief Society	Tara Fulmer
Sunday School	Aaron Lauritzen
Young Men	Jay Holcomb
Young Women	Brittany Filetti
Ward Missionary	Kevin Sommerfeldt

TO CONTACT MISSIONARIES SERVING IN KATY 1ST WARD:

CALL 832–578-7166

This is the phone number to reach the missionaries who have been assigned to serve in our ward

in the building of a mighty commonwealth in these mountain valleys.
* * * On all great occasions promptness and decision were characteristics of his organization; and let a question arise where it might, all Israel felt when it reached God's prophet-leader, it would find proper solution, and when solved would be endorsed by wisdom.—*Moses Thatcher.*

4. **Succession of the Twelve on the Death of President Young:**
—On the 4th of September, 1877, the two counselors of the late President Young and ten of the Twelve Apostles—Orson Pratt and Joseph F. Smith, the other two members, were absent in England—held a meeting and waited upon the Lord. With humble, contrite and saddened hearts they earnestly sought to learn his will concerning themselves and the Church. The Lord blessed them with the spirit of union, and revealed to them what steps should be taken, and the following is what was done: Elder Taylor was unanimously sustained as the President of the Twelve; and with the same unanimity it was voted that the Twelve Apostles should be sustained as the presiding authority in the church, while the counselors to the late President Young, John W. Young and Daniel H. Wells, were sustained as one with, counselors to, and associated in action with the Twelve Apostles. To facilitate the transaction of business it was also voted that for the time being President Taylor should be assisted by John W. Young, Daniel H. Wells and George Q. Cannon, in attending to business connected with the temples, the public works and other financial affairs of the Church.—*Life of John Taylor.*

5. **John Taylor:**—There was a beautiful harmony in the character of his mind and the lineaments of his person. If the habitation was splendid, the inmate was worthy of it. His noble form and bearing were but the outward expression of the spirit within. A universal benevolence, powerful intellect, splendid courage, physical as well as moral, a noble independence of spirit, coupled with implicit faith and trust in God, a high sense of honor, unimpeachable integrity, indomitable determination, and a passionate love of liberty, justice and truth marked the outlines of his character.—*Life of John Taylor.*

6. **The Discontinuance of Plural Marriage:**—The clause in President Woodruff's manifesto which discontinued plural marriage is as follows: "Inasmuch as laws have been enacted by Congress forbidding plural marriages, which laws have been pronounced constitutional by the court of last resort, I hereby declare my intention to submit to those laws, and to use my influence with the members of the church over which I preside to have them do likewise. * * * And I now publicly declare that my advice to the Latter-day Saints is to refrain from contracting any marriage forbidden by the law of the land."

Following is the resolution presented to the semi-annual Conference in the October following. It was presented by Lorenzo Snow, the President of the Twelve Apostles:—"I move that, recognizing Wilford Woodruff as the President of the Church of Jesus Christ of Latter-day Saints, and the only man on the earth at the present time who holds the keys of the sealing ordinances, we consider him fully authorized by virtue of his position to issue the manifesto which has been read in our hearing, and which is dated September 24, 1890; and that as a church in general conference assembled, we accept his declaration concerning plural marriage as authoritative and binding." The vote to sustain the foregoing motion was unanimous.

7. Basis on Which the Manifesto Was Issued:—"Verily, verily I say unto you, that when I give a commandment to any of the sons of men, to do a work unto my name, and those sons of men go with all their might, and with all they have to perform that work, and cease not their diligence, and their enemies come upon them, and hinder them from performing that work, behold it behoveth me to require that work no more at the hands of those sons of men, but to accept of their offerings." [Revelation given 19th Jan., 1841. Doc. and Cov., Sec. cxxiv.] It is on this basis that President Woodruff has felt himself justified in issuing this manifesto. * * * We have waited for the Lord to move in this matter, and on the 24th of September, President Woodruff made up his mind that he would write something, and he had the spirit of it. He had prayed about it and had besought the Lord repeatedly to show him what to do. At that time the Spirit came upon him, and the document that has been read in your hearing was the result. I know that it was right, much as it has gone against the grain with me in many respects. * * * But when God speaks, and when God makes known his mind and will, I hope that I and all Latter-day Saints will bow in submission to it.—*Geo. Q. Cannon, in a sermon Oct.* 6th, 1890.

"I want to say to all Israel that the step which I have taken in issuing this manifesto has not been done without earnest prayer before the Lord. * * * I have done my duty, and the nation of which we form a part must be responsible for that which has been done in relation to that principle [plural marriage.]—*President Woodruff, in a Sermon Oct.* 6th, 1890.

8. Testimony from God Promised that the Manifesto was Inspired:—"I have received a revelation and a commandment from the Lord, which I have not revealed to any man, which I shall reveal to this assembly, and the command of the Lord I shall give to this people, which is this: The Lord has revealed to me that there are many in the church who feel badly tried about the manifesto, and also about the testimony of the presidency and Apostles before the master in chancery. The Lord has commanded me to put the following question to the Saints, and those who will give strict attention to it shall have the Holy Ghost to be with them to inspire them to answer that question for themselves, and the Lord has promised that the answer will be to all alike. The question is this: Which is the wisest course for the Latter-day Saints to pursue—to continue to attempt to practice plural marriage, with the laws of the nation against it and the opposition of 60,000,000 of people, [this in 1890] and at the cost of the confiscation and loss of all the temples, and the stopping of the ordinances therein, both for the living and the dead; and the imprisonment of the First Presidency and Twelve, and the leaders or heads of families in the church, and the confiscation of the personal property of the people (all of which of themselves would stop the practice), or after doing and suffering what we have through our adherence to this principle, to cease the practice and submit to the law, and through doing so leave the prophets, apostles and fathers at home, so that they can instruct the people and attend to the duties of the Church, and also leave the temples in the hands of the Saints so that they can attend to the ordinances of the gospel, both for the living and the dead?   Now the inspiration of the Lord will reveal to any person which course wisdom would dictate us to pursue.   And the Latter-day Saints throughout all Israel should understand that the First Presidency of the Church and the Twelve Apostles are led and guided by the inspiration of the Lord, and the Lord will not permit me nor any other man to lead the people astray.— *President Woodruff, at Box Elder Quarterly Conference, Oct. 25th. 1891. Juvenile Instructor, vol. xxvi, p. 671.*

REVIEW.

1.   Relate the circumstances connected with the martyrdom of Joseph and Hyrum Smith.

2.   Who succeeded to the Presidency of the Church after the death of the Prophet Joseph?

3.   Give an account of the expulsion of the Church from Illinois?

4.   State the reasons why the Church in its flight went westward.

5.   Give an account of the arrival in Salt Lake valley.

6.   When and where was the First Presidency of the Church reorganized?

7.   State the leading achievements in the career of Brigham Young.

8.   What was the character of President Young?   (Note 3.)

9.   Who again took the Presidency of the Church at the death of Brigham Young?

10.   When was the First Presidency again organized?

11.   State what you can of the life and character of John Taylor.

12.   For what is John Taylor's administration noted?

13.   Who succeeded to the Presidency of the Church after the death of President Taylor?

14.   What led to the discontinuance of the practice of plural marriage?

15.   When was plural marriage publicly announced as a doctrine of the Church?

16.   Give an account of the enactments of Congress against plural marriage.

17.   State in what spirit these laws were enforced.

18.   State in what way plural marriage was finally discontinued.

19.   What was the basis of this action of the Church?   (Notes 6, 7, 8.)

20.   Give an account of the laying of the cap-stone on the Salt Lake Temple.

21. Make a statement of the growth and present position of the Church.

22. What is the immediate purpose of the work began by the Prophet Joseph Smith?

23. State several promises to be found in the Jewish scriptures respecting the glorious return of Messiah.

24. Quote those that predict Messiah will come to judgment.

25. What hath God decreed concerning the time of his coming? (Note 9.)

26. For what especial purpose hath God sent forth his servants to the world in this dispensation?

27. What will be the crowning event to the work of this dispensation?

28. State what is contemplated by the work of God in the dispensation of the fullness of times.

THE END.

INDEX.

Charles V, rupture with pope, 235.
"		decides against Prot-
		estants, 238.
Christian II. King of Sweden and
		Denmark, 275.
Christian II. driven from Sweden,
		275.
"		Invites Reynard, Carol-
		stadt and Luther to
		Denmark, 275, 276.
Christian banished from Den-
		mark, 276.
Christian III. of Denmark regu-
		lates religious affairs of
		his kingdom, 276.
Christians, Unwise zeal of, 134.
Church, A corrupt, 263.
"		Organization of, by
		Joseph Smith, 319.
Church, Conferences of, 380.
"		Government, Reflections
		on, 380.
Church, in America, 68, 106, 107.
Church, Condition of, 2nd cen-
		tury, 124.
"		Early decline of, 168.
"		Progress of, under Con-
		stantine, 132.
Church, condition of, in 10th
		cent., 204.
Church destroyed, 205.
"		Nephite, 215.
"		Anti-Christian Nephite,
		215.
"		Attempt to reorganize
		Nephite, 217.
Church, Distinct Protestant,
		founded, 235.
Church, division of, 9th century,
		165.
"		Immoral condition of,
		199.
"		Moral condition of, in
		4th cent., 200.
"		Condition in 5th cent.,
		201; subsequent to 3rd
		cent., 203.
Church, Establishment of, by
		apostles, 151.
Church, Government of, modeled
		on plan of civil govern-
		ment, 155.
Church government, opinions of,
		109.
Church, Growth and present
		condition of, 439.

Church, members of, Duties of,
		325.
"		The, what it is, etc., 364.
"		Territorial divisions of,
		373.
"		Judiciary system of, 377-
		78-79.
Church organization not perpet-
		uated, 151.
Church, The, 101.
"		Officers of, divinely call-
		ed, 104, 105.
Clement VII. succeeds Leo X.,
		235.
"		rupture with Charles V.,
		235.
"		proposes council in Italy,
		239.
Clergy, Celibacy of, 198.
Commerce, afterwards Nauvoo,
		423, 428.
Conferences appointed, 328.
"		The first, 330.
Confirmation, Manner of, 324.
Consecration, Law of, 344-5-6-7-8.
Constantine, 129, 130, 132.
"		Friendliness to
		Christians, 130.
Cnostantinople taken by Turks,
		222.
Cornelius, 83.
Councils, Rise of, 154.
"		Usurpations of, 169.
"		Nicene, The, 189.
"		General, appeal to, 229.
"		Desire for general, 229
		(note).
"		Difficulty of locating
		one, 239.
"		Trent, The, 240, 244.
"		Attempt to settle diffi-
		culties by, 262.
"		High, organized, 356.
"		High, how organized,
		356.
"		Different kinds of, 357.
"		Traveling High, The, 358.
"		High, Standing, The 358.
"		High, Temporary, 358.
"		High, Fair dealing in,
		361.
"		High, Order in, 361.
"		High, Just judgment
		in, 362.
Cowdery, Oliver, involved in
		errors, 331.